Mike Meyers' Certification
Passport ★

MCSE Windows®
XP Professional

EXAM 70-270

BRIAN CULP

OSBORNE

New York • Chicago • San Francisco
Lisbon • London • Madrid • Mexico City
Milan • New Delhi • San Juan
Seoul • Singapore • Sydney • Toronto

McGraw-Hill/Osborne
2600 Tenth Street
Berkeley, California 94710
U.S.A.

To arrange bulk purchase discounts for sales promotions, premiums, or fund-raisers, please contact **McGraw-Hill/Osborne** at the above address. For information on translations or book distributors outside the U.S.A., please see the International Contact Information page immediately following the Index of this book.

Mike Meyers' MCSE Windows® XP Professional Certification Passport
(Exam 70-270)

1234567890 DOC DOC 0198765432

Book p/n 0-07-222509-2 and CD p/n 0-07-222510-6
parts of
ISBN 0-07-222508-4

Publisher
Brandon A. Nordin

Vice President & Associate Publisher
Scott Rogers

Acquisitions Editor
Nancy Maragioglio

Senior Project Editor
Pamela Woolf

Acquisitions Coordinator
Jessica Wilson

Technical Editor
Rodney Fournier

Copy Editor
Carl Wikander

Proofreader
Mike McGee

Indexer
Karin Arrigoni

Computer Designers
George Toma Charbak
Elizabeth Jang

Illustrators
Kelly Stanton-Scott
Lyssa Sieben-Wald
Michael Mueller

Series Designers
Peter Hancik, epic

Cover Series Design
Ted Holladay

This book was composed with Corel VENTURA™ Publisher.

About the Author

Brian Culp cut his teeth in the IT world in a small networking outfit called IBM before gaining his MCSE certification and stepping into the classroom. He is currently president and CEO of LANscape, Inc., and no, they won't trim your shrubbery or build you a berm. LANscape provides training services to companies big and small, and also provides network administration. He has written or contributed to several computer books.

About the Technical Editor

Rodney Fournier, MCP, MCSE, MCSA is currently the president and lead consultant of Net Working America, Inc. He has been a Microsoft Certified Trainer for the past five years and consults on Microsoft Windows 9x/ME/NT/2000/XP, Novell 3/4/5/6, Linux, UNIX, and all kinds of desktop software.

Acknowledgments

There were many people involved in bringing this book to completion. Thanks to the technical editor Rodney Fournier for his excellent, thorough technical edits. He made sure that none of the many changes to the XP operating system slipped my attention. This book is much better than it was in draft form, and most of the credit for that belongs to him. I also need to thank Pamela Woolf for her edits, for improving the clarity of what was first written, and for saying at times, in essence, "This stinks. Rewrite it." Again, the book is better because of her. Thanks again to David Fugate for his guidance and support. And once again I wish to thank all the good folks at the KC Starbucks, especially the one on College Blvd. As much as I would like to rail about the corporate homogenization of America, of which Starbucks is a shining example, they do make a damn good cup of joe, and it's a great place to write.

Furthermore, I want to acknowledge specifically the efforts of Nancy Maragioglio. If it is true that people don't quit their jobs, they quit their bosses, then I hope to be writing books for McGraw-Hill/Osborne for a long time.

Thanks to Steve and Nancy Lind and the Lind family, for letting me hole up in their place as I was cranking through all the new material Windows XP has in store. The time and quiet provided there was invaluable, and the dinners were great. Everyone should be lucky enough to have friends like these.

Thanks to my family for all they've done.

Dedication

For Griffin

Once, there was a young boy who went outside with his daddy. It was a bright, clear winter day and everything was covered in a blanket of white snow, so deep that it came up mid-thigh. They could barely walk. Then the boy had an idea: "What if we make some snowshoes using old tennis rackets?" And so they did. Striding on top of the powdery white snow they made their way deep into the forest, walking along peacefully, telling stories. They had wrapped themselves in long brown coats made from heavy cloth, and stocking caps to cover their heads. They each wore wide belts around their waists and tucked into the belts, both the boy and his daddy carried a big, long sword.

They walked along peacefully when they heard a faint snap of twigs. "Did you hear that?" asked daddy. That's when the snow monster jumped out of the tree. The huge beast landed on daddy's back, knocking his sword out of his belt, and the monster and daddy wrestled around, daddy trying to avoid the sharp claws.

The boy quickly ran over and drew his sword. "Don't panic! Don't panic!" he yelled at his dad. "I've got my sword!"

With a great whistle, the blade of the boy's great sword sliced through the air, and there was a yelp of pain from the snow monster. Daddy was able to free himself and draw his own sword. The monster looked down at his claws ... gone. The boy had cut off the sharp points of the monster's fierce weapons. Daddy lowered his sword, aiming it at the beast's shaggy torso, and glared down the length of his sword. "Be on your way monster, and don't ever come here to scare us again."

The monster saw the look in daddy's eyes, looked once over at the boy, then once more over at daddy. Then the snow monster turned and ran, deep into the woods.

Daddy and the boy sat down together and started a fire, roasted some marshmallows and made some s'mores. While they ate the s'mores, the boy told a really long story with lots of chapters about their long day. Then they went to sleep in their sleeping bags. *The end.*

To Clint Hurdle, my former hitting instructor, whose most valuable instruction to me had noting to do with batting. It dealt with how to turn the page to the next chapter of life, even though he was talking about himself and we were trying to get him to take batting practice. I can't repeat exactly what the words of advice were on these pages, but let's just say that it had to do with a campfire and an empty bladder. (And Clint, I may have had seven knee surgeries, but I can still rake it, by the way. I think I could give you a couple of years of .300-30-100, and I've checked the standings. Give me a call when the National League institutes the DH... Well, now you've gone and won the first 8 games or so of you managerial tenure, and are probably on the horn right now with some jeweler being fitted for World Series rings, but the offer still stands.)

Contents

Check-In

May I See Your Passport?

What do you mean you don't have a passport? Why, it's sitting right in your hands, even as you read! This book is your passport to a special place. You're about to begin a journey, my friend, toward that magical place called *certification*! You don't need a ticket, you don't need a suitcase—just snuggle up and read this Passport—it's all you need to get there. Are you ready? Let's go!

Your Travel Agent: Mike Meyers

Hello! My name's Mike Meyers and I'm proud to introduce myself to you as the series editor for the *Mike Meyers' Certification Passport* series. I've written a number of popular certification books, and this is my dream of the perfect certification book! Every book in this series combines easy readability with a condensed format—in other words, the kind of book I always wanted when I did my certifications.

I designed this series to do one thing and only one thing: to get you the information you need to achieve your certification. You won't find any fluff in here; your author, Brian Culp, packed every page with nothing but the real nitty-gritty of the certification exam. I hope you enjoy the casual, friendly style; I want you to feel as though Brian is speaking to you, discussing the certification. My e-mail address is mikem@totalsem.com. Please feel free to contact me directly if you have any questions, complaints, or compliments.

Your Destination: Windows XP Professional Exam 70-270

Although you don't have to take the Microsoft Windows MCSE exams in any particular order, it is generally accepted practice that this one will be your first. The Windows XP Professional exam is a good starting point, as the knowledge that you gain here will provide a good conceptual base upon which you will build. This test will measure your ability to implement, administer, and troubleshoot information systems that incorporate Microsoft Windows XP Professional.

You can expect to be tested on topics such as installing Windows XP Professional, configuring hardware such as network cards and hard drives, configuring the desktop environment for end users, implementing the networking protocols, establishing connectivity between computers, and troubleshooting security settings. In addition, MCSE candidates are expected to have at least one year of experience implementing and administering network operating systems.

The MCSE certification is one of the industry's most powerful certifications—it always has been. Now that the exams have been updated to incorporate the Windows XP operating system, some significant changes have been made to their difficulty level. Microsoft has changed test questions to reduce the emphasis on learning facts, instead requiring synthesis of information in real-world scenarios. Nearly half the items in the core exams demand that you have troubleshooting skills acquired through hands-on experience and working knowledge. Because of this new difficulty, the MCSE will carry more clout than ever, as the numbers of people who achieve certification will surely be fewer.

Your Guide: Brian Culp

Brian Culp is one of those people who just have to buck trends. Unlike the majority of his fellow nerds, Brian is also a certified jock! Let's first point out his major nerdish accomplishments. Before teaching computers, Brian learned the IT ropes in Seattle, Washington, at a small outfit called IBM. Brian currently holds three certifications: the MCSE, MCT, and A+.

He has been teaching the Windows XP MCSE track to students far and wide since the operating system hit the shelves. Along with the standard core MCSE track and design courses, he has taught and written courseware for Microsoft Systems Management Server 2.0. Today, Brian's students' scores of his conversational teaching style and technical knowledge consistently rank him as one of the Midwest region's top technical instructors.

Prior to his life in front of a computer, Brian played baseball in the Colorado Rockies organization, where several knee surgeries and general lack of talent (*his* words, not mine) conspired to force his retirement in 1996.

Brian is always eager to hear feedback and comments from readers in an effort to improve the style and content of this and future projects. You can contact Brian at one of two e-mail addresses to discuss any issues or questions relating to the book: bculp@lanscapecomputer.com, or bculp23@hotmail.com.

Why the Travel Theme?

One of my favorite topics is the metaphor of gaining a certification to a taking a trip. Many of the elements are the same: preparation, an itinerary, a route—even mishaps along the way. Let me show you how it all works.

This book is divided into eight chapters. Each chapter begins with an Itinerary that provides objectives and an ETA to give you an idea of the time involved in learning the skills in that chapter. Each chapter is broken down by real exam objectives, either those officially stated by the certifying body, or if the vendor doesn't provide these, our expert takes on the best way to approach the topics.

The end of each chapter gives you two handy tools. The Checkpoint reviews each objective in the chapter with a handy synopsis—a great way to review quickly. Plus, you'll find end-of-chapter Review Questions and Answers to test your newly acquired knowledge.

But the fun doesn't stop there! After you've read the book, pull out the CD and take advantage of the free practice questions! Use the full practice exam to hone your skills, and keep the book handy to check answers. When you've mastered the practice questions, you're ready to take the exam—go get certified!

The End of the Trail

The IT industry changes and grows constantly, and so should you. Finishing one certification is just a step in an ongoing process of gaining more and more certifications to match your constantly changing and growing skills. Read the "Career Flight Path" appendix to see where this certification fits into your personal certification goals. Remember, in the IT business, if you're not moving forward, you are way behind! Good luck on your certification! Stay in touch!

Mike Meyers
Series Editor
Mike Meyers' Certification Passport

Installing Windows XP Professional

ETA	NEWBIE	SOME EXPERIENCE	EXPERT
	4 hours	2 hours	1 hour

Start here. This familiar phrase might tempt you to insert the shiny new Windows XP CD-ROM disc and begin installing the operating system. Resist this temptation! You have quite a few factors to consider before and during an installation, all of which you should nail down before you insert the disc.

Microsoft provides numerous ways to install Windows XP and, not surprisingly, the MCP Exam 70-270 tests heavily for your knowledge of these methods. This chapter first examines issues related to performing attended installations, such as the minimum hardware requirements for the operating system and overall hardware compatibility. You also need to decide what sort of attended installation to employ, either a clean install or an upgrade from a previous version of Windows.

You will make important decisions during installation about the partitioning scheme for your hard disk and the file system those partitions will use. These decisions can have a great impact on how you use XP, and they will be especially important if you want to create a dual-boot machine, running both Windows XP and some other, *lesser* operating system.

If you have used cloning technologies before (for computers, that is; not sheep, cats, or other quadrupeds), you also know that you don't have to sit by the computer the entire time during an installation. The 70-270 exam also focuses substantially on the technologies that Microsoft makes available to facilitate unattended installations, and the second part of the chapter focuses on these tools. You will find out all about the System Prep tool and about the Remote Installation Service (RIS), both of which help make unattended installations easier.

Windows XP comes with the Files and Settings Transfer Wizard, an excellent tool that enables you to import easily and quickly most of the settings from an older Windows computer to the fresh Windows XP installation. This new wizard can save you a lot of time and headaches, especially when upgrading a network of PCs. And, of course, it comes up on the 70-270 exam.

Microsoft expects you to understand some things that can go wrong at installation time. Knowledge of troubleshooting will also serve you well in real-life administration environments. A portion of this chapter identifies some of the common pitfalls and the steps you can take to avoid/repair them.

Microsoft also expects you to know a thing or two about its new product activation, and despite what you may have heard, it won't require you to jump through too many hoops. It's just an anti-piracy thing, as you will see.

Even though many installations won't require the depth of knowledge presented in this chapter, installing Windows XP Professional is a task that you will perform dozens, perhaps hundreds, of times over the course of your administrative career.

The journey to Microsoft certification is a long one. But, as with all journeys—as the adage goes—it begins with a single step. So consider this chapter the first step on that path. To begin our trip, we will indeed, *Start here.*

Perform an Attended Installation of Windows XP Professional

Objective 1.01

Installing Windows XP the first time and *getting it right* so you don't have to reinstall requires you to know quite a bit about the operating system. Microsoft's design considerations for the operating system led directly to changes from Windows 2000, and some of these changes have a huge impact on installation tasks. Let's look at Microsoft's goals first and then dive into the features of Windows XP. Once the basics are out of the way, we'll plunge into the steps of an attended installation.

To make a more informed choice about installing the Windows XP Professional operating system (OS), it is useful to know some of Microsoft's stated design goals. Even though you won't see this information on the XP exam, familiarity with these objectives can help you make a better business case for a Windows XP Professional installation, and further sets the backdrop against which you will begin your understanding of the OS. The architects of Windows XP had the following design goals in mind when they developed their code:

1. Integration of the best features of Windows 98 and Windows Me: features that contribute to ease-of-use and that include certain system utilities.

2. Integration of the best features of Windows 2000: a reliable, crash resistant Windows engine that has done away with all previous remnants of MS-DOS–compatible code, which has security features such as support for NTFS partitions, and that has system management tools that provide a familiar interface and are intuitive to use.

3. Combining these two operating system families has led to lower Total Cost of Ownership (TCO) for an operating system.

Travel Assistance

The list and related discussion provide only an overview of all things wonderful, shiny, and new about Windows XP. For a more in-depth discussion, please refer to the following website: http://www.microsoft.com/windowsxp/pro/evaluation/features.asp.

If you keep these three goals in mind, you will better understand some of the changes that have been made in XP, and there are literally hundreds. Many of these changes begin with the basic raw materials of previous Windows versions—the Start menu is still there, and you still have a My Computer icon on the desktop, but other features have been given a complete facelift to make Windows easier for novice users. If you are upgrading to XP from Windows 2000, many of the architecture changes are subtle, if noticeable at all. In other words, while the user interface has changed quite a bit, what's going on under the hood—how the operating system will be managed—hasn't changed all that much from Windows 2000. (One thing you might notice right away is a faster boot process. You'll no longer have time to do the New York Times Sunday crossword waiting for Windows to boot. You won't see any test question on this—like "Which boots faster, Windows 2000 or Windows XP?"—but you will notice it.)

If you are one of these upgraders, always using the latest version of Microsoft's operating system, you might find the "Classic" Windows interface the most comfortable and cost-effective way to use your computer. It's a page from the "If it ain't broke, don't fix it" school of thought. You can easily switch to the "Classic" interface by taking the following steps:

1. Right-click your desktop; then click Properties.
2. Click the Appearance tab.
3. On the Windows and Buttons menu, select Windows Classic. Click OK.

Now you can make the transition to XP while keeping the old Windows look, and you'll still get the full functionality out of Windows XP, new look or old. Note, however, that doing this does not configure everything on your system to look like Windows 2000. You will still have the new Start menu when using the Windows Classic theme, and your folders will still default to the new task-based view. Both of these things are changeable with a few more clicks, as you will see later.

> ## Local Lingo
>
> Just a quick note before we go on: most of the technologies mentioned here in this chapter are given further attention throughout the course of this book. I try to include definitions for technologies, acronyms, and such whenever possible, especially when they are first introduced. However, you might not read this book front to back, so I'll give you a quick reference that you should find very valuable whenever you come across something in this book, or any other, that doesn't ring a bell. For a great website that dispenses concise definitions, check out Webopedia, which you can find at http://www.webopedia.com.

An overriding aim of Windows XP Professional is to fulfill the third design goal in the previous list: to reduce the cost of owning, maintaining, and upgrading the operating system. Windows XP includes easy-to-use administrative interfaces through the Microsoft Management Console (MMC) snap-ins and, as we'll discuss in this chapter, provides multiple deployment options, including the use of unattended installations and the Remote Installation Service (RIS).

What's New in Windows XP?

It's a good question, and the short answer is *a lot*. This can be good news and bad news for users of previous versions of Windows. If you are familiar with the evolution of the Microsoft product line, you are probably already aware of the changes made when Windows NT became Windows 2000. These changes really did not affect the end-user experience; if you were comfortable with any of the Windows operating systems from Windows 95 on, you could probably sit down and use a Windows 2000 computer just fine. The real changes made in 2000 occurred under the hood, and the Windows 2000 code made *dramatic* changes to the way Windows computers were administered. In other words, if you were a network admin, or were updating your support skills from Windows NT or 9x to Windows 2000, or were preparing to update your MCSE certification, you had a lot of new information to tackle. End users, by design, had it easy.

Now, both families of Windows desktop operating systems (9x and NT) have evolved to XP. And from the moment you install, a user will find that its "look and feel" is substantially different from its Microsoft predecessors and may even find it disorienting at first. Users will have to learn a new way of interacting with the computer, and many of the old ways employed to make Windows behave the way they wanted it to—hacking the Registry, creating intricate workarounds, and sharing secrets within a cloister of Windows gurus—are now pretty much obsolete. That's the bad news.

The good news is that, to generalize just a bit, from an administrator's point of view, not much has changed in the way XP behaves behind its graphical interface, as was the case when upgrading from NT to 2000. You will still use most of the same concepts that served you when administering Windows 2000 computers (or studying for 2000 exams).

More good news about XP: the changes that have been made allow this latest iteration of Windows to run faster, more securely, more smoothly, and more intuitively for everyday chores than ever before. These new benefits are well worth the time and effort spent to understand and master this new OS. But first you'll have to roll up your sleeves, install the new OS, and open your mind to the new capabilities. But that's why you're reading this book, isn't it, young Jedi? I will be your Master Yoda in your exploration of XP: first you must "unlearn what you have learned." (Okay, there it is: my geeky *Star Wars* reference. I authored the entire 2000 Professional title without making even one of those, at times having to chew the flesh off my knuckles at the keyboard to keep from doing so. I will keep them to a minimum.)

Overview of New Features
As was mentioned, the entire "fit and finish" of Windows XP differs dramatically from that of any version of Windows before it. But the changes are not only cosmetic; it also offers many new features that were not available on previous versions of Windows, especially in the Windows 9x product line. These changes and additional features give Windows XP a competitive edge in the OS market. This book, as well as the Windows 2000 and the Windows.NET MCP core exams, focus heavily on these new features. These features, all of which are discussed at some point in this book, include the following:

- Disk quota support (on NTFS partitions)
- Internet printing support
- Encrypting File System (EFS) support (on NTFS partitions)
- Wizard-based administration and configuration
- Enhanced virtual private networking (VPN) support
- Offline file support
- Slipstreaming of service packs

Exam Tip

As a rule of thumb, any time a new feature of Windows XP is mentioned, you can bet that it will be the subject of a test question or two. Microsoft, in order to bolster the credibility and prestige of the MCSE, has really emphasized tougher tests for the new Windows MCSE track, and testing on concepts that apply to NT 4, even though they may be critical for real-world administration, wouldn't make the exams very hard for NT veterans.

What's the Difference Between XP Professional and Home Edition?

XP Home is the operating system designed for, obviously, home use. However, that does not mean it can't be used in a corporate setting. Some users in your network might not require all the features of XP Professional and will be able to perform all necessary tasks with XP Home Edition, just as they were able to do with Windows 98. However, one of the limitations of XP Home is that it cannot *join* a domain, just as Windows 98 could not. Windows XP Professional, on the other hand, can.

Travel Assistance

For a full discussion of the differences between the two versions of XP, Home and Professional, please see http://www.microsoft.com/windowsxp/pro/howtobuy/choosing.asp. There are several pages that discuss this issue at great length in order to help you decide which version is the right one.

Quite simply, Windows XP Professional can do everything Home can do, plus much more. It is a "nesting toy" approach, one that Microsoft has used before in Windows 2000; that is, everything 2000 Pro can do, 2000 Server can do; Server builds on the Pro code base to support a list of other technologies that 2000 Pro does not. For example, 2000 Pro and 2000 Server can both be clients of a Microsoft network, and they can both share a folder, but only on Server can you install Active Directory and behave as a domain controller. Same goes for the relationship between XP Home and XP Professional. They both run on the same Windows engine, or kernel, and all file and folder management tasks will look the same.

Much of what you learn here will carry over seamlessly to the XP Home environment. But, since the focus of this book—and of the exam you are preparing for—is solely on the Professional flavor, you should be aware of some of the key features that are *only* available in Windows XP Professional. They are listed in Table 1-1.

Local Lingo

Windows 9x   I've already made a few references to this, so I better define it: *Windows 9x* refers to the line of Microsoft operating systems beginning with Windows 95. There is nothing substantially different about the code base in these versions, so for most discussions what applies to one applies to all. Hence the reference to Windows 9x.

Beginning the Attended Installation

After you've made the decision to install XP to run your computer and have educated yourself about some of the benefits you should expect to see from Microsoft's latest and greatest, you are ready to begin that first critical administrative task of performing the installation. (Just a quick note here: it is assumed for purposes of the attended installation discussion that the installation is being performed on a new or relatively new computer and that the hardware is robust enough to support XP. You can certainly install XP on somewhat older computers and components, but there are some compatibility issues in doing so.)

| **TABLE 1.1** | Advantages of the XP Professional Version |

Feature	What It Does
Multiple processor support	Only XP Pro supports Symmetric Multiprocessing (SMP).
Support for 64-bit (Intel's Itanium) processors	Home edition is unable to work with this type of CPU.
Advanced Security Features	XP Pro supports EFS and IPSec.
Internet Information Services	Only XP Pro lets you set up IIS to share out a website.
Domain Membership	XP Pro can join a domain to take advantage of Group Policies.
Dynamic Disks	XP Home supports only basic disks, which follow the partitioning rules of Windows 9x.

executables just mentioned. One of the simplest methods is to just boot from the Setup CD if your computer's BIOS supports this capability (most computers able to run XP will).

Other methods include installing over the network. During a network install, clients will connect to a location that holds the contents of the XP Setup CD's \i386 directory, then launch the Setup program. This will require, of course, that there is some kind of operating system already on the computer (a simple DOS Setup floppy with a DOS networking client installed will do, if you know your way around the command prompt) and that the OS has some kind of network connectivity. This procedure is usually done in organizations where large numbers of computers need to be installed at once and it is impractical to go from computer to computer with the Setup CD.

Travel Advisory

There is a 64-bit version of XP Professional as well, and its installation files are housed in a different place than the 32-bit version. The installation files directory for the 64-bit version is \ia64, and you will only see it if you have the 64-bit version's CD-ROM.

And there are many other ways to install over the network. Additional network-dependant installation methods, especially in use with large organizations, include Systems Management Server, as well as cloning programs such as Symantec's Ghost, SysPrep, and Remote Installation Services (RIS). We discuss RIS and SysPrep in Objective 1.02.

You can also simply run the Setup utility from the CD without the splash screen by using the command prompt or the Run dialog box (again, you could specify a network location here as well). Once more, you will navigate to the \i386 directory and then choose one of the Setup programs. The advantage of using either of the Setup utilities from the command or Run interface is that they are much more flexible when used in this way. Winnt.exe and the winnt32.exe installation programs support a number of switches that can be used to configure a variety of options, including the option not to sit there providing answers to Setup questions.

Exam Tip

You can count on the Setup switches to provide material for a test question or two on your XP Pro exam.

The winnt.exe Setup switches supported by the Windows XP installation are listed in Table 1-2.

To use any of these switches, you pass the switch to the winnt.exe program like so:

```
winnt.exe /s:d:\i386 /u:acct.inf
```

In this example, Setup will look to the d drive, and then in the \i386 directory for the XP installation files. During installation, Setup will also get information it needs for Setup questions answered by the file acct.inf when necessary. It will then begin copying the necessary files for the Windows XP installation to a temporary folder on your hard drive. Once the files are copied to the hard disk, you are prompted to remove any floppy disks and reboot the computer.

TABLE 1.2	Setup Switches Supported by the Windows XP Installation
Switch	**Description**
/s: [sourcepath]	Specifies the location to the i386 folder, which contains the Windows XP Setup source files; usually used with unattended installations. If you do not specify a location, Setup attempts to locate a drive for you.
/u: [answer filename]	Performs an unattended installation using an answer file, which contains all the answers to questions you are asked during installation. You can put the answers in the unattend file and tell Setup to use the answers from this file with the /u switch. If you use the /u switch, you must also use /s to specify where the Setup files are.
/udf:ID [,UDB_file]	Some Windows XP install settings must be unique— for example, the computer name. The UDB overrides values in the answer file, and the identifier (ID) determines which values in the UDB file are used. You can configure a "uniqueness database file" (udb) and tell Setup to use this file with the /udb switch. If no UDB_file is specified, Setup prompts you to insert a disk that contains the $Unique$.udb file.
/r: [foldername]	Installs an additional folder to the system with Setup. The folder remains on the system after installation is complete.
/rx: [foldername]	Installs an additional folder to the system with Setup. The folder is removed from the system after the installation is complete.
/a	Enables accessibility options during installation.
/e: [command]	Executes a command after the graphical portion of Setup has completed.

Travel Advisory

It's impossible to memorize the necessary syntax for every command utility, so you'll have to learn to be resourceful. There is, however, a help command that will come in very handy. When using the command environment, always remember you can type **/?** at the end of any command for help. For example, say you would like to set up Windows XP using the Uniqueness Database File in conjunction with an unattended setup to provide unique answers to Setup questions, but you can't quite remember the syntax of the winnt.exe utility. To get the exact syntax, at the Command Prompt type **winnt /?**.

You should also be familiar with the switches used for the WINNT32 utility. Notice in Table 1-3 that they perform most of the same functions that the WINNT switches do, only most of the WINNT32 switches need to be spelled out.

Using the /unattend command-line option to automate Setup affirms that you have read and accepted the Microsoft License Agreement for Windows XP. Before using this command-line option to install Windows XP on behalf of an organization other than your own, you must confirm that the end user (whether an individual or a single entity) has received, read, and accepted the terms of the Microsoft License Agreement for Windows XP. OEMs may not specify this key on machines being sold to end users.

Travel Advisory

It is good computing practice to disable virus-scanning software prior to beginning a Windows XP Professional upgrade. This is because the Setup program will access the Partition table of the hard disk, something that rankles most antivirus software programs.

Upon the first reboot, Windows XP Setup launches the text-based portion of the installation, where you can repair an installation by pressing R or continue with the installation by pressing ENTER. This portion is shown in Figure 1-2. Note that this is also the first screen you see if you perform the installation by booting from the XP Professional CD-ROM, which will likely be the case as you complete your first several installations. The MCSE test is geared to those installation techniques that require more extensive understanding.

After you have selected to continue the installation, you should read the Windows XP License Agreement. At the end of the agreement, press F8 to acknowledge that you've read it. *Thoroughly.*

TABLE 1.3   Commonly Used winnt32.exe Switches

Switch	Description
/checkupgradeonly	Does not perform an install, but rather just checks your computer for upgrade compatibility with Windows XP. The results of the check are saved by default to a file called Upgrade.txt, which is saved in the *systemroot* folder. If you use this option with /unattend, no user input is required.
/cmd:command_line	Instructs Setup to carry out a specific command before the final phase of Setup. This would occur after your computer has restarted and after Setup has collected the necessary configuration information, but before Setup is complete.
/cmdcons	Also does not perform installation of XP, but instead installs the Recovery Console as a startup option. The Recovery Console is a command-line interface from which you can perform tasks such as starting and stopping services and accessing the local drive (including drives formatted with NTFS). Note that you can use only the /cmdcons option after normal Setup is finished (we will come back to this one in Chapter 6).
/dudisable	Prevents Dynamic Update from running. Dynamic Update tries to grab the latest Setup files from the Windows Update website before performing installation. Without Dynamic Update, Setup runs only with the original Setup files. This option has trump-card power—it will disable Dynamic Update even if you use an answer file and specify Dynamic Update options in that file.
/duprepare:*pathname*	Carries out preparations on an installation share so that it can be used with Dynamic Update files that you have downloaded from the Windows Update website. This share can then be used for installing Windows XP for multiple clients.
/dushare:*pathname*	Specifies a share on which you previously downloaded Dynamic Update files from the Windows Update website and on which you previously ran /duprepare:pathname. When run on a client, it specifies that the client installation will make use of the updated files on the share specified in pathname.

TABLE 1.3   Commonly Used winnt32.exe Switches *(continued)*

Switch	Description
/makelocalsource	Instructs Setup to copy all installation source files to your local hard disk. Use /makelocalsource when installing from a CD to provide installation files when the CD is not available later in the installation.
/noreboot	Instructs Setup to not restart the computer after the file copy phase of Setup is completed so that you can run another command.
/s:*SourcePath*	Directs Setup to the location of the Windows XP files (like the /s: switch with WINNT). To simultaneously copy files from multiple servers, type the /s:*SourcePath* option multiple times (up to a maximum of eight). If you type the option multiple times, the first server specified must be available, or Setup will fail.
/udf:*id* [,UDB_file]	Serves the same purpose as it does for the WINNT command. Indicates an identifier (*id*) that Setup uses to specify how a Uniqueness Database (UDB) file modifies an answer file (see the /unattend entry). The UDB overrides values in the answer file, and the identifier determines which values in the UDB file are used. If no UDB_file is specified, Setup prompts the user to insert a disk that contains the $Unique$.udb file.
/unattend	Causes WINNT32 to upgrade your previous version of Windows 98, Windows Millennium Edition, Windows NT 4.0, or Windows 2000 in unattended Setup mode (when used without arguments). All user settings are taken from the previous installation, so no user intervention is required during Setup.
/unattend[*num*]:[answer_file]	Performs a fresh installation in unattended Setup mode. The specified answer_file provides Setup with your custom specifications. *Num* is the number of seconds between the time that Setup finishes copying the files and when it restarts your computer. You can use *num* on any computer running Windows 98, Windows Millennium Edition, Windows NT, Windows 2000, or Windows XP.

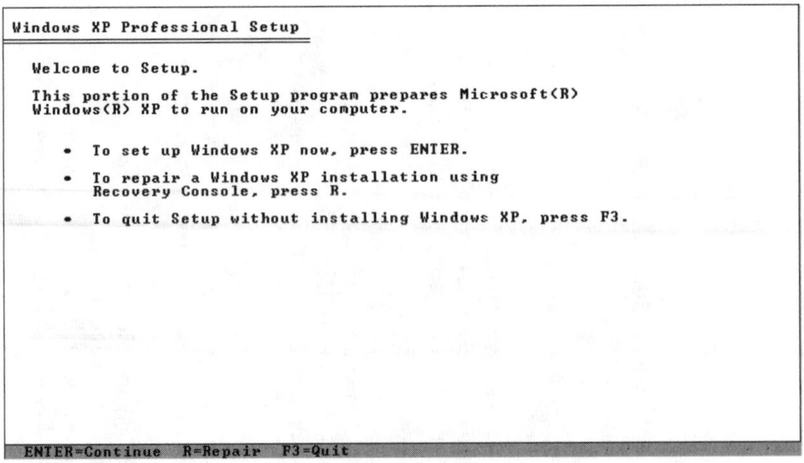

```
Windows XP Professional Setup

  Welcome to Setup.

  This portion of the Setup program prepares Microsoft(R)
  Windows(R) XP to run on your computer.

      • To set up Windows XP now, press ENTER.

      • To repair a Windows XP installation using
        Recovery Console, press R.

      • To quit Setup without installing Windows XP, press F3.
```

ENTER=Continue   R=Repair   F3=Quit

FIGURE 1.2   Starting the Windows XP installation

Your next stop, whether you have installed XP from an existing installation of Windows or have booted from the CD, will be a significant one, and one that will determine what happens to the data already on your hard drive (if applicable). Depending on how your disk has been partitioned before, you will see choices about Creating a partition, Deleting an existing partition, or Installing on an already existing partition.

For example, to create a partition from unpartitioned space, press C on your keyboard, and to delete a partition, press D (Figure 1-3).

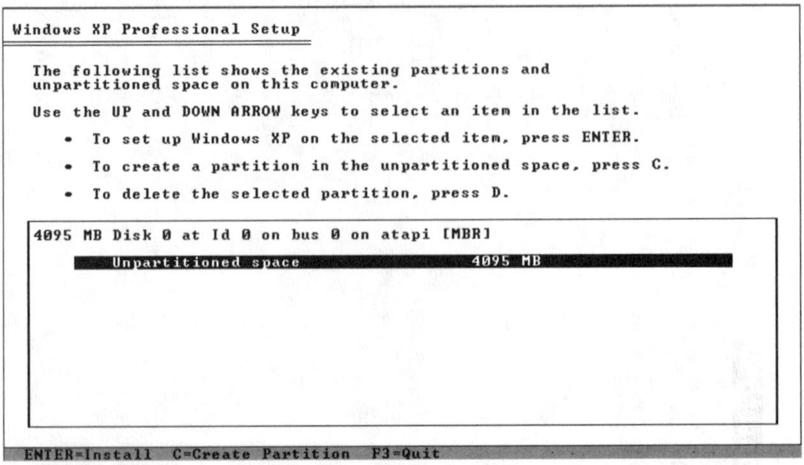

```
Windows XP Professional Setup

  The following list shows the existing partitions and
  unpartitioned space on this computer.

  Use the UP and DOWN ARROW keys to select an item in the list.

      • To set up Windows XP on the selected item, press ENTER.

      • To create a partition in the unpartitioned space, press C.

      • To delete the selected partition, press D.

  4095 MB Disk 0 at Id 0 on bus 0 on atapi [MBR]
       Unpartitioned space                     4095 MB
```

ENTER=Install   C=Create Partition   F3=Quit

FIGURE 1.3   Making the partition selection

After you have considered the data preservation consequences of your choices and have made your partitioning decisions, select the partition where you want to install Windows XP.

To install Windows XP on all the free space as one partition, highlight that free space and press ENTER. Windows XP will automatically make a single partition out of all the selected free space and install the operating system to the \WINDOWS folder. After you have selected a partition, you can select the file system that will be used. Windows XP supports FAT16, FAT32, and NTFS for the installation partition, and the file system chosen here will have a large impact on the features available with XP. We talk more about these important file system considerations in Chapter 2.

After these decisions are made, the Setup program will copy more files and reboot your computer; then the Setup Wizard (shown in Figure 1-4) will start. As the Setup Wizard runs, you will be asked a series of questions that will help Setup configure your system. You will be asked to supply user and computer names, product ID keycode information, network settings, and other information that will ensure a smooth installation.

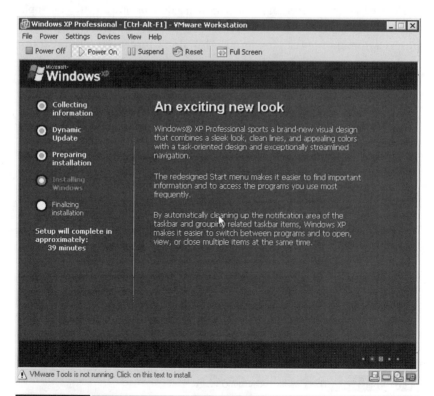

FIGURE 1.4 The Windows XP Setup Wizard

The Setup Wizard begins by detecting the hardware in the system and installing the appropriate device drivers. After the installation of your hardware is complete, Setup will ask you to make regional settings, where you change your locale and your keyboard layout.

If you decide not to change your local settings at this point, you may later make the change through Regional Options in the Control Panel. After you select locales, you are asked to provide your name and organization.

The Product Key dialog box, shown in Figure 1-5, appears next. This is an important dialog box, because it's where you type your 25-character product key, located on the back of the Windows XP Professional Setup CD case. Without this key code, installation is impossible.

Another vital dialog box, the Computer Name and Administrator Password dialog box (see Figure 1-6), contains fields used to create an identity, or an account, for the computer. In a Workgroup environment, computer names must be unique to the specific Workgroup. In larger environments, the computer account can be added to an existing Windows domain. You will be asked to provide this network participation information later in Setup. Computer accounts represent a significant level of participation in a domain and are used for application of Group Policies. For example, they can be used to restrict which computers a domain user can log on to. Also, don't forget the Administrator

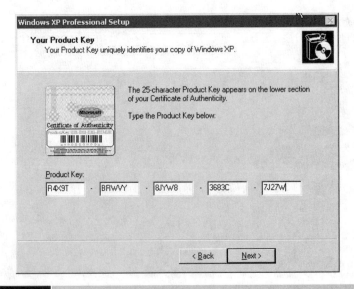

FIGURE 1.5 The Product Key dialog box

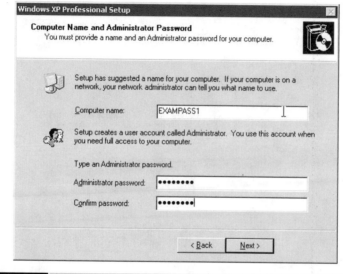

FIGURE 1.6 Naming your computer and selecting an Admin password—you can change both later

Password that you type in this dialog box; you will need it to log on to Windows XP Professional for the first time.

If a Plug and Play modem is detected and its drivers are installed, the Modem Dialing Information dialog box will appear. If one is not detected, the Date and Time Settings dialog box appears, where you configure the time zone and ensure that the correct time is set.

The Network Settings dialog box, shown in Figure 1-7, is where you specify how you want to connect to other computers. Choose Typical Settings to install network connections and the Workstation and Server components. (The significance of these two networking components is fleshed out in Chapter 2.) Doing this will also set up TCP/IP with the addressing information to be assigned automatically. Choosing Custom Settings allows you to install and configure each of these networking components separately, as well as install others.

The Workgroup or Computer Domain dialog box is your next waypoint, and it asks whether your system is going to be part of a workgroup or domain. As mentioned, this dialog box (see Figure 1-8) is another "biggie" in terms of making your computer behave as you want. But don't worry if you get it wrong the first time (or any time). Workgroup and domain membership for XP Professional computers is very flexible; you will be able to go back and change workgroup or domain membership as well as the computer name once installation is complete.

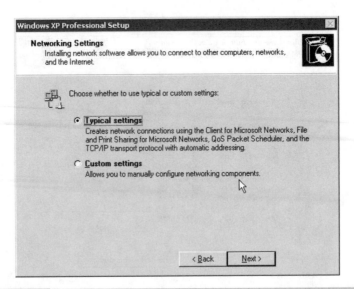

FIGURE 1.7 Configuring how XP will communicate with the Network Settings dialog box

The Windows XP Setup program then progresses by installing the necessary Windows components; this will take some time. After it has installed the components, it performs "Final Tasks." The Setup Wizard creates the Start menu,

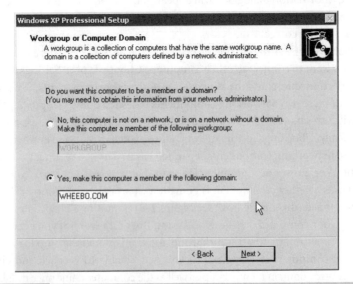

FIGURE 1.8 Selecting domain or workgroup membership

Network Identification Wizard

User Account
You can add a user to this computer.

Adding a user to this computer grants the user access to all the resources on this computer and to all shared resources on the network.

Type your network user account information, or type the account information of another user on your network.

○ Add the following user:

User name: bculp

User domain: WHEEBO.COM

○ Do not add a user at this time.

[< Back] [Next >] [Cancel]

FIGURE 1.9   The Network Identification Wizard

registers components into the system Registry, and removes any temporary files created by the Setup Wizard.

The Setup Wizard will inform you when the installation of Windows XP is complete, and it will ask you to remove the CD and click Finish.

The system restarts with the Network Identification Wizard, shown in Figure 1-9, which helps you set up the computer for networking by asking whether the system should log in automatically as the same user every time or whether each user must provide a valid user name and password to access the system.

For networks with security concerns, it is recommended that you not automatically log on to the system as the same user account each time. It is better to choose User Must Enter a Username and Password to Use This Computer. After the Network Identification Wizard is finished, the installation of Windows XP is complete.

Travel Assistance

For exhaustive information about the installation process, see the *Microsoft Windows XP Professional Resource Kit Documentation*, Chapters 1–4, from Microsoft Press.

Perform an Unattended Installation of Windows XP Professional

If our attended installation involved us manually supplying the answers to the Setup questions, then an unattended installation is designed to make sure those questions are answered automatically. In other words, it's setting up a computer with Windows XP Professional (and potentially any desired applications) without a user's intervention. As we will see, there are several mechanisms available to help you achieve this objective. If you have been performing installs in the field for any length of time, you probably know of a third-party software package or two that will perform this task without any assistance from Microsoft. Most admins will continue to use these familiar software packages because of their ease of use. However, because the tools mentioned here are relatively new, and because performing unattended installations is an advanced task for administrators of large computing environments, Microsoft can be expected to test you on its way of installing Windows XP on multiple computers at once. (One of these installation mechanisms even requires that you use a third-party tool, as we will soon learn.)

For success on the Windows XP Professional exam, you should be familiar with three areas of unattended installation:

- Remote Installation Services (RIS)
- SysPrep
- Creation of unattended installation files

We will spend time with each of these in the following sections.

Install Windows XP Professional Using Remote Installation Services

Another way that automated installations of Windows XP Professional can be performed is through the Remote Installation Service (RIS). This area of expertise is one that you will be tested on throughout your MCSE track, so it is in your best interest to get familiar with this technology as quickly as possible.

Exam Tip

You are likely to see questions covering this topic on all four of your core exams, because the technology crosses so many disciplines. You will see a few questions on the 70-270 (XP Professional), a few more on the 70-215 (2000 Server), a couple on the 70-216 (2000 Network Infrastructure), and quite a few on the 70-217 (Active Directory) test.

RIS installations work by letting a client computer simply boot up and find an image of the OS that is then downloaded and installed. This client-server technology includes a RIS server, which must have the RIS software installed and house the Windows XP Professional installation image(s). The RIS client, in order to boot up, grab an IP address, locate a RIS server, and then receive the RIS image, needs to use one of the following technologies:

- The NetPC specification
- A Pre-Boot Execution Environment (PXE) network card v.99c or greater
- A RIS boot disk

Local Lingo

NetPC A set of specifications developed jointly by Windows and Intel that allows for a computer to boot to the network and run Windows applications locally. The important feature as far as RIS is concerned is the ability to easily connect to the network without an operating system already installed.

With a RIS installation, if properly configured, there is little if any need for user interaction. However, several procedural steps need to be completed when performing an installation using RIS. Some of these procedures will involve preparing a Windows 2000 Server to house the RIS image. Some involve the correct authorization of the DHCP and RIS services in Active Directory, and others involve making sure the client computer can boot up and locate a RIS server.

Since the purpose of this book is to give you the basics of what you need to prepare for an exam, the following discussion will be an overview, not a lesson, in RIS.

Travel Assistance

For more detailed information on RIS, please refer to the *Windows XP Resource Kit Documentation*, Chapter 2, from Microsoft Press.

As mentioned, the RIS server is the computer running the 2000 Server that will also be running the RIS service and hold the images that will be used for client installation. Two kinds of images can be stored on a RIS server: CD-based images and RIPrep images. CD-based images contain the Windows XP Professional OS files and can be customized through the use of answer files. RIPrep images are based on a preconfigured computer and can contain application installations as well. RIS with a RIPrep image is Microsoft's version of a cloning program, like Symantec's Ghost.

To prepare the RIS server, the following *must* occur:

1. The RIS service must be installed. This can be done with the Add/Remove Windows Components section of the Add/Remove Programs applet in the Control Panel. The RIS server must then be authorized in Active Directory through DHCP Manager.

2. After RIS is installed, you will configure RIS by typing **RISETUP** in the Run dialog box. The Remote Installation Services Setup Wizard starts. After you click the Next button from the Welcome screen, the Remote Installation Folder Location dialog box appears. This is just the folder that holds the RIS images.

3. The Initial Settings dialog box appears next, allowing you to configure the RIS server to respond to client requests. Notice that the server does not respond to client requests until you tell it to do so. It is enabled with a check box, as seen in Figure 1-10.

4. The next steps will depend on what type of image you are setting up on the RIS server. You will be prompted in the next few screens for the installation files location, the image folder name, and the friendly name. When you are finished, a Review Settings dialog box gathers all your choices for review.

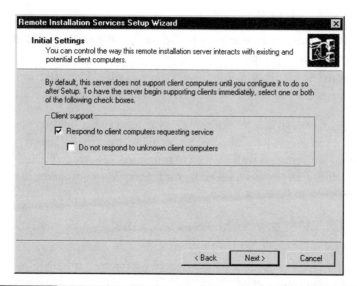

FIGURE 1.10   Configuring the RIS server to respond to image requests

5. The installation files will be copied at this time, a process that can take several minutes to complete. Click the Done button when through.

6. Next, users who will perform RIS installations must be granted the right to create computer accounts. These users must also have the right to Log On As A Batch Job user. (The details of how to grant user accounts rights to perform system tasks are covered in the Chapter 8 discussion of user accounts.)

Exam Tip

The Remote Installation Folder in step 2 must reside on a partition separate from the operating system, and furthermore must use NTFS.

A successful RIS implementation relies on the following network services to be in place:

• DCHP, which is used to assign IP addresses to RIS clients.
• A Domain Name Service (DNS) server, which is used to locate Active Directory.

- Active Directory, which is used to find the authorized RIS servers and RIS clients as well as to manage RIS configuration settings and client installation options.
- A RIS Server is also needed, which appears self-evident, but don't forget that you need to have a server running RIS in order to use RIS.

All right, enough acronyms already. (As an aside, regarding accepted social etiquette, you should know that you're not going to get many dates if you start peppering conversation with a bunch of computer acronyms.) The integration of these three technologies is necessary for RIS to perform properly. In order of operation, the RIS client will:

1. Boot and be leased an IP address from a DHCP server. It can then communicate on the network.

2. IP address in hand, query the DNS server for the Active Directory domain controller.

3. Once the IP address of the domain controller is returned, query Active Directory for a list of RIS servers in the network. It will then contact the RIS server and request (from a possible list of OS choices, as discussed later) that the operating system be sent.

As you can see, this technology crosses many boundaries, a number of which exist on the server side, which is why this won't be the last you hear of RIS.

The computer that will connect to the RIS server for the install of Windows XP Professional is the RIS client. To complete the first step of the RIS process just listed, it is necessary that the RIS clients rely on a network card technology called PXE (Pre-Boot Execution Environment). The magic of a PXE-compliant network card is that it can go out and find an IP address without the aid of an operating system. In other words, it's a bootable network card. Once this card has an IP address, it can eventually connect to a RIS server and be sent an installation image.

Exam Tip

As mentioned earlier, if your potential RIS client cannot boot from the network card, you can create and use a RIS boot disk to start that client computer. The utility used for the generation of the RIS boot disk is called Remote Boot Floppy Generator, and it will be run from the RIS Server by typing **rbfg.exe** from the Run dialog box.

After the PXE-compliant system has been started and has located a RIS server, you will answer a series of questions to complete the installation. Here are the steps involved to install the RIS image:

1. Press the proper key, if necessary (this will usually be preset by your manufacturer or just configured through the BIOS), to start a network service boot on the client computer. The RIS server will be found, and the Client Installation Wizard will start.

2. After you press ENTER, the Windows XP Logon dialog box appears. You will be prompted for the user name and password and a valid domain name.

3. A menu will appear showing you the setup options available. These options include Automatic Setup, Custom Setup, and Restart a Previous Setup Attempt. You will most likely choose the Automatic Setup option.

4. After selecting which Setup option to run, the image on the RIS server will be installed if only one image is available. If multiple images are available on the RIS server, you will be able to choose which one to apply to your machine.

5. The remote installation will now begin. What happens next during Setup depends on whether or not you have configured the use of unattended installation files.

Create Unattended Answer Files Using the Setup Manager to Automate the Installation of Windows XP Professional

The goal of any automated setup is to provide answers to Setup's questions, so that you don't have to be sitting at the computer providing the answers. One of the methods by which this can be accomplished is with a file called an *answer file*. An answer file's job is to store answers to questions that Setup normally poses during an attended installation. For a long time, Windows users have been able to use answer files, but the creation of these files was such torture that few bothered to do so; it wasn't really worth the effort. The manual creation of answer files is still available, but Microsoft has made it much easier with the creation of the Setup Manager. First introduced in the NT 4 Resource Kit, the Setup Manager's help with automation of the installation process represents a significant improvement to the Windows family.

The Setup Manager provides a wizard-based interface that leads you through a series of questions (as all wizards do) for quickly creating a script for a customized installation of Windows XP. This is a big improvement over the use in Windows NT 4 of cryptic script-file syntax (unless, that is, cryptic script syntax is your bag).

And, if you're into that kind of masochistic torture, you can let out a sigh of relief. As mentioned, you can still create the script files the old-fashioned way by editing the unattend.txt file that installs with Windows. You can find it in the \i386 directory on the installation CD-ROM. However, the Setup Manager makes this file creation much easier and eliminates errors in syntax.

Here's how to use the Setup Manager:

1. Extract the Windows XP deployment tools from the deploy.cab file that is found in the \Support\Tools folder on the Windows XP Professional _CD-ROM. Double-click this cabinet file and you should see a list of deployment tools and help items in the details pane (if you have used Windows Explorer, as I have in Figure 1-11).

2. Right-click the files you want to extract (you can just lasso the entire contents of the deploy.cab file as well), and then select Extract from the context menu. It is a good idea to have the destination folder already created before the Extract procedure, as the extract utility does not let you create folders.

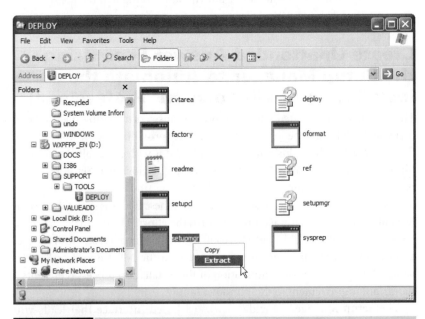

FIGURE 1.11 The Deploy Tools that are stored in the deploy.cab file

3. After you have extracted the Windows XP deployment tools, you can run the Setup Manager by double-clicking setupmgr.exe from the location you have extracted the tools to. You will then be presented with the first fork in the road, and you will be able to do one of two things, as shown in Figure 1-12: create a new answer file or edit an existing answer file.

4. Click the Next button. For this example, it is assumed that you want to create a new answer file. The Product to Install dialog box appears next. You can select a Windows XP Unattended Installation, a SysPrep Install (discussed later), or a Remote Installation Services install, as shown in Figure 1-13. For this example, choose Remote Installation Services.

5. In the User Interaction dialog box that appears next, select one of five levels of user interaction during the install. Each option is described when you select its respective radio button. Assume that the Provide Defaults options is selected and click Next.

6. The Administrator password dialog box appears, as shown in Figure 1-14. You can have the user prompted for the Administrator password, specify an account and password, or choose to log on automatically as Administrator when the computer starts. Make a choice and click Next.

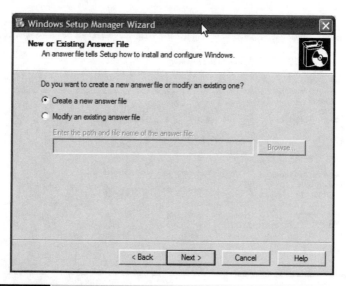

FIGURE 1.12   The answer file options

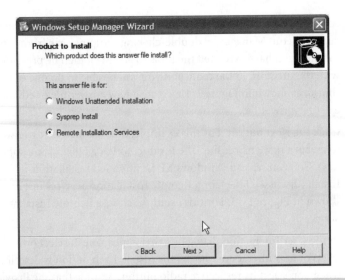

FIGURE 1.13 The Product to Install dialog box

7. In the Display Settings dialog box , configure your display settings. Each of the drop-down boxes will configure the user's display without the user having to change settings through the Display applet of the Control Panel.

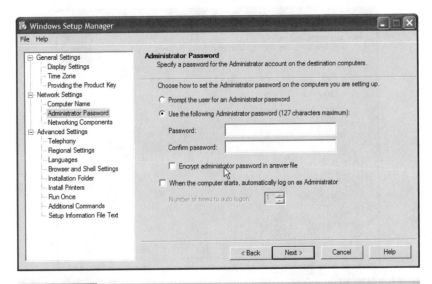

FIGURE 1.14 The Administrator Password dialog box

8. In the Network Settings dialog box, you provide answer file information about how the computer will interact with the network. Notice that you are essentially going through Windows XP Professional Setup, except that rather than configuring the computer on the spot, these answers are used to generate a file that can be used in the configuration.

9. Click Next to configure the Time Zone; then click Next again. The Additional Settings dialog box then lets you edit settings like these:

   - Telephony settings
   - Regional settings
   - Languages
   - Browser administrator shell settings
   - The location of the installation folder
   - Installed printers
   - A command (if any) that will be run the first time a user logs on

10. The default selection is No, Do Not Edit the Additional Settings, which we'll select. Click Next to continue.

11. In the Setup Information File Text dialog box, provide the answer file with a descriptive name and any other text that might be helpful. You might want to include information here that would let you quickly recognize what kinds of information are contained in the file. After entering this information, click Next.

12. The Answer File Name dialog box appears, as shown in Figure 1-15. This is the filename and storage location that will be saved to the hard disk. The default name for the file is remboot.sif. Click Save and then click the Next button.

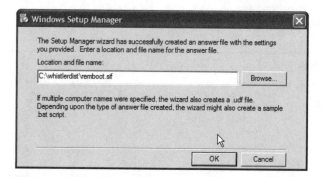

FIGURE 1.15 The Answer File Name dialog box

13. After completing the Windows XP Setup Manager Wizard, a dialog box appears to verify the successful creation of the answer file. Click the Finish button after you have reviewed this information.

Install Windows XP Professional Using the System Preparation Tool

If your goal is to install Windows XP Professional with identical configurations on several computers, the most efficient installation method is to use disk duplication. You may have heard this called *ghosting*, *cloning*, or *imaging* in the workplace. The image refers to the snapshot of the computer configuration that will be copied to other systems on the network, giving each system a consistent configuration. Windows XP includes a slick little utility that will help create these images, called SysPrep. It is extracted from the \Support\Tools folder in the same way that the Setup Manager is, as shown in Figure 1-16.

The main job of SysPrep is to remove the security identifier (SID) of the source computer, which is essentially the thumbprint of the computer. When you delete an account, you are deleting the SID, which is why if you delete an account and then create another account with the same name, you must reset all permissions for that account—to the computer, the new account is a different account. Without getting too technical about it, if you have a network in which computers' SIDs are the same, you have problems.

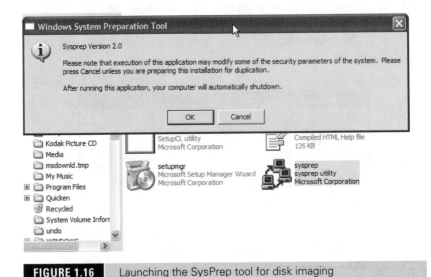

FIGURE 1.16   Launching the SysPrep tool for disk imaging

Local Lingo

SID A unique number that identifies user, group, and computer accounts. Internal processes used by Windows XP refer to the SID of the computer account, not its name.

After you've used SysPrep to prepare the system for image creation, you can then copy it to destination computers through third-party software or through disk duplication.

SysPrep is also responsible for generating a mini-Setup wizard that is added to the master image of the operating system. After you have installed the image on the target computer, this mini-Setup wizard guides the user through the process of entering user-specific information during setup, such as:

- Product ID
- Regional settings
- User name
- Company name
- Network configuration

What's key about the use of the SysPrep tool is that you have an understanding of the required components on the clients who want to use the target copy of the operating system. Although it used to be the case that where a client using a SysPrep image needed the hard disk controller and hardware abstraction layer (HAL) as the SysPrepped machine, this is no longer the case. The current version of SysPrep, Version 2.0, does away with these requirements. The other hardware components, such as the video card and the network adapter, do not need to be the same because the SysPrep tool will cause all the clients using the master image to run a full Plug and Play detection as a part of the OS setup.

Travel Assistance

If you plan on using SysPrep for real-world installations, you are going to want more information than presented in this test overview. Please refer to the *XP Resource Kit* from Microsoft Press. However, be aware that there are many more deployment options than the ones covered here.

The four switches listed in Table 1-4 can be used to modify how SysPrep behaves, and knowing them is a good idea as you prepare for the exam.

TABLE 1.4	Command-Line Switches for Use with SysPrep
Switch	**What It Does**
/quiet	With this switch, SysPrep requires no user interaction.
/pnp	Forces Setup to detect Plug and Play devices on the destination computer.
/reboot	Restarts the source computer upon completion of SysPrep.
/nosidgen	Doesn't regenerate SIDs on the destination computers.

We've talked quite a bit about using SysPrep and preparing a computer for the creation of the master image. To make sure you understand this technology, let's review the steps:

1. Install Windows XP Professional on a source computer. Extract the deploy.cab file from the CD-ROM, as described previously.

2. Log on to the source computer as the Administrator to install any other applications as desired.

3. Run the SysPrep utility from the extraction folder.

4. The Windows XP Professional System Preparation Tool dialog box appears, warning you that security parameters will be modified. Click OK, and then you will be prompted to shut down your system.

5. Now use a third-party imaging tool to create the image.

Now the image is ready for use. Copy the image to a shared folder or CD-ROM for distribution computers.

Local Lingo

Shared folder A place on a network computer that other computers can connect to and get stuff, like image files. A more thorough discussion of shared folders can be found in Chapter 3.

Once this third-party image has made it to the destination computers, your end users can start up their computers. The mini-Setup wizard will prompt each user for the variables mentioned, and the install is on its way. You can also automate the completion of the mini-Setup wizard by creating a sysprep.inf file with the Setup Manager Wizard.

Exam Tip

Make sure you remember that the Setup Manager creates a file called sysprep.inf for use with SysPrep-imaged installations.

 **Objective 1.03** # Upgrade from a Previous Version of Windows to Windows XP Professional

Remember that you will have three options after assessing the compatibility of the hardware to receive a Windows XP Professional installation:

- Perform a clean install of Windows XP Professional.
- Upgrade a previous installation.
- Preserve the existing installation of whatever OS is there by installing Windows XP Professional in a separate disk or partition. Although technically possible, Microsoft does not support a separate install of XP into the same partition as an existing operating system.

Objective 1.01 assumed that you are performing a clean install of XP onto a system that does not have any operating system, or an install where the current OS will be wiped out. This next section discusses in further detail the last two options you will have at Setup time, which are outlined in the splash screen that appears when you insert the Windows XP Professional Setup CD-ROM into a computer with a preexisting operating system like Windows 98, and you choose the option to Install Windows XP.

Prepare a Computer to Meet Windows XP Requirements

The first order of business when performing an installation of Windows XP Professional is to make sure it will play nicely with your existing hardware and software. One thing you are sure to discover relatively quickly is that many programs written for the Windows 9x environment won't run the way they're supposed to under Windows XP. Also, if you've got old hardware lying around and intend to use it with your new OS, you may be set up for either 1) disappointment or 2) a trip to a computer store. Because so much is new in this game,

Windows XP can be a little finicky about who gets to play, and the time to discover this is *before* you've completed the setup process, not after. You can ignore this advice at your peril, as I have explained to many clients of mine after receiving calls like, "My [insert hardware device here] does not work, and I've been on hold with [insert company name here] for the last hour and a half, so could you please come fix this?"

Travel Advisory

One great new feature of XP is Application Compatibility, which means you are far less likely to have software compatibility problems than hardware compatibility problems. It can be used to make a variety of applications work, even though they were written without XP in mind. To use Application Compatibility, right-click the Start menu shortcut that launches the program and choose Properties. Then select the Compatibility tab and the compatibility mode that is appropriate for the app. By doing this, you can trick an application into thinking it's running on a machine with a previous version of Windows. Alternatively, you could use the Program Compatibility Wizard, which can be launched through Start | All Programs | Accessories | Program Compatibility Wizard.

Fortunately, to help you determine what software and hardware components Windows XP Professional will and won't work with, Microsoft publishes and continually updates its Hardware Compatibility List (HCL), a database of the currently tested hardware components on which Windows XP Professional will run. You can search through the most recent revision of the HCL at the Microsoft site (http://www.microsoft.com/hcl/). There are several ways to search the HCL from this site, and you can also get the HCL in a plain text format from a Microsoft FTP site.

The good folks in Redmond recommend that you check the HCL prior to performing an installation of Windows XP Professional; they might even think that most people actually do. The best rule of thumb is that a check of the HCL is warranted if you're considering an upgrade of an older computer. Most modern computers will support Windows XP Professional quite nicely (refer to the list of minimum hardware requirements in Table 1-1), regardless of whether or not hardware components exist on the HCL. And not every piece of hardware will appear on the HCL, even though it might get along with Windows XP just fine.

Of course, this brings us to the other method of verifying whether or not the hardware you are considering will support Windows XP Professional: just install the darned thing on the intended computer. If it works, the hardware is supported. If not, well, you can always try to find new drivers or wait for a service pack release. This will be a problem, however, if you don't have the luxury of a test computer or a removable hard drive on which to perform an install.

Travel Advisory

Here's a quick note about removable hard drives: get them. Removable drives allow you to experiment with multiple configurations without fear of messing something up. You can keep a "production" hard drive for storing all your work and critical data and a "test" hard drive where you can try out all the features of Windows XP, or anything else, for that matter.

So again, the caveat here is: be careful on older hardware. Installation "issues" have been known to arise. For example, I have an older printer that is great for laptops because it is easily moved. Actually, it's great on laptops running Windows 98, because no driver for it exists on the Windows XP installation media and the manufacturer won't bother to write one. I have seen numerous other problems with older hardware, from network cards to scanners, which flat-out won't work on Windows XP.

Travel Advisory

New hardware components and peripherals are usually just fine with Windows XP, but you should be prepared to shell out some extra money to upgrade hardware if you are using older stuff.

To determine software compatibility, you will need to check with the application vendor, check the Microsoft compatibility list, or check both. You can find the software compatibility list by searching on the keywords "software compatibility" at http://www.microsoft.com/windowsXP/. But, as with hardware, probably the best way to check application compatibility is just through old-fashioned trial and error—of course, away from a production environment. Again, if it's new, it's likely supported on XP.

The Upgrade Advisor

Along with the HCL, Microsoft included a utility called the Windows XP Upgrade Advisor, and this is a favorite test topic. The Upgrade Advisor is really a subset of the XP Setup utility, and is intended to check for hardware compatibility, software compatibility, or both.

There are two ways to run the Upgrade Advisor. One is to launch it directly from the installation CD's splash screen. You will choose Check System Compatibility and then click Check My System Automatically.

The other way you can run the utility is from the command line. You can do this if your CD's splash screen doesn't appear or if you have done other things since inserting the CD-ROM. The syntax of the Upgrade Advisor command is

```
D:\i386\winnt32 /checkupgradeonly
```

where *d* is the letter of your CD-ROM drive

Both of these methods accomplish essentially the same thing—they run the Advisor, which in turn prepares an Upgrade Compatibility Report, as shown in Figure 1-17. The report lists potential problems you may encounter during an upgrade. If the report reveals a significant compatibility issue, such as a problem with the I/O drivers for the hard drive (which would be rare), you should cancel Setup and address the issues. If the report lists only minor issues, you can safely proceed. Either of these two utilities checks your computer for upgrade compatibility with Windows XP.

Exam Tip	

Microsoft loves to test on the use of the /checkupgradeonly switch.

As mentioned, most newer hardware will support XP without incident. For testing purposes, it is essential to know the requirements for installation. Table 1-5 shows the minimum and recommended requirements for an installation of

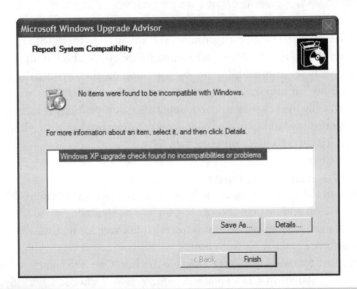

FIGURE 1.17   The Upgrade Compatibility Report lists any potential compatibility problems before installation.

Windows XP Professional. Note that this table is based on published Microsoft requirements current as of the date of this publication. However, Microsoft has been known to update this table, so a double-check of the Microsoft website with regards to the minimums isn't a bad idea.

As you can see, these installation requirements leave plenty of breathing room on any new system, and Windows XP Professional will run beautifully on modern computers. Peripherals, especially older ones, are the thing you have to worry about the most.

> **Travel Advisory**
>
> The most important component, by the way, for real-world performance of XP, is memory. Consensus among the top XP minds is to have at least 192MB for best performance.

For application compatibility issues, apps that work on Windows 2000 machines generally should work with XP. Applications that were written specifically for Windows 9x computers can potentially be problematic—some of these programs install differently on Windows 9x than they do on 2000 and XP. The Upgrade Advisor should flag these potential problems, and it may even offer to download updated service packs during XP installation (if the service packs are available). This is a process called *Dynamic Updates*, which is also offered as a part of Setup, as described later.

When you choose to upgrade your installation of Windows, Setup offers to check the Internet for any updates of service packs, hotfixes, or updated drivers for the hardware and software detected on your system. The Dynamic Update process is highly recommended while performing Setup, as it gives you the very

TABLE 1.5   Minimum Installation Requirements

Component	Minimum Requirement	Recommended Requirement
Processor	Pentium-class 233MHz processor	Pentium-class 300MHz processor
Memory	64MB RAM	128MB RAM
Hard drive space	1.5GB free disk space	1.5GB free disk space
Network	None required	Network card as required by your network topology (usually a card on the PCI bus)
Display	Super VGA (800×600) or higher resolution video adapter	Super VGA (800×600) or higher resolution video adapter

best chance for problem-free installation. By making installation inclusive of these latest patches, Dynamic Update can save you the headache of having to install a bunch of updates the first time you run XP.

Travel Advisory

Windows 16-bit and 32-bit applications that use *virtual device drivers* (VxDs) will not run properly in Windows XP.

As a last upgrade note, you should assume that any programs that work at the system level, like disk partitioning tools or antivirus programs that were written for prior versions of Windows, will not work with XP. My copy of Partition Commander, for example, has been rendered useless on my XP machine.

Configuring Dual Boot

When you install Windows XP Professional into a different folder than the one with the current OS, you will have configured a computer that can multiboot (or dual-boot). This second OS folder can be located on the same partition as the current OS or on a different one. Be mindful, however, of your file system considerations when configuring a system for dual-boot. For example, remember that Windows 9x cannot read any data locally from an NTFS partition without the addition of a third-party utility. Also, the NTFS file system version native to NT 4.0 is not fully compatible with the NTFS version in use with XP. Here are some other important considerations when setting up a dual-boot configuration:

- If you will be dual-booting to Windows NT 4, make sure that disk compression is turned off. Windows XP will not be able to read the drive properly if it is on.

- Never upgrade to dynamic disks, unless you are booting between XP and 2000 only. Dynamic disks are seen only by Windows XP Professional and 2000 Professional and Server computers; they are not recognized by earlier Microsoft operating systems, such as Windows 98.

- Perform the install of Windows 9x or DOS before installing Windows XP. If you install Windows XP first, you can't install a previous OS without trashing the Windows XP installation.

- Make sure you have enough disk space. An additional OS will take up a lot of room, and you will have to install applications twice to be used with both of them.

Travel Advisory

When setting up a dual-boot computer, if Windows NT 4.0 contains no service pack or a version prior to SP6, the Windows XP Setup routine will warn you not to continue the installation. If you plow ahead anyway, you will not be able to boot into Windows NT 4.0 after Windows XP is installed.

We will also be discussing additional dual-booting issues in Chapter 2, as we talk about disk and file system management. Before you install Windows 2000 and XP on the same system, even if you've performed dual-boot installations before, I recommend that you take a look at that chapter.

Performing the Upgrade to Windows XP Professional

When you think about it, the computer's OS is nothing more than another piece of software installed on a computer, just like any other application. And just like other applications, the OS has an installation directory where the bulk of the files are placed. When you install over the current folder holding the computer's OS, you are performing an upgrade. You will be able to perform an upgrade to Windows XP Professional on the following operating systems: Windows 98, Me, NT Workstation 4.0, Windows 2000 Professional, and XP Home edition. Conceptually, it's like going from Office 97 to Office XP—out with the old, in with the new. The data and applications on the computer should be unaffected—that is, unless they are incompatible with Windows XP Professional, which you should have found out beforehand if you had done your homework!

Remember, while it's possible to get XP on a machine that's running Windows 95, it isn't considered an *upgrade*, because there is the intermediary step of first progressing to Windows 98 (or Me, or 2000 Pro…). You could also do a clean install on such a system.

Want to upgrade from DOS or Windows 3.x? Tough. In the first place, such a computer's hardware probably won't suffice. There is no upgrade from DOS or Windows 3.1, but if you want to do a clean install of Windows XP on a computer running DOS, you may run the 16-bit version of the Windows XP Setup program, winnt.exe.

Exam Tip

If you're upgrading a computer running Windows 98 or Me that lives in an NT 4.0 or Windows 2000 domain to Windows XP, make sure that you create an account for the computer object in that domain. This can be done either prior to or during the upgrade of the OS.

Migrate Existing User Environments to a New User Installation

When you perform an upgrade to Windows XP from a previous version of Windows, all of your previous programs and settings should remain intact. You should see all the same items on the Start menu as before.

But suppose your Windows XP will *not* be on the same disk that has all your working files and the programs you want to keep. For instance, you may be installing Windows XP on a new computer or separate disk drive, or you may have purchased a new computer with Windows XP already installed. What then? Enter the Files and Settings Transfer Wizard, which by itself might be worth the price of XP.

In the past, when you migrated from one computer to another, you either had to use third-party utilities or go through a laborious backup and restore process in order to get the old environment transferred to the new. Now with the Files and Settings Transfer Wizard, you can take the files and program settings from any 32-bit version of Windows and apply them to your new installation of XP with a minimum of effort. This feature saves hours of headache when configuring a new system and is available on both XP Pro and Home editions.

Travel Advisory

The Files and Settings Transfer Wizard is an update of the User Settings Migration tool, which is still available on the Microsoft website if you search from the Windows 2000 home page. Both tools do essentially the same thing, but the Files and Settings Transfer Wizard utilizes the Wizard interface.

There are two ways to get your files and settings from one computer to another using the Wizard:

- **A direct network connection** This option is the easiest to execute and often takes advantage of an existing network. You can connect two computers together using the LAN or via a null modem cable and take settings directly from the one system to the other. If possible, use the Fast Ethernet option, especially when transferring lots of data files from old system to new.

- **Saving the settings to a file**   If a direct connection isn't practical, you can use the Files and Settings Transfer Wizard to save the settings to a file and then apply this file after you have finished installing XP on the new system. You can think of this option as making a backup of all your current settings, then restoring that backup on the new system. You can save the output to any removable media, including Zip disks, floppies, and CD-R devices, and also to a network location (although this would be rarely done, as you would just choose the first option if a network was available).

For the example that follows, we will assume that a network connection between an old and a new computer is in place. This will give you the overview necessary to understand the purpose and function of the Wizard, which is what you will need for the exam. For real-world use, there are many forks in the road that can be taken when using the Wizard. However, if you understand the following example, you shouldn't have any trouble using any of the other options. To start the Files and Settings Transfer Wizard, install XP on the target computer (the one that will *receive* the transferred settings), then complete the following:

1. On the target XP system, choose Start | All Programs | System Tools | Files and Settings Transfer Wizard. (You can also type **migwiz** from the Run dialog box, or follow the Perform Additional Tasks button when you insert the Windows XP CD. Or you can even double-click the fastwiz.exe icon in the CD's \Support\Tools folder.)

2. Click Next to get the Files and Settings Transfer Wizard started.

3. Choose the New Computer Option and click Next.

4. Specify where the Files and Settings Transfer Wizard will be run from, as shown in Figure 1-18. This will usually be the XP Setup CD.

5. At the old computer, insert the Windows XP Professional CD and, from the Welcome splash screen, choose the option to Perform Additional Tasks and then Transfer Files and Settings.

6. Choose Old Computer when given the option about which computer this is, if running XP on the old system. If you are running a previous

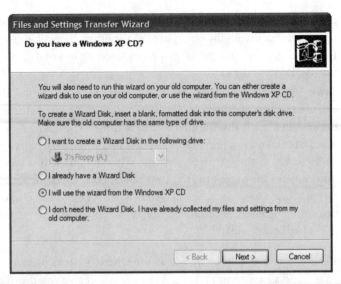

FIGURE 1.18 Choose the source files of the Files and Settings Transfer Wizard

Windows version, the Old Computer option is automatically selected and this page does not appear.

7. Make your choice about how the operation will proceed. We are using the network in this example.

What has transpired so far in the Files and Settings Transfer Wizard is sizzle; now you're to the steak. The next screen you see is where you begin to define exactly what will be traveling to its new home. As shown in Figure 1-19, you will be able to bring over Files, Settings, or Both. Each of these selections is inclusive of the items on the right side of the dialog box. However, the checkbox at the bottom lets you make changes to the defaults. Most of the time, you will use this selection, because it offers the most control over what's being transferred.

When you click Next, you will be taken to a dialog box where you are able to make your selections. It is not important to memorize each and every setting that can be transferred to each folder location that is suggested for relocation. The choices are fairly intuitive. For example, you can bring over your settings from Internet Explorer, preserving your Favorites list, but not the Display settings, because the new system has a better monitor and video adapter.

You will then be prompted to return to your new computer and retrieve a password that has been randomly generated. You will enter this password at the old computer, and the settings and files you have designated will be taken from

Files and Settings Transfer Wizard

What do you want to transfer?

What do you want to transfer?

   ○ Settings only
   ○ Files only
   ◉ Both files and settings

Based on your current selection, the following items will be transferred:

Settings
Accessibility
Adobe Acrobat Reader
Command Prompt settings
Folder options
Internet Explorer settings
Microsoft Messenger
Microsoft Netmeeting
Microsoft Office
Mouse and keyboard
Network printer and drives

   ☐ Let me select a custom list of files and settings when I click Next (for advanced users)

      < Back   Next >   Cancel

FIGURE 1.19   Choosing what to transfer

one system to the other. Depending on your file selections and the speed of your network, the transfer will take anywhere from a few seconds to several minutes.

Travel Advisory

Avoid at all cost using a serial cable connection. It's slow and not much better than a dial-up connection. If you do use a serial cable and have a large amount of data to move, bring your Snickers bar. Even floppies are a better choice. You can also use a Zip disk, which would be faster than both.

Objective 1.04

Perform Post-Installation Updates and Product Activation

There are still a couple of items to take care of after your installation is complete to ensure problem-free operation and maximum exam readiness. These include the application of operating system updates, which you will be performing throughout the XP Professionial product cycle. This task is certainly not unique to the XP operating system, and examples abound. Prior versions of Windows as well as most other applications (antivirus applications and the Office suite come immediately to mind) undergo this constant update procedure. You likely have experience with product updates with Windows or other software by now, usually involving downloading files over the Internet, and the process in XP shouldn't present that great of a challenge to anyone with this experience.

The other task necessary, new to XP, is product activation.

Post installation Updates

No operating system is a static entity; all are constructed with code, and that code is constantly improving, evolving, changing. Windows XP is certainly no exception, and by the time you read this, a major update to XP will have been published. You will perform a majority of these updates by applying service packs. The first thing you need to understand about service packs is that their name is misleading. When Microsoft hires me to run the company, I am going to start calling them Operating System Updates, because that's what they are. You can locate them on the Windows update website, a centralized, online resource for Windows Updates that, in my opinion, is just one of the smartest, easiest to use, greatest little things that Microsoft has ever put together. You will find it at http://windowsupdate.microsoft.com, which is the site opened with the shortcut that appears on the Start menu. On this site, you can find hotfixes, drivers, and service packs for all kinds of Windows products, and the interface even suggests the best ones to download and install automatically.

An operating system update is meant to address a specific feature, something Microsoft recommends be installed right away rather than being included in a service pack release. A recent example of this was the hotfix that was released for IIS 4, which fixed an issue that left the web server vulnerable to attack.

New to Windows XP is a feature that lets you choose how and when Windows Updates are installed. From a tab in the System Properties dialog box (right-click My Computer and choose Properties), you can adjust the settings of Automatic Updates, as shown in Figure 1-20.

The Automatic Updates tab presents you with three choices:

- **Download the Updates and Notify Me When They Are Ready to Be Installed** This option is especially tailored to users with persistent Internet connections. When OS updates are downloaded, the notification area in the system tray alerts you. Note that you aren't forced to install the update. You can always reject any download.

- **Notify Me Before Downloading Any Updates and Notify Me Again Before Installing Them On My Computer** With this option, you will

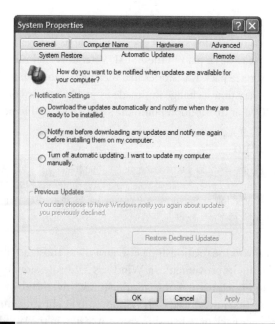

FIGURE 1.20 XP will check automatically for hotfixes and service packs when you select either of the first two options.

be notified when updates are available from the Windows Update website, but you are given the choice of whether or not to download. This choice is more suited for users with dial-up connections, because they need to have more control over bandwidth use.

- **Turn Off Automatic Updating. I Want to Update My Computer Manually**   This is the old way of performing OS updates, used in Windows 98 and Windows 2000. You can use this option to centrally manage Windows Updates, which is better suited to most business environments (where OS Updates will be downloaded once, and then scheduled for off-hours installation, rather than to all individual computers in an enterprise).

Oh Yeah, I *Did* Want to Install that Patch...

The Automatic Updates tab also lets you review downloaded updates that did not make the cut the first time around. Downloaded updates are not deleted automatically from your hard drive, and with the Restore Declined Updates button, you can choose from a list and perform the installation you have previously rejected. Notice that in Figure 1-20 this button is grayed out. Why? At the time the screen shot was taken, I had not rejected any updates.

Slipstreaming

In earlier versions of Windows 32-bit operating systems like NT 4.0, the application of service packs was a pain in the ASCII. Veteran NT administrators can sit around telling service pack war stories like the crew of the fishing boat in *Jaws*. That's because every time a change was made from what existed on the operating system's CD-ROM or distribution point, the service pack had to be reapplied.

Local Lingo

Distribution Point   A folder where the installation files for the operating system are stored and shared. For example, if you copied the contents of the \i386 directory to a shared folder called \W2K Pro, you would have just set up a distribution point.

Figure 1-21 shows the relationship between a client and a distribution point.

Now for the big improvement. In Windows XP Professional, a technology called *slipstreaming* eliminates the administrative overhead of service pack reapplication. As first introduced with Windows 2000, slipstreaming allows you to apply the service pack update just to the source files in the Windows XP Professional distribution point. Any installations made from this distribution point also include the application of the service pack. Further, any services or drivers added to the local installation come from the distribution point, again avoiding the need to reapply the service pack to the local machine.

Exam Tip

The important thing to remember, and the thing about service packs that you are likely to be tested on, is that you need to apply the service pack to a distribution point, even if the distribution point is the local machine, to take advantage of slipstreaming.

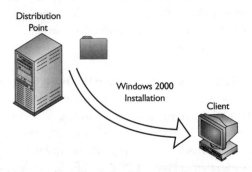

Distribution
Point

Windows 2000
Installation

Client

FIGURE 1.21   Client and distribution point

To implement slipstreaming, you must modify the default behavior of update.exe, the service pack installation utility. From the command line, type

```
update -s: distribution folder
```

where *distribution folder* is the location of the OS files. This command will execute slipstreaming. From then on, use the distribution point to perform any changes to services or drivers on the local installation.

Exam Tip

Even though most administrative tasks can be accomplished from Windows' graphical interface, Microsoft loves to ask you questions about the times when they cannot. You are expected to know the commands and important switches used for many of these command-line utilities.

Activating Windows XP

By now you've probably heard of the donnybrook caused by Microsoft's activation feature. Built into Windows XP is a new antipiracy technology called Windows Product Activation (WPA), that was introduced to a chorus of…well a chorus of *something* on Internet bulletin boards—in my opinion, it's not that big a deal. Whatever your personal feeling towards this new technology, its intent is very simple and very understandable: to make it harder for people to steal Microsoft's software.

WPA works by associating the Product Key you enter at Setup time (in reality just a portion thereof) to the hardware configuration. The hardware configuration information comes from a "hardware hash," which is derived from a number of elements that characterize the machine. These components include your video card, primary hard drive, CPU, RAM, network adapter, and CD-ROM drive. It ignores peripherals such as printers and digital cameras. These two values are combined to generate an installation ID.

In order to activate the machine, the installation ID is sent to Microsoft, which validates it. After Microsoft's WPA clearinghouse clears the installation ID, Windows XP is good to go, and reactivation should be necessary only if the operating system is completely reinstalled or if the machine's hardware is substantially changed. What "substantially" means is that, if you upgrade four or more components on one machine from the list above within 120 days of each other, you will be required to call the WPA clearinghouse and obtain a new activation code. In other words, if you want to slap in a new video card, or upgrade your hard drive, go ahead—everything should still work just fine.

You will have 30 days to activate your installation of Windows XP, and, trust me, they are not going to give you a chance to forget that you're supposed to register. You will see pesky reminders to activate each time you log on. After expiration, Windows will disallow interactive logons until the system is activated. Because you have 30 days, it is probably a good idea to wait a week or two before activating. That way, you can make sure that all the hardware and software you plan to use is operational. Also, it lets you make configuration changes before activation, without affecting the installation ID.

Microsoft provides a volume licensing agreement for businesses and large organizations, and these volume agreements supply administrators with distribution media that are exempt from Product Activation.

Remember, the idea is to prevent casual copying: they don't want you purchasing a copy of XP and then running a cloning program to upgrade your entire network of 20 users with that single copy of Windows. Unlike many dot-coms long since out of business, Microsoft actually wants you to pay for its products.

Also, keep in mind that activation and registration are not the same thing. Product activation is completely anonymous, and no personal information is divulged. Really. Microsoft does not get your name, phone number, address, or Social Security benefits. (Microsoft has saved that for when you sign up for a Passport and try to get support.)

Travel Advisory

For more information about Windows Product Activation, please check what Microsoft has to say about it at http://www.microsoft.com/windowsxp, and search for "WPA."

 **Objective 1.05** ## Troubleshoot Failed Installations

To borrow a phrase from Austin Powers, "This organization will not tolerate failure!" The same can be said for the setup of Windows XP Professional. Following are a few guidelines that will help you overcome many installation pitfalls.

First, make sure all of the hardware is supported. Most technicians start to look at the HCL only after a failed install. And at the risk of repeating the obvious,

Microsoft recommends that you remove or upgrade the components not on the HCL *before* attempting installation again.

Another important task is to make sure that the computer's basic input/ output system (the BIOS) is up to date. Vendor-provided BIOS updates can resolve many installation failures. One example of this: disabling the Plug and Play Operation System setting in the BIOS is important before installing Windows XP Professional on computers that don't support the Advanced Configuration and Power Interface (ACPI) specification. (Most newer computers will support ACPI.)

Your next step in troubleshooting installation failures is to determine at which point of the setup process the failure is occurring. Three distinct installation phases can be evaluated, as shown here:

- In the Setup Loader phase, some of the installation files are copied from the source to the local disk that is to receive the OS.
- In the Text-Mode Setup phase, you see white text against a blue background. Installation and configuration of hardware drivers continues. Minimum system requirements are verified here before Setup continues.
- The GUI-Mode Setup phase is the conclusion of the setup process. Additional device drivers are detected, installed, and configured.

If installation fails at the last phase, restarting the computer may resolve the problem, allowing Setup to continue. However, rebooting to resolve installation failure isn't an option during the first two phases of Setup. If installation fails during either of these phases, rebooting the computer will just bring you back to the same error.

A couple of information log files are created during setup that can be of assistance in troubleshooting the installation process. These files are a record of all the essential setup information:

- **setupact.log**   This is a listing of all the actions that were performed during installation and a description of each. The actions will be listed in chronological order.
- **setuperr.log**   This lists any errors encountered by Windows XP Setup. For each error, an indication of the severity of the error along with its description is included.

Several device-specific or component-specific log files also may be generated during the setup process or when a new Plug and Play device is added. These log files are stored in the *systemroot* directory (it's usually \WINDOWS). Here is a listing of a few you will want to be familiar with:

- **Comsetup.log**   Logs the COM setup routines
- **Mmdet.log**   Logs multimedia installation and resource definition
- **Netsetup.log**   Logs network computer name, workgroup, and domain validation
- **Iis5.log**   Logs the installation and configuration of Internet Information Services 5, if you've chosen to install this component.

CHECKPOINT

✔**Objective 1.01: Perform an Attended Installation of Windows XP Professional**   In this objective, we looked at some of the new features offered by XP, outlining reasons why one may choose XP as their computer's operating system. It then presented an overview of the attended installation options. We also examined important setup decisions involving such issues as installing into a workgroup or domain, choosing the language and locale settings, and partitioning your disk.

✔**Objective 1.02: Perform an Unattended Installation of Windows XP Professional**   In this objective, we looked at how to get XP on a system without providing answers to Setup questions, as is the case during an attended install. These unattended choices are of greater importance as organizations begin to grow. We looked at the role of the unattended script files (unattend.txt), and how these script files are used to provide answers to common installation questions. We also looked here at the Remote Installation technologies available to get Windows XP Professional on many computers with a minimum of administrative effort. We learned the basics of how to set up and configure RIS, and we looked at some of the RIS client requirements.

✔**Objective 1.03: Upgrade from a Previous Version of Windows to Windows XP**   We looked at some of the upgrade paths available for upgrading installations of Windows XP Professional from previous operating systems. We also identified several of the steps necessary to ensure a successful upgrade from previous Windows operating systems to Windows XP.

These include running the Upgrade Compatibility Report with the command winnt32 /checkupgradeonly. Additionally, we learned how to use the Files and Settings Transfer Wizard to easily migrate existing user environments to a new user installation.

✔**Objective 1.04: Perform Post-Installation Updates and Product Activation**   In this objective, we examined the process for applying service pack updates to the Windows XP operating system. We also looked at some new features that make the application of service packs much easier. We then looked at the controversial topic of Windows Product Activation and its implications for system use and hardware upgrades.

✔**Objective 1.05: Troubleshoot Failed Installation**   This objective identified a few of the common problems that can occur during installations, and what to do should these problems occur. We looked at some of the resources, such as log files created during installation, that can help us in our troubleshooting efforts.

REVIEW QUESTIONS

1. Setup Manager comes on the XP Setup CD, but you cannot run it from there. To run the Setup Manager for the easy creation of unattended setup files, the following tasks must be completed:

   A. Copy the Windows XP deployment tools by extracting the files in the Wintools32.cab file on the Windows XP Professional CD-ROM.

   B. Copy the Windows XP deployment tools by extracting the files in Deploy.cab file on the Windows XP Professional CD-ROM.

   C. Run the autoset.exe application in the directory to which you extracted the file.

   D. Run the setupmgr.exe application in the directory to which you extracted the file.

2. You are the administrator of a large network, and want to quickly install Windows XP on several systems. You have three Windows 2000 servers at your disposal and decide that RIS will be a cost-effective solution. What two kinds of images can you distribute from your RIS server?

   A. PXE-compliant

   B. RIPrep

   C. CD-based

   D. Published images

   E. Third-party images

3. The boss has given you the OK: it's time to upgrade the computers on your network to Windows XP Professional for the 30 employees of the company. Currently, they are running Windows 98 machines. You have procured the Windows XP Professional Setup CD and have also downloaded Service Pack 1. You copy the contents of the I386 directory to your Windows XP machine in a folder called \New OS and share it out with a sharename matching that of the distribution folder. You are now going to deploy Windows XP Professional on your client machines from that network share. How will you apply the service pack to all the Windows XP Professional deployment machines seamlessly as a part of the upgrade process?

   A. Type **update Windows XP**

   B. Type **update -s: New OS**

   C. Type **update /syspart -s**

   D. Type **update /slip: New OS**

4. Oliver has set up a RIS server on his network to distribute images to 50 PXE-compliant computers in an Active Directory domain. These client computers are currently running Windows 98, but the computer accounts will be added to the domain after installation. To the user accounts, he has set the proper user rights for OS installation. All of the clients in the network are DHCP clients. Additionally, the network is running WINS for name resolution on the 98 clients. However, upon boot-up, none of the intended RIS clients are being offered RIS images. What can you do to help Oliver fix this situation?

   A. Authorize the RIS server in Active Directory.

   B. Install the DNS service; RIS requires DNS.

   C. Create RIS boot disks for the intended clients.

   D. Remove the WINS server from the network.

5. On a home computer with a cable Internet connection, you installed Windows XP Professional. Months later, you notice that a service pack is available, so you download and install it. A few months later, you add another service from the original Windows XP Professional installation CD-ROM. What should you now do?

   A. Do nothing. The service pack is not affected.

   B. Type **update /refreshservicepack** at the command prompt.

   C. Run setupmgr.exe –s.

   D. Reapply the service pack.

6. Which of the following automated installation options can make use of an answer file? (Choose all that apply.)

   A. Unattended installations

   B. Attended installations

   C. SysPrep tool disk images

   D. RIS image installations

7. You are administering a large network, and are using RIS to distribute Windows XP Professional. However, the machines in the call center are older machines and are not NetPC compatible, nor do they have network cards that are PXE-compliant. What utility should you run to create a RIS boot disk for these clients?

   A. MAKEBOOT.EXE

   B. WINNT32 /RIS

   C. PXEBOOTR.EXE

   D. RBFG.EXE

8. You are setting up a Windows XP Professional OS for use at your office, Russell International. The install fails. Where will you start looking to determine the severity of the setup error?

   A. COMSETUP.LOG

   B. MMDET.LOG

   C. NETSETUP.LOG

   D. SETUPERR.LOG

9. As the admin of an international marketing firm, you are planning to deploy Windows XP Professional on several computers on your network. You would like to first check to see if any hardware or software upgrades are necessary before rolling out the new operating system. How can you quickly generate a report that will check that the computers you are considering for deployment are compatible with Windows XP?

   A. Run COMPATCHK.EXE from the \Support folder of the installation CD-ROM.

   B. Download and run the Upgrade Advisor from the Windows XP website.

   C. Use the winnt32 /checkupgradeonly switch of the installation utility.

   D. Use the winnt32 /checkupgradenow switch of the installation utility.

10. You will be performing an upgrade of your client workstations rather than a clean install. Which of the following Operating Systems support an OS upgrade to Windows XP Professional? (Choose all the apply.)

    A. Windows 95

    B. Windows 98 and Me

    C. Windows 2000 Professional

    D. Linux workstations

    E. NT 4 workstations

    F. NT 3.51 and NT 3.5 workstations

11. You have just installed a brand new system with the XP Professional operating system. You want your new computer to use all the settings the old computer had, and you also want to quickly move all of your working data from the old computer to the new. You decide to use the Files and Settings Transfer Wizard to do this. What means will you have from this Wizard to moves your files and settings.

    A. A set of floppy disks

    B. A writeable CD-ROM

    C. A network connection

    D. A crossover cable connection

    E. All of the above

REVIEW ANSWERS

1. **B** **D** To run the Setup Manager, you must first extract the tools from Deploy.cab, which is located in the \Support\Tools folder on the Windows XP Professional installation CD-ROM. Then, after the Setup Manager is extracted, start it by running setupmgr.exe. You will then be guided by a wizard through the process of generating an unattended setup file for a fully automated installation. A is incorrect because there is no such .cab file on the installation CD-ROM. C is incorrect because that is not the file used to start Setup Manager (it is also a make-believe file).

2. **B** **C** These two images can work with a RIS implementation. A is incorrect because, while PXE is a technology that is essential to (most) RIS installations, it describes the network card and not the image of the operating system. D is incorrect because Published is a term that applies to applications installed by Group Policy, not to RIS images. E doesn't apply because the RIS technology is Microsoft-specific.

3. **B**   This is the command needed to enable service pack slipstreaming. The command will apply the service pack files to the distribution folder. Any clients that then perform an installation from this shared directory will have the service pack automatically installed as well. A, C, and D are all incorrect because of the syntax of the command. This is one of the areas for which you must know syntax exactly to answer the question correctly. Update by itself can be used to apply a service pack on a local machine that is already running Windows XP Professional.

4. **A**   For the RIS server to offer installation images, it must first be authorized in Active Directory. B, while a true statement, is not necessary, because you can assume from the question that the network has access to DNS. You would not be able to install Active Directory without DNS. C is incorrect because the computers are PXE-compliant, so a boot disk should not be necessary. D is incorrect because WINS is a smokescreen here: it will not affect the operation of RIS in any way. This is a common Microsoft exam tactic.

5. **D**   When a new service is added to Windows XP Professional from the installation CD-ROM, you must reapply the previously installed service pack to ensure functionality. A is incorrect for this reason. B is incorrect because, while the update utility will be used to apply the service pack, this switch is not necessary. C is incorrect because this is not the correct utility to update service packs. Setup Manager is used to help generate automated installation scripts.

6. **A C D**   All these installation methods, with the exception of an attended installation, can use an answer file. B doesn't fit because, by its nature, an installation that is attended will not need an answer file.

7. **D**   RBFG.EXE is the utility to create a RIS boot disk. You can find it by connecting to the \\RIS_Server\Reminst\Admin\I386 directory. A is used to make boot disks, but the disks you make with this tool are the Windows XP Setup disks. B is incorrect because there is no such switch for WINNT32, and it's not the correct utility anyway. C is, well, let me know if you ever find the PXEBOOR utility.

8. **D**   This is the log file that is generated when errors are encountered during the setup process. You can view this log by finding it in the *systemroot* directory and opening it with a text editor. The rest are legitimate log files, but they are used for other troubleshooting purposes. A is wrong because COMSETUP.LOG logs COM component problems. B is the log file that will help troubleshoot multimedia device detection. C is also wrong because it is used to troubleshoot computer name registration and workgroup or domain detection.

9. **B C**   Windows XP Upgrade advisor can be found at the Microsoft website and will check to see if your hardware and software are ready. This program will run a minimal version of WINNT32.EXE to check the upgrade capability of the computer. The same thing applies to running winnt32 /checkupgradeonly. This switch will cause the winnt32 upgrade utility to generate a log file to report upgrade readiness. The file will be called UPGRADE.TXT on Windows 9x computers and WINNT32.LOG on NT 4 systems. A is incorrect because that utility does not exist, and the same goes for answer D. The /checkupgradenow switch is close, but this is not horseshoes.

10. **B C E**   You will almost certainly be asked which operating systems can be upgraded to Windows XP Professional. You can upgrade Windows 98, Me, 2000, and NT 4 machines to XP Professional. A is incorrect because upgrades from Windows 95 are not possible. You will have to upgrade to another operating systems first. D is incorrect because no upgrade path is defined for any UNIX system. (I guess I will get e-mails from Linux gurus about whether installing Windows XP Professional on a Linux box constitutes an upgrade.) E is incorrect because you cannot upgrade directly from NT 3.5 or 3.51. You must first upgrade those systems to NT 4 before an upgrade is possible.

11. **E**   All the choices are possible options when moving files and settings with the Files and Settings Transfer Wizard. You are taking files from one computer to another and can do that in a number of ways.

Managing Disk Drives, Volumes, and File Systems

	NEWBIE	SOME EXPERIENCE	EXPERT
ETA	4 hours	2 hours	1 hour

As you know, a hard disk is a piece of hardware, slapped in to your computer somewhere so that it can store data. It is a *physical* device that can do nothing more than hold "ones" and "zeros." But, before the platters of the hard drive can actually perform the function for which they were designed, they have to be prepared in such a way that the "ones" and "zeros" they hold make sense to the operating system. We prepare hard drives by performing two discrete steps: first we divide the disks into *logical* devices called *partitions* (or *volumes*), and then we format those partitions or volumes so that they can accept data in a format that the OS understands. But before we talk about the specifics of drive management, let's first lay the foundation with a closer look at two important disk management concepts: *partitioning* and *formatting*.

Partitioning

A physical drive cannot be recognized by the OS—it simply does not know it is there unless there is some way to manifest that drive so that the OS can see it. As was mentioned, partitioning is the process where we take a physical drive and convert it into one or more logical drives called partitions. These logical spaces are then assigned a drive letter. For example, you may have a system that has only one physical disk, but when you look at Windows Explorer, you see a C:\ drive, a D:\ drive, an E:\ drive, and so on. One drive, multiple logical storage locations.

You should also be aware from the outset that these logical divisions have different names when configured on Windows XP dynamic disks. Even though they serve the same purpose—storing data—they are called *volumes* on dynamic disks. We will talk much more about the implications of using volumes versus partitions (that is, basic versus dynamic storage) later in this chapter.

Formatting

However, more than just defining these logical divisions needs to be done before you can begin working with the hard drive. You must take things one step further. In order for the partitions to store and retrieve files, including the files of the operating system (OS) itself, the logical spaces must be *formatted* with a *file system*. These file systems represent the "rules and regulations" for storing information and are a necessary interface through which the OS functions with the sometimes diverse range of storage media present on your computer. Another way to think about file systems is to consider that they work much like an index or table of contents of a book; they help you find what is where and help you do it quickly. Sounds simple enough, but the underlying task really isn't.

These file systems do their work by means of various file system *drivers*— sometimes included within the operating system, sometimes loaded from external sources—which are responsible for the retrieval of information from the file systems they support. Remember, the job of a driver is to help the operating system work with a device. In the case of file system drivers, that device is the file system. In other words, they help build the index on a particular file system.

An example of this is the installation of CD-ROM file system drivers. CD-ROM media stores information on optical media (the CD) differently than magnetic media (hard drive or floppy) stores its information. Therefore, CD-ROM File System (CDFS) drivers are needed to access the information stored on a CD, while NT file system (NTFS) drivers must be loaded to read data from an NTFS partition.

Fortunately, you don't have to give this a moment's thought, because all of this driver configuration business is done automatically by Windows XP at installation time. This was not the case, however, back in the DOS days. Because DOS was written before CDs became ubiquitous, the capability to read CDs was not built into the MS-DOS operating system. Therefore, before CDs could be accessed, administrators had to make sure that DOS was "told" to load the Microsoft CD-ROM Extension (MSCDEX.EXE) as a part of the autoexec.bat configuration. This driver enabled DOS to see and read the contents of a CD-ROM. The CDFS 32-bit driver replaced MSCDEX.EXE in the Windows 95 release and has been incorporated into every Microsoft OS since, and, as a result, we don't need to give such CD drivers a whole lot of thought today.

What we've learned up to this point is that Windows XP supports multiple types of partitions (and volumes) and supports multiple file systems. But even though most of the drive stuff is automated, you still need to know how to make, edit, and remove your own partitions/file systems in Windows XP!

Further, as an administrator, you need to be keenly aware of the file system in use, because it plays such a large role in how XP Professional functions. Many of the file system choices you make will be determined by how you intend to use XP. As you will learn here and throughout your Windows MSCE training, Professional will not be able to take advantage of all available technologies without one particular file system, NTFS.

This chapter takes a look at the different file systems that are available on a Windows XP computer and also at how physical media is prepared for formatting in these file systems. We spend a good portion of time discussing the different ways to manage the logical spaces of your hard disks and the tools used to perform this management. We also cover configuring XP to restrict disk usage and to reduce the space files occupy. As always, much of our focus is on some of the new capabilities of Windows XP Professional. Special emphasis is placed on the new version of NTFS, NTFS version 5.x, and all that it can do.

By the time you've finished the chapter, you're going to have a thorough understanding of the power of Windows file systems and the amazing control you have over them. You'll be able to talk about these file systems the same way that morticians can talk about embalming fluids.

Objective 2.01   Configure and Manage File Systems

As touched on previously, the task of a file system is to help the OS interact with the storage media of a computer. One purpose of the "rules and regulations" of a file system is to define how the logical space should be divided up. It achieves this by dividing the space on a logical portion of physical media into "storage boxes," by assigning numbers to these boxes, and then by keeping track of which of these numbered "boxes" are storing which files and folders. It also keeps track of what storage locations are free (or more precisely which ones can be reused) and when new files are added and deleted.

As mentioned in the previous chapter, Windows XP will support three types of file systems for partitions (or volumes) on a hard disk: FAT16, FAT32, and NTFS. (Technically speaking , FAT12 is also supported, but that file system is used for floppies. This chapter's focus is on partitioning for hard drives, and FAT12 is not available for hard drives, so besides in this parenthetical, it won't be discussed.) Each usable drive letter on a system's hard drive(s) will be formatted with one of these supported file systems.

What's a Drive Letter?

Glad you asked. Every primary partition, logical drive of an extended partition, volume on a dynamic disk and removable disk (such as floppies, CD-ROMs, tape devices, and so on) are, by default, assigned drive letters. Storage devices get drive letters so that XP knows what file system drivers to "call" when information is requested from a program. On our typical store-bought, preinstalled computers, the floppy drive is assigned A, the hard disk is C, and the CD-ROM gets D.

By keeping track of the drive letters, and keeping track of what devices are where, Windows is, in effect, telling itself, "All right, now. If a program or command asks me to get information from drive D, I need to go get the CDFS file system drivers to get that information. And the Department of Justice is really a pain." (Okay, XP really doesn't say that last part.)

One of the things you will first squirrel away in these storage locations are the installation files of the operating system, and how you use XP will depend to a great extent on what file system you select for the installation. In fact, that decision at setup time is one of the most important decisions associated with file management you will face. Let's take a look at each of these file system considerations in further detail.

Configure FAT16, FAT32, or FAT File Systems

In this section, we'll take a more detailed look at each of the three file systems and discuss what happens if you have a change of heart about your file system decision.

FAT16

FAT16 was first used with DOS way back when I was in parachute pants (that would be 1981). FAT16 divides the space on a fixed disk into 2^{16} storage locations, or *clusters*, and each of these locations is assigned a number. A cluster is the smallest unit of storage space on a FAT partition. A cluster can be used to store a single file, even if the file does not use up all the storage space, or just a part of a single file. If might help to use a storage box analogy: think of a cluster as storage space for the stuff that won't fit into your house—you have to rent out the entire space, even if you're going to store only a few things and use just a fraction of the available space; you can't go to the manager and just rent out half of a storage locker.

Like our storage containers, hard disk space can be allocated to a file that doesn't use up all the space. Therefore, it is usually best to keep cluster sizes as small as possible, especially when formatting larger volumes, as we'll see when we look at FAT32 or NTFS.

The location of files in these storage spaces is tracked by the use of a File Allocation Table (hence the acronym), which, as mentioned, works in a way that is similar to the index of a book. It says, "File x is stored in the location starting with the number y and then uses storage boxes a, b, and c." The read/write heads of the disk then know exactly where to travel to quickly find and retrieve data from storage locations y through c.

The main advantage of FAT is that almost all operating systems support it. This makes FAT a good choice if the computer will be dual-booting with other operating systems (more on that later in this chapter). It is also a good choice for small partitions, 500MB or less, which will operate with better performance when formatted with FAT16 instead of NTFS. This is because the overhead associated with the storage of files on FAT partitions is much smaller than with NTFS. The FAT16 file system has two key drawbacks, however, that make it an unlikely choice for most installations of Windows XP Professional: first, it was designed to be a single-user file system and does not support any kind of local security, and second, the maximum partition size is limited to 4GB, reached when the system uses the maximum number of storage locations and the largest possible cluster size. Maximum FAT partition size is applicable under Windows NT and 2000 as well.

FAT32

FAT32 is an updated version of FAT16 that uses smaller cluster sizes, because it creates more of them (2^{32}, to be exact). Smaller cluster sizes result in a more efficient use of disk space, especially on larger drives. The average space saved when comparing data stored on a FAT32 partition versus a FAT16 partition is about 20 to 30 percent. One of the most appealing benefits of FAT32 over FAT16 is its ability to be used with today's much larger hard drive capacities. Using FAT32, you are able to create partitions up to 32GB in size, which is also the case with Windows 2000 machines.

The FAT32 file system was first introduced with the release of Windows 95 OEM Service Release 2 (OSR2), and it has been supported on all versions of Windows since, including Windows XP. However, it is not compatible with earlier versions of Windows NT, which includes Windows NT 4.0. If your goal is to create a dual-booting system with XP and NT 4 as your operating systems, you will probably want to steer clear of FAT32. Other than that, however, there is little reason not to use FAT32 over FAT.

FAT32 is the default choice of the XP Setup program, both on the Home and Professional versions.

NTFS

NTFS was first used with the NT operating system (the general consensus is that it stands for—or at least it used to stand for—New Technology File System, although you'd have better luck getting the formula for Coca-Cola than getting the definitive word from Microsoft about that).

NTFS provides the highest level of performance and features for Windows XP computers. NTFS version 5.10, which installs with Windows XP, includes some significant enhancements. In fact, many of the technologies discussed in this book—such as compression, quotas, and encryption—are specific to NTFS, and more specifically to NTFS version 5.10.

Travel Advisory

Microsoft is constantly making improvements to the NTFS file system, so it is released in versions much like applications or operating systems. The version that Windows 2000 installed on was NTFS 5. XP now installs—as of this writing—with the NTFS version 5.10. Because there is no distinction between versions, when dealing with most of the technologies presented in this book, you can assume that if NTFS version 5 is mentioned, I am referring to any version thereof.

NTFS supports partitions up to 2TB in size, and as with FAT32, cluster size is relatively small. This means that NTFS makes efficient use of disk space and is well suited for larger drives. One other significant advantage of NTFS is that it allows for local security of files and folders, which is especially important when two or more users are accessing the same computer. With NTFS, these users can be assigned different levels of permission to a resource, so that, for example, one user may have access to a particular file while the other user does not. This kind of security is not possible with either version of FAT.

You're not really taking full advantage of the Windows XP operating system capabilities unless you are using NTFS. NTFS includes technologies such as disk quotas, file encryption, local security, compression, and the hosting of a mounted drive, to name just a few. The longer you study the Windows XP operating system, the more you will realize the benefits of NTFS. For example, remember from Chapter 1 that Remote Installation Services required an NTFS partition to install. In fact, certain BackOffice Products, like Systems Management Server 2.0 and Internet Security and Acceleration Server (in caching mode), simply won't install without an NTFS partition handy.

The main disadvantage of using NTFS is that only the NT, 2000, and Windows XP operating systems can recognize the NTFS file system. Windows 9x does not have the necessary file system drivers to access information on NTFS partitions, so if your computer dual-boots with Windows 9x, the NTFS partition will not even be seen on that installation.

> ### Travel Advisory
>
> You can still access information that is stored on an NTFS partition from a Windows 9x computer over the network. That's because the client request is serviced by the server, and the server calls the appropriate file system drivers necessary to retrieve the data before sending it back over the network. The client is not aware of what file system is being used to service the request.

Partitioning for Dual Booting

Many administrators need more than one operating system, especially in a test environment. One solution to this is removable hard drives, but a more common one is dual booting. Some everyday users also need more than one OS. If this is the case, you will need to be mindful of certain dual-boot partitioning considerations.

If you want to boot to a previous version of Windows that supports only FAT (16 or 32), you must make sure that the system partition is formatted with the FAT file system. If the system partition is formatted with NTFS and you are booting to Windows 98, for example, Windows 98 will not be able to read the files necessary to start up the operating system, and the boot process will fail. (We'll discuss the system partition later; for now, just assume it's the C: drive. It will be 99 times out of 100 anyway.)

If booting to both Windows 2000 and XP, NTFS can be used across the board.

> ### Travel Advisory
>
> If configuring a computer to boot into both XP and 2000, install XP last. If you don't, you will run into an installation "issue" (Microsoft's term, not mine; I tend to shun euphemism) that is documented in Microsoft Knowledge Base article Q283433. To paraphrase: it's fixable; you will just need to start the computer in Windows 2000, and then copy the NTLDR and Ntdetect. com files from the I386 folder on the Windows XP CD-ROM to the root of the system drive.

Also, if you are configuring a dual-boot machine, you should, if at all possible, install XP into a separate partition. Microsoft's recommendation on this subject cannot be overstated—it will not support configurations that do not heed this advice.

Convert from One File System to Another File System

So what if you've set up you partitions, dual-boot or no, and now change your mind about the file system in use and want to use another? The most common scenario for this would be a case where you have accepted the defaults and installed XP using the FAT32 file system, and now you want to take advantage of all that XP Professional has to offer. To do so, you will need to make the switch to NTFS.

Fortunately, Windows XP Professional provides a utility that allows you to convert both FAT16 and FAT32 volumes to NTFS volumes without affecting any of the data stored there. This is a big departure—saving time and headaches—when compared to your other option for file system conversion: reformatting. As you have no doubt experienced when formatting a floppy disk, any time you format a logical storage location, you will destroy any data on that drive and will have to restore from a backup.

The FAT to NTFS conversion utility is called convert.exe, and it is run from the Command Prompt. Here is the syntax of the command (where *volume* is the drive letter that you want to convert):

```
convert volume /fs:ntfs
```

Here, *volume* is the logical FAT drive you want to make NTFS. Note that floppies cannot undergo this conversion. Of course, you can use the convert /? command to jog your memory about correct syntax when using this tool. For example, to convert the C:\ drive to NTFS, you would enter the command shown in Figure 2-1.

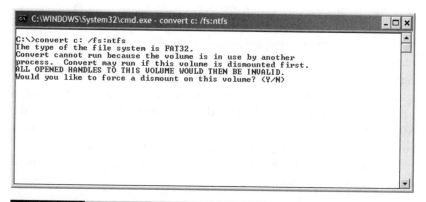

```
C:\WINDOWS\System32\cmd.exe - convert c: /fs:ntfs                    _ □ ×

C:\>convert c: /fs:ntfs
The type of the file system is FAT32.
Convert cannot run because the volume is in use by another
process.  Convert may run if this volume is dismounted first.
ALL OPENED HANDLES TO THIS VOLUME WOULD THEN BE INVALID.
Would you like to force a dismount on this volume? (Y/N)
```

FIGURE 2.1   Converting a partition from FAT to NTFS

When the conversion process begins, it will attempt to lock the partition from use while the conversion is in process. If it cannot, as when trying to convert a partition with an open file, the conversion will begin the next time you boot the computer.

Travel Advisory

The conversion of a FAT volume to an NTFS volume is a one-way process. There is really no other conversion option offered from within Windows XP. For example, you cannot convert NTFS to FAT without third-party utilities such as Partition Commander or Partition Magic, and many versions of these popular programs do not work on XP yet. In Windows XP, the only way to make an NTFS volume a FAT volume is to reformat, which would wipe out all the data on the volume. As is usually the case, a little planning in this area can go a long way.

Now that we've set up our file systems, we need to consider *where* we will be configuring these—on disk devices. As administrators, we will be faced with decisions every day about how to best use the disks on our computers, and we will need to have a thorough understanding of the options available. Microsoft also expects you to have command of this knowledge.

Objective 2.02 Implement, Manage, and Troubleshoot Disk Devices

A computer's reason for existence is to work with data—to input, output, process, and store data. How an operating system works with storage devices is one of the first things you need to understand, because one of the items stored on such devices is the operating system itself. In other words, to perform that first XP installation, you will usually be working with two storage types right off the bat: the hard disk and, more times than not, a CD-ROM.

But before we launch into our discussion of disk management, it's worth a brief sidebar to discuss the framework of Windows XP management, the Microsoft Management Console (MMC)! It will be the most important tool at your disposal as you manage your disks—in fact, it will be the most important tool for managing *anything* in Windows XP. Let's take a look at an important piece of the XP puzzle now.

Using the Microsoft Management Console

You will absolutely be required to have a thorough command of the MMC, as it is the foundation on top of which all tools to manage Windows XP are built. Fortunately, the MMC should not be difficult to grasp for the majority of Windows users, as it provides a standard look and feel to management tools that is similar to the file management utility Windows Explorer. Further, the MMC interface was first incorporated into the Windows 2000 operating system, so users familiar with administration on Windows 2000 machines should find little to trip them up.

By itself, the MMC has no functionality; it is just scaffolding around which the management tools are designed. The MMC's particular utility depends on which *snap-in* is loaded.

The MMC is not new to Windows XP. The technology was first used to manage Microsoft BackOffice products such as Internet Information Server (IIS) 4.0 (where the MMC made its premiere), Systems Management Server (SMS) 2.0, Systems Network Architecture (SNA) 2.0, and SQL Server 7. Anyone who studied or used those products is familiar with the MMC interface and with Microsoft's pledge that all future releases of Windows would be managed with MMC snap-ins. You might also be aware that with the launch of Windows 2000, Microsoft has kept its promise. All management tools are now developed using this template as the basis.

Those familiar with any of the just-mentioned products are also aware of how different (and easier to use) the MMC tools are than previous management utilities, such as NT 4's Server Manager and User Manager for Domains. Use of these tools required extensive memorization of the available menus, whereas use of the MMC utilities can be done much more intuitively and visually by examining the contents of the console tree (the left pane) of a given snap-in.

The preconfigured MMC tools are meant to give you easy access to the most commonly performed management tasks without the hassle of adding snap-ins to an MMC each time you want to do something like add a user. Some of these preconfigured consoles give you access to one snap-in, and others, like Computer Management, give you access to several.

The MMC management interface offers many additional benefits, including:

- It's highly customizable.
- MMC consoles can be saved and shared with other administrators, and snap-ins can be sent as e-mail attachments.
- Most snap-ins can be used for remote computer management.

- You can configure permissions so that MMC runs in author mode, which an administrator can manage, or in user mode, which limits what users can access.

On Windows XP computers, no default snap-ins are loaded when you launch the MMC. To open up a blank MMC, select Start | Run, and type **mmc** in the Run dialog box. When you first run the MMC, you will see a blank template, waiting for you to specify a snap-in. Figure 2-2 shows an MMC waiting for instructions on what to manage.

To add a snap-in to an MMC, you need to perform the following:

1. From the main console window, select Console | Add/Remove Snap-in; this opens the Add/Remove Snap-in dialog box.

2. Click the Add button to open the Add Standalone snap-in dialog box.

3. Select the snap-in you wish to add, then click the Add button.

4. You might be prompted here about which computer you wish to manage. In most cases, you will select the Local computer. When you are done, click Finish.

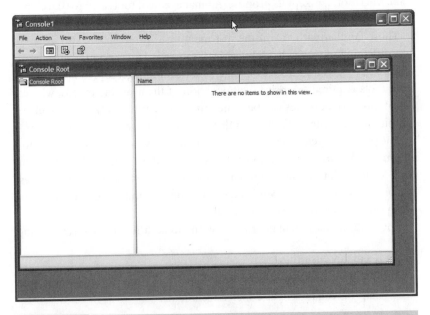

FIGURE 2.2   The MMC window before the addition of a snap-in

5. Keep repeating steps 2, 3, and 4 to add snap-ins. In this way, you can create a single MMC that will gather all the tools you commonly use in a single location.

6. After you have added the snap-ins for creating a console, you can save the console by selecting Console | Save As. Enter a name for your console. The custom consoles will be saved with an .msc extension by default.

The best place to save the console (in this author's opinion) is on your desktop, where it becomes a part of the user profile. In the case of an administrator, the custom MMC tool can be accessed anywhere with the implementation of a roaming profile (which is discussed in Chapter 4). From then on, double-click one icon from the desktop to access all your day-to-day administrative tasks, as shown in Figure 2-3.

To make things easier on you, a collection of *preconfigured* MMCs is grouped in a folder called Administrative Tools on a Windows XP Professional machine. These preconfigured MMCs contain the tools that are most commonly accessed when performing day-to-day tasks, so you don't have to go through the steps

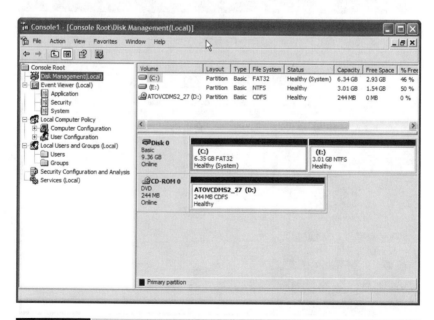

FIGURE 2.3   An MMC now fully armed for Windows network administration

listed earlier each time you want to add a user, start a service, or partition a disk. These administrative tools can be accessed from the Control Panel, as shown in Figure 2-4.

Travel Advisory

A quick note about the new Control Panel interface: it will default to the Category view, which is great for newbies because it helps these users find the right tool based on the end result they want to achieve. Windows graybeards like myself, who have been using Windows 2000 for *three whole years* now, will probably be much more comfortable with the "Classic" Control Panel, which can be enabled by first clicking the Switch to Classic View link in the upper-left corner of the Control Panel.

If you have installed Windows 2000 Server, you have no doubt noticed the Administrative Tools Start menu shortcut that is placed under the Programs menu, and you have probably also used this method to launch these utilities. If you click the XP Start menu, however, the Administrative tools are nowhere to

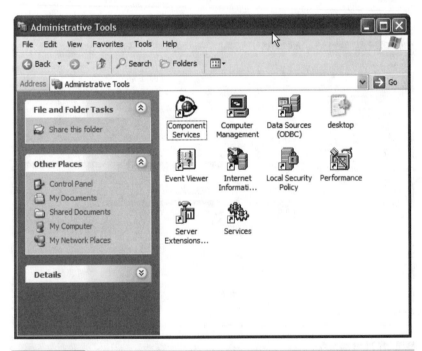

| FIGURE 2.4 | Accessing Administrative tools |

be found when you first install. Microsoft is assuming here that most users of XP Pro aren't going to use these tools on an everyday basis, as you do, Mr. Admin, and so have kept them hidden away in an attempt to keep users from hurting themselves. "But I want the Administrative tools on the Start menu," you say. No problem.

To avoid the hassle of opening the Control Panel each and every time you want to open up an administrative MMC, you can enable a menu item called Administrative Tools to appear on the Start menu. To do so, execute the following:

1. Right-click the Start menu, and then click Properties.

2. On the Start Menu tab, click Customize.

3. Click the Advanced tab and, under Start menu items, scroll to System Administrative Tools.

4. Click Display on the All Programs and the Start menu.

Simpler now? Of course! You can now navigate to the Administrative tools right from the familiar interface of the Start menu. You will also probably now find it easier to rearrange the Administrative tools from the Start menu so that the most commonly used tools are easily accessible. (As in previous Windows iterations, the Start menu can be easily customized with drag-and-drop techniques.)

Now, let's start to get our hands dirty with this management interface.

Configuring Disk Storage

The tool for managing and configuring the real estate on your network—that is, the disks and partitions—is a snap-in called Disk Management, which can be loaded in a custom MMC, using the steps just outlined or run from a special preconfigured MMC that includes the Disk Management snap-in.

Most people launch the Disk Management tool from the preconfigured Computer Management MMC snap-in. You can find this MMC in the Administrative Tools folder in the Control Panel, but a much faster way to launch this tool is simply to right-click My Computer from the desktop (if it's not there, use the Start menu) and choose Manage. From the Computer Management MMC, the Disk Management utility is easily accessible as one of the nodes on the console tree under the Computer Management tools. You can also add the Disk Management snap-in by itself into a blank MMC. Figure 2-5 displays the Disk Management tool as seen from the Computer Management preconfigured snap-in.

This Disk Management tool will be discussed in further detail later in this chapter, under the section "Upgrading from Basic Storage to Dynamic Storage." In the following section, you'll learn how to use the tool to upgrade disk storage.

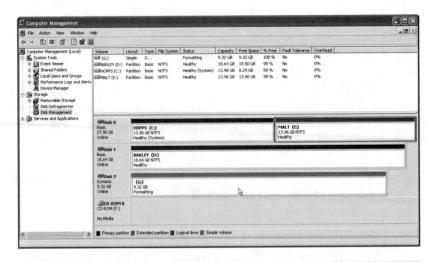

FIGURE 2.5 The Disk Management MMC

Monitor and Configure Disks

Most computer users who have purchased a computer with Windows preinstalled haven't had to give disk drives much thought. That's because on these computers, the entire space of the physical hard drive is partitioned into a single large partition, and it will remain so for its whole life because the vast majority of computer users never make any hard drive adjustments. But, even if you never plan on changing the configuration of the C:\ drive after you take the computer out of the box, you may need to eventually add more storage space. Familiarity with partitioning and formatting is essential for this task—when you add another disk to such a system—because you'll be unable to take advantage of the new space until you partition and format. And, as an administrator, you have to perform this task on a more regular basis—hence its emphasis on the test.

To understand hard drive management under XP, let's start with this facet: Windows XP supports two hard disk storage types, basic disks and dynamic disks. *Basic disks* use *partition*-based storage, which lets you divide a hard disk into up to four partitions, just as is the practice in NT 4.0, Windows 9x, and even DOS. *Dynamic storage*, first introduced in the Windows 2000 family, is a new system of storage that divides hard disk space into *volumes*. Both storage types, no matter what we call them, are concerned with converting the physical real estate on your hard drive into one or more usable parts called *logical drives* that will be formatted with a file system. In the next sections, we'll tackle basic disks first, and then move on to a discussion of dynamic disks.

Basic Storage

Basic storage is a continuation of the disk storage that was used by earlier versions of Windows and is therefore backward compatible with these and other operating systems. All Windows operating systems support basic storage. It works, as mentioned, by setting up boundaries on the usable hard disk space called partitions. There are two types of partitions that can be configured on a basic disk: *primary* partitions and *extended* partitions.

The first partition on a hard drive will be a *primary* partition, and all the usable space in that primary partition will be assigned a drive letter. This brings up an important aspect with regard to primary partitions: they are assigned a single logical drive letter. Keep this in mind as the discussion turns to extended partitions. We will then format the logical drive with a single file system so that it may store files. You can't mix and match file systems on a single logical drive.

Further, with basic storage, you can configure up to four primary partitions on a single disk. This limits you to using four drive letters to address the storage there. To get around this drive letter restriction, however, *extended* partitions can be used.

After the first primary partition has been configured, an extended partition may then be set up. Unlike primary partitions, the usable space in an extended partition can be further subdivided. Each subdivision of space in an extended partition is assigned a drive letter and called a *logical drive*. As a result of the subdivision possible in an extended partition, you can get around the four-drive-letter constraint that would be in effect by using primary partitions only.

When you use an extended partition, you reduce the number of primary partitions available by one, so that the new partitioning rule thus becomes: up to *three* primary partitions and *one* extended partition. It is not possible to have more than one extended partition on a single disk.

However, because you can divide extended partitions into multiple logical drives, one of the more common basic disk configurations is to have a single primary partition and a single extended partition. (Of course, the *most* common disk configuration for disks is the one handed to most computer users out of the box: the entire drive is configured as a single primary partition that uses all of the available space.) This one primary and one extended composition gives administrators almost all the partitioning flexibility they will ever need. This common drive configuration is represented in Figure 2-6.

Each logical drive on an extended partition can be formatted with different file systems, if necessary, and each can serve as the boot partition for the operating system—that is, they can hold the operating system's installation directory. In this way, it is possible for a Windows XP computer to boot to a primary

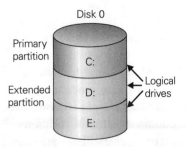

FIGURE 2.6   A single disk divided into two partitions and multiple logical drives

system partition that is formatted with FAT and then run off an extended boot partition that is formatted with NTFS.

The only restriction on extended partitions is that they can't be the system partition (the partition containing the hardware boot files), because extended partitions can't be marked as active. You will need to have your system partition on a primary partition for the computer to boot.

Travel Advisory

This is kind of backward, and very confusing, but the *system* partition is used to hold necessary files to boot the computer. The operating system installation itself, the partition that holds the \WINDOWS (in XP) or \WINNT (in 2000) directory is actually called the *boot* partition. Got it? The system partition holds the boot files, while the boot partition holds the operating system. Confused yet? I sure was the first three times someone explained it to me.

Can these two partitions be one and the same? You bet. In fact, for most home computers, they are. (If your hard drive is just configured as one big C:\ drive, your system and boot partitions are the same drive.) This is also another topic that is explored in more detail in the A+ material, so for further discussion, I again point you to the wonderful book, *Mike Meyers' A+ Certification Passport*.

Basic disks are also an important consideration when you want to configure a computer for dual booting with non-Windows XP operating systems. That's because basic partitions are supported by operating systems other than Windows XP (like NT), which means that if you want to boot using an OS other than Windows XP, you must configure the system partition on a basic disk.

Dynamic Storage

With dynamic storage, you have the most control over your disk storage. You are able to take advantage of technologies that wipe out the drive letter restrictions of basic disk partitions, and you can add space to your logical drives without wiping out data and having to start from scratch. On Windows XP machines, dynamic storage is the preferred method of holding data on a disk.

The new wrinkle in the area of disk storage, first appearing on Windows 2000 systems, and now with Windows XP, is a disk configuration feature called *dynamic disks*, which divide the usable space on a hard disk into dynamic *volumes*. What's the difference between a partition and a volume? To most users, nothing. Both partitions and volumes divide up physical space on a disk.

When you first install Windows XP, the default type of disk will be a basic disk, and the space will be divided into partitions. XP will let you upgrade these basic disks, though, and once upgraded to a dynamic disk, those primary and extended partitions will become simple volumes (which are explained in the next section). But to an end user accessing these storage areas, nothing will have changed. There won't be any more or any less room on that volume than was on the partition, and it can still be addressed by the same drive letter. A volume looks and acts much the way that a partition does to everyday users, but to an administrator, and to a test candidate, there are some significant differences between the two.

One of these differences is that dynamic disks do not, and cannot, contain partitions or logical drives (subdivisions of extended partitions). This removes almost all restrictions placed by partition-based disk storage—for example, with dynamic disks you can have an unlimited number of volumes per disk. This storage type is also important to understand if you want to implement advanced disk configurations. Dynamic storage supports three volume types: simple volumes, spanned volumes, and striped volumes. Most of these advanced configurations were available with Windows NT 4.0 on basic disks (although that's not technically correct; there was no distinction back then between the two types of disks) but are available now in Windows XP only on dynamic disks. If you are familiar with these kinds of disk configurations in NT 4, there isn't really much new to learn. Names have changed; functionality hasn't. Now let's take a look at each of these in more detail.

Simple Volumes

A simple volume is simply storage space from a single dynamic drive. The cool part is that the space can come from either contiguous or noncontiguous space from that drive. These volume types are analogous to a primary partition on a basic disk, and your end users will probably never know the difference. You would use a simple volume when you have enough space on a single disk to hold your entire volume.

Spanned Volumes

A spanned volume contains space that is located on multiple dynamic drives (from 2 to 32); one could even say that the logical storage location space *spans* many drives. Spanned volumes can be used to increase the size of a dynamic volume. When you create a spanned volume, the data is written sequentially across the drive set, filling up the available space on one physical drive before moving on to use the space on the next drive on the set. For example, you can configure a 1GB space from one drive, another 500MB from another drive, and 500MB more from a third drive for a total volume size of 2GB. All the space would be addressed by a single name, usually a drive letter like D:\, and again, end users would have no idea of which physical drive stores the data, nor would they ever need to know.

Administrators would usually set up a spanned volume when available space on a disk is getting low. When a volume is running out of disk space from one hard drive and you need to extend a volume's storage capacity by using space from another one, spanned volumes are the answer.

One of the drawbacks to spanned volumes is that they do not provide fault tolerance. In fact, because multiple drives are involved, it is a bit less fault tolerant than a simple volume. If one of the drives in the spanned set fails, you lose the entire volume and will have to restore the set from a backup. You will also not see any increase in performance because the data is being written sequentially, accessing only one physical disk per I/O request.

Striped Volumes

A striped volume stores its data by writing data across dynamic drives (from 2 to 32) in equal portions. The important thing to understand about striped volumes is that the areas of free space in a volume set must be of equal size, even though the disks that they exist on are not. This is because the operating system writes the data across all disks in the stripe set as it fills up. To help you visualize, think of a how a dealer deals out a hand of poker. Each player is going to get the same amount of cards, one card at a time. The dealer does not hand out two to one person, three to the next, and then skip the next. When the dealer is done dealing the "set," players have exactly five cards in front of them. The drivers controlling I/O operations on a striped volume act the same way. A single stripe in a stripe set can only be as big as the smallest area of free space on one of the disks on the set. Figure 2-7 illustrates a striped volume.

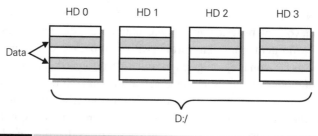

FIGURE 2.7 A striped volume

As with simple volumes and spanned volumes, the striped volume will be addressed as a single entity to end users, usually as a drive letter. The drawback to using striped sets is also the same: if you lose any of the disks in the set, the entire volume fails, and you must restore from backup.

So why would anyone use a striped set? Performance. Because the data is written across all the stripes in a set, you can take advantage of multiple I/O performance and increase the speed at which data reads and writes take place. You can also combine free space on multiple disks—but be careful when doing this; for example, if you combined space from three disks, two with 1GB of free space, and one with 100MB of free space, you don't get 2100MB of storage, as you would with a spanned volume. You would instead have 300MB of space on your striped volume.

Mirrored Volumes and RAID 5 Volumes

Two other volume sets are worthy of mention here but are *not* available with Windows XP: Mirrored volumes and RAID 5 volumes (RAID stands for redundant array of independent disks). Both volume types are *fault tolerant*, but neither is available on Windows XP Professional computers. There are two reasons why it doesn't hurt, however, to give them some attention.

Local Lingo

Fault tolerant in the computer world refers to the ability of something to withstand the loss of data and keep performing, without the need to restore from a saved backup set. In the case of fault tolerant volume configurations, one of the disks could fail and need to be replaced, but an end user would never know the difference.

The first is that they are available on Windows 2000 Server implementations and will certainly also be configurable on the .NET platform (in likely the same manner; NET is the next generation of Microsoft server operating systems). For this reason, you will be tested on the two volume types during the MSCE track and may encounter them when working with your back-end systems.

The second reason they are given so much attention is that they are *software* implementations, not *hardware* implementations, of fault tolerance. We don't have the space to go into a great amount of detail, but it's important to understand that there are many other fault-tolerant disk configurations out there, and most of them are hardware-based. What that means is that during a hardware fault-tolerant instance, Windows won't know, for example, that the logical C:\ drive is really being written to three separate hard disks. If a software-based fault-tolerance solution is being used, however, Windows *is* conscious of the underlying disk array infrastructure.

You shouldn't see any questions on the 70-270 exam on these fault-tolerant volumes, but you will certainly see related questions on the 70-215 (Server) exam. We will discuss these volumes briefly, because it won't hurt for you to have some understanding of these volume types now. You can't be overprepared or have too much understanding of how Windows works, as you sit for the 270.

Mirrored Mirrored volumes work by creating a duplicate copy of data across two physical drives. A standby copy of a hard drive is waiting in the event of a disk failure. When a disk failure occurs, the mirrored volume must be "broken" and then rebuilt, but access to the volume will continue uninterrupted (except in the event that a computer must be shut down to replace the failed drive).

RAID 5 (Formerly Disk Striping with Parity) RAID 5 volumes are striped sets that work across 3 to 32 physical dynamic disks that store the duplicate copies of data across the entire set in the form of parity. These RAID 5 sets, in fact, were known as striping with parity sets when configured in NT 4 Server computers. The parity information can be used to regenerate lost data in the event of the failure of a single disk in the RAID 5 array. Again, data access will remain uninterrupted even though a component has failed.

Using Dynamic Disks with other OS's So now here's the dilemma: you've configured a dynamic disk on an XP machine, and you want to use the information in that disk on another machine. A machine with a different operating system. Can you do this? The answer is the same as for almost any computer question. Depends.

Windows XP and Windows 2000 are the only Microsoft operating systems that support dynamic disks. So if you create a dynamic disk and want to use it in one of these systems, be my guest. However, prior versions of Windows don't know what to do with a dynamic disk, so you can't take a dynamic disk created in XP and plop it into an NT 4 machine. They also can't be directly accessed by computers running 98, Me, or XP Home Edition. However, these other operating systems can get to data stored on a dynamic disk when accessing the data over the network.

You also have to be careful when performing the inverse operation. Windows 2000 and Windows XP no longer support fault-tolerant disk sets that were created using Windows NT 4.0 or earlier. These multidisk volumes include RAID 1 arrays (mirror sets), RAID 0 arrays (stripe sets), or RAID 5 arrays (stripe sets with parity). These multidisk basic volumes must be backed up and deleted prior to installing Windows XP or moving disks to a computer running these operating systems. In Windows 2000, you can restore the data to a basic disk, convert the basic disk to a dynamic disk, and then use dynamic storage to create new spanned volumes, striped volumes, mirrored volumes, or RAID 5 volumes. Remember that you have only a few of these volume options available on an XP Professional machine.

So now that we understand some of the capabilities of dynamic disks, our reasons for performing an upgrade from basic to dynamic storage are more clear. There are a few other issues that we must keep in mind. Lets look at some of these dynamic storage considerations and examine the technique to make our storage dynamic.

Upgrading from Basic Storage to Dynamic Storage

As you recall, a disk is configured as a basic disk when you install Windows XP Professional or perform an upgrade from a previous operating system. All partitioning information on the existing drive is carried over from the upgrade. To take advantage of the new features offered by dynamic disks, you must perform an *upgrade* of your basic disks.

Exam Tip

One very important consideration to keep in mind as you study for the Windows XP Professional exam, as well as something you'll use in the real world, is that a single physical disk can be either basic *or* dynamic, but not both. The process of configuring the disk as either basic or dynamic is done at the disk level, not at the partition level.

To perform a disk upgrade, you use the Disk Management MMC snap-in, which can be found under the Computer Management tools in the console. From the Disk Management utility, just right-click the drive you want to convert and choose Upgrade to Dynamic Disk, as shown in Figure 2-8.

The Upgrade to Dynamic Disk dialog box appears, where you can select the disk you want to upgrade (I know that seems a little redundant) with a check box and then click the OK button. After your selection, the next box will ask you to click Upgrade to proceed, and then a confirmation dialog box appears, warning you that there is no chicken exit for this procedure, as seen in Figure 2-9. Another confirmation dialog box warns you that any file systems mounted on the disk will be dismounted. You will need to click Yes to continue. The last warning you will receive is that a reboot will take place to complete the operation.

Travel Advisory

Be sure to test any upgrades to dynamic storage before implementing in production. I won't name names here (other than Microsoft's, because taking shots at Microsoft has become something of a pastime for computer nerds like me), but I've seen some very well-known computer maker's hard disks become very grumpy ("inoperable" or "hosed") when they were upgraded to dynamic storage. (This particular situation was resolved by installing the manufacturer-supplied hard disk I/O drivers, but it's not like you're going to get a call beforehand from Microsoft or the company that sells the computers telling you not to do this.) So test, just to be sure. (And by the way, Microsoft, I did come to your aid on the Windows Product Activation thing, back in Chapter 1, which isn't exactly leading the technological "Q" rating races right now, so we're even.)

Local Lingo

Hosed   A highly technical acronym that stands for Hardware Or Software Error Detected. Hosed.

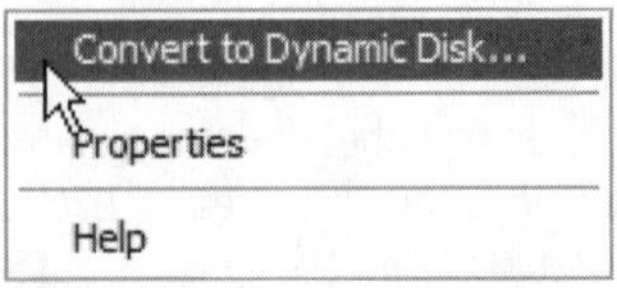

| Convert to Dynamic Disk... |
| Properties |
| Help |

FIGURE 2.8   Converting to a dynamic disk

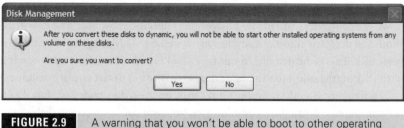

| FIGURE 2.9 | A warning that you won't be able to boot to other operating systems after the upgrade |

As a last point about dynamic disks, note that to upgrade a disk from basic to dynamic storage, the target disk needs at least 1MB of free, non-partitioned space for the operation to complete. This space is needed for Windows to re-create and store the volume information of the upgraded disk. This means that some computers—it will depend on how the manufacturer partitions the hard drive—with Windows XP Professional out of the box will not be candidates for an upgrade to dynamic disks immediately.

> **Travel Advisory**
>
> Usually, if you want to implement dynamic disks, it's better to start from scratch with a non-partitioned hard drive. On a clean install, XP checks for this and will leave enough free space for the upgrade.

Monitor, Configure, and Troubleshoot Volumes

The Disk Management utility allows you to perform all your physical and logical disk space management. You will use Disk Management when you are adding new storage space to a computer, a fairly common administrative task as programs and files grow larger. How you will use Disk Management to help you add more space depends on whether or not the computer supports hot swapping.

> **Local Lingo**
>
> **Hot swapping** The capability of a device to be added without shutting down the computer. Most hot-swappable hard drives, come in special hardware arrays that are part of a high-end server package. These machines are not designed for end users to play Solitaire really fast—they are built to be servers and run a Server operating system. In most cases, a computer running Windows XP Professional will not support the hot swapping of disk drives.

If your computer does not support hot swapping, you first need to shut down the computer. Add the new drive and restart the computer. The new drive should be detected automatically and listed in the Disk Management utility as a basic disk. This is the default storage type. You can now create partitions on the basic disk or upgrade it to a dynamic disk so that you can start creating volumes.

If your computer does support hot swapping, you don't need to shut down the computer. (If you did, it wouldn't be hot swappable.) Add the disk to the system and then, from the Action menu of Disk Management, choose the Rescan Disks command. The new drive should be detected and appear in the display. You will then have the same partitioning or volume management options as mentioned earlier.

As you know now, after you add a new disk to the computer, you need to divide that space into logical storage areas and format those areas before use. Disk Management offers the ability to create, delete, and format partitions on basic drives, and it lets you create simple, spanned, or striped volumes on dynamic disks. The processes for creating new partitions and new volumes are similar. Both processes start with right-clicking an area of free space on a drive, which launches a wizard to help create the partition or volume on that drive. (General rule of thumb when using any MMC: when in doubt, right-click.) We'll illustrate how this works with the creation of a volume.

1. Right-click an area of free space and choose Create Volume. The Create Volume Wizard appears. Click Next to continue.

2. Select the type of volume to create, as shown in Figure 2-10. Note that only the volume types supported by your computer's hardware configuration are available. Choose the radio button of the volume you want to create and click the Next button.

3. The Select Disks dialog box appears, where you will set the size of your new volume. The maximum volume size possible will be the amount of free space recognized. Choose the size of the volume and the disk you want it created on, then click Next.

4. The Assign Drive Letter or Path dialog box is next, where you will specify a drive letter or choose to mount the volume in an empty folder. Being able to assign an empty folder from another partition for this new drive will allow you to browse one folder hierarchy to get access to all your resources. For example, if you have drive C and you are in the process of building drive D, you could mount drive D to an

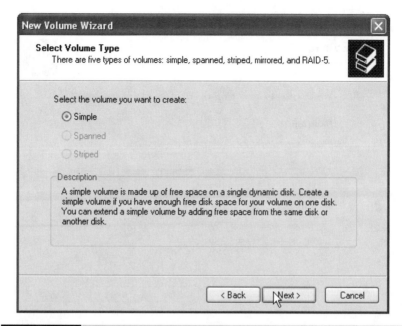

FIGURE 2.10   Select which type of volume you want to create

empty folder in drive C. This would allow someone who is browsing the folder contents of drive C to double-click the empty folder and be transparently redirected to drive D.

Travel Advisory

To mount a volume to an empty folder, the drive that will hold the empty folder *must* use NTFS.

5. Next, the Format Volume dialog box appears (see Figure 2-11), and you will choose to format the volume with FAT16, FAT32, or NTFS. You can give the volume a label for informative purposes (your volume will still be accessed with the information you provided in the previous step) and perform a quick format. The quick format, however, does not scan the disk for potential bad sectors, so it is recommended that you use it only in test environments. After you've made your choice, click the Next button.

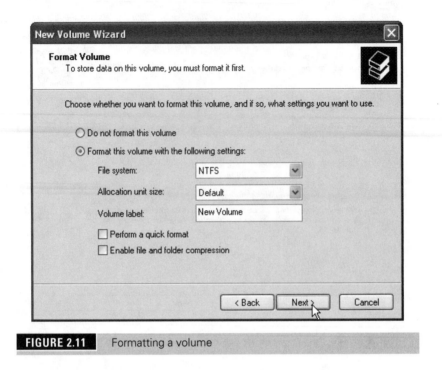

FIGURE 2.11   Formatting a volume

6. The Completing the Create Volume Wizard appears, which summarizes your selections. If you need to change any of them, click the Back button to return to the appropriate dialog box and make changes. If all is well, click the Finish button.

When you are creating a new partition on a basic disk, these steps will look pretty much the same. You right-click an area of free space and select a partition type to create, which will launch the Create Partition Wizard. You will then be asked, much as in the preceding example, to select the partition type, specify the partition size, assign a drive letter or path, and then format the partition.

Additional Volume Management: Extending a Volume

One of the big advantages of third-party disk management utilities like Partition Magic or Partition Commander is the ability to add space to partitions without having to first delete and then re-create the partition, thereby destroying the data contained therein. Windows XP's dynamic storage now allows you to add space to partitions with the ability to *extend* a volume.

When you extend a volume, you are taking a single simple volume and adding more storage area to that volume from free space that exists on the same physical drive. Other than that, nothing else will change when accessing a volume that has been extended. The drive letter will remain unchanged; only the volume's capacity will have changed.

Travel Advisory

To extend a volume, the simple volume must be formatted as NTFS. You also cannot extend a system or boot partition, so this option will not be available on most C:\ drives.

Disk Quotas

Disk quotas are a powerful feature available for managing storage on Windows XP NTFS volumes. Like many of the disk management features presented in this chapter, it was first introduced in Windows 2000, so if you have experience using that OS, you definitely have a leg up here.

Quotas let you determine who is hogging all of the disk space on Windows XP Professional computers with all of their multi-gigabyte downloads (read: Napster et. al.). However, you should recognize that even though it is available on any Windows XP computer with an NTFS volume, quota management is usually done only on file servers, where many network users may be storing files and your goal is to set limits on how much storage an individual can use. Disk quotas are not typically set on individual end-user workstations, so you may end up configuring this on a 2000 or .NET server, not on an XP Pro box. Another example of where test knowledge doesn't exactly map precisely to real-world use.

Disk quotas will allow for a high degree of flexibility in their implementation, although this flexibility is not enough for some administrators, as we will see. You can set disk quotas for all users, or you can limit disk usage on a per-user basis. You cannot, however, set quota limits on a per-group basis. I'll explain why in just a bit.

You enable quotas on a per-volume or per-partition basis. In other words, you configure quota tracking for the C:\ drive or the E:\ drive, but you will not set it up for hard disk 1. Further, there's no way to set up quotas for a specific folder. The quota feature will be tracked for the contents of an entire volume.

So how are disk quotas monitored? They work by tracking file and folder *ownership*, which is why monitoring can occur only on a per-user basis, and not per group—groups do not own files or folders, individual user accounts do. The significance of file and folder ownership extends far beyond the topic of Quotas, and we discuss the importance of ownership in complete detail during Chapter 3.

A further consideration is that quota limits are based on the *uncompressed* size of files or folders. A user up against his or her quota limit cannot compress files to free up space; the files will have to be deleted. (We will get to the compression attribute of a file or folder in the next section.)

Travel Advisory

There is an exception to these quota rules, of course. The local Administrators group is the default owner of all files on a volume formatted with NTFS, and the Administrator account is exempt from all quota limits. This includes ownership of all files associated with a program installation. If the Administrator account were not exempt, it would severely limit what the Administrator could do.

You configure quota limits from an NTFS volume's Properties dialog. You can configure the quota entries from Disk Administrator in either the top or bottom pane of the details pane by accessing a volume's Properties dialog box, but you can also access this dialog by right-clicking a drive letter in Windows Explorer.

After opening the Properties dialog box for a volume (again, I stress that you're working with a volume or partition, not a physical disk), click the Quota tab, shown in Figure 2-12. Quota tracking is disabled by default. You can turn it on by checking the Enable Quota Management box.

Once you have turned on quota tracking for a volume, it will be effective for all new users of that drive. Three general quota configuration options can be set from this tab, as described in the following table.

Quota Tab Option	What It Does
Deny Disk Space To Users Exceeding The Quota Limit	Users who try to save more information than their quota limit allows will receive an "out of disk space" message.
Select The Default Quota Limit For New Users On This Volume	Sets the quota for new users of the volume. You can limit disk space and use the drop-down boxes to set quotas and warning levels for disk usage.
Select The Quota Logging Options For This Volume	Specifies whether log events will be recorded when users exceed warning or quota limits. You may view these events in the system log.

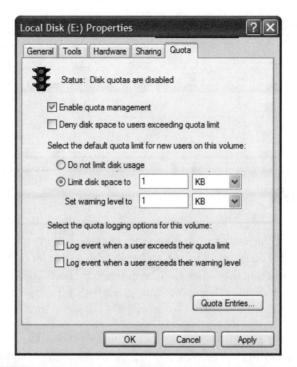

FIGURE 2.12 Enabling Windows XP's Quota feature

After you enable quota entries, an interesting thing happens from the perspective of the end user. The size of the drive they are saving their work to becomes exactly the same as their quota entry. So, even though you might have set up a 10GB D:\ volume for file storage, if you have set quota limits of 100MB, any user with that quota limit who logs on will see a D:\ drive under Windows Explorer of 100MB in size. What they don't know can' t hurt them.

You will also note from an examination of the Quota tab that the utility can be used as a monitoring tool only, rather than to enforce disk usage rules. In fact, the default choice by the operating system is that no disk space will be denied to new users until you set the configuration parameters.

You can monitor the disk space usage of each user by viewing the quota entries for the partition or drive. To view the quota entries, open the Properties window of the drive and open the Quota tab. At the bottom of the tab, you can click the Quota Entries button to view the list of users using hard drive space on that partition (shown in Figure 2-13). If you would like to change a user's quota limit, you can double-click the entry and modify the quota limit value.

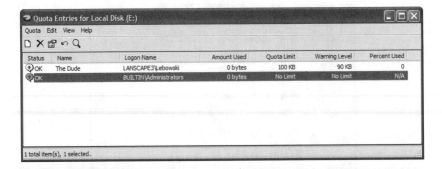

FIGURE 2.13   Examining individual quota entries

This Quota Entries dialog box is also your management interface to monitor disk usage. Now that quota tracking has been enabled and you've told it how to behave, the results of that activity will be summarized here. The Status column next to the user's name will graphically display whether the user has exceeded a quota threshold.

- A green arrow means that the user's quota status is OK.
- An exclamation point indicates that the warning threshold has been tripped.
- An exclamation point in a red circle indicates that the user has exceeded allocated storage space.

You can also configure a higher degree of granularity for your quota settings from this tab. To modify an individual's quota, double-click a user name to bring up the individual quota entry dialog box shown in Figure 2-14. The options here mirror those that appear on the Quota tab. Remember that setting a quota entry but not limiting disk space lets you see how much space a user is using, which is in many instances all the administrative leverage you will need.

Local Lingo

Granularity   Tech-speak for being able to set a high degree of individuality—setting something one way for one user and another way for another user. If you hear this word used in a meeting in the same sentence as *drill down*, and/or have it suggested that you should address an issue *offline*, you are in a meeting whose participants are not really trying to communicate, but are suffering from technical prolixity. You have my permission to finish the rest of the meeting outside the box.

The individual quotas entry page

Finally, what should you do when a user's quota limits have been reached and that user wants to save more stuff to your precious disk space? There are several ways to handle this situation. You can, as the Administrator, take ownership of the files. The files then would not be charged against the user's quota limit. Or you can tell the user to delete files that he or she no longer needs. As a last option, if the user does need all of the files, you could modify the quota entry settings for that user by increasing the quota value.

Travel Advisory

Remember that you are only human, and your first assumption of a quota limit may not have been realistic for all users. It is also important to know that you can change the quota value for a particular user after the initial set up of quotas.

As a final note regarding quotas, you should know that a user's quota entry cannot be deleted while he or she still owns any files or folders. To make a deletion of a quota entry, the files that the user owns must either be deleted or file ownership must be taken by another user.

Exam Tip
You are likely to see a troubleshooting question regarding what to do when a user is up against his or her quota limit.

To summarize our discussion on quotas, here are a few main points you should know about setting and configuring disk quotas as you sit down to take the Windows XP Professional exam:

- Quotas are available only on NTFS partitions or volumes. Quotas are one of those features of Windows XP that will not work on drives formatted with the FAT file system. You must be using NTFS on drives that you wish to enable quotas on.

- Disk usage is based on ownership. An understanding of quotas requires that you be familiar with the concept of NTFS file and folder ownership. Recall that every file and folder on an NTFS volume has an owner, and quotas use this owner attribute to track disk usage. When a user creates or copies a file on an NTFS volume, Windows XP charges the disk space used against the user's quota limit.

- Disk quotas ignore compression. Users are charged against their quota limit based on the uncompressed size of the files they own.

- Free space for applications is based on quota limits. When you enable quotas for a user, the free space for the volume that Windows XP reports to applications is the amount of space remaining for the user's quota limit.

- Administrators are not charged against quota limits. Since most of the files on an NTFS volume are owned by the local Administrators group by default (including the installation of the operating system, if applicable), it would be pointless to track usage by the administrator. For this reason, you should perform all application installs when logged on as the Administrator.

File and Folder Compression

Each file and folder on an NTFS-formatted volume maintains a compression state (a compression attribute) that is either *compressed* or *uncompressed*. This feature of an NTFS volume enables you to compress files or folders and will ultimately let you store more data on an NTFS volume. The compression attribute on files and folders are managed independently, which means that a compressed folder can contain uncompressed files, and an uncompressed folder can hold a compressed file.

The setting to enable file and folder compression is accessed by clicking the Advanced button on the General tab of the Properties dialog box of a file or folder. After choosing to look at the Advanced Properties, you can set the attribute with a simple click of the mouse, as shown in Figure 2-15.

A quick note here is necessary about the Compression attribute as it relates to the Encryption attribute, since you will configure them both from the same location. (We discuss encryption in Chapter 8.) These attributes are mutually exclusive: you can either enable compression or encryption, but not both at the same time.

The compression that NTFS applies is invisible to users and even to applications accessing the compressed files. When a compressed file is requested by an application like Microsoft Word or even by an older DOS application, NTFS takes care of the decompression before presenting the file contents to a user.

Exam Tip

And what about the compression attribute on a FAT or FAT32 volume? You won't find a setting for compression on these FAT volumes because compression is available only on NTFS volumes. Don't let this trip you up on the exam!

Some file formats, such as JPG, MP3, and ZIP, exist in an already highly compressed state, and compressing them on an NTFS volume will have little

| FIGURE 2.15 | Compressing a file or folder

impact on the space they use. Large ASCII text files (if you have any on your computer), graphics formats like .BMP and .TIF that don't include much native compression, and some executables are usually good candidates for compression.

Moving and Copying Considerations   Here is a summary of what happens when compressed files and folders are copied and moved between and within NTFS volumes You will see this discussed in much more detail in Chapter 3:

- More often than not, the compression attribute changes when files and folders are moved or copied (similar to security attributes in this way).

- When you perform a copy from within the same NTFS volume, the copied files and folders inherit the compression attribute of the destination folder. This is true for copies between different NTFS volumes.

- When you perform move operations within the same NTFS volume, the moved files and folders retain their original compression attribute.

- When you perform a move between different NTFS volumes, the moved files and folders inherit the compression attribute of the destination folder. Windows XP treats the move between volumes as a copy operation and then deletes the original file or folder (as it does with security attributes).

- And what about moves or copies to non-NTFS volumes, like to FAT drives or to floppy disks? As mentioned, the compression attribute is not supported on these file systems, so the copied or moved file is uncompressed before being copied or moved.

You can also easily determine which files and folders are compressed from Windows Explorer by setting compressed files and folders to display in a different color. Simply select Tools | Folder Options from Windows Explorer. Then, from the View tab, select the Display Compressed Files And Folders With Alternate Color check box. From then on, compressed files and folders are displayed in blue.

So far, we've only talked about storage in terms of a computer's fixed hard disks. And while the management of hard disks will make up the bulk of your storage administration, there are other storage media that Microsoft expects you to know a thing or two about. Let's take a look at some of these other storage types now.

Install, Configure, and Manage DVD and CD-ROM Devices

Windows XP Professional uses two file systems to see and use optical (read by a beam of light) media. The CDFS is used for access to CD-ROM drives, and the

Universal Disk Format (UDF) is used to access DVD drives. Both file systems are standards-based, which means that they comply with guidelines set forth by the International Standards Organization (ISO).

CDs and DVDs are both listed in the DVD/CD-ROM Drives area in Device Manager, which you use to manage the devices connected to your computer. Later in this chapter, we'll discuss the Device Manager in detail as you learn to set the properties of other devices.

It is likely that you already have extensive experience with the Device Manager, as it has been around in the Windows 9x operating systems and was ported over to Windows 2000. To quickly review the opening of Device Manager, follow these steps:

1. From the Start menu, right-click the My Computer shortcut and choose Properties from the context menu, which will display the System Properties dialog box. (It seems there are always dozens of ways to accomplish the same task. For example, you could choose the Show On Desktop option when you right-click the Start menu shortcut and then just right-click that. Or, you can access this same window through the Control Panel's System applet. The WINDOWS KEY + BREAK also works. You get the drift.)

2. However you get to the System Properties dialog box, you will next click the Hardware tab, then click the Device Manager in the middle-right of the window. As shown in Figure 2-16, the Device Manager dialog box will then be displayed, where you can access the properties of a particular device. For the time being, we will keep our focus on the storage devices.

To start management of your DVD and CD-ROM devices, simply double-click the DVD/CD-ROM Drives node of Device Manager, then double-click the device you want to manage. (You could also right-click the device and choose Properties.) You will then see at least three tabs in the Device Properties dialog box: General, Properties, and Driver. The other tabs will be specific to the device selected, so while it is likely that you will see a tab or two that will differ from what is in the screen shots here, the important tabs to be familiar with for exam purposes are the three everyone should see, no matter what device you are examining.

- **General tab** This tab lists the device type, manufacturer, and location (see Figure 2-17). It also shows the device status, indicating whether the device is working properly. If the device is not working properly, you can click the Troubleshooter button. Unfortunately, the Troubleshooter does

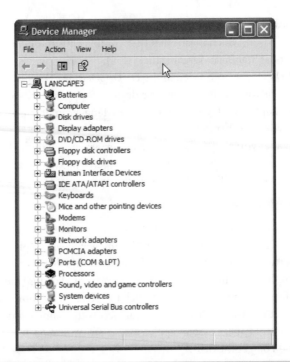

FIGURE 2.16   Viewing the Device Manager from the System Properties window

little in the way of actual troubleshooting beyond asking you to make sure that a device is plugged in and has power. It is next to useless for experienced administrators. The General tab of any device can also be used to configure the device's usage in a particular hardware profile. In the Device Usage area at the bottom of the window, you can set this behavior.

- **Properties tab**   This tab allows you to set device-specific options, such as volume and playback settings. (An optional tab, called Advanced Settings, is used to program a DVD device for the playback of any regionalized DVD media. From this tab, you can select a country and click OK. Usually, you can change the regional settings for the DVD device a limited number of times.)

- **Driver tab**   This tab shows you information about the currently loaded driver, as well as buttons that let you see more driver details, uninstall the driver, or update the driver. If you click the Update Driver button, you will launch the Hardware Update Wizard, which will prompt you for the location of the driver(s) you wish to update.

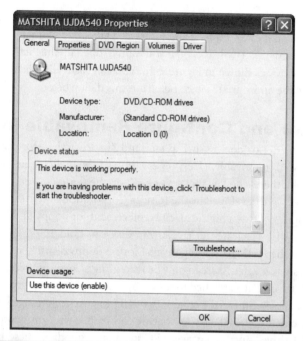

FIGURE 2.17   The General tab gives you basic information about a device.

You will find the Device Manager an indispensable tool when troubleshooting hardware problems on your XP system. We will also be using it later to configure the properties of Hardware Profiles, so this won't be the last time you see it. There is one more thing, then, worth mentioning before we close out this section on CD devices.

New CD Autorun Behavior   As a general note about CD-ROM usage, you have no doubt noticed that most CDs you drop into your system's cup holder start to play automatically. That's because most CDs have a file called autorun.inf, which contains instructions about what to launch when the CD is inserted, and Windows has instructions to look for and run this file whenever a CD is inserted. Unlike in previous versions of Windows, there is no way to disable the Autorun feature through the CD device's Properties dialog box. If you want to disable Autorun, you have to hold down the SHIFT key as the CD is spinning up. (You also need to be logged on as a Power User or Administrator for this to work.)

Also, there's a new wrinkle in the behavior of Windows upon CD-ROM recognition: Windows XP is trained to look for media files, such as MP3 or AVI, and will display a dialog box asking you what you want to do with the media once recognized. For example, if you insert a CD that has a bunch of files from your digital camera, XP will ask you if you want to open up the Picture viewer to view a slideshow, as shown in Figure 2-18. You can easily disable this behavior by checking the appropriate check box from this dialog box.

Monitor and Configure Removable Media

Removable media are devices such as tape and Zip drives that store data on media that is, well, removable. (Hey, observation of the obvious has worked for Jerry Seinfeld; there's no law that says I can't do the same.)

Zip drives were developed by the Iomega Corporation and first hit the market in the mid-1990s as a high-capacity replacement for floppy drives (depending on what disk version you have, a Zip disk can hold 100–250MB of data compared to the 1.44MB of storage available on a floppy disk). Removable storage media, such as Zip disks, can only be read using a corresponding reader device (a Zip drive) that's attached to the computer. Such devices have since been usurped by the commercial availability of CD-burner technologies, which let folks easily create 650–700MB CDs that are compatible with any computer with a CD-ROM drive—just about every PC in existence today. These removable types of storage can also be managed through the Device Manager.

FIGURE 2.18   The New Autorun options give you many choices.

Removable media devices are listed under the Disk Drives node, where you can double-click a device icon to manage the removable drive of your choice. Double-clicking will open the Properties window that contains General and Driver tabs that look pretty much the same as what you found when examining your CD-ROM and DVD devices. The Disk Properties tab contains options specific to the particular removable device you are managing. Whether or not other tabs appear in this Properties page will depend on the type of device installed.

Tape drives are managed the same way. If you have one installed, Device Manager will keep track of it with a node in the list of devices. You will manage it with the same properties dialog box interface as is the case with other removable media, and you will store data on the tape via a drive letter that will be assigned to the device. Further, most tape backup solutions will ship with their own backup software and management utilities. There is really no rocket science involved with the configuration of tape drives, and Microsoft will not grill you on the particulars of performing tape backups, or on the contents of a specific dialog box.

Exam Tip

Know about backups, described in the next section and in Chapter 6. There is plenty of test material on various aspects of backups—scheduling backups, types of backups, and so on. What media you choose for your backup, however, is of secondary concern; on the exam, it won't matter *where* the backups are performed.

Using the Windows XP Backup Utility

Windows XP also includes a backup utility called Windows Backup. The purpose of a backup is to protect your data in the event of a system failure, like the failure of a device, or any other disaster such as the theft of a machine or a really angry user with a sledgehammer. But you know that already, don't you?

Windows Backup is run interactively through a graphical interface, which, if you've ever backed up anything in your life, you'll find intuitive to use. This interface can be configured either manually or via a series of wizards. The wizards can be used to back up, restore, and schedule backup jobs. Simply specify what you want to back up, with a few check boxes, select what kind of backup to perform, and where the backup job should be saved.

In Chapter 6, we discuss in more detail the mechanics of the Backup utility, including the various types of data that can be backed up and the different kinds of backup operations that are possible.

What may be the most confusing thing about the Backup utility is where to find it. Most management tasks on a Windows XP computer are configured from a MMC snap-in. As mentioned earlier, many of these preconfigured MMC snap-ins are found under Start | Programs | Administrative Tools. To access the Backup utility, however, you will need to select Start | Programs | Accessories | System Tools | Backup. In XP, unlike in Windows 2000, the Backup utility starts in Wizard Mode. To begin in Advanced Mode, as most administrators do, select the Advanced Mode link in the Welcome dialog box. Figure 2-19 shows you where the configuration of backup jobs will start from Advanced Mode.

From this window, you can start the Backup Wizard, start the Restore Wizard, and create an Automated System Recovery (ASR) backup job. The ASR is a special type of backup that is used to restore the working state of an XP Professional computer (it is covered in detail in Chapter 6 as well).

There's no law that says you have to use the Windows Backup utility. Almost every tape drive vendor supplies its own software package for configuring backups. In fact, the Windows Backup that is included with Windows XP was written by Veritas, Inc.

You can schedule backup jobs from the Backup utility or manually configure backups to run by adding a task to the Windows XP Task Scheduler. I think you'll find the Backup utility the easier of the two to use for scheduling automated backups.

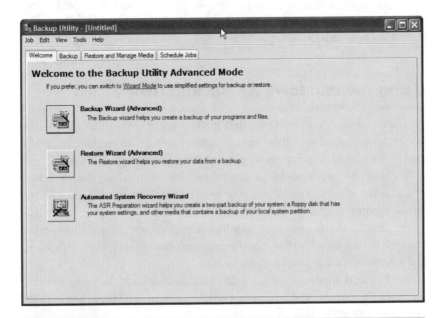

FIGURE 2.19   The Windows Backup utility

CHECKPOINT

✔**Objective 2.01: Configure and Manage File Systems**   In this section, we looked at issues you need to consider when making your formatting choices. We also introduced partitioning choices, preparing for the discussion of Disk Devices that followed.

✔**Objective 2.02: Implement, Manage, and Troubleshoot Disk Devices**   We discussed storage management considerations for DVD, CD-ROM, fixed disks, basic disks, and dynamic disks. We also looked at technologies for NTFS volumes that allow administrators to further control the network environment, including setting disk quotas for network users, setting compression on files and folders on a partition, and configuring backups on removable media.

REVIEW QUESTIONS

1. Artie Fufkin has just installed Windows XP Professional on a brand new computer running an Athlon 2GHz processor. He has two 30GB hard drives to work with and wants to set up a D: drive for the storage of his extensive music collection. He doesn't want to use all the available space right away, yet he wants to reserve the right to extend a volume on his first disk to use the space on the second disk if necessary. There are two factors Artie must plan for if he is to accomplish his goal. What are they?

   A. Basic disk

   B. Dynamic disk

   C. Simple volume

   D. Striped volume

2. You have been given a management directive to monitor disk usage by the users in your network. It seems that the file server's G: drive is filling up fast with bad jokes, chain letters, and urban legends saved from forwarded e-mails. You try to enable disk quotas but are unsuccessful. What is the problem?

   A. Quota tracking doesn't set any limits on usage when you first enable it.

   B. The G: drive isn't using NTFS. Quotas only work on NTFS volumes.

   C. You have not specified the users to track in the disk quotas configuration dialog box.

   D. Quota tracking, by default, applies only to new users in Windows XP. Until new users use the system, you won't be able to manage their storage use.

3. Pete Hogswallop wants to change the file system on his C: drive from NTFS to FAT32 so that he can configure the system to dual-boot between Windows XP Professional and Windows 98. He also wants to preserve the existing data on that drive. How will Pete accomplish this?

   A. Type **convert drive_letter /fs: fat** from the Command Prompt.

   B. Type **convert drive_letter /fs: ntfs to /fs: fat** from the Command Prompt.

   C. Delete the partition and reformat with NTFS; the NTFS format leaves files unharmed.

   D. Back up all data, reformat the partition as FAT32, and restore from backup.

4. You want to implement a fault tolerant storage solution on your XP Professional computer, but are wondering whether or not this is possible. Which of the following volume types are not supported on a Windows XP Professional computer? (Choose all that apply.)

   A. Striped volumes

   B. Mirrored volumes

   C. Spanned volumes

   D. RAID 5 volumes

5. Which of the following cannot be upgraded to dynamic disks?

   A. Disks from laptops

   B. Disks that don't have at least 1MB of unallocated free space

   C. Disks that are part of a striped set created in NT 4

   D. Disks that are part of a volume set created in NT 4

6. XP Professional includes support for a number of file system drivers. Which of the following file systems can you select for the system partition when installing the operating system? (Choose all that apply.)

   A. FAT16

   B. FAT32

   C. CDFS

D. HPFS

E. NTFS

7. You have compressed a 50MB file into 25MB. Now, you want to copy that file to a FAT32 partition. You are aware that, by default, during a copy the file will inherit the destination directory's compression attribute. What procedure is necessary to ensure that the file maintains its compression state during the copy operation?

   A. You must perform the copy operation from the command line with the XCOPY command, using the /retain switch.

   B. You really can't change the default behavior; you must make sure to go back and set the compression attribute after the copy has taken place.

   C. Right-click and choose Cut, and then at the destination directory right-click again and choose Paste Special. Then specify that the compression attribute be retained.

   D. You can't maintain compression of a file on non-NTFS partitions.

8. You are running out of storage space on your XP Professional system and decide to add a brand new hard disk to the array. Your system supports hot-swapping, so you expect to see the new disk space right away, but do not see the disk when you go to set up a partition in Disk Management. To start using the disk right away, what should you do?

   A. Reboot the computer. Plug and Play will pick up the new disk and install appropriate drivers.

   B. In Disk Management, choose Action | Rescan Disk.

   C. In Disk Management, choose Action | Import New Drive.

   D. From the Control Panel, run the Add New Hardware Wizard.

9. You are the administrator of a network of Windows XP computers. You have a \Public storage folder shared out on an NTFS volume of a Windows XP Professional computer. You want to configure quota management on that folder so that the Sales group does not take up too much of the space. How should you configure quota management?

   A. Set a quota limit for the Sales group on the NTFS volume.

   B. Set quota limits for the \Public share for individual accounts of the Sales group.

   C. Set quota limits for the Sales group on the \Public folder.

   D. Set quota limits for the individual members of the Sales group on the NTFS volume.

10. Your boss is vaguely aware of some of the possibilities on a Windows
    XP Professional dynamic disk and is peppering you with questions
    about when and where they can be used. Which of the following are
    not possible regarding Windows XP Professional dynamic disks?
    (Choose all that apply.)

    A. Dynamic disks are supported only by Windows XP and Windows
    2000 systems.

    B. You can add a dynamic disk to a NT 4 computer.

    C. Dynamic disks support division of disk space into partitions.

    D. Dynamic disks support division of disk space into volumes.

REVIEW ANSWERS

1. **B C**   Free space from another disk can be added to a simple volume
   by extending the simple volume into a spanned volume. A spanned
   volume is composed of regions of free space on from 2 to 32 dynamic
   disks. A is incorrect because none of the volume options are available
   on basic disks. Partitioning is the only method of dividing space on a
   basic disk, and a basic disk does not allow for extending the partition
   without third-party tools. D is not correct because a striped volume
   and a spanned volume are mutually exclusive. You will begin the
   process of creating spanned and striped volumes in the same way,
   but you will not be able to choose both when you select an area of
   unallocated space and run the Create Volume Wizard. Further, you
   will not be able to extend the striped volume once it is in place.

2. **B**   Quotas can be configured only on NTFS volumes. All of the other
   answers are true statements that apply to quotas, but none apply to this
   scenario.

3. **D**   You can't convert NTFS to FAT, and deleting the partition and
   reformatting with any file system would certainly harm the data. The
   only way to accomplish this task is to restore from backup. A is incorrect
   because this is not an option of the Convert command. B is incorrect
   for the same reason. C is incorrect because reformatting would blow
   away the data, not leave it unharmed.

4. **B D**   Windows XP Professional does not support fault tolerant
   volumes. B is correct because a mirrored volume provides fault
   tolerance by making duplicate copies of data across two physical disks.
   D is also correct because RAID 5 provides fault tolerance by storing

parity information, which can be used to regenerate data on a failed disk, across from 3 to 32 drives in an array. Answers A and C are incorrect because neither striped nor spanned volumes provide fault tolerance for data—only one copy of data is kept on the drives. Normal backup is the only way to guard data from disaster using these volume configurations.

5. **A** **B** Upgrading to dynamic disks is not supported on laptops or on disks with less than 1MB of free space. C and D are incorrect because it is possible, however, to upgrade any disks that are part of a striped set or volume set.

6. **A** **B** **E** Windows XP Professional can be installed on hard drives that have been formatted in any of the listed file systems. C is incorrect because while Windows XP can read from CDFS media (CD-ROMs), you can't perform the installation on CDFS media. D is incorrect because HPFS is no longer supported by Windows XP.

7. **D** Only NTFS drives support compression. This is the sort of head-fake that is likely on exams. Answer A *sounds* good, for example, but the command switch doesn't exist with the XCOPY utility. None of the other possibilities exist, either. You can choose Paste Special from Microsoft Word, but not in file copy operations.

8. **B** All that is necessary if the computer supports hot swapping is for you to select Action | Rescan Disk from the Disk Manager utility. A is incorrect because a reboot, while it should work, is not the most efficient solution. C won't work because it's not a menu option. D is also unnecessary because the hot-swappable device would have already been detected and set up. A trip to Add Hardware is not needed.

9. **D** Here you need to remember that quota limits are set for individual users and on entire volumes only. There is no way to set limits for groups of users, because quotas are based on ownership, and things are owned by individuals, not groups (with the exception of the Administrators group). Nor is there a way to set quota limits on folders; it's the whole volume or nothing. Therefore, only choice D will let you accomplish your goal.

10. **B** **C** These statements do not describe the behavior of XP Professional dynamic disks. NT 4 does not support dynamic disks, and partitioning is only supported on basic disks, not dynamic disks. A and D are incorrect because both statements are accurate regarding dynamic disks.

Implementing and Conducting Administration of Resources

C H A P T E R 3

	NEWBIE	SOME EXPERIENCE	EXPERT
ETA	4 hours	2 hours	1 hour

Now that you have installed Windows XP Professional on a system, you need to start making decisions about what is going to be accessed. Simply stated, *resource access* refers to what the operating system (OS) makes available to a user and what level of access that user has. To understand these vital file and folder operations, you first need to understand that there are two ways file and folder resources can be accessed: locally and over a network.

A user who is sitting down and opening a file from the C:\ drive, D:\ drive, and so on—that is, on a local disk—is said to access that resource *locally*. That same user, using the same computer, can also access a file resource that lives on a different computer. (If you'v'e ever surfed the Internet, you've done just that.) This user is accessing a *shared* resource, and that pathway to files and folders can be further subdivided into one of two flavors: 1) *web sharing*, and 2) well, there really isn't a specific name given to the other kind; it's just referred to as *sharing*, period.

But whether you're talking about local resource access or shared folder resource access, one thing holds true: varying levels of security can be applied to let certain users in, and keep other users out. And, as you'll see later in the chapter, your administrative control over security extends far beyond the either/or choice illustrated above. Additionally, we will look at how the file system used to store the resource determines exactly how it can be secured.

This chapter also has very striking real-world implications. One of your main functions as an admin is to make sure that users can get to the files they need to work on, while protecting files that they don't need access to from being overwritten or otherwise damaged. Much of what is discussed in this chapter will directly correlate with how you actually use the OS.

A number of file systems are supported by Windows XP. The two fixed-disk file types it supports are the file allocation table (FAT) and the NT File System (NTFS). The FAT file system support is kept for backward compatibility, floppy access, and dual-boot configuration. NTFS is a more feature-rich file system, as you will be learning in this chapter and throughout your entire Windows XP education. Only computers running Windows NT, 2000, or Windows XP support it. As we have discussed in Chapter 2, the type of file system used for the installation of XP and the storage of your data has a huge impact on the technologies available.

Objective 3.01 Manage and Troubleshoot Access to Shared Folders

When you share something on your system, you are making a resource available to others. This begs the following question: What's a resource?

Resources are the software objects on your computer made available to other users, regardless of whether those other users are local or remote. More simply put, it's something on your computer. Most often, when we talk about resources, we are talking about files and folders stored on our fixed disks. As you recall from Chapter 2, these fixed disks have been prepared to hold the resources by formatting them with *file systems*. Devices attached to your computer can be resources as well, like a printer or a CD-ROM device. Resource implementation tasks, then, include preparing the partitions with file systems and creating folders, shares, and Internet-accessible resources. It also includes configuring security permissions to these resources. Administration tasks include modifying these permissions and removing unnecessary partitions, folders, files, and shares. It also includes troubleshooting resource access problems for the users in your network.

These resources are made available from the servers on your network. So, then: What's a server?

I often begin Windows 2000 or XP Professional classes with this simple question, because it helps clarify some of the concepts that will follow. Did you know that when you're sitting down at your Windows XP Professional installation, you are also sitting at a server? That's because the server service is running, which allows files and folders to be shared on Microsoft networks. XP Professional is just the title of the operating system. Of course, the 2000 and .NET Server products, which are the titles of other operating systems, run the server service as well, but the point is that what constitutes a server is the behavior of the computer in the network, not what it looks like, or what the name of the operating system is.

Put another way, a server is simply a function of a chunk of software. What's more, as you will see throughout your admin career, different pieces of server software share out different things.

So What's a Share?

A *share* is a portion of your computer's resources that is specifically made available to other computers on the network. The share is central to a network's functionality, and the network is the important thing to keep in mind. There is no such thing as a local share. After all, that's why we hook all of these computers up in the first place, so that files on one computer can be accessed, used, and modified by someone on another. With sharing, we make disk resources (folders and drives) network accessible. Without sharing, we have little more than *sneakernet* to get files back and forth between computers. And when properly implemented, using network resources in XP is just as simple and easy as using resources on your own. (You can even use network resources when there's no network available, as discussed in Chapter 6.)

Local Lingo

Sneakernet   The process of transporting files from one computer to another using floppy disks by walking files from one computer to another. It's networking using your sneakers. Sneakernet. Get it? No one said the computer industry wasn't full of hilarity.

You'll be able to share resources in Windows XP Professional in two ways: through regular network sharing or through a totally different beast called web sharing. We'll talk more extensively about web sharing in Chapter 7. As we get familiar with this topic, let's focus just on regular network sharing—that is, a couple of computers in a room or office building talking to each other and exchanging files.

What's the Difference Between Web Sharing and ... the Other Thing?

Alright, I've opened up a can of worms, and an explanation is needed here to help keep the sharing types separate. Let me try to summarize:

Since sharing is a function of software, the two different constructs of resource sharing are controlled by different pieces of server software. Sharing is made possible through the Server service, which is installed and started automatically on all Windows XP (as well as 2000 and NT) computers, by default. Further, the Server service, by default, is configured to start automatically each time the system boots up, and it runs in the background. This means that files that have already been shared will remain shared even if no one is logged on at the computer. You can just turn on the computer and others will have access to shared folders, even if no one is logged onto the machine.

You can view the properties of the Server service by examining the Services program in the Administrative Tools group. If you want to make changes to the way the Server service starts, that is certainly your prerogative. From the Services utility, double-click the Server service icon to access the Properties dialog box, as shown in Figure 3-1.

Travel Advisory

To make your computer more secure, you can disable the Server service (or not enable File and Printer Sharing for Microsoft Networks on a Windows 9x or XP computer—they are the same function but go by different names—on the network adapter that's exposed to the Internet). This is especially significant on a computer with "always on" Internet access, as with a cable or DSL connection.

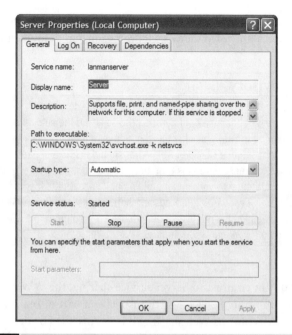

FIGURE 3.1   Configuring the Server service

From the General tab, you can configure startup behavior of the Server service (or any service, for that matter) to be either automatic or manual, and you can disable the service completely. You can also associate the startup of the service with a particular hardware profile from the Log On tab. This might be useful when a computer is not sharing any files at all, such as when a laptop is using a profile that is off the network. We will cover hardware profiles in Chapter 6.

Sharing on Microsoft Networks   If you look closely at the description of the Server service from the Services MMC snap-in, you might notice that the stated job of the Server service is to make a file or print resource available on Microsoft networks. (I'm paraphrasing just a bit.) But what does that mean? The Server software component actually makes shared resources available through a protocol called Server Message Blocks (SMBs), which is the "language" that Windows computers speak to one another in when they are requesting and delivering shared files and printers. In other words, the client makes the request using the SMB protocol, and the request is answered because the server also "speaks" SMB.

So what is the client component that speaks SMB? The Workstation service. The Workstation service is the software that allows access to files that have been made available through the Server service. The Workstation service, like the Server service, installs and runs at startup time, by default. These client-server communication topics will be revisited later in this book in Chapter 7 when we discuss interoperability of Windows XP Professional in a Novell environment.

Travel Advisory

I realize that I often say, "We'll talk about this in more detail later," or something like that. This is not because I am putting off discussing the subject matter; rather, I am trying to keep this chapter, the longest one of the book to begin with, somewhat shorter than a Clancy novel. What should become apparent from all the references to other material is that much of the information presented in this chapter is foundational to your understanding of Windows XP. If you don't "get" sharing, or how shares are accessed, or how resources are secured, for example, you are likely going to have a hard time understanding other Windows XP topics.

Web Sharing   In contrast to Server service sharing, the WWW (for World Wide Web) Publishing Service, which installs as a part of Internet Information Server (IIS), controls Web sharing. It is *not* installed by default on Windows XP Professional, unless you've upgraded a system that was already running the Personal Web Server. The WWW Publishing Service's job is to make files available through a different protocol, in this case the Hypertext Transport Protocol (HTTP). But again, our focus for now is squarely on SMB sharing, via the Server service.

For the time being, let's concentrate on what this looks like from the client's point of view. From an end user standpoint, the big difference between SMB (regular) sharing and web sharing is the program used when the user connects to a shared resource.

Local Lingo

SMB (Server Message Blocks)   An application-layer protocol used by Windows computers to share files and printers. SMB is not compatible with other vendor's client software, like the Novell client.

HTTP (Hypertext Transfer Protocol)   Also can be used for the purposes of sharing files and printers. It is compatible with any computer that has a web browser.

As you probably know, a client connects to a Web resource using a web browser. Resources are located using the Uniform Resource Locator (URL) syntax, which looks something like this: http://*computername/alias/file.*

Okay, enough of this web talk for now. While a web resource is usually accessed using only the standard syntax just shown, users can access a "normally" shared resource in several ways. Here are three of the most common ways, which we will discuss later in the chapter in greater detail.

- By browsing the network using My Network Places
- By mapping a drive letter to a share and then accessing it through Windows Explorer
- By using the NET USE utility from the command line

But first things first. Let's figure out how to set up these shares before worrying about how to access them.

Create and Remove Shared Folders

It's not enough anymore just to learn about sharing. Previously, a discussion about sharing concepts could be applied to any Windows product used to make a resource available. Unfortunately, such knowledge is no longer cross-platform, so to speak.

There is a new beast in Windows XP that is intended, as are many of the innovations of the OS, to make the sophisticated simple. This new beast throws a monkey wrench into our previous model of sharing learned on previous versions of Windows. It's called *Simple File Sharing*, and it makes setting the security for shared resources easy to implement for single installations of XP that are shared by multiple users.

This new version means that there are now two distinctly different sharing models in use in Windows XP:

- **Simple File Sharing**   Sharing resources with Windows XP is easy, but the configuration options are limited once you do. To illustrate, look at the way a resource is shared with SFS turned on. You perform the share with a single click of a check box, and then XP takes over from there. The OS will automatically set the share permissions and NTFS permissions it feels appropriate without further intervention. However, you are making the resource available to all network users, so you can't selectively set different permissions for different users. Also, Windows will use the Guest account for all network access.

- **Classic Sharing**   The classic sharing model is the one that has been implemented all the way back to Windows 3.0. When you share a folder, the default share permission given to the Everyone group has Full Control, but you are free to modify the permissions for individual users and groups at your will. Using this model, you are also able to set limits on the number of simultaneous connections. The drawback of this model is that you are required to have a better knowledge of how sharing works and the ways in which share permissions interact; it is more complex than its younger vintage. You will also need to create individual accounts, and possibly groups, for each computer that allows network access.

Travel Advisory

If you are studying for the XP exam from a Home Edition computer, you are working at a technological disadvantage. The Home edition uses Simple File Sharing exclusively. Only Professional gives you the option to use either SFS or classic sharing.

On a clean installation of XP, sharing is disabled. This is because sharing in a workgroup relies on the Guest account, which is also disabled until an administrator changes this. You can verify this when you look at the Properties dialog box of a folder, as shown in Figure 3-2. To set your computer up to share, you will first need to run the Network Setup Wizard, which will ensure that computers in your network use the same workgroup name and will try to set up a shared firewall-protected Internet connection, among other things.

If you want to bypass the Network Setup Wizard, you can just click the second link at the bottom of this dialog box. You will still be begged to start the Wizard, but if you've already configured your computers so that they see each other on the network (usually done at Setup time), you can choose the second option in the dialog box, as shown in Figure 3-3.

Be aware that when you click this option, two things will happen behind the scenes:

- The Guest account will be enabled. It will not, however, be displayed on the Welcome screen. To have it displayed at startup time, open User Accounts from the Control Panel and turn on the Guest account.

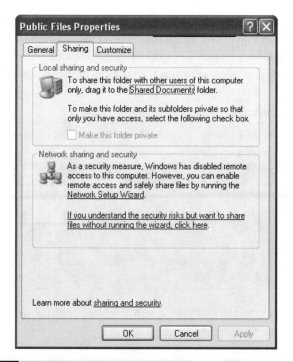

FIGURE 3.2 The Properties dialog box will indicate whether or not you have previously configured sharing.

FIGURE 3.3 Bypassing the wizard

- The guest account will also be removed from the list of accounts with the Ability to Access This Computer from the Network user right (for more information on user rights, refer to Chapter 8). You can also change this manually through the Local Security Settings MMC.

Travel Advisory

In Windows versions prior to XP, every folder showed a Sharing tab as long as File and Print Sharing for Microsoft Networks (the Server service in NT and 2000 computers) was installed. However, this is not automatic when working with XP. If you are looking for the sharing tab of a folder's Properties dialog box and can't find it, make sure your system has been set up for sharing. First, look at the Properties dialog box for the network connection and make sure that File and Printer Sharing for Microsoft networks has been installed. (This sets up SMB on the computer, as described earlier.) Then, use the Services MMC snap-in to make sure that the Server service is started.

Here's what Windows XP does with a shared folder when Simple File Sharing is the sharing method in effect:

- It creates shared resource permission to the built-in Everyone group. Depending on the choice you make in the Allow Network users to Change My Files check box, XP will grant the Read permissions or the Full Control permission to the Everyone group. (The Guest account, if you are wondering, is a part of the Everyone group.)
- If the shared folder lives on an NTFS partition, Windows will also assign an entry for the Everyone group to the Access Control List (ACL) of the resource (the ACL is discussed later in this chapter). If the Allow Network Users To Change My files check box is not selected, the ACL allows the Read and Execute permissions. If it is selected, the ACL allows the Modify permission. Whatever the setting, it is wise to remember that NTFS permissions are inherited, by default, by all child objects of the resource in question.

As you can see, Simple File Sharing is a convenient shortcut to granting access to resources on your system. However, it does not give you nearly the level of administrative flexibility available with classic sharing. Because access is made through the Guest account, what you lose with SFS is the power to restrict access to individual users or to give certain users different levels of access than others. For this reason, the majority of the questions on the exam should be related to the classic sharing model, as it will require more advanced administrative know-how than SFS, and it will likely be the model used in any corporate environment.

Classic Sharing

In the Windows XP implementation of classic sharing, you can make files and folders available to network users by using the same methods previously at your disposal: Windows Explorer, the Shared Folders utility, or the command line using the NET SHARE utility. To begin this process, first make sure that you are logged on as a member of the Administrators or the Power Users group. Only a member of at least one of these two groups can create shares.

Exam Tip

For the Windows XP Professional exam, know that a user must be a member of the Administrators or Power Users group to share a resource.

To make a folder and *all* of its contents available to other Microsoft clients, take the following steps:

1. From Windows Explorer, right-click the folder you want to make available and choose Sharing and Security.

2. From the Sharing and Security tab, which for space considerations is titled only Sharing (shown in Figure 3-4), select the check box to Share this folder on the Network, then give the share a name.

3. Click Apply when you are finished.

Travel Advisory

I should also mention that if your XP Professional computer is joined to a Windows XP domain (remember that Home edition computers cannot do this), it will always use classic mode when sharing, no matter what your setting in Folder Options.

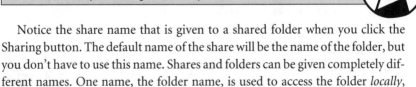

Notice the share name that is given to a shared folder when you click the Sharing button. The default name of the share will be the name of the folder, but you don't have to use this name. Shares and folders can be given completely different names. One name, the folder name, is used to access the folder *locally*, and the other name, the share name, is used to access the folder over the *network*.

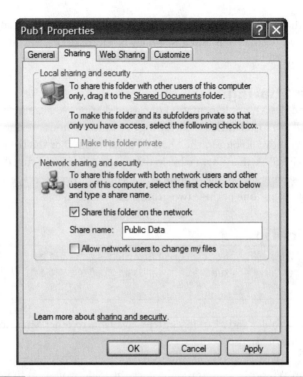

FIGURE 3.4   Setting up a share

For example, you could have a folder named "Pub1" on your system and share it under the name "Public Data."

You can also set up sharing through the command prompt if you're into this kind of thing. Using the NET SHARE command, you can create, delete, or display shared resources. The syntax of the NET SHARE command is shown here:

```
NET SHARE sharename=drive:path
```

where *sharename* is the network name of the shared resource (remember that it does not have to match the actual folder name of the resource) and *drive:path* is the way that the local machine addresses this resource (that is, what drive letter it's on and what folders and subfolders it lives in).

Travel Advisory

Remember that you can use the NET SHARE /? command for a quick reference of the proper syntax.

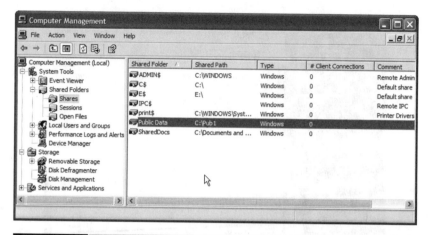

Shared Folder △	Shared Path	Type	# Client Connections	Comment
ADMIN$	C:\WINDOWS	Windows	0	Remote Admin
C$	C:\	Windows	0	Default share
E$	E:\	Windows	0	Default share
IPC$		Windows	0	Remote IPC
print$	C:\WINDOWS\Syst...	Windows	0	Printer Drivers
Public Data	C:\Pub1	Windows	0	
SharedDocs	C:\Documents and ...	Windows	0	

Computer Management (Local)
- System Tools
  - Event Viewer
  - Shared Folders
    - Shares
    - Sessions
    - Open Files
  - Local Users and Groups
  - Performance Logs and Alerts
  - Device Manager
- Storage
  - Removable Storage
  - Disk Defragmenter
  - Disk Management
- Services and Applications

FIGURE 3.5   The shares listed in the Shared Folders utility

A third way of setting up a share on Windows XP Professional computers is to use the Shared Folders utility, which is found in Computer Management. To launch Computer Management from the desktop, right-click My Computer and choose Manage. The Shared Folders node will appear in the left panel, between the Event Viewer and Local Users and Groups, as shown in Figure 3-5.

The Shared Folders utility exhibits all the shares that have been created on the computer and will also show you the sessions that are accessing the share, listed by user. Remember, you won't see the Shared Folders utility unless Simple File Sharing is turned off.

In the Shared Folders utility, you can create new shares by completing the following steps:

1. Right-click the Shared folder and from the context menu choose New File Share. The Create Shared Folder Wizard starts, as shown in Figure 3-6, which will guide you the rest of the way.

2. From this dialog box, you will specify the path to the folder that you wish to be shared, or you can just browse to your hard drive and click on the folder you are after. Then fill in the name of the share (it doesn't have to be the same as the folder name) and click the Next button.

3. The next dialog box will allow you to assign initial permissions for the share. You can select from one of the predefined permissions or customize the share permissions that will be set. (More about share permissions in "Control Access to Shared Folders Using Permissions," a little later in this chapter.) When you are done, click the Finish button to set up the share.

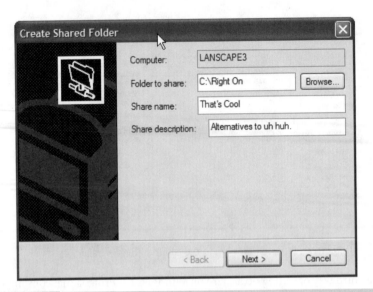

Create Shared Folder

Computer:	LANSCAPE3
Folder to share:	C:\Right On [Browse...]
Share name:	That's Cool
Share description:	Alternatives to uh huh.

[< Back] [Next >] [Cancel]

FIGURE 3.6   The Create Shared Folder Wizard

4. The Create Shared Folder dialog box appears, verifying that the share had been successfully created and asking you if you'd like to create another. To stop sharing a folder from the Shared Folders utility, simply right-click the share and select Stop Sharing from the context menu, as shown in Figure 3-7.

Travel Advisory

You must not be using Simple File Sharing in order to use the Shared Folders utility to share out a resource.

What's the Deal with Simple File Sharing?

There are three fundamental differences that distinguish classic sharing from Simple File sharing. You should know these differences. They are

- Classic sharing lets you set up, or more correctly requires you to set up, permissions on a per user basis. Recall that SFS specifies permissions only for the Everyone group. (You need to keep in mind, though, that the default behavior of classic sharing is to let the Everyone group have Full Control, so be careful.)

- Users who connect to your server using classic sharing are not automatically authenticated as the computer's Guest account. (In this way, SFS works very much like web sharing, as we'll later see. All users, by

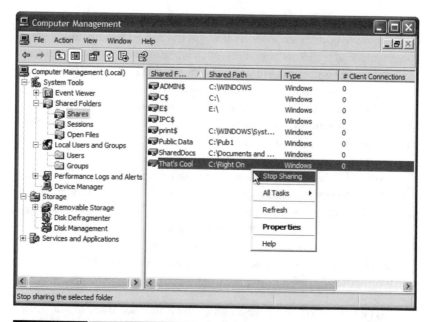

FIGURE 3.7   How to stop sharing a folder

default, access a website anonymously until this setting is changed by the administrator.) Each connection attempt is submitted with its own unique set of credentials, and if there is a match for a local computer account, Windows authenticates using that account. Otherwise, the Guest account is used for the connection attempt, and that account might not have any access at all to resources. As a result, security is much greater when using classic sharing.

- If the shared resource lives on an NTFS partition, an administrator (or the owner) can specify access through Access Control List entries. (Ownership and ACLs are discussed in Objective 3.02.)

Travel Advisory

Here's a common real-world scenario many administrators new to XP encounter: when you access an NTFS resource for the first time, there is no Security tab where NTFS permissions are set. This is because Simple File Sharing is enabled out of the box, and SFS sets permissions only for the Everyone group, and those settings match what was set at the share level. In fact, when SFS is on, it will hide even the Security tab. So if you have wondered where the NTFS permissions have gone, make sure that SFS is disabled.

Hidden and Administrative Shares

You may have noticed some shares listed in the Shared Folders utility whose share names end with a dollar sign ($). What is that all about? Who set those up? Well, the answer is not who, but what. The Windows XP OS set up those shares, and they are your computer's *administrative shares*.

Windows XP automatically sets up these administrative shares to facilitate system administration from remote computers. It does, however, hide these shares from view as users are browsing the network.

The significance of the dollar sign ($) after the share name means that the share will be hidden from view when using share access utilities like My Network Places. In fact, any share you create will be hidden from view if you append a dollar sign to the share name. This can be a good way to store software programs and other utilities that you may regularly use as a network administrator while keeping these files safe from the curious.

The following administrative shares are created on a Windows XP Professional computer, by default:

- The *Driveletter*$ share, where *driveletter* is the root of any logical drive. In Figure 3-5, you can see that the C:\ and E:\ drives have been shared.
- The ADMIN$ share points to the Windows XP installation folder, which is \WINNT if the defaults were kept at installation time.
- The IPC$ (Interprocess Communications) share allows remote administration of a computer and is used to view shared resources.
- The PRINT$ share may be present for remote printer administration.

If you go back through either Windows Explorer or the Shared Folders utility and try to administer the administrative shares, you may be in for a surprise. You cannot change any of the settings of the administrative shares, such as the permissions. You might even notice that if you try to stop sharing an administrative share, it will be shared out again if the computer reboots. Does this mean that just anyone who has knowledge of these hidden shares can access your drive and wreak untold havoc? Not to worry. Only certain groups have access to the administrative shares.

If you protect the user name and passwords of the users with access to the administrative shares, you are protecting these shares.

Connecting to Shared Resources

Once you've got a folder shared on the network, users can gain access to it in several ways. The list earlier in this chapter showed some of the common ways, one of which was by browsing through My Network Places.

My Network Places is probably the most intuitive tool for novice users to employ to gain shared folder access. By double-clicking network objects, such as groups of computers and then servers, users can be presented a listing of the shares that live on these servers. You can also use the My Network Places to map a network location through the use of the Add Network Place Wizard; doing this will create an easy-to-access method for you to connect to shared resources on the network.

1. To start the wizard, click the Add a Network Place task (if using the classic interface, choose the icon) from the first My Network Places window. Figure 3-8 shows the wizard's Welcome screen.

2. You can either enter the name of the network place to which you want to connect or click Browse and search for it. You can use a URL path to a web folder, a File Transfer Protocol (FTP) path to an FTP site, or a Universal Naming Convention (UNC) pathname. Notice that when you browse for a shared folder and select it, the UNC pathname will be entered for your convenience.

FIGURE 3.8 The Add Network Place Wizard opening screen

Before going any further, it is important that you understand completely the UNC syntax for addressing network resources. A *UNC path* is a method that you can use to connect to any resource on the network (that you have permission to access) by specifying a unique path, called the UNC path.

This syntax is vital to understand as we work with Windows XP, because it is used so often to specify network resources. If you don't know what you're looking at when seeing a UNC path, not much else will make sense.

The UNC path syntax to access a network share is as follows:

`\\computername\sharename`

The *computername* is the name of the computer, or server, to which you would like to connect, while the *sharename* is the name of the share on that specific computer.

It is important that you not confuse this syntax with the MS-DOS pathname, which will look like this: *C:\folder\subfolder1\subfolder2*. The UNC path is used to access the resource over the network, while the MS-DOS path is how the same resource is addressed locally. Notice that the UNC syntax makes no reference to a drive letter or to how deep in the folder hierarchy the resource may live. In Figure 3-9, you can see how resources on a computer look when accessed over the network compared to when accessed locally.

In Figure 3-9, the window on the left shows the contents of my hard drive when accessed locally. On the right, inside the window titled Lanscape3, it

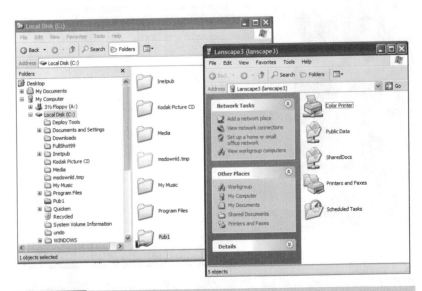

FIGURE 3.9   Viewing a resource locally and over the network

shows the resources available to someone accessing the computer using the syntax *computername* (you can use just the first half of the UNC syntax to see a list of all shares on a given server). Notice that from the network side, you don't see all the folders, only those folders that have been shared.

You can also access network resources by mapping a network drive using Windows Explorer. After you have mapped a network drive, it will appear as another drive letter when the user accesses My Computer or Windows Explorer. You can map a network drive in several ways. Here's one:

1. Either right-click My Computer or My Network Places and choose Map Network Drive.

2. The Map Network Drive dialog box appears, as shown in Figure 3-10, choose the drive letter that will be associated with this network connection and the path to the location. You can use any letter for the drive that is not already taken. You can then specify the folder location by typing the UNC pathname of the folder or click Browse to search for the folder location. Notice that the UNC pathname syntax is used even if you Browse for the folder.

3. If you want this mapped network connection to be persistent, make sure the Reconnect At Logon check box remains selected. (It will be selected by default.) This will ensure that the mapped connection is part of a

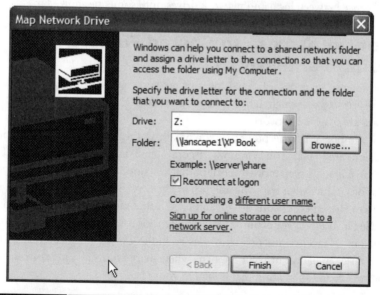

FIGURE 3.10   Mapping a network drive

user profile, which means that it will be a part of the drives seen in Windows Explorer each time the user logs on.

4. You can also specify a different user name that will be used to make this connection if you wish. To do this, click the hyperlink called Different User Name and then designate the account used for the connection.

Additionally, Mavis Beacon disciples can use the NET USE command to assign a user name, which is actually a fairly quick and painless way to map a network drive to a shared location. Similar to the NET SHARE command, the NET USE utility uses the following syntax

```
NET USE x: \\computername\sharename
```

where x is the drive letter that will be used for the mapped connection and \\computername\sharename is the UNC address of the share. (I'm not one to say I told you so, but I told you so: you have to know the UNC path.)

Your users will probably never have to know what the UNC syntax is or what it means. That's fine, as they will most likely use graphical applications, like Explorer, to access shared resources. One of the benefits of a GUI-based OS like Windows is that any resources needed are just a few intuitive double-clicks away. In the workplace, you might even hear complaints from end users about the "H:\ drive going bad." The confusion is understandable. I didn't know the difference between local and network drives until someone showed me.

Control Access to Shared Folders Using Permissions

Sharing also provides a limited form of network security through the use of *share permissions,* which define what kind of access a user has when connecting to a share over the network.

It's important at this point to take a breath and realize that two kinds of permissions are available on Windows XP computers: share permissions and NTFS permissions. It's even more important that you not confuse the two. Share permissions define what happens only when a *network* user is connecting to a resource. These permissions are meaningless if that same user were to sit down and log in *locally* at your computer. To control local access, you need NTFS permissions. NTFS permissions are discussed in the Objective 2.02 section, along with an explanation of what happens when share and NTFS permissions are combined, an explanation that is vital to your test success.

The three levels of share permissions are described in this table:

Permission	Characteristics
Read	Allows users to view files in a folder; lets users execute programs in the shared folder
Change	Allows users to change the data in a file; lets users delete a file within a share, so be judicious about who has change permission
Full Control	Allows full access to the shared folder, including all permissions from Change; allows users to change permissions on the share

Further, these three permissions are restricted by two conditions, called *Allow* and *Deny*. Allow grants the specific permission to a shared resource, and it is the default selection for a permission setting. Deny will explicitly block the permission from being applied to a resource. The Deny condition adds another layer of complexity to shared resources and, therefore, should be used sparingly. For example, it is possible to deny Read access to a resource while still allowing Change access to be in effect. It wouldn't earn you a happy face on your dissertation on good administrative practice, but it's possible. The result would be a folder in which a user could delete a file that he or she could not read.

Exam Tip

Remember that the Deny permission overrides the Allow permission. This concept will remain consistent throughout many other aspects of the operating system, so it's a good thing to have clear in your mind.

To configure share-level permissions to a network resource, you will edit the *Access Control List* (ACL) for that resource. The ACL is a list of user accounts and groups that are allowed to access a resource, and it lists what level of access is allowed. Each and every *object* in Windows XP Professional has an ACL associated with it that it checks every time an account needs access to the resource. Examples of objects include folders, files, network shares, and printers.

Travel Advisory

For practical purposes, when you don't want a user or group to access a resource, you simply do not include them in the list of users and groups in the Access Control List (ACL) that you are building. You don't need to add a group and then deny that group a given permission. Just don't add it in the first place.

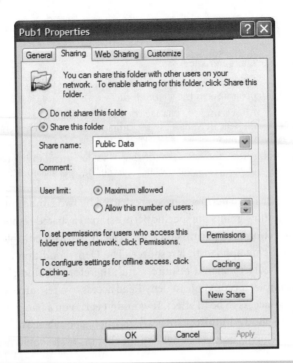

FIGURE 3.11   The Permissions button lets you lock down a share.

To access the ACL, start from the Sharing tab of a folder's Properties dialog box. Click the Permissions button, as shown in Figure 3-11, to begin editing the ACL.

When you first share out a folder, you will notice that the ACL consists of only one entry that says the Everyone group is granted Full Control. If you want to edit the list of users and groups who can access the share and how they can access it, click the Add button and add a group or individual account. You can also remove groups by selecting them in the ACL and clicking Remove.

After the user or group appears in the ACL, you can modify its level of access by either checking or unchecking the appropriate check boxes in the Permissions property page, as shown in Figure 3-12.

For example, if you want the local Administrator to have Full Control and the Everyone group to have the Read permission, you first uncheck the Full Control and Change permissions of the Everyone group. Then add the Administrator account and grant it Full Control by checking the Full Control box (Full Change and Read will automatically be checked when you select Full Control).

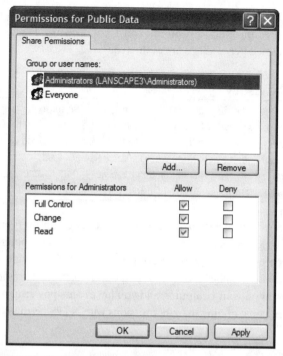

FIGURE 3.12   Setting share permissions

The share will then let Everyone read files in the share, and the Administrator will be allowed Full Control to all files and subfolders within the share, as explained next.

Exam Tip

You should know that the default permission on a shared resource is that the Everyone group has Full Control. As a best practice, you will typically remove this permission and then build the ACL to your own needs.

It is, of course, possible for a user to be a part of two or more groups within Windows XP. And when those groups have different levels of access to a resource, the share permissions for that user are cumulative—that is, the permissions are added together.

To illustrate, suppose user Brian is a part of the Sales group, which has Read access to the \Commissions shared folder. That same user is in the Management group(of course), which has the Full Control permission. What is Brian's permission when connecting to \Commissions? Full Control. Figure 3-13 shows how the combined permissions are evaluated.

Travel Advisory

Remember that if the Deny permission is in effect, either through group membership or by individual assignment, the Deny becomes effective for that particular permission. In the Brian example, if the Sales group were denied the Read permission, Brian would also be denied Read permission by virtue of his membership in the Sales group. In other words, the Deny permission overrides the Allow permission.

As mentioned, when a share is created, the special group Everyone is granted the Allow Full Control access permission to the share. This is a potential security hole, but it represents a design philosophy of Microsoft. Why share something if you don't want it accessible? It is up to you, the administrator, to tighten the security of resources on your computer, and you have some powerful options to do just that when you combine share permissions with NTFS permissions.

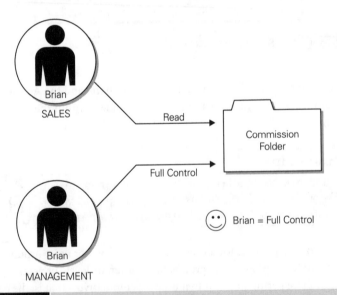

FIGURE 3.13   Share + share permissions

Travel Advisory

Be aware of the default behaviors of sharing (and those for just about anything else). Defaults might not be the type of behavior you want the operating system to display, and, in the case of sharing permissions, the wrong sharing choices may leave you open to security breaches.

One more point about sharing on a Windows XP Professional computer that must be mentioned: The number of concurrent connections is limited to a maximum of 10. In the case of Windows 2000/.NET Server, the connections are unlimited by default. For this reason, dedicated file servers on larger networks usually use XP Server as their operating system. Windows XP Professional is more suited for smaller peer-to-peer networks.

Exam Tip

Remember the following about share permissions:

- They are not effective locally when a user is sitting down at a computer. They are effective only when other systems access folders over the network.
- They can be applied only to folders, not to individual files. (As a corollary, everything within a share is available, files and subfolders included.)
- Share permissions can be applied to any file system that is supported by Windows XP Professional.
- Share permissions, when combined, are cumulative. (The caveat here is that the Deny permission overrides the Allow permission.)

And, as a coda about sharing, remember that sharing is not a function of the file system. It is a function of the Server service. You can implement sharing on both FAT and NTFS partitions. (You can also share out resources that the server retrieves using CDFS—the file system for CD-ROM drives.) Sharing is just a way to make something accessible on the network. The Server service will call the appropriate file system drivers necessary to retrieve the resource being asked for.

As you'll see in the next objective, NTFS security is specific to a resource on an NTFS partition. Higher levels of security are one of the several features available on NTFS that aren't on any other file system. Something to keep in the back of your mind as we press on.

Manage and Troubleshoot
Web Server Resources

In order to make resources available on the Web, Windows XP uses the services of Internet Information Services (IIS), which can be installed as an additional component of Windows XP Professional computers. When installed on an XP Professional system, IIS is intended to act as a small-scale Web server for a small intranet or Internet site with limited traffic. It won't be able to do everything that an installation of IIS can do when installed on Windows 2000/.NET Servers. For example, the XP Professional installation of IIS makes available the services of Hypertext Transport Protocol (HTTP) and the Simple Mail Transport Protocol (SMTP), but not the services of Network News Transport Protocol (NNTP). In other words, you cannot host a newsgroup on an XP Professional system.

Web sharing will be dealt with in further detail in Chapter 7. One could argue that since it is, in essence, a file sharing technology, it would be more appropriate to discuss it here, but I think it's best to focus on smaller scale file and print sharing for now.

Objective 3.02 Monitor, Manage, and Troubleshoot Access to Files and Folders

On a volume or partition formatted with NTFS, each file or folder has associated with it a set of NTFS *attributes*. Some of these attributes are the NTFS security permissions that are granted to users and groups when accessing the file or folder. Other attributes include the compression attribute, the encryption attribute, and the owner attribute. The important thing to remember is that these attributes are available only on NTFS partitions, which is one of the many reasons that Microsoft strongly recommends that Windows XP be installed on an NTFS partition where possible.

The decision to format a drive is usually made at installation time, although you can convert a drive from the FAT file system to NTFS even after you've performed the Windows XP installation. (The conversion from FAT to NTFS was detailed in Chapter 2.) To determine whether you're working with an NTFS partition, right-click the drive letter from Windows Explorer and choose Properties to look at the properties of the drive. The General tab will list what kind of file system the drive is using. Another quick way to know whether the drive is NTFS is to look at the properties of any folder or file (this works on the drive letter itself, as it is really a folder in its own right). If you see a Security tab listed, you're in business.

On the Security tab of a file or folder, you will configure the NTFS permissions, and most of the time you will be working with the standard permissions. But before we define these standard permissions, you should understand that the NTFS standard permissions are collections of *individual* NTFS security *attributes*. Click the Advanced button on the Security tab to see a complete, somewhat overwhelming listing of these individual security attributes, as shown in Figure 3-14.

Control Access to Files and Folders Using NTFS Permissions

With NTFS permissions, you have a wide range of security possibilities for the file resources on your system. For example, you can configure private storage locations for users. We'll discuss other possibilities here.

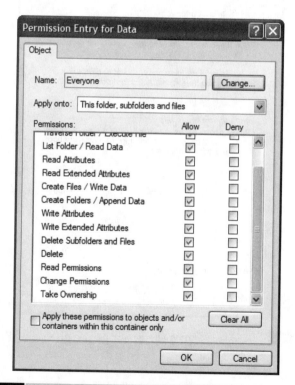

FIGURE 3.14 The individual NTFS security attributes

Keeping Your Files Private

When you are using Simple File Sharing, you can make a folder resource private with a single click of the mouse (see Figure 3-15).

So what does this dialog box mean? First of all, understand that you will not have this option available if your user profile is stored on a FAT or FAT32 drive. That's because the option uses NTFS permissions to restrict access to files accessed locally from anyone other than the account being configured, including administrators of the system. Once this option is set, only you (the account) can open and view the files that have been created by you. (Admins: there is still a way to get at the files. An administrator, or someone with the Take Ownership user right, could still commandeer the ownership attribute, and then change the ACL permissions for the file or folder.)

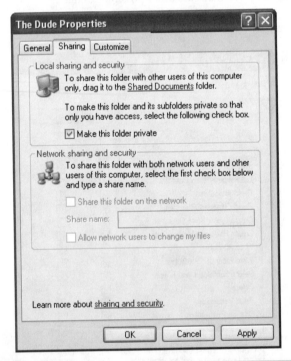

| FIGURE 3.15 | Private storage might be a good idea on shared XP installations. |

Travel Advisory

The Make This Folder Private option is pretty much useless unless you have configured the account with a password. A dialog box will remind you of this as you are setting up the private location. Without a password, someone could easily access the computer using your account by clicking it in the Welcome screen.

You can also do this the long way, by setting individual NTFS permissions for the folder or file. To do so, you need to first make sure two things have been done (both possible only from XP Pro):

- Format the desired volume using the NTFS file system.
- Disable Simple File Sharing.

To make the switch, open up any Windows Explorer window and choose Tools | Options. Then from the View tab, scroll to the bottom of the list and clear the Use Simple File Sharing (recommended) check box.

Once this change has been made, you will see a new Security tab on each and every file and folder stored on the NTFS volume, including the volume root, as was the case with NTFS-formatted volumes in Windows NT and Windows 2000. From there, much of the NTFS security settings should look and behave exactly the same way as in previous versions, especially Windows 2000.

Setting Permissions Through the Command Line

You also have the ability to set permissions through the command line with a utility called cacls, available with both the XP Pro and XP Home versions. With this utility, you can view permissions by typing **cacls** *filename*, where filename is the name of the file or folder whose ACL you are looking up.

Next to each user account name, the output of cacls will display a letter or letters, with each letter representing a level of permission for the particular resource. *F* for Full Control, *C* for Change, *W* for Write, *R* for Read, and so on. Any other settings produce output that is too complex to be effectively interpreted and that is outside the scope of the XP exam.

Cacls is useful for quickly finding the permissions for an object if you're working on a Command Prompt interface and is especially useful when working from the XP Home edition. Like most every command utility, cacls can be used with one or more switches to modify its behavior. This table lists some of the command switches you should be familiar with:

Switch	Use
/T	Changes permissions in the current directory and all subdirectories.
/E	Edits the Access Control List instead of replacing.
/C	Continues on "access denied" errors.
/G user:perm	Grants user rights. If used without /Explorer, it will replace the existing permissions.
/R user	Revokes specified user's access rights (this one must be used with /Explorer).
/P user:perm	Replaces specified user's access rights.
/D user	Denies access to a specific user.

For example, the cacls utility could be used to give the Full Control permission to a user, Lindsey, for a folder called Patient Records from the command line in this way:

```
Cacls Patient Records /g lindsey:f
```

Note that you would be performing the command from whatever directory the files were located in.

There is also an extended version of cacls called Xcacls, found with the support tools that are included with the Windows XP and XP Setup CDs. It is more flexible and supports alternate switches to make it work. Knowledge of this tool should not be important for testing purposes, but you can find it under the following path from the XP CD: \Support\Tools\Support.cab.

NTFS Permission Behavior

One of the hallmarks of the NTFS permissions is that, unlike shared folder permissions, *they can be configured at the folder level and the individual file level.* Table 3-1 lists the standard folder permissions that can be assigned with the click of a mouse from the Security tab of the Properties dialog box for a folder. These standard folder permissions are collections of the security attributes mentioned previously.

As with share permissions, each of the NTFS standard permissions (as well as individual attributes) has an Allow setting and a Deny setting. Also, as with shares, the Deny trumps the Allow. To explicitly deny all access to a user or group to a particular resource, deny the Full Control permission. This turns off all other access to the resource.

TABLE 3.1	Standard Folder Permissions
NTFS Folder Permission	**Lets a User...**
Read	See files and subfolders and view folder ownership, permissions, and attributes
Write	Create new files and subfolders within the folder, change folder attributes, and view folder ownership and permissions
List Folder Contents	See names of the files and subfolders within a folder
Read and Execute	Move through folders to reach other files and folders, even if the users don't have permission for those folders; perform actions permitted by the Read permission and the List Folder Contents permission
Modify	Delete the folder, plus perform actions permitted by the Write, Read, and Execute permission
Full Control	Change permissions, take ownership, and delete subfolders and files, plus perform actions permitted by all other NTFS permissions

So, from the Security tab, you will build the Access Control Lists. This turns off all other access to the resource specific for the NTFS permissions for a file or folder. The process will look almost exactly the same as when you built the ACL for shared resources using the Sharing tab.

Exam Tip

You should know that the default NTFS permission in the Everyone group is Full Control. As with shared folder permissions, a best practice when setting NTFS permissions is to remove the default permission and create your own ACL of users who may access the resource.

Here's how to begin to modify this default NTFS security behavior:

1. On the Security tab, click the Add button to open the Select Users or Groups, and you will see another new XP dialog box shown in Figure 3-16. It does the same thing that its earlier cousins do, just in a slightly different interface. From this dialog box, you can select users and groups from the computer's local accounts database or from a domain, depending on your configuration. You can click the Locations button to browse these other locations.

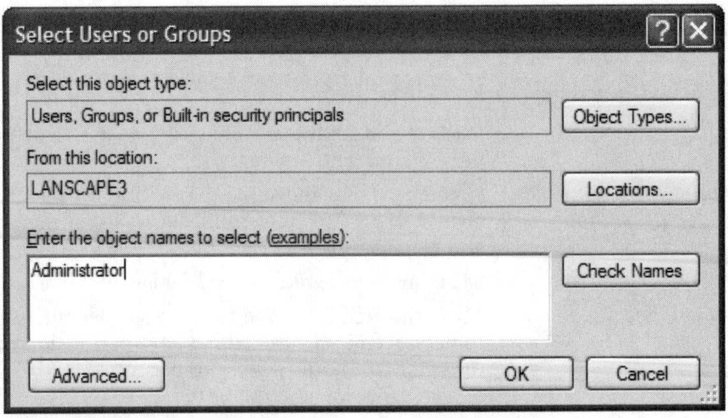

Select Users or Groups

Select this object type:

| Users, Groups, or Built-in security principals | Object Types... |

From this location:

| LANSCAPE3 | Locations... |

Enter the object names to select (examples):

| Administrator | Check Names |

Advanced...   OK   Cancel

FIGURE 3.16   Adding a group or user to the ACL

Choosing Advanced will let you run a Search, just as if you had run one from the Start menu. This will let you look for objects without having to type the name exactly, as you do from the Select Users and Groups dialog box.

2. Select the user or group you want to add and then click the Add button. If you are selecting an account from a domain, you will notice that the list presented can grow quite large.

    A shortcut in navigating the accounts list in Windows XP comes in handy. Instead of scrolling through the list, you can type the first letter or first few letters of an account or group you are trying to find. When you press ENTER on your keyboard, you will see a shortened list of all groups and accounts that start with the letters you just typed, making it much easier to find the intended account. If only one account or group starts with the letters you typed, it will automatically be added to the ACL without your having to click Add. To see how this works, type **u** and then press ENTER. (Make sure that your computer name is listed in the Look In drop-down box.) One of the accounts that should appear is the Users group, as well as any other groups and accounts that start with the letter *u*.

3. After you have made an addition to the ACL, configure access to the resource by highlighting a group or user account and selecting or deselecting the check boxes that correspond to the level of access you wish to allow or deny.

Travel Advisory

It is possible to configure the ACL so that nobody has access to a resource. If you remove all groups and accounts from the ACL, nobody will be granted any kind of access whatsoever. That goes for you, too! (We'll discuss how to fix this if it occurs, later in this Exam Objective, when we talk about NTFS ownership.)

Although the file permissions are, by default, inherited from the parent folder in which the files live (more about this in the "NTFS Permissions Inheritance" section to follow), NTFS permissions can also be used to secure individual files. Table 3-2 lists the standard NTFS file-level permissions that you can assign and the type of access that each permission implies.

As you can see, the only significant difference between folder and file permissions is that List Folder Contents is not one of the standard file permissions. What is really significant about the two NTFS sets of permissions for folders and files is that *file permissions override folder permissions.*

It is possible, then, for a folder's NTFS permissions to be set to allow a user Read access, yet that same user would have Full Control to a file within that folder. That's because the file's ACL would be king of the mountain when the account was used to access the file.

Further, like its relative the share permissions, NTFS permissions are *cumulative.* That is, a user's effective permission is a combination of the group permissions that an account has been assigned to, plus any individual permissions specifically assigned to that user.

TABLE 3.2   Standard NTFS File-Level Permissions

NTFS File Permission	Lets a User...
Read	Read the file and view file attributes, ownership, and permissions
Write	Overwrite the file, change file attributes, and view file ownership and permissions
Read and Execute	Run applications and perform the actions permitted by the Read permission
Modify	Modify and delete the file, plus perform all actions permitted by the Write, Read, and Execute permissions
Full Control	Change permissions and take ownership, plus perform the actions permitted by all other NTFS permissions

To illustrate, using the same example used in the discussion of shares, suppose that Brian is a part of the Sales group that has NTFS Read access to the \Bonuses folder. Brian is also part of the Management group, which has the NTFS Full Control permission. What is Brian's permission when connecting to \Bonuses? It's Full Control. This example is shown in Figure 3-17.

Optimize Access to Files and Folders

NTFS permissions differ from share permissions in two significant ways:

- **NTFS permissions are effective locally when a user accesses a resource.** Share permissions apply only when network connections are made to a resource.

- **NTFS permissions can be applied to both folders and individual files.** Share permissions can be granted at the folder level only. The share permissions then apply to any files and subfolders within the share.

Local access means that the user is using the local machine. Local access to a file is made through the file system pathname, and shared folder access is made

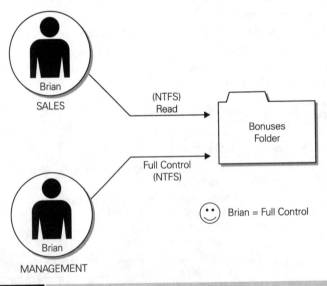

| FIGURE 3.17 | Applying NTFS + NTFS permissions |

using the UNC path. This fact also highlights one of the core differences between the Windows XP Professional and the Windows 9x operating system families. Because Windows 9x is not capable of supporting NTFS locally, there is no way for a user of a shared machine to restrict local access to a file or folder. Anything on a partition that is formatted with the FAT (or FAT32) file system can be seen, changed, or deleted by *any* user who is able to log on to the machine. In the case of Windows 9x, no logon is even necessary. You can just press the ESC key while in any logon dialog box and then delete files to your heart's content. This is one of the many reasons that Windows XP Professional is considered a *secure* platform and Windows 9x is not. The only way to make sure people don't have access to files on a Windows 9x machine is to make sure they can only access them over the network; that way, you can at least apply share permissions.

As for the second point—NTFS permissions can be applied to both folders and individual files—does that mean that NTFS permissions are effective *only* locally? A good question, but the answer is *no*; they are effective *both* locally and when making connections over the network. This brings us to one of the most significant pieces of the resource permissions puzzle.

When share-level permissions and NTFS permissions are combined, the *most restrictive permission becomes the effective permission.* This is *crucial* information for you to know both for taking the exam and for troubleshooting real-world access problems in a network. You will not have much success at either if you don't understand this point.

The permission settings behave in this way because ACLs are evaluated independently of one another. The Windows XP operating system is saying, in effect, "You may have *this* set of permissions at this level, but you only have *that* set of permissions at another level. So you only get *that* level of permission." This way of combining two sets of permissions, especially when joined with the capability to set individual file permissions on NTFS volumes, gives the administrator a powerful mechanism for controlling the granularity of access to network resources.

Let's illustrate again with the example used previously: suppose that Brian is a part of the Sales group, which has the Read share access to the \Bonuses folder. He's also in the Management group, which has the NTFS Full Control permission. What is Brian's permission when connecting to \Bonuses? It's Read. This example is illustrated in Figure 3-18.

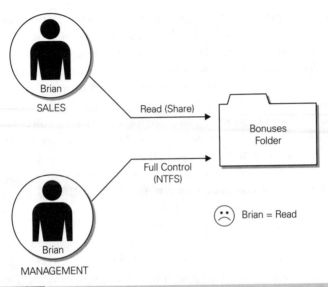

Brian
SALES

Read (Share)

Bonuses
Folder

Full Control
(NTFS)

Brian = Read

Brian
MANAGEMENT

FIGURE 3.18   Combining Share + NTFS permissions

I can't stress enough how many times you are likely to be asked questions that test your understanding of how permissions interact, both on the 70-270 test and in others, especially the 70-215 (Server) test.

> ### Exam Tip
>
> Things you must remember about NTFS permissions (unless you plan to write off your test fees as charitable contributions):
> - NTFS permissions are effective locally, unlike share permissions.
> - NTFS permissions can be applied to files as well as folders.
> - File permissions override folder permissions.
> - NTFS permissions are cumulative, with the exception of Deny, which overrides Allow.
> - When NTFS and share permissions are combined, the effective permission is the most restrictive permission.

So, then, the advice given to new administrators: share the disk resources you want users to access on an NTFS volume with the default network permissions (Everyone, Full Control) and then tighten down security via NTFS permissions. Don't bother setting share permissions because doing so adds another level of permissions to track and document, and they aren't effective locally anyway.

This strategy is recommended for a few reasons:

- It gives administrators maximum flexibility when designing and implementing file servers in a network.

- It ensures that files and folders will remain secure on computers that are shared by several users.

- It lets an administrator set security on files before they are even available on the network (assuming that you, the administrator, take the step of configuring NTFS permissions before sharing out the resource, which is a step you should take).

NTFS Permissions Inheritance

It's important in the MCSE track that you have a clear understanding of how NTFS permissions are inherited from parent folders. Not only will this understanding help you when answering questions regarding NTFS permissions, but it will set the foundation for understanding other types of permission inheritance, especially when dealing with Active Directory.

The default behavior of NTFS permissions is that the permissions you assign at the parent folder level are propagated to the subfolders and files that are contained in the parent. This default behavior is consistent throughout many other Windows XP technologies, so you will see this practice repeated time and again.

The good people at Microsoft have given us a visual cue, however, that permissions on a given folder or file have been inherited. When you look at the Security tab of the Properties dialog box, as shown in Figure 3-19, the boxes that have a gray shading indicate that the permissions checked have been inherited from the parent.

But what if you want this inheritance behavior to be prevented? What if you want to set NTFS permissions for individual files and folders, so that a user can be granted Full Control over a file that is stored in a folder that he or she has Read permission for? You can easily prevent this default permission inheritance from parent folder to subfolders and files that are contained within the parent. And when you configure this behavior, the folder for which you prevent permission inheritance becomes the new parent, and any new files or subfolders created in this new parent folder will inherit the new permissions just set.

This inheritance blocking is done with a single click: just uncheck the box at the bottom of the Security tab that says Allow Inheritable Permissions From Parent To Propagate To This Object. You will be given two options when you perform this task: whether to copy previously inherited permissions or to remove existing permissions, as shown in Figure 3-20.

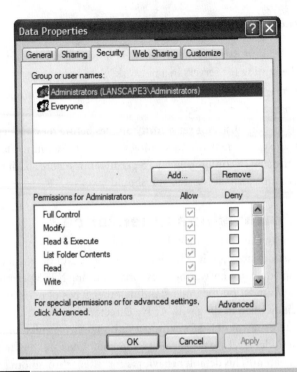

FIGURE 3.19 The gray shading indicates inheritance.

Copying existing permissions is preferred, because you can then edit the ACL that is already present. Most of the time, you will be making a few minor tweaks to the ACL. Choosing Remove will empty out the ACL, and you will have to start from scratch.

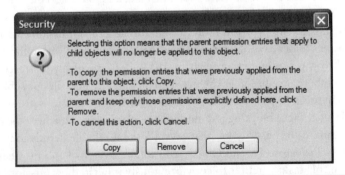

FIGURE 3.20 Options when preventing permission inheritance

Copying and Moving Considerations

When you copy or move files and folders, the NTFS permissions set on those objects might change. In fact, they often do. You must understand the specific rules that control how and when permissions change during copy and move operations. Like the discussion about NTFS permission inheritance, an understanding of concepts presented here will help you understand what happens to other NTFS attributes as *they* are copied or moved.

Whenever you perform a *copy* from one folder to another, the permissions change. The file or folder copied inherits the permissions set for the destination folder. This behavior occurs regardless of whether your copy is from folder to folder on the same partition or the copy is from one partition to another.

Also, when a copy is performed, the user making the copy becomes the Owner of the copy and can modify the NTFS permissions on the copied resource. (More on this Ownership power is discussed later in "Special Access Permissions"—for now, just think of this behavior as analogous to copying someone's report on a Xerox machine. You take the copy with you and do whatever you want with it and return the original to it owner.)

When a *move* is performed on a file or folder, the NTFS permissions may or may not change, depending on the destination directory of the move. It can get a little confusing, but here's how a move operation works:

- If you move a file or folder *within* the same NTFS partition—say from one folder to another on the C:\ drive—the file or folder *retains* its original permissions. The Owner attribute of the object also remains the same.

- If you move a file or folder *between* NTFS partitions—like when you drag and drop something from the C:\ drive to the D:\ drive—the file or folder *inherits* the permissions of the destination folder, and the Ownership also changes to the user performing the action. Windows treats a move between partitions, like from a folder on the C:\ drive to a folder on the D:\ drive, as first a Copy and then a Delete. Thus, what is really happening is that the move operation between different partitions follows the rules of a Copy, which to the OS is what the file management operation actually is.

Travel Advisory

You must have at least the Modify permission for the source file or folder for a move, and you must have the Write permission for the destination folder to perform the move operation.

Finally, when you perform a move *or* copy of files and folders from an NTFS partition to a FAT partition, the files and folders *lose their NTFS permissions*. Why? FAT partitions don't support NTFS permissions. So take care when moving files and folders to FAT volumes, because carefully implemented NTFS permissions could be lost instantly.

Special Access Permissions

Some 14 special access permissions—14 security attributes—can be assigned to a NTFS folder or file. If you assign the standard NTFS permissions to a resource and then look at the Advanced properties from the Security tab, you will notice that some or all (in the case of Full Control) are checked, as shown earlier in Figure 3-14. Two special permissions are particularly useful when governing access to resources: the Change Permissions and Take Ownership permissions.

The *Change Permissions* attribute is useful for assigning to others the ability to control access to files and folders without giving them the Full Control permission. In this way, a user who has the Change Permissions permission won't be able to delete or write to the file but can set user access, including setting the user's own account to include the permission to delete the file. (This paradox is one reason that special permissions are used infrequently.)

Take Ownership is a somewhat more powerful permission because of the inherent ability that an Owner has over a file or folder. The next section will cover this issue.

Ownership

The Owner attribute is set for every file and folder on an NTFS partition. Each and every file placed on an NTFS partition is placed there by its Owner, and this owner of a disk resource has the ability to edit the ACL permissions for that resource. That means that the owner of a file can lock everyone out, even the administrator. The Owner attribute is another of the attributes tracked by Windows on an NTFS partition. It is not tracked on FAT volumes.

The Owner attribute is also used for several additional Windows functions, such as for tracking disk quota usage (which was discussed in Chapter 2) and identifying system events.

Ownership of a resource can be taken, but never assigned. It's a one-way street, and this is a point that is important for you to understand. What can be assigned by the current Owner of a file or folder, an Administrator, or anyone with the Full Control permission, is the Take Ownership *permission*, which allows the assignees to take ownership of the resource. Users or groups with this permission will be duly noted, but only when viewing the Advanced security permissions, as seen in Figure 3-21. A user called The Dude has been explicitly granted the special permission to Take Ownership. This ownership behavior assures accountability for files created on an NTFS partition.

Like a million shares of Enron stock, there are some things you might not want to own. For example, I can't create a file called "My Grand Plan for a Hostile Takeover of the McGraw-Hill Publishing Company" and then assign ownership of that file to one of the Executive VPs. I am the owner of that particular piece of invective until the VP (probably after reading it and sizing up the opportunity) takes ownership from me (if he or she even has the ability). Figure 3-22 illustrates the principle of NTFS Ownership.

To view the current owner of a folder or file, open the Access Control Settings dialog box by clicking the Advanced button of the Security tab of an NTFS resource. As seen in Figure 3-23, the Owner tab of this dialog box will show the current owner of the resource. If the current user (or group) has the ability to take ownership, they will see their name listed just below, in the section labeled Change Owner To.

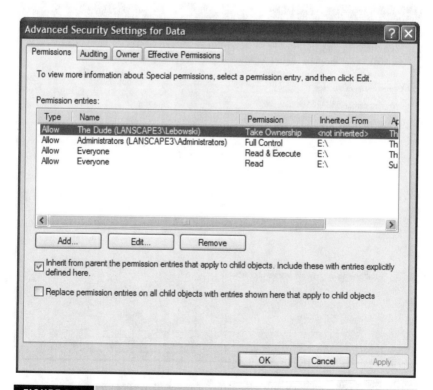

FIGURE 3.21 Advanced security options

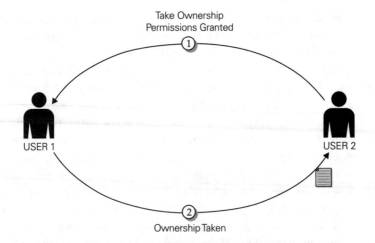

FIGURE 3.22 Ownership taken; only the ability to own is given

FIGURE 3.23 Viewing and changing the current owner of a file

Additionally, the permission to Take Ownership is given to users or groups by editing the special permissions of the ACL. The users given the NTFS permission Take Ownership will then be able to take ownership through the Owner tab.

This "one-way street" characteristic of Ownership is also important when considering disk quotas. It's not hard to imagine how ineffective quotas would be at limiting disk usage if every time a user was up against his or her quota limit, the user just gave away ownership of a couple megabytes' worth of files.

Exam Tip

Don't forget: to become the owner of a resource, a user or group member with the Take Ownership permission must explicitly take ownership.

Ownership may never be given to another user. Notice in Figures 3-22 and 3-23 that even though a user named The Dude has the ability to take ownership, his account does not appear in the Change Owner To section, because at the time the screenshot was taken, I was logged on as the Administrator. That's why only the Administrator account (and Administrators group, as noted below) appears. So even though I'm the Admin, I can't change the owner to The Dude without his knowledge. The Dude (who abides, despite not being in the Administrators local group) will have to log on and take ownership, if he wishes.

Remember at test time that you can give someone the right to take ownership of a file and then have that person perform the act of taking ownership, but you cannot give ownership to an individual without his or her knowledge.

Exam Tip

For the exam, know that only members of the Administrators group have the right to take ownership of resources by default.

As I mentioned in the first paragraph of this section, the owner of a file can lock everyone out, even the administrator. What does an administrator do when a user has a file that's locked out to everyone, and the administrator needs to see what's in that file? What if that user has left the company? One of the most omnipotent powers of the Administrator account, as well as the Administrators local group, is the capability to take ownership of anything on a disk, regardless of the assigned permissions. So, then, to resolve such a situation, the administrator takes ownership from the user and then, as the new owner, the administrator can modify the ACL.

Travel Advisory

When an Administrator takes ownership of a resource in Windows XP, she may decide whether her account specifically will be the owner of the resource or whether the entire Administrators group is to be the owner.

The Effective Permission

In classrooms, I have been asked this question many, many times: is there an easy way to see what a user's effective permission for a resource is? I had the annoying habit of answering with another question: is there an easy way to prove string theory?

Prior to XP, figuring out a user's effective permissions was a matter of keeping track of what permissions had been assigned where, and to what groups. You had to have a full understanding of how permissions combine, and how permission inheritance behaves, to explain why or why not a particular user had access to a file. It was just a little less complex than trying to figure out college football's BCS poll. Now, however, it no longer requires a degree in applied mathematics.

XP's new Effective Permission tab performs these calculations for you. To use it, perform the following steps:

1. Open the Properties dialog box for a file or folder you want to check.

2. Click the Advanced button from the Security tab. Then click the Effective Permissions tab, as shown in Figure 3-24.

3. Next, click the Select button, which will prompt you for either a User or Group account.

4. Enter the name of the users or group you want to check effective permissions for, then click OK.

The result of the preceding steps shows the effective permission for your selected user (or group). Notice that the dialog box shows you a complete listing for all of the NTFS attributes that are effective for the user, so reading and understanding this dialog box can take some getting used to. You will have to be familiar with the NTFS Special Permissions to understand what a Change permission would look like if listed individually in the Special Permissions tab.

FIGURE 3.24   The Effective Permissions tab...at last!

Also note that you won't be able to change permissions from this dialog box.

 **Objective 3.03**

Connect to Local and Network Print Devices

When it comes to printing in the Windows XP environment, Microsoft uses a bunch of terms most folks wouldn't find very obvious—it's kind of like a whole new language. So, for the purposes of this lesson, we will be using all new language. Consider this your language lesson. A quick question to get us started: what is that thing on your desk that spits out a printed page? That's a printer, right? Wrong. It is, at least for the purposes of this chapter and the exam, a print device.

Local Lingo

Print device What used to be (before this section, anyway) called the printer. The piece of equipment that prints your electronic files.
Printer A piece of software that provides the necessary translation so that an application can send information to a print device. The printer is there to provide access to the print device on your desk.

Now that we have established that a printer is a piece of software and not a piece of hardware (again, don't walk around correcting your grandmother on this; the social consequences can be harsh), it really shouldn't be too much a leap of faith to imagine that this piece of software, the printer, is just another disk resource that can be shared on a network, just like other resources such as files and folders. And when this bundle of code is shared and available for other users to submit a print job to, that printer is known as a *shared printer*.

A computer providing this shared printer is a *print server*. Lots of Microsoft OSs can be set up as print servers. A Windows 9*x* box can be a print server, as can a Windows XP Professional machine. Both of these OS flavors can quite capably handle the print server needs of most Microsoft-only networks. In addition, Windows XP Server print servers have the potential to become print servers for non-Microsoft client computers. (You should be aware of this now, but you won't need this information again until the Windows.NET or 2000 Server exams.)

Some print devices are connected directly to the network, just like any other computer. These types of print devices that are not directly connected to other computers are called *network print devices*. Figure 3-25 shows all the components of a Microsoft network printing environment.

Here we have the building blocks of network printing, which is probably a close second on the list of why networks were designed in the first place. With network printing, we don't need printers…pardon me…print devices at every desk in an organization.

A printer needs a way to get its translated information to the print device. It accomplishes this through a specifically defined pathway known as a *port*. These pathways of information can be one of several varieties, as you'll soon learn.

Connecting to Local and Network Printers

A print device attached directly to the computer is known as a *local printer*, because it makes use of a *local port*. The local printer usually uses the LPT1 (parallel)

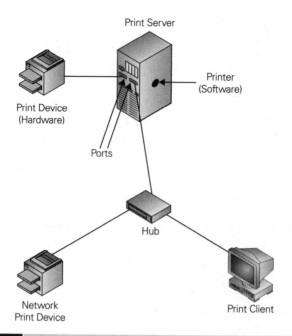

Print Server

Print Device
(Hardware)

Printer
(Software)

Ports

Hub

Network
Print Device

Print Client

FIGURE 3.25 The components of network printing

port, but other ports qualify. The USB port also comes to mind as an example of a commonly used local printing port. This port selection simply defines which copper wires the 1's and 0's use to get from the printer to the print device. Most people who have home computers with a print device handy have set up a printer to use a local port.

Local Lingo

Port An interface through which a device—for instance, a print device—is connected to a computer. Ports can be thought of as the byway by which instructions are sent from a piece of software to a piece of hardware.

To access the physical print device in Windows XP Professional, you must first create a logical printer. To do so, you must be logged on as a member of the Administrators or Power Users group for the machine. You'll create a logical printer using the Add Printer Wizard, which can be found in the Printers folder either via the Control Panel, My Computer, or the Start menu under Settings.

> ### Exam Tip
>
> For the Windows XP Professional exam, know that only members of the Administrators group and the Power Users group can install a local printer.

Click Add a Printer task, the first task listed—double-click Add Printer if using the classic interface—and the Add Printer Wizard will launch. After clicking the Next button to get things started, you will be given the choice of adding either a local printer or a network printer, depending on where the printer is located, as shown in Figure 3-26.

The remaining questions in the Add Printer Wizard depend on whether you choose to install a local printer or network printer. If you are setting up a local printer, you will select a port that the print device is connected to and then find the print drivers to install.

The second way to get access to a print device is over a network connection. In the Local or Network Printer dialog box, if you choose to connect to a network printer, the wizard asks where the printer lives, as shown in Figure 3-27.

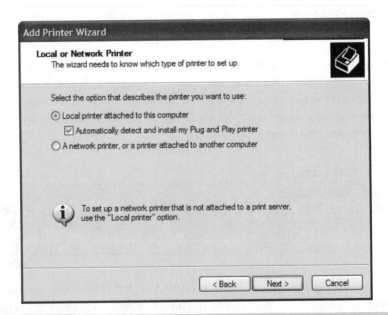

FIGURE 3.26   Choosing a local or network printer

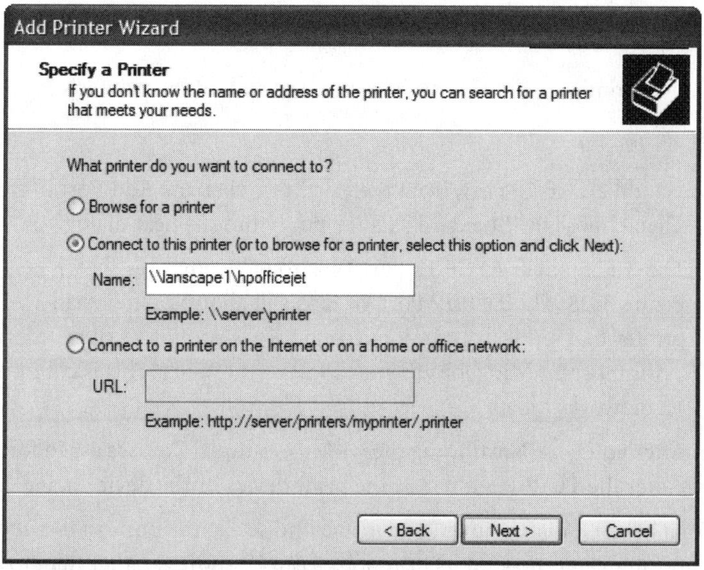

Add Printer Wizard

Specify a Printer
If you don't know the name or address of the printer, you can search for a printer that meets your needs.

What printer do you want to connect to?

○ Browse for a printer

◉ Connect to this printer (or to browse for a printer, select this option and click Next):

Name: \\lanscape1\hpofficejet

Example: \\server\printer

○ Connect to a printer on the Internet or on a home or office network:

URL:

Example: http://server/printers/myprinter/.printer

[< Back] [Next >] [Cancel]

FIGURE 3.27   Connecting to a shared printer

The Specify a Printer dialog box will let you connect to and install a shared printer by specifying a UNC pathname (here's that UNC stuff again) or a Uniform Resource Locator address or by browsing through a list of shared printers. Note that when you browse for a printer, the network printer will appear as just another share on the network, *servername**printername*, when the selection is made.

There is an even easier way to set up a network printer. A print client can connect and submit jobs to a printer that is shared using the exact same process that a client would use to connect to other shared resources. By simply browsing the network through My Network Places and double-clicking a shared printer, or by entering the UNC path to a printer in the Run dialog box from the Start menu, the client will automatically perform the installation without further user interaction. It's pretty cool.

Port Properties

Windows XP Professional supports local ports and TCP/IP logical ports. A TCP/IP port is used when a printer needs to send a print job to a network-interface print device, which is connected to the network with a network interface card (NIC).

You will configure your ports from the Ports tab of the printer's Properties dialog box.

1. To add a TCP/IP port, from the Ports tab, click the Add Port button. Then choose the Standard TCP/IP port from the next dialog box.

2. The Add Standard TCP/IP Port Wizard will launch, as shown in Figure 3-28. The TCP/IP Port Wizard will allow you to install a printer that sends its print jobs to a network printer, as opposed to a printer submitting jobs to your local printer port. This is common on networks today.

3. After you click Next, using the wizard is simple. You are asked for either the TCP/IP address of the print device or the device name.

4. In the next dialog boxes, you install and set up the port, so that the printer can now send its print jobs to an IP address rather than to a local port.

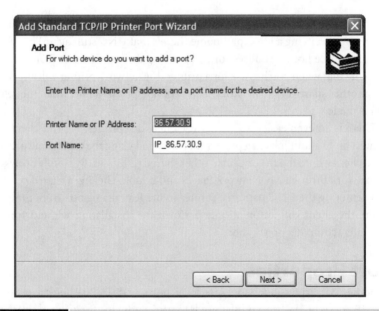

FIGURE 3.28 Adding a network print device

Managing Printers

After you have set up a local printer on your computer, you will configure its settings through the Properties dialog box, which is accessed by right-clicking the printer from the Printers folder and choosing Properties.

From the Sharing tab, you can make available a local printer the same way you make folder resources available. When you share out an existing printer, you will specify the share name, which is the name that will be seen by network users when they browse the resources on your server. Additionally, you can configure driver support for Microsoft clients other than Windows XP if necessary. By default, the only driver that loads when setting up a shared printer on a Windows XP Professional box is the Intel print driver for Windows XP. A Windows XP client connecting to this shared printer will then automatically download and install these drivers when the connection to the shared printer is made. To provide additional print driver support, click the Additional Drivers button at the bottom of the Sharing tab, which will bring up the Additional Drivers dialog box, as shown in Figure 3-29.

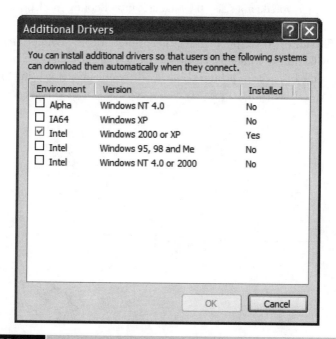

FIGURE 3.29   Configuring additional driver support

Print Pooling and Priorities

Printer pools and *print priorities* are typically used in high-volume printing environments, where many printers or print devices are needed to service the printing needs of network users. The two technologies are really two sides of the same coin, as you will see.

Print pooling is used to associate a *single printer* with *multiple print devices*. You would typically use a printer pool if many print devices of the same type are located on the network, so that they would all understand the instructions of one type of print driver. The first available print device will service print jobs submitted to a printer, as illustrated in Figure 3-30. When you configure printer pools, however, you cannot specify what print device will be receiving the job. For that reason, it is wise to place the print devices in close physical proximity to one another, unless you are trying to incorporate your printing scheme into some kind of corporate exercise program.

To configure a printer pool, access the Ports tab from the Properties of a printer, as shown in Figure 3-31. At the bottom of this tab, check Enable Printer Pooling and then select all the ports you want the logical printer to send its 1's and 0's from. If you do not select the Enable Printer Pooling check box, you will be able to configure only one port per printer.

The flip side of printer pooling is setting printer priority. With printer priority, you will configure *multiple printers* to use a *single print device*. Catch that? Priority is the opposite of printer pooling, where one printer is using multiple print devices. When you set priority, you specify *how* print jobs are sent to the

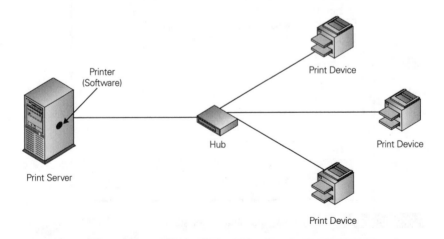

FIGURE 3.30   One printer, many print devices

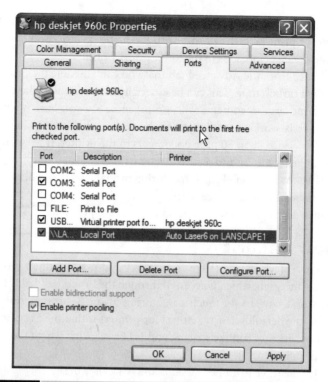

Enabling printer pooling

device. In this example, you have two logical printers that are pointed to the same physical port to submit their jobs, as illustrated in Figure 3-32.

You set the priority of a given printer from the Advanced tab of the Properties dialog box for the printer. From this tab, you will be able to rank the priority of the printer from 1 to 99. The default priority for a printer is 1, which is the lowest ranking. Any printer that has a higher ranking gets first dibs on the print

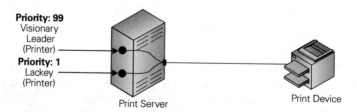

FIGURE 3.32   Many printers, one print device

device that is associated with the printers. When the print manager on the system polls for print jobs, the printer with the higher priority will always print jobs in the queue before jobs in the lower priority printer.

Also notice from the Advanced tab that you can schedule the printer to be available at a certain time. This can be especially useful for users or groups that typically print large documents with no urgency. Say you have a network in which a user is working on drafts of a book, and this user—who we'll call *Brian*—often sends 40 to 50 page documents to the printer. If we set up a specific printer just for Brian and set this printer with a schedule of 11 P.M. to 5 A.M., the large documents won't be printed during the day, but they will be ready for Brian when he gets to the office in the morning. This frees up the normal network printer from Brian's time-consuming 50-page printouts.

Printer Security

You will control which users have access to a Windows XP printer through the printer's Security tab, which is accessed through the Properties dialog box. You typically won't have to do much configuring of the Security permissions of printers, as the default security settings for printers is that the Everyone group has Print permission (unlike sharing and NTFS security, where the Everyone group gets Full Control).

Here are the three print permissions and what they mean:

Print Permission	Lets a User...
Print	Connect to a printer and send print jobs to the printer
Manage Printers	Have administrative control over the printer, pause and restart the printer, share and unshare the printer, and change printer properties
Manage Documents	Pause, restart, resume, and delete queued documents, but with no management of the properties of the printer

So what's the worst breach of print security that normal user accounts could have? They could send a job to the printer. No big deal, at least to everyday network security. Users do have the ability to manage the documents they own—the documents they have sent to the printer.

Travel Assistance

For further information about network printing options and possible configurations, please see Chapter 11 of *Microsoft Windows XP Resource Kit Documentation* from Microsoft Press.

Internet Printing

Windows XP supports the Internet Printing Protocol (IPP), which lets documents be sent over the Internet to printers that are available. This relatively new protocol allows users to print directly to a URL.

So exactly how are printers available on the Internet? Glad you asked. The ability to print over the Internet is an integral part of the setup of Internet Information Services (IIS). By default, the installation of IIS makes shared printers accessible through the Internet, and any subsequent printers that are added and shared will be Internet-available as well.

Users who have the appropriate permission levels will be able to view and manage printers from a web browser window. All they have to do to connect to a printer over the Internet (this works in an Intranet just the same, by the way) is open a browser window and type **http://***hostname***/printers**, where *hostname* is the name of the print server where IIS is installed. The hostname can be either a name or an IP address, just as when connecting to a website. (Note that "printers" in this syntax is literal: you type the word "printers.") This will cause the browser to bring up the window shown in Figure 3-33. From there, the printing options are fairly intuitive—if you can click around on Yahoo to get information, you should have little trouble with the options presented here.

This web page also presents an easy way to set up a network printer on your system. The Printers home page will present you with a hyperlinked list of all shared printers. Just follow the link of the printer you want to install and then choose Connect from the next page (it will be at the bottom of the Printer Actions list, as shown in Figure 3-34) to install and set up the printer for your use. You might be prompted to select drivers for the printer you are setting up as part of the installation.

Alternatively, you could also specify the URL of a known printer when working through the Add Printer Wizard, whose steps were outlined earlier.

You can also modify the syntax in the address bar slightly if you want to connect directly to an available printer, bypassing the home page: http://*servername*/printers/.

After the Internet printer is installed, you can use the IPP printer exactly the same as you would any other printer installed on your system, either attached locally or available on the network.

Finally, it is not uncommon in many networks to have a computer that is dedicated as a print server. This machine does not need to be one of your latest and greatest machines—in fact, it can be one of the oldest. Doesn't matter.

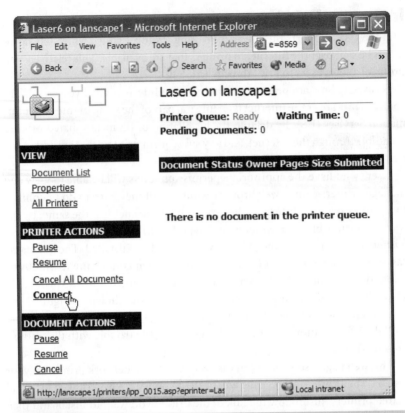

FIGURE 3.33 The "Home Page" of Internet Printing on a print server with IIS installed—follow the hyperlinks to install and manage printers.

Travel Advisory

Take one of your older computers, possibly even one that has been pulled from production, and make it the dedicated print server. The speed of the processor is of little importance; the bottleneck in printing is always the speed of the print device.

A Final Word or Two about the Test

Microsoft certification exams are famous for using disguises when testing your understanding of permissions. Some questions will look like they are asking you

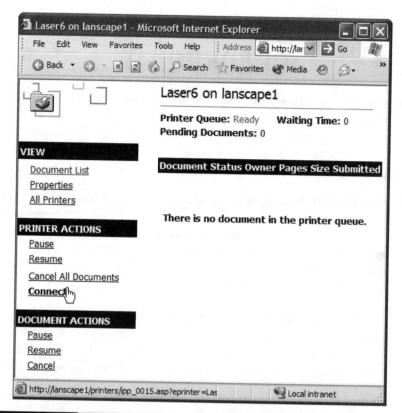

FIGURE 3.34 You can install the printer if it is not already set up.

about moving and copying considerations, or about almost anything else, but they are really testing whether or not you grasp the security considerations discussed in this chapter. The trick is to read the question carefully to determine what is being asked, not to go for the head fake.

It cannot be overstated: *You almost certainly will not pass the exam without knowledge of the material covered in this chapter.* To the best of this author's recollection, a good 20 percent of the questions from both the Professional and Server tests covered these topics. You will give yourself a huge boost and a little margin for error with a thorough understanding of share and NTFS permissions.

I now step down from my soapbox.

CHECKPOINT

✔**Objective 3.01: Manage and Troubleshoot Access to Shared Folders** In this objective, we looked at the significance of setting up network shares and then managing access with shared folder permissions. We also looked at considerations when share permissions are combined when users are part of groups that have different levels of share access to a resource.

✔**Objective 3.02: Monitor, Manage, and Troubleshoot Access to Files and Folders** This objective examined what security attributes are available in NTFS partitions. We distinguished between NTFS and share permissions and also looked at what happens when share and NTFS permissions are combined. We looked at NTFS permission inheritance and at some advanced NTFS attributes such as ownership.

✔**Objective 3.03: Connect to Local and Network Print Devices** We discussed the characteristics of the Microsoft network print environment. Once we understand the terminology involved, we can set up local and network printers. We can then further manage our network printers so that they best meet our printing needs.

REVIEW QUESTIONS

1. You are the administrator of a small Memphis law firm called Bendidi, Lambert, and Locke. Matt is a new lawyer assigned to a case. The case files are stored in a folder called \Laundry, and you make the folder available on a computer running Windows XP Professional over the network, assigning a share name that matches the folder. You assign the Read share permission to user Matt and assign the Change share permission to the Research Scientists group. Matt is a member of the Rookie Lawyers group. What will Matt's effective permission be to the folder when accessing it over the network?

   A. Read
   B. Change
   C. Full Control
   D. No Access

2. The respected firm now wants to move the folder referred to in question 1 to a newer computer, but one also running Windows XP Professional. After the move is made, Matt calls to complain he can no longer access the \Laundry folder. What is the most likely cause of the problem?

   A. The disk signature on the target volume is corrupt.

   B. When you move a shared folder, Windows XP stops sharing the folder.

   C. Users must log off and log back on before being able to access a shared folder that was moved.

   D. To be able to move a shared folder, you must download the Microsoft Windows XP High Encryption Pack and apply it from the Windows Update site.

3. Dr. Lindsey is a veterinarian at a prominent land-grant university, and she has NTFS Read permission to the \Prescriptions folder. You are the administrator at this clinic, and you put a Clinical Trials.doc file in that folder and assign Lindsey the Full Control permission to that file so that she can make regular updates to it. You don't change anything on the \Prescriptions folder. What is Dr. Lindsey's effective permission when she accesses the Clinical Trials file?

   A. No Access

   B. Read

   C. Full Control

   D. None for now, but she will be able to change this because she has Full Control to the file.

4. Using the example in question 3, you decide to reorganize the directory structure of your NTFS partition to reflect your current business needs. You create a new folder called \Testing on the same partition and share out that folder, giving the group Everyone Read permission. You then move the Clinical Trials document over to this new folder. What now is Lindsey's permission to the file?

   A. Full Control. Because the move occurs within the same partition, the NTFS permissions are unaffected by a move.

   B. No Access. You need to create a new ACL for the file because of the deletion from the original location.

   C. Read. The share permission is now effective.

D. This operation is not allowed because of the conflicting permissions.

5. You are the admin of a Windows XP peer-to-peer network for your small business. You would like to make sure that users have the ability to share out working folders from their XP Professional computers. What groups can you put them in and meet your objective?

A. Administrators

B. Backup Operators

C. Power Users

D. Server Operators

6. You set NTFS permissions on a folder named \Public on your Windows XP Professional computer. This folder contains several subfolders. Which folders inherit the permissions set on the \Public folder by default?

A. \Public

B. \Public and any first-tier folders

C. \Public, first-tier subfolders, and any second-tier subfolders

D. All subfolders

7. You have given a user the NTFS Change permission to a file in the \Data folder. You then move the file to a folder on a FAT partition that the user has the Read permission to. What now will be the user's effective NTFS permissions after this move operation?

A. Read

B. Change

C. Full Control

D. All NTFS permissions will be lost.

8. You are creating a new printer in Windows XP Professional through the Add Printer Wizard. What settings are required during printer installation?

A. Printer Name

B. Share Name

C. Port Location

D. Location and Comment

9. You are the administrator of a Windows environment that includes a Windows XP Server domain and Windows 9x clients. The Windows 9x clients are not running the Windows XP Directory Service client or

Microsoft Internet Print Services. Taking this into consideration, what methods can clients running Windows 9x use to connect to a network printer using the Add Printer Wizard?

A. Enter a UNC name.

B. Browse the network.

C. Use a URL name.

D. Search Active Directory directory services.

10. You are the admin of a Windows XP Professional computer called LEBOWSKI. An HP LaserJet 5 print device is connected to LPT 1 and shared out as LaserPrt. The accountant, who uses an MS-DOS client computer, calls to ask how she can connect to the network printer to print end-of-month reports. What is the syntax you should tell her to use?

A. Net use lpt1: \\lebowski\laserprt

B. Net use lpt1: \\laserprt\lebowski

C. Net print lpt1: \\lebowski\laserprt

D. Net print lpt1: \\laserprt\lebowski

11. On your Windows XP Professional computer, you want to connect to a network-interface print device using the Add Standard TCP/IP Printer Port Wizard. What can you specify to identify the port?

A. A TCP/IP host name

B. An IP address

C. A Media Access Control (MAC) address

D. A Windows Internet Naming Convention (WINS) computer name

REVIEW ANSWERS

1. **B** The effective permissions to a shared folder are the combination of the user and group permissions, with the least restrictive permission being the effective permission. The Deny permission will override the Allow permission, but that is not mentioned here. All other answers are incorrect because of this behavior of share permissions.

2. **B** Any time you move a shared folder, the Windows XP operating system stops sharing that folder. It must then be shared out from its new location. A is incorrect because a corrupt disk signature would most likely make the drive inaccessible in the first place, as it is an indicator of disk problems. It is written when the drive is viewed for the first

time in Disk Administrator. C is incorrect because this will have no effect on whether or not the folder is shared after it has moved. D is incorrect for the same reason. The 128-bit High Encryption Pack can be applied to secure access, but it does not affect the actual sharing of the folder.

3. **C** Here you must remember that file permissions override folder permissions on NTFS volumes. Since she has Full Control to the file, that will be the effective permission. A and B are, therefore, wrong. D is partially true: she will be able to change the permissions because she has Full Control, but she won't have to change any configurations to make changes to the file.

4. **C** When Share and NTFS permissions are combined, the effective permission will be the most restrictive of the combination of permissions. A is a true statement; the NTFS permissions will not be affected, but when combined with the share permissions, Full Control will not be the effective permission. B is incorrect because a new ACL creation is not necessary after a move; the ACL will travel with the moved item as long as it is within the same partition. D is just a false statement altogether.

5. **A C** Only these two groups can share out folders in a Windows XP workgroup. The Administrators local group has unrestricted access to the local machine. The Power Users local group doesn't have quite as many rights to the machine that an Administrator does, but close. One of these rights is the ability to share out resources. B is wrong because Backup Operators are pretty much limited to being able to back up and restore files. D is wrong because that group exists in Windows XP domains, not in workgroups.

6. **D** The default behavior for inheritance on NTFS volumes is that child objects inherit the permissions—or, more technically, the ACLs—of the parent. Any new folders and subfolders in the \Public folder get the permissions of \Public until these permissions are changed. A, B, and C are all incorrect because of this default inheritance behavior. You can block the inheritance by clearing the Allow Inheritable Permissions From Parent to Propagate To This Object check box.

7. **D** NTFS permissions will not be retained when you move a file or folder from an NTFS partition to a FAT partition. You should be especially careful of this when moving folders and files to a FAT partition. Any security you have on the resource could be lost. A, B, and C

are all wrong because they assume a certain NTFS security, which will be nonexistent.

8. **A** **C**   You must give the printer a logical name that will be used by applications to address the printer as they submit jobs. The printer queue will also use this name. You must also specify a physical location for the print job to get to the print device. Specifying the port does this. B is incorrect because a printer need not be shared at setup time, if ever. D is also incorrect because this is optional information that makes it easier to search for a printer in Active Directory, but again it is not required.

9. **A** **B**   When a client computer connects to a network printer, it is just connecting to another shared resource, and the addressing convention is the same as if the client had connected to a folder. If you know the print server name and the printer share name, you can speed up the printer installation process by not having to browse around the network. In fact, you don't even have to run the Add Printer Wizard to perform the install. Just choose Start | Run and then enter the UNC path to the printer from the Run command line. Browsing the network is also a perfectly acceptable way to connect. C is incorrect because while a down-level client will be able to view the properties of a printer via a Uniform Resource Locator (URL), a printer cannot be installed in this way. D is incorrect because your down-level clients cannot search the Active Directory unless they have Active Directory Services client installed, and the question makes no mention of that.

10. **A**   The NET USE command line syntax for connecting to a shared printer is **net use lptx: *servername\printsharename*** , where *x* is the port number of the shared printer. B is wrong because the syntax of the utility has been reversed. C and D are wrong because *print* is not a valid parameter of the NET USE utility.

11. **A** **B**   It helps in this question if you understand what a network-interface print device is. Because a network print device will have its own IP address, it stands to reason that it can be accessed by either a host name or an IP address. Both the name and IP address can be used to locate the port that will be used for the submission of print jobs. C is incorrect because a print device's MAC address is not used to establish a port connection when running the TCP/IP protocol. D is incorrect because the Windows XP port monitor uses either a host name or IP address to establish the port connection, not the NetBIOS name.

Configuring and Troubleshooting the Desktop Environment

	NEWBIE	SOME EXPERIENCE	EXPERT
ETA	3 hours	2 hours	1 hour

This chapter focuses not only on ways in which to change the overall look and feel of the desktop, but also on technologies that make XP usable in almost any locale and in almost any language. Furthermore, we'll gain exposure to the tools for managing software installations.

To accomplish the objectives of this chapter, we will:

- Look at user profiles.
- Look at installing applications through the use of Group Policy and Microsoft Installer software packages.
- Examine how to install and configure MultiLanguage support, enabling Windows XP to speak many languages, adjusting itself to the needs of the user. (In other words, for example, we will tell Windows to use *Empezar* instead of Start in the menu at the lower-left-hand corner.)

This chapter discusses the technologies that Windows XP provides to give both end users and administrators control over the operating system interface. These technologies allow a user to configure the desktop colors and mouse settings, and they extend to management capabilities, such as deploying software to all users from a remote computer.

We like to do things our own way. We also like to feel a sense of mastery over our machines; we like to get the computer system to do what we want, and we like it to look the way we want it to. User profiles are designed with this in mind. They are used to distinguish between different computing environments and are intended to personalize the Windows XP experience for each individual. For example, it's the user profile that allows one user to have a ZZ Top desktop wallpaper while another user might have a Chia Pet wallpaper. User profiles are read when the user logs in and configures the desktop wallpaper (along with a number of other settings) to the user's personal preferences.

User profiles are great for configuring the overall look of the Windows XP Professional operating system, but there are many tools that will help make more meaningful changes to the user environment—like the Control Panel. The Control Panel allows users to configure a variety of settings that help define interaction with the OS. Administrators can also lock down the user desktop through the employment of Group Policies. Group Policies are a powerful new tool set in Windows XP that works in many different ways to ease the burden of administration, thus reducing overall total cost of ownership for an operating system. One of the ways Group Policies can accomplish this, as we'll see later in the chapter, is to revoke the user's authority to make certain changes.

This chapter concludes with a discussion of fax support and Accessibility Services. Accessibility Services are another important part of customizing the experience for users with special needs.

Configure and Manage Desktop Settings and User Profiles

In this opening objective, we will take a look at the composition of the user desktop, the way users interact with the Windows XP operating system, and at some of the many ways that it can be manipulated.

We will then move on to better understand that this collection of desktop settings is stored by XP for later use. These settings are stored in a folder, just like anything else that is stored on a computer, and there are a couple of ways we can manage these folders administratively. We will do this through the use of Local and Roaming user profiles, and we can make the profiles mandatory for our end users.

Desktop Settings

There is a considerable difference between the Windows XP interface and all versions of Windows that preceded it. What has not changed from Windows NT and 2000, however, is that users are presented the desktop only *after* they have successfully logged on by entering a user name and password. Once logged on, these desktop settings are generated by using the contents of a user profile. The user has many options for configuring the desktop to suit personal preferences. When users configure desktop settings, they are customizing the computing experience to best suit their needs. They are creating a workspace that will, presumably, make them more efficient. So what desktop settings are configurable? Almost every single one of them, including elements such as the Start menu, taskbar, toolbars, and the desktop background. These settings are then saved, by default (you can change the profile behavior as an admin), in a folder for the next time a user accesses the computer.

Two common methods exist for configuring the desktop settings:

- Through the various user interface components that support the desktop
- Through Group Policy

These two methods accomplish the same things, but they differ in their approach to desktop administration. Generally speaking, the user interface components let *end users* manage their desktops, while Group Policies are applied so that *administrators* can do the desktop management. We start with a discussion of these user interface components, then we'll turn the discussion to Group Policy.

Exam Tip

Group Policy is a feature of Windows XP that's available in Windows 2000 or .NET Active Directory domains. This technology serves as a cornerstone to managing Windows domains.

You can expect to see Group Policy covered in great detail throughout your study of the Microsoft MCSE track. So even though you might not be expected to know volumes about Group Policy for *this* exam, the sooner you have an understanding of Group Policy, the sooner you will understand the new Windows operating system platforms.

Customizing the Taskbar and Start Menu

Upon first running XP, you will notice that Microsoft completely redesigned the Start menu. That's because Microsoft, presumably overwhelmed with pride in their new accomplishment, has programmed XP so that the Start menu is already open the first time you see the desktop. The Taskbar has also changed, but not as substantially.

Although the look of these two items has undergone a facelift, the *function* of both remains constant. You will still *use* them for the same purpose that you did before, even though they look rather different. As you probably are well aware, the Taskbar and Start menu are important launching points for modifying system settings and running applications, and modifying the contents of these areas has a great impact on overall user friendliness.

Now, if there's one constant about the Windows experience since Windows 95, it's that if there is one way to accomplish a task, there's probably three of four other ways that will produce the same result. So, while there are several ways to modify the contents and behavior of both the Taskbar and Start Menu, the easiest way, in this author's opinion (read: the right way), to customize the Taskbar and Start menu is by right-clicking any blank area of the Taskbar and choosing Properties from the context menu.

The Taskbar and Start Menu Properties dialog box, as shown in Figure 4-1, has two tabs on its initial page: Taskbar and Start menu, which are discussed in detail next.

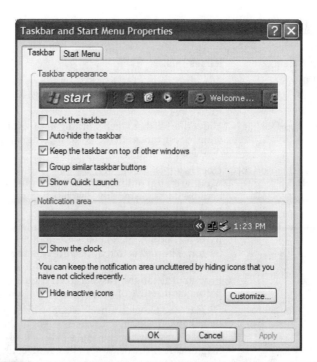

FIGURE 4.1   A look at the Start Menu and Taskbar Properties dialog box

Taskbar   On the Taskbar tab of the Taskbar and Start Menu Properties dialog box, you specify what the taskbar will look like and what items will display in the Notification area. There are two new items of particular interest that weren't configurable on the Taskbar before: the grouping of similar Taskbar buttons and the hiding of inactive icons. Table 4-1 describes the options configurable from the Taskbar tab.

Clicking the Customize button will let you further configure the behavior of the inactive icons in the System tray. You could configure certain ones, for example, to never display an icon even though the program is loaded and running in the background.

Start Menu   The Start Menu tab of the Taskbar and Start Menu Properties dialog box allows you to customize your Start menu.

Now, before we get too far into a discussion of the Start menu, I should mention that the new XP Start menu will perform plenty of customizing on its own, if the default settings are left alone. That's because, among other things, it uses

TABLE 4.1	Taskbar Tab Options
When You Select...	**It Does This...**
Lock the Taskbar	Specifies that the Taskbar stays in its current position and cannot be modified, mover, or resized—enabled by default.
Auto Hide the Taskbar	Hides the Taskbar when working in programs unless your mouse travels to the bottom of the screen—disabled by default.
Keep the Taskbar on top of other windows	Does just this. An application will not draw its window on top of the Taskbar. I prefer this option because it lets me quickly switch between open programs.
Group similar Taskbar buttons	New to XP, this gathers all open windows of a particular program and places them in one Taskbar button. The idea is to reduce clutter on the Taskbar. To switch between programs, you will first click the Program title on the Taskbar, then choose a particular instance of the program from a list.
Show Quick Launch	Displays the Quick Launch section, which, by default, will be located just to the right of the Start menu. Many have been using this area for years to help unclutter the desktop of Program icons.
Show Clock	Displays the clock in the right corner of the Taskbar (unless you've moved the Taskbar somewhere else). This area is known as the Notification Area; you can adjust the date and time by double-clicking the clock—enabled by default.
Hide inactive icons	Helps simplify display and clean up messy icons. When selected, only active programs will display in the System Tray area, located, by default, on the far right-hand side of the Taskbar.

an algorithm to determine what you have used recently and what you have used most often and places those items at your ready disposal on the Start menu's left side. Again, the idea is to reduce confusion and clutter on the desktop by reducing the need to place frequently used program icons there for handy access. They should all be there now on the Start menu, or at least that's the idea.

But just as in ancient times, XP's new Start menu lets you add or remove shortcuts, re-sort the menu's contents, and specify other appearance settings. You can modify much of this behavior through the Start Menu tab. From here, for example, you can enable the display of the Administrative Tools group from the Start menu, something that most administrators like to have enabled. Figure 4-2 shows the Advanced tab of this dialog box, where you can set many of the Start menu options.

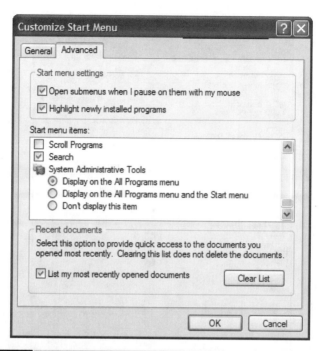

FIGURE 4.2   Configuring the Start menu

First, let's take a closer look at the items appearing on the Start menu under normal circumstances (and, because you can customize the Start menu, you will get to define what is normal). Here's what you are sure to see the first time XP presents the desktop—Microsoft is showing off its new creation. Figure 4-3 shows the new Start menu.

- **All Programs**   As alluded to previously, there is a process XP uses to populate what is readily available on the Start menu. The All Programs menu, then, is where your *less* frequently used programs will live quiet lives, waiting to be found. (The more frequently used ones will be here as well; this is just where they reside until XP decides they are one of your favorites.) These program shortcuts live in the Programs folder of your user profile (more on profiles in the following section.) You can change the contents of the All Programs menu at will.

- **Frequently Used Programs**   This is where all the cool programs hang out. The area on the middle-left of the Start menu, above the All Programs selection, lists the programs you use most frequently. Here again is where that algorithm thing comes into play, running

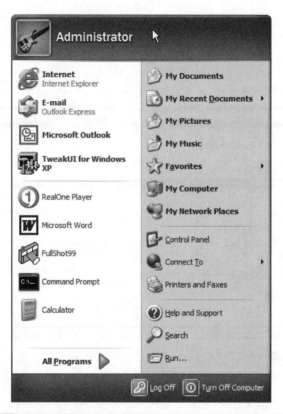

FIGURE 4.3   The new Windows XP Start menu

in the background and populating this area based on how often and how recently you have used these programs.

- **Pinned Programs**   At the top-left portion of the Start menu, these programs are the ones you have designated to be "pinned," just as you might pin something to a bulletin board. These are the programs you have made a commitment to and that will always appear in the Start menu, regardless of the number of times you have used them. You can add and remove pinned programs as you please.

Pinning also ensures that the program will not be bumped by other programs, even if you use the others more frequently. To pin a program, right-click the link to your favorite program on the Start menu and select Pin To Start Menu. Your program will be moved permanently to the top part of the list, just below your browser and e-mail programs.

- **Folders**   This lists the special folders that a Windows XP installation creates: My Documents, My Pictures, My Music, My Network Places, My Recent Documents, and My Computer. You can click any of these selections to see the contents of the folder in a Windows Explorer interface.

- **Control Panel**   This item launches the Control Panel, which helps make a host of configuration changes to your computer, including installing software and changing Windows settings.

- **Help And Support**   Clicking here displays the online help. Use of the Windows XP Help options will be discussed later in this chapter.

- **Search**   This word opens a Windows Explorer window in which you can search for files, folders, and other computers.

- **Run**   This link lets you launch a program by typing the name of the file that contains the executable. It is a favorite for opening up a command prompt and for connecting directly to other computers.

- **Log Off**   This enables a user to end a session, so that another user can log on and establish a session of their own.

- **Turn Off Computer**   When you select this item, you get three options: Stand By (or Hibernate or Suspend), Turn Off, and Restart. These Turn Off options are part of understanding mobile computer administration, and are discussed in greater detail in Chapter 6.

You've probably played around with some of these features on either Windows 9x or 2000 computers, and while a few different bells and whistles can be configured here, this isn't considered meat and potatoes Windows XP administration. You will become comfortable with the options to manage the desktop environment mostly by trying out a few of the features. It's all part of taking the operating system out for a test drive.

As mentioned, the new Start menu will work on your behalf to keep the most frequently used programs close at hand when opening up the Start menu. But one of the first things you can do to make the Start menu more useful is to make sure that frequently accessed programs are available right away, without having to wait for the Windows algorithm to add it to your list of Favorites.

You will also notice that the Start menu comes in one of two flavors: the XP variety or the Classic version. These can be selected with the corresponding radio button, and the preview panel will generate a picture of how it will appear. The Classic interface, as you will see, looks exactly the way the Windows 2000 Start menu does and can be used independently of the Windows 2000 "theme," which can be specified by selecting the Windows Classic theme from the Display Properties dialog box (discussed next).

Using the Classic Interface   You will also notice when using the new Start menu—it's technical name is Personal menu—that with Windows XP, Microsoft has jettisoned the "smart menu" feature, which hid many of the menu options that were infrequently used under chevrons, ostensibly to simplify the interface. It had the effect, however, of annoying several users who suddenly couldn't find the Programs they were looking for. If you still pine for the feature, it will be enabled automatically when you use the Windows Classic interface.

The Windows Classic interface is actually a theme that can be set from the Display Properties dialog box. To use this interface, perform the following:

1. Right-click the desktop and choose Properties.

2. The first tab of this dialog box is the Themes tab; make sure it's selected.

3. In the drop-down menu, choose the Windows Classic theme and then click OK.

Now, Windows is set back to use the stately, bankerly cornflower-blue and gray of Windows 2000. Ahhh! Be aware, however, that when you configure XP to use the Classic theme, you will also be making changes to the desktop. By default, Windows Classic will add the My Documents, My Computer, My Network Places, and Internet Explorer icons to your desktop.

The Control Panel

Another utility used to configure a wide range of computer options is the Control Panel. And, like many of its user interface cousins, it looks a lot different than it did before. Also like its kin, though, it can be easily switched back to the look and feel that Windows veterans are familiar with. You can access the Control Panel in three ways:

- Select Start | Control Panel.

- Open Windows Explorer and choose Control Panel from the left pane of the window.

- Open My Computer and choose the Control Panel link from the list of Other Places.

If familiar with Windows, you'll notice right away that the Control Panel has a completely new look, as shown in Figure 4-4.

The Control Panel's new interface is designed so that it can be used as long as users have the end result in mind when they start, which they usually do. This new interface is called the task-based interface, because that's exactly what it's meant to do: help users accomplish *tasks*. Using this task-based interface is indeed very intuitive, so much so that it is an exercise in redundancy to list what

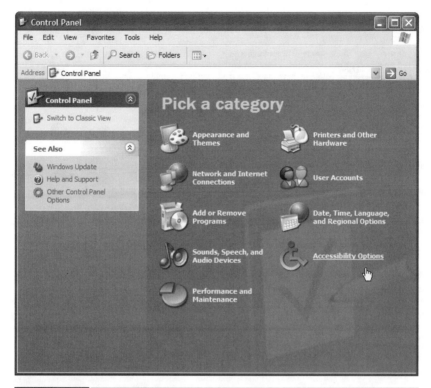

FIGURE 4.4   The new Control Panel window

kinds of things are configurable where. In other words, I'm not going to insult your intelligence, my fingers, or this good publisher's press time by stating the obvious: "To change the appearance or theme of Windows XP, click on the Appearance and Themes link."

Travel Advisory

Sometimes, applications and utilities will install their own Control Panel icons (installing Apple's video viewer QuickTime, for example, does this). If this is the case, and you are looking at the task-based Control Panel interface, you will click the Other Control Panel Options link to access these management icons.

To switch back to the old Control Panel interface, select the Switch to Classic View link on the left side. It's this classic interface that you will likely become most familiar with as an administrator, and it's the one that you'll have to be

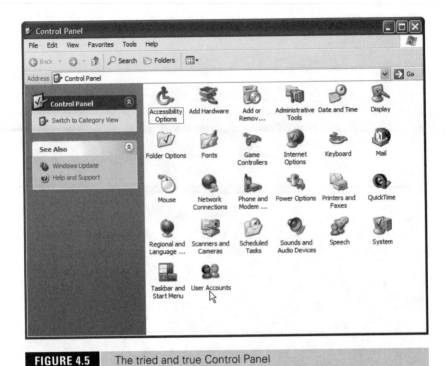

FIGURE 4.5 The tried and true Control Panel

comfortable with for exam success. Moreover, the Control Panel skills you learn here will serve you better when configuring Microsoft operating systems other than Windows XP. The Classic Control Panel is shown in Figure 4-5.

Table 4-2 gives you a succinct overview of all the Control Panel icons and what configuration settings they manage. It will serve as a valuable reference as you are working with Windows XP Professional. Most of these programs will be discussed in detail throughout this book.

TABLE 4.2 Items in the Control Panel

When You Select...	You Can Do This...
Accessibility Options	Configure options to make Windows XP more accessible to users with limited vision, hearing, or mobility.
Add/Remove Hardware	Install, remove, or troubleshoot hardware, especially hardware that is not Plug-and-Play compliant.
Add/Remove Programs	Change or remove programs that are currently installed on your computer (accessed when adding Windows XP components).

TABLE 4.2	Items in the Control Panel *(continued)*
Administrative Tools	Access the preconfigured MMC snap-ins that are most useful for managing day-to-day administrative operations—Event Viewer, Performance, Local Security Policy, and Computer Management.
Date/Time	Set the time and date, as well as the time zone for your computer—handy when you're traveling.
Display	Configure the computer's background, screen resolution, color scheme, and multiple monitor support with appropriate hardware.
Folder Options	Set folder options, such as the look of folder contents, general folder properties, file associations, and support for offline files.
Fonts	Manage the fonts installed on your computer.
Game Controllers	Add, remove, and configure game controllers, including joysticks and game pads.
Internet Options	Set Internet connection settings, including security, content settings, and Internet programs.
Keyboard	Configure keyboard settings, including speed and input locales. Configure mouse settings, including button configuration, pointer appearance, and motion settings.
Network and Dial-up Connections	Set network connectivity, including which protocols to use, and includes a Wizard to create new network connections. Administrators will use this dialog box often.
Phone and Modem Options	Set telephone dialing options, such as what area code you are dialing from, which modem to use, and the properties of that modem.
Power Options	Configure power schemes, enable hibernation, and set UPS options.
Regional and Language Options	Set regional settings, such as the currency used in money calculations, and set input locales.
Scanners and Cameras	Add a scanner or digital camera device to the computer and configure and troubleshoot its operation.
Scheduled Tasks	Configure tasks to be run according to customized schedules.
Sounds and Multimedia	Set up audio options, such as what sounds occur at specified events, and set the output and input devices.
System	Change a computer's identity, configure virtual memory settings, and manage user profiles.
Users and Passwords	Create and manage users and passwords. (You can also use Local Users and Groups, found in Computer Management.)

Several Control Panel programs can be accessed from places other than the desktop. Most of these access methods will be mentioned when the applicable settings are discussed in this book, and some of them have already been addressed, but I'll give you a few examples here:

- To access the Internet options, right-click the Internet Explorer icon and choose Properties.
- To access the Date/Time options, double-click the time display in the Notification Area.
- To access the System options, right-click My Computer and choose Properties.
- To access the Network and Dial-up Connections options, right-click My Network Places and choose Properties.

You also need to be aware that the real purpose of the Control Panel is to provide a safe and user-friendly way to edit the Registry, because that's where all the changes that matter to the operating system take place. Let's discuss the Registry now.

The Registry

The Registry is a database of settings the operating system uses as a central repository of configuration information. The Registry information is the DNA of the system; it tells the computer how to look and act. For example, when you change the theme on your Windows XP Professional system to use the Classic Theme, the changes to the window bars, screen, and other interface elements are recorded in the Registry.

You can edit the Registry directly with the Registry Editor, which can be launched using either of two commands from the Run dialog box: *regedit* or *regedt32*. (Because of the command used to launch it, you might see the Registry Editor referred to as Regedit.) These used to be two separate programs, but that is no longer the case. In XP, both commands will launch the one and only (text) Registry Editor shipped with XP; the regedit32 command is just a pointer to the regedit executable. Somewhat surprisingly, the Registry Editor version used by Windows XP is the one carried over from the Windows 9x family, not the NT family. This version of the Registry Editor includes a robust search capability and is visually arranged like Windows Explorer, which makes it easy to navigate. The Registry Editor is shown in Figure 4-6.

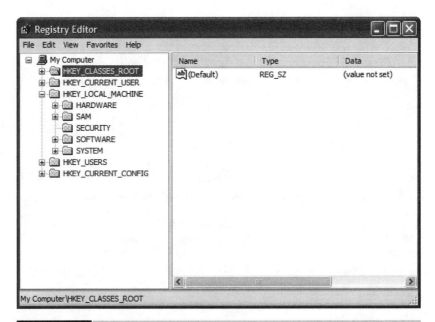

FIGURE 4.6   The Registry Editor utility

Travel Advisory

The regedit32 command opened the NT versions of the Registry Editor on Windows 2000 machines. The NT version had a few security features that were not previously available in the regedit version. Now, however, you can set permissions on the Registry keys and subkeys through the Permissions dialog box, which will look exactly like setting NTFS or Share permissions, as discussed in Chapter 3. To set permissions on any of the objects in the Registry, choose Edit | Permissions. An ACL dialog box will appear for the selected key.

Registry Structure

The Registry is organized into a hierarchical tree format of *keys* and *subkeys* that represent logical areas of computer configuration. By default, you will see five keys, sometimes called *Root* keys, when you open the Registry Editor. The registry keys and their configuration information are listed in Table 4-3.

TABLE 4.3	The Registry Configuration Keys
Registry Key	**Configuration Information**
HKEY_CLASSES_ROOT	Information associated with Windows Explorer to properly associate file types with applications. For example, this area of the Registry will store a setting that tells the system that .doc files are to be opened with Microsoft Word.
HKEY_CURRENT_USER	Information about the user currently logged on to the computer.
HKEY_LOCAL_MACHINE	Hardware and software configuration information: how hardware is used, startup parameters, bindings, drivers used, and so on.
HKEY_USERS	Configuration information that is not specific to any one user of the machine.
HKEY_CURRENT_CONFIG	Hardware profile information that is used during system startup.

Travel Advisory

You've heard this warning before: treat editing the Registry like brain surgery on your computer. It is meant for configuration changes that can't be made through the Control Panel. You won't need to make many of these changes in day-to-day administration.

If you have to edit the Registry manually, you will usually be working with the HKEY_LOCAL_MACHINE key, which contains all the settings that tell hardware and services how to behave. For example, a Registry setting here tells the network card what Internet Protocol (IP) address to use at startup time and what services are bound to it.

Now, as the purpose of this book is to prepare you for the 70-270 exam, I will not go into exhaustive detail about each and every registry setting. That feat would require another 500 to 700 pages, and there are reference books that deal with nothing other than making neat little Registry edits. As with most areas of test preparation, you will be better served by an understanding of the topics involved, not by rote memorization of buttons, keys, or dialog boxes. Remember, as I mentioned in the Introduction of this book, to ask yourself: "What is this for? What purpose does this serve?"

You will not be asked any questions that require direct knowledge of Registry particulars, perhaps because Microsoft understands that many of the keys and entries in the Registry are cryptic. The first couple of times you have to edit the

Registry, you will likely be performing the changes from some kind of reference material. Even Steve Ballmer would have to do the same. It is not necessary to have a mastery of the Registry to pass the Windows XP Professional exam.

You should know that making the wrong change to the Registry can have disastrous results, such as rendering the computer inoperable. There is also no Undo command. For this reason, it is critical that you have backups of Registry keys, and you are likely to be tested on this point.

Fortunately, it is a relatively simple exercise to make a backup of your Registry keys—not much different than saving a document in Microsoft Word. To back up a key, you will choose the Registry Editor's File | Export command. You will then be given a standard Save dialog box, with the option to save the Registry key in one of several formats. For failsafe backup and restore, you should choose the Registry Hive Files option. This option will create a binary image of the selected portion of the Registry; all subkeys and values will be saved. You won't be able to view or edit the contents of this file, but if you need to perform a restore, you can have confidence that this format will get the job done without a snag.

The other Registry file options will create text files, which can be edited in a text editor like Notepad. The Registration Files option creates a .reg file, which can be edited "offline" and then imported back into the Registry. There is also a Win 9x/NT4 Registration Files option, which creates a file able to be imported into older Windows machines. The Text Files option also creates a text file, but this file cannot be merged back into the active Registry. You can use this file to take a snapshot of the Registry, without being concerned that changes to the file will ever affect Registry settings. It can't be accidentally merged with an existing Registry, as can the .reg files, by a curious user.

If you need to restore the Registry, or a portion thereof, select the key you wish to restore (or, more correctly, revert back to the saved version) and choose the File | Import command. Then specify the file and then confirm in a dialog box telling you that you are about to overwrite the current key and subkeys.

Group Policies

Up to now, we've been dealing with the configuration settings applied by an individual user at his or her computer, or with changes made by an administrator affecting all users of a machine. But what if the administrator wants to take more control of the user environment, dictating the look and feel of the desktop experience? What if, for example, the administrator of a computer—or even a network—wants to remove access to the Control Panel altogether for ordinary users? What if she wanted all users, for purposes of professionalism, to use a uniform desktop theme? Group Policy is the answer.

Group Policy is a powerful new technology built into Windows XP that lets an administrator manage the Windows XP computing experience. It is the command center from which Information Technology department policies and rules will be implemented to effect overall computing practice.

Now, before we get too far along in the discussion, you should know that the topic of Group Policies is a large one, and you will be spending a great amount of time getting familiar with Group Policies as you continue to study Windows XP, 2000, and .NET. In fact, the 2000/.NET Active Directory core exams (70-217 and 70-277) that you will likely be ramping up for soon cover little else besides Group Policy. Fortunately, Microsoft has recognized the expanse of this topic, and for that reason you will see only a small portion of Group Policy covered in the Windows XP Professional exam (and in this book). To try and cover all the Group Policy material for this exam would be like trying to take a sip of water from a fire hose. There's plenty to learn here besides all the information relating to Group Policies.

You should recognize for now that Group Policy Objects (GPOs) can be applied to many objects in a modern Windows computing enterprise. They can be applied to *local machines*, to *domains*, to *sites*, and to *organizational units* (OUs). Three of these objects, however, are specific to Windows 2000 or .NET Active Directory domains and are not applicable to the 70-270 Exam, which assumes that you are installing Windows XP Professional in a Workgroup environment. When that is the case, only the Local Group Policy settings apply to the user environment.

Local Policies

When you start up Windows XP Professional, there are security settings being applied in the background. These settings aren't really all that secure, but just set a baseline of secure operation so that you can tighten security further if it suits your needs. For example, one of the settings is that blank passwords are allowed, a security setting you would almost surely change if you were concerned with a secure environment. So what else do these security settings do?

The desktop settings of a computer not on a Windows XP domain running Active Directory are enforced with a default Local Security Policy that is created at installation time. In this way, the Local Security Policy behaves like a user profile (discussed next): you get one before you're presented with the desktop. The user profile specifies what the desktop will look like, and the Local Security Policy specifies what you can do on that desktop. These default Local Security Policy settings can be viewed and managed using the Local Computer Policy node of the Group Policy snap-in, as shown in Figure 4-7.

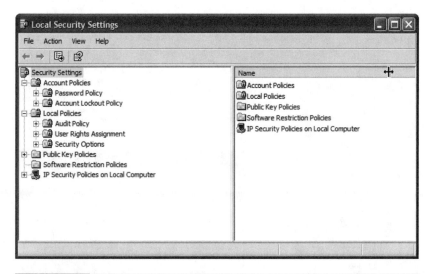

FIGURE 4.7   The Local Security settings

You can begin working with the Local Security Policy of a system in two ways: you can add the Group Policy snap-in to a custom MMC, and you can launch the Local Security Settings preconfigured snap-in. However, the Local Security Policy is just a subset of the configurable options available with a Local Policy. To see all that a Local Policy has to offer, you will use a blank MMC with the Group Policy snap-in added.

When using the MMC option in adding the Group Policy snap-in, make sure that the Group Policy will apply to the Local Machine. The Local Security Settings preconfigured snap-in is found in the Administrative Tools folder in the Control Panel. Note that the Local Security Settings tool is actually a subset of the Group Policy settings. The security settings can be found in the Group Policy snap-in by expanding Local Computer Policy, Computer Configuration, and then Windows Settings, which will then show you the Security Settings node.

With the Local Security Settings, you can configure the user rights on a given computer, such as who can shut down the system or who can increase quotas. You can also set passwords and account policies from their respective nodes. For example, you can specify that passwords for users on a machine must be at least six characters in length. To configure a policy, just double-click a setting to open its Properties dialog box, as shown in Figure 4-8.

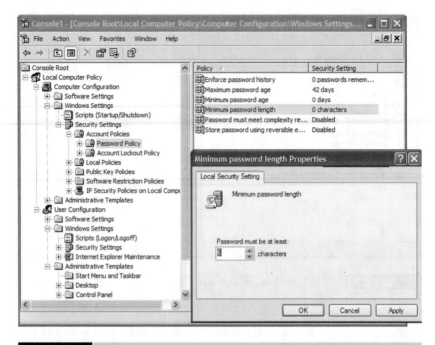

Configuring a policy

You can further configure almost all aspects of the user environment through the settings of the Local GPO. To do this, make sure that the interface you are using is the Group Policy snap-in, which gives you a huge range of management options, including the administrative templates, which are used mostly to manage the desktop environment. They contain many of the settings that we associate with a user profile. The Local Security Settings are specific to, well, security options.

Let's return to our earlier scenario where an administrator might not want users to access the Control Panel. This can be enabled in Group Policy (and this can be a bit hard to follow) by enabling the policy that disables the display of the Control Panel. This setting can be found under the User Configuration node of Group Policy by expanding Administrative Templates and then clicking the Control Panel node, as shown in Figure 4-9. The setting can then be enabled by double-clicking the policy option and choosing to enable the policy.

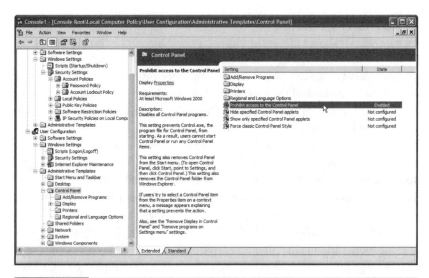

FIGURE 4.9 Turning off the Control Panel with Group Policy

Exam Tip

These are just a few examples of the settings possible with Group Policy. You won't be expected to memorize any part of the Group Policy snap-in; just know what it is used for. We will be returning to the Group Policy editor from time to time throughout this book to configure different management tasks where appropriate.

User Profiles

Every user who has used Windows XP has worked with a user profile. That's because a user couldn't even get to the desktop without a profile. In other words, Windows XP will never present the desktop to a user without using a user profile, because part of a profile's job is to define how that desktop will look. User profiles make it possible to personalize the desktop environment based on the user's account name. In fact, profiles are so ingrained in the Windows experience that each and every time a new user account successfully logs on, a profile is created for that user account if one hasn't been configured by the administrator already.

What Is a Profile?

So what all is included in a user profile? A profile includes settings that are vital to the end user experience, such as the color and resolution of the desktop, the size and shape of the mouse pointer, any network connections or printers that have been mapped, and the location of the My Documents folder, to name a few. In brief, pretty much everything that's part of the user's interaction with the OS will be found in a user's profile. Further, these settings are stored in a folder somewhere, usually on the local machine, and the user's account is configured to retrieve the desktop settings from this folder. Profiles can be assigned to a single user, or an entire group of users can be pointed to a single profile. If a profile is assigned to an entire group of users, each of the users in the group will receive a consistent desktop every time he or she logs on.

Two *types* of profiles are available: local and roaming. By default, user profiles are local, meaning that they are stored and accessed locally at the computer the user logs on from. Users access their roaming profiles on a network server, which means that they will receive the same desktop environment from any computer on the network.

Also, by default, users can make changes to their profiles. For example, they can change the screen saver and appearance of the icons as they please. An administrator can decide to make each of the two types of profiles mandatory, which restricts user modifications to the desktop somewhat, as we'll see in just a minute.

Local Profiles

As mentioned, when a user first logs on to a computer, a profile is created for that user locally, right there on the hard disk of the machine (unless that user has been previously configured to use a roaming profile). This includes the Administrator account the first time it's used to log on to the computer. These profile folders are stored, by default, as subfolders in the *systemroot*\Documents and Settings folder. Also by default, a new users local profile is stored in a folder that is titled with the same name as the account (that is, the Administrator account creates the Administrator Profile folder, Brian creates a folder called Brian, and so on).

This new local profile, created the first time a user logs on, is generated by making a copy of two profile folders created when Windows XP is installed. The two profile folders involved in this process are the All Users profile folder and the Default User profile folder. (The Default User folder might be hidden, depending on the settings you have configured from the View tab of Tools | Folder Options.) A quick glance at the contents of these two folders gives you an idea of

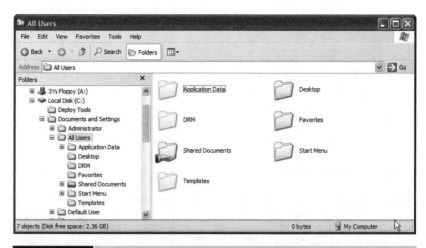

The settings of the All Users profile folder

the kinds of settings that define a profile, as shown in Figure 4-10. As you can see in the figure, the settings of the All Users folder will define what shortcuts are found on the Start menu for *all* users of this computer.

Travel Advisory

If you have upgraded from Windows NT 4 to XP, the profiles folders are stored under *systemroot*\Profiles, not in the Documents and Settings\Profiles folder. The Documents and Settings folder is used for upgrades of 2000 and on clean XP installs.

Here's how it all shakes out:

1. When a user logs on for the first time, the system checks to see whether a local user profile exists, which appears as a folder with the user's account name located under Documents and Settings. This Documents and Settings folder is created on the boot partition when you install the Windows XP Professional operating system.

2. If a folder for that user is not present at logon time, a profile folder that matches the account name is automatically created by copying the contents of the Default User folder to a new folder created just for that user account. This new folder's name is the same as the account.

3. The user's profile and the All Users profile from this point on remain in distinct folders, but their contents are merged when a user's desktop environment is generated. For example, after I created a user called The Dude, a folder is created for that user when he logs on, as shown in Figure 4-11.

You can even manage the contents of desktops for new users by adding and deleting from the contents of the All Users folder and the Default Users folder, although I recommend messing around only with the Default User folder, whose contents affect only those users who have no user profile created.

Travel Advisory

Be careful about what you change in the All Users folder, because changes made here will affect all users of the computer. This includes you, the administrator.

FIGURE 4.11   The Dude's user profile folder is created when logging on the first time.

Windows XP keeps track of all the profiles that have been created on the local machine in the System Properties dialog box. To launch this Control Panel program, you can right-click My Computer and choose Properties. The list of profiles contained on a particular system is kept on the User Profiles dialog box, found by clicking the Advanced tab of System Properties in the User profiles section. If you want to configure roaming profiles, this is where you go. Figure 4-12 displays the profiles that exist on my system.

The drawback of the local user profile is that it is available only at the computer where the profile was created. This becomes unwieldy in an environment where users are constantly moving among computers, because a new profile gets created for the user at every computer he or she uses. In this scenario, a user would have a hard time maintaining a consistent desktop environment and may spend otherwise productive time rearranging the look and feel of each desktop. To provide an efficient way for users to maintain a consistent desktop environment, you should use a roaming profile.

Roaming Profiles

You can copy any of the local user profiles to a network server so that it's available no matter what computer they use. This feature is called a *roaming profile*.

FIGURE 4.12 The User Profiles dialog box

Roaming profiles allow a user to move from one computer to another in a network and get a consistent desktop no matter what computer they are logging on from. When a user is using a roaming profile, the contents of the profile are retrieved from a network share at logon time and downloaded to the local computer to generate the user's desktop.

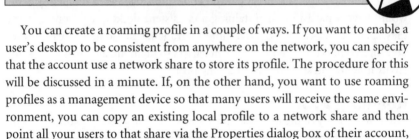

Travel Advisory

When you are setting up the share to store user profiles, be sure that users have the ability to read and write to this share; if they can't read from the share, they can't get their profile, and if they make changes to their desktop, they can't be saved without having the write permission.

You can create a roaming profile in a couple of ways. If you want to enable a user's desktop to be consistent from anywhere on the network, you can specify that the account use a network share to store its profile. The procedure for this will be discussed in a minute. If, on the other hand, you want to use roaming profiles as a management device so that many users will receive the same environment, you can copy an existing local profile to a network share and then point all your users to that share via the Properties dialog box of their account, as described next (you will also usually make this profile mandatory, so multiple users can't make changes to the same profile).

It's usually wise to create a user profile that will be used as a template for the roaming profile. After you have the desktop settings the way you want, use the System applet in the Control Panel to copy the profile to the network location.

1. From the Advanced tab of the System Properties window, click the Settings button under the User Profiles section. The User Profiles dialog box will appear.

2. Next, select the profile you wish to make available as a Roaming Profile and click the Copy To button.

3. In the Copy To dialog that opens, click the Browse button.

4. Select a shared directory where you want to place the profile, as shown in Figure 4-13. Click OK.

Travel Advisory

Always use the System applet to do the copying of the user profile. You cannot just drag and drop profile folders from Windows Explorer. (Well, you *can*, but the profiles won't work. Part of the profile settings are registry-specific, and the System program provides a graphical interface to the registry, whereas Windows Explorer does not. See "The Registry" section earlier in this chapter.)

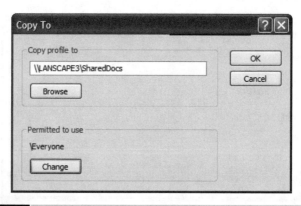

FIGURE 4.13   Copying a profile

After the profile you want to use has been copied to the network share, it is ready for use as a roaming profile. A user needs to be pointed to that profile folder at logon time.

To configure this second part of the roaming profile process, you'll work from the Properties page of a user account.

1. On a Windows XP Professional computer in a workgroup, open Computer Management by right-clicking My Computer and choosing Manage.

2. Access the Properties dialog box for the user account by double-clicking the user account in the Users folder of the Users and Groups node.

3. From the Profile tab (shown in Figure 4-14), enter the share location in the Profile Path text box, using the UNC path to that location.

Although we are looking at how to configure profiles in a Workgroup environment, it is unlikely that you will configure this in the real world. It is much more likely that roaming profiles will be used in conjunction with a Windows 2000 or .NET Active Directory domain environment, and when this is the case, the tool used to configure user accounts is called Active Directory Users and Computers. The Computer Management tool is used only to illustrate how to specify a profile path because, if you're studying at home, you are far less likely to belong to a domain.

Also, it is good practice to use the *username* variable when configuring roaming profiles for individual accounts. The *username* variable takes the user's account name and creates a private folder for that user's profile using that name.

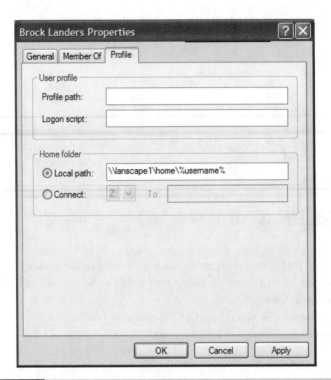

FIGURE 4.14   Specifying a profile path

For example, you can create a share called \profiles on a server called \\server1. The Profile Path box would be filled in with \\server1\profiles\%username%. The folder for that user will be created as a subfolder of the \profiles folder, and only the user would have the Full Control permission to the folder.

Now the magic happens. When that user logs on to the domain from any computer using the domain account, the user's profile will be accessed from the server holding the profile, and a local copy of the roaming user profile is copied to the user's computer. Any changes that are made to the desktop environment during the session are saved back to the server when the user logs off. The next time the user logs on, the desktop settings will appear just as they were at the user's last session.

Mandatory Profiles

If the user has been set up to use a *mandatory* profile, the changes made during the last session will not be saved as the user logs off. Mandatory profiles are an ideal solution when many users share the same profile, such as might be found in a computer kiosk or in a highly secure environment where you do not want users making changes to the desktop.

Saving changes made to desktop settings at logoff time or not saving them (there's a Hamlet reference here somewhere) is the difference between a normal user profile—either local or roaming—and a mandatory profile. Users of a mandatory profile will still be able to manipulate desktops to their heart's content during their session, but the changes that are made during that session are not saved to the network version of the profile. As a result, the next time the user logs on, the original desktop will appear.

But we still haven't discussed how to make a profile mandatory. You can make a profile of either type mandatory in one of two ways: by renaming the NTUSER.DAT file NTUSER.MAN or by renaming the profile folder by adding a .man extension to it. For example, you can configure a mandatory profile for a user named The Dude by renaming the \The Dude folder to \The Dude.man, or by looking in the \The Dude folder for the NTUSER.DAT file and renaming it to NTUSER.MAN. It's up to you.

If you haven't modified the default settings for the display of hidden files, you won't see the NTUSER.DAT file in Windows Explorer. Well, that's not really accurate. You will see the file; it just won't have the .DAT extension that you are looking for. You must enable the display of hidden files before you can find NTUSER.DAT. To do this, open the Folder Options dialog box, which is accessed by choosing Tools | Folder Options from Windows Explorer (or by selecting the Folder Options icon in the Control Panel).

You still aren't done. When you first look in a folder where you want to set a mandatory profile, the NTUSER.DAT file that you see is not what it seems. It is really a text file called NTUSER.DAT.LOG, and renaming it will do nothing toward configuring a mandatory profile. To see all the file extensions correctly, you might want to uncheck the Hide File Extensions For Known File Types box in Folder Options. You'll then see the NTUSER.DAT file that you will rename to make your user profile mandatory.

If you mistakenly rename the .LOG file, you'll end up creating a new file called NTUSER.MAN.TXT, and you know what that means—no more dinners at the Gates' residence for you. Actually, Windows will just create a new NTUSER.DAT.LOG file next time the user logs on, resulting in multiple NTUSER files in the same folder, and a result that is not what you're looking for: the user profile will not be mandatory.

If, on the other hand, you append the profile folder with a .man extension as your method of configuring mandatory profiles, be cautioned that if the server holding the profile is not available, the user will not be able to log on. Conversely, if you rename the NTUSER.DAT file and the profile server is unavailable, the user will log on using a locally cached version of the profile.

Configure and Troubleshoot Fax Support

Windows XP Professional includes the software needed to send and receive faxes through a fax-capable modem. If Windows XP detects the presence of a fax device, it installs the Fax Service and the Windows XP fax driver. The Fax Service will then appear in the Services window, and the Windows NT fax driver will appear in the Printers folder as a printer named Fax. After the Fax Service has been installed, you need to start it through the Services node of Computer Management, which is launched by right-clicking My Computer and choosing Manage. Click Services and Applications and then click Services. Then find the Fax Service and start it, as shown in Figure 4-15.

After your fax device has been set up and configured, documents to be faxed from an application are treated in the same way that they are when printed, except the destination printer for faxed documents becomes the Fax device.

FIGURE 4.15   Starting the Fax Service

Faxes can also be received through the fax device. The Windows XP Fax Monitor listens for incoming faxes and receives the fax as a TIF graphical image. When the image file is received, it can be saved to a folder, sent via e-mail, or sent along to a print device. Any of these three options are available, but routing the TIF file to the Received Faxes folder is the default setting.

Local Lingo

TIF or **TIFF** An acronym for *tagged image file format*, one of the most widely supported file formats for storing bitmapped images on personal computers. TIF graphics can be any resolution, and they can be black and white, gray-scaled, or color. Files in TIF format often end with a *.tif* extension.

The image files can either be read by the Imaging for Windows Preview utility or by any installed application capable of viewing TIF files.

Travel Advisory

To route faxes to a network printer or to an e-mail profile, the Fax Service must be configured with a logon account with the necessary rights to read the user's e-mail profile, to access a network printer, or both. You need to be aware of this when considering the default behavior: the Fax Service is configured to use the Local System account, which does not support network printing or local e-mail profile access.

You can further manage and customize fax support from two places: from the Fax applet in the Control Panel and from icons in the Fax program group by choosing Start | Programs | Accessories | Communications. For example, extensive user information can be added to outgoing faxes by double-clicking the Fax icon on the Control Panel to open the Fax Properties window, shown in Figure 4-16.

It is not important to know the specific tabs of the fax properties dialog box, as they are likely to vary depending on the type of device you have installed. Once the fax is installed, however, you can manage it through the Fax Console, which is the faxing equivalent of the Print Manager and will launch when you double-click the fax device in the Printers and Faxes window. If you have used an e-mail program before, you shouldn't find the Fax Console to be any trouble.

The first time you run the Fax Console, the Fax Configuration Wizard starts, letting you configure how, and if, the fax device is to send and receive faxes and what to do once the fax has been received. If the Wizard detects that the new Fax Console is an upgrade from the Personal Fax for Windows, the Wizard will offer

The Fax Properties window

the capability to import existing fax archives. As shown in Figure 4-17, I have configured the fax to send all received fax jobs directly to the printer.

If you ever need to run the Fax Configuration Wizard again, just choose Tools | Configure Fax from the Fax Console.

Now that we've looked more closely at some of the output devices and their configuration options, it's time to turn our attention to some of the ways we can make *input* easier on a Windows XP Professional machine.

Configure and Troubleshoot Accessibility Services

The keyboard is not the ideal input device for everybody. And not everyone can hear the beep and bell sounds made by Windows XP. To accommodate preferences and alternative accessibilities, Windows XP includes Accessibility Services, which makes it easier for people with disabilities to interact with the OS. These tools are installed by default at setup time. The Accessibility Options

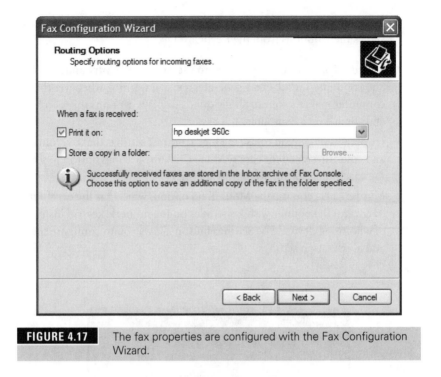

FIGURE 4.17   The fax properties are configured with the Fax Configuration Wizard.

applet in the Control Panel is one of these tools, and you can find the others in the Start menu under the Accessibility program group.

Accessibility Options

You can use five tabs in the Accessibility Options program in the Control Panel to manage many of these accessibility features: Keyboard, Sound, Display, Mouse, and General. The options on these tabs can be used to assist people with various hearing, sight, and mobility challenges. The special behavior options that can be set from these five tabs are summarized here:

- **Keyboard**   Allows you to specify the use of StickyKeys, FilterKeys, and ToggleKeys. StickyKeys will let a user press a multiple-key combination without having to hold down all the keys at the same time. This is especially useful for users who can't press more that one key at a time, yet need to access a keystroke command like CTRL-ALT-DELETE. FilterKeys ignores repeated keystrokes. ToggleKeys makes a noise when CAPS LOCK, NUM LOCK, or SCROLL LOCK keys are pressed. The Settings buttons for each of these further modify the behavior of each. Figure 4-18 shows these options from the Keyboard tab.

- **Sound** Lets you specify whether to use the SoundSentry and ShowSounds. SoundSentry generates a visual warning whenever the computer makes a sound. ShowSounds displays captions for speech and sounds on a computer.
- **Display** Allows you to use the high-contrast settings that use fonts and colors designed for easy reading. Click the Settings button to set the specifics of the high-contrast setting.
- **Mouse** Lets you use the MouseKeys option, which has the capability to control the pointer with keystrokes on the numeric keypad instead of a pointing device. The Settings button allows you to configure speed and acceleration settings.

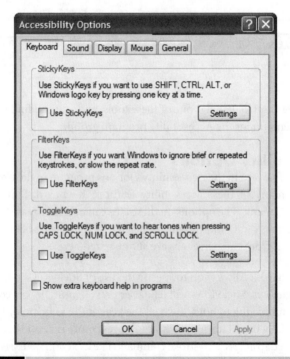

FIGURE 4.18   Configuring keyboard accessibility

- **General** Used to control how the computer will react to idle time and to control how notifications are delivered when an accessibility feature is enabled or disabled. From here, you can also configure whether or not the accessibility features will apply only to the logged-on user or to all users of the system. You can also specify a SerialKey device, an alternative keyboard and mouse hardware used as the input device that connects to a computer's serial port.

Other Accessibility Utilities

Other important accessibility features can be configured via the Start menu. (Again, the path is Start | Programs | Accessories | Accessibility.) Three important accessibility utilities for people with limited sight, hearing, and mobility are readily available: the Magnifier, the Narrator, and the On-Screen Keyboard. Here is a summation of these three utilities.

- **The Narrator** A text-to-speech converter that reads the text displayed on the desktop, including contents of an active window and any text you select or type. The Narrator is not guaranteed to work with all applications; however, it usually does.
- **The Magnifier** Makes anything appearing on the desktop more readable by creating a separate window that follows the movements of the mouse to display a greatly magnified view of the desktop, a high-contrast view of the desktop, or both.
- **The On-Screen Keyboard** Helps people who have difficulty using a keyboard to enter text strings. It displays a keyboard on the desktop to enable users with mobility impairments to type data using a pointing device or joystick.

You can manage the startup of these applications by selecting the application individually or by starting the Utility Manager application, which is found in Start | Programs | Accessories | Accessibility. From the Utility Manager application, you can select to start the Narrator, Magnifier, or the On-Screen Keyboard utility.

Each of these utilities can be started independently of one another, and independently of the Utility Manager, by clicking their corresponding icon in the Accessibility program group. However, most users with visual or mobility impairments will need greater capabilities than these three utilities can offer. The Microsoft Accessibility website (http://www.microsoft.com/enable) contains a comprehensive list of hardware and software designed to assist computer users with visual, auditory, or mobility impairments.

Configure Support for Multiple Languages and Multiple Locations

Objective 4.02

There are two technologies in operation that allow Windows XP to support Multilanguage environments:

- Multilingual editing and viewing, which is called upon if a user is editing or printing a file in a language other than the one used for the user interface.

- Multilanguage user interfaces, which allow XP Professional to present the user interface in a variety of languages, depending on who is using the system.

Let's take a look at some of the important (that is to say, testable) considerations when implementing Windows XP for many languages and/or locations.

Enable Multiple Language Support

As the focus of this chapter has to do with the end user experience, you will notice that a great deal of time is spent on the appearance of the desktop. That's because, to a great extent, the desktop defines the end user experience. It is the user's portal to accessing their system, and the less time users have to worry about the desktop, the more productive they can be.

We typically don't give the language settings much thought on a day-to-day basis, but the language that the desktop uses is one of the key factors in defining the end user experience. Believe me, you would give it a lot of thought if you came in and your desktop was in Greek one day (unless you were Greek). So, to allow the Windows XP Professional OS to be understood by almost anyone on the globe, it has the capability to use and understand almost any language on the planet. It actually comes in three different multilingual versions: the English version, the Translated version, and the MultiLanguage version. Each version offers varying degrees of language support:

- The English version allows a user to view, edit, and print information in more than 60 languages.

- The Translated version provides the same support as the English version, and it also includes a language-specific interface for menus, help files, dialog boxes, and file system components.
- The MultiLanguage version provides the same support as the Translated version, and it allows the (presumably multilingual) user to switch the user interface language.

Configure XP Professional for Multiple Settings

While it will take you years of study to learn new languages, it takes a Windows XP computer a matter of seconds. You will perform your configuration of multiple languages in the Regional and Language Options program accessed from the Control Panel. Here's how:

1. In the Regional and Language Options window, you can select from the drop-down box the language used to display numbers, currencies, dates and times, as shown in Figure 4-19. You can also set your Location here for delivery of specialized information, such as news and weather.

2. Clicking the Language tab will allow you to change the default input language and methods for inputting text. For example, if you were using a Chinese character keyboard, you could set it as the input keyboard device here.

3. Additionally, you can set other programs (non-Unicode) to display menus and dialog boxes in their native language by choosing a language from the Advanced tab. Be aware that changes made here will affect all users of the computer.

Which version you choose will, of course, be dependent on the multilingual needs of your organization. The MultiLanguage version, for example, is ideal when full multilingual support is necessary to ensure the smooth execution of the business model.

Finally, when you have the MultiLanguage version of Windows XP Professional installed, you will see a Menus and Dialogs drop-down list on the General tab in the Regional and Language Options dialog box. You can select any installed language from this drop-down list. This new language can apply to a particular user logging on or to all users accessing that computer.

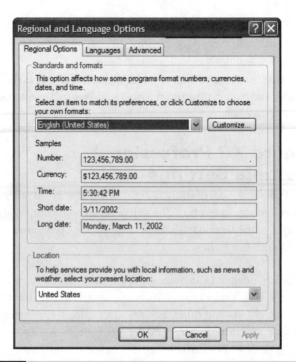

FIGURE 4.19 Setting the Regional and Language Options

Travel Advisory

Selecting a different language in the Menus and Dialogs drop-down list affects only menu items, help files, and such that are bundled with the operating system. The language for files not bundled with the operating system, including some of the desktop icons, will not be affected by the change in language.

Manage Applications Using Windows Installer Packages

Objective 4.03

The proper use of the Windows Installer can help you take great strides in lowering the much-talked-about Total Cost of Ownership (TCO) of your network. Its purpose is to reduce the cost of software deployment by reducing the number of administrative visits made to the desk side. An understanding of the Windows Installer calls into play several areas of Windows XP expertise, and most of these areas deal with new technologies. This means that you are likely to be peppered with questions about this feature on both the Windows XP Professional and .NET (and 2000) Server exams. It's a good idea to become familiar with this service, even if there are other ways of getting software to your clients in a real-world network.

The Windows Installer is an operating system service that helps manage or repair software installations. The Windows Installer can be set to manage the features and components of an application that is to be deployed—for example, you can configure some components not to install or to run right from the CD-ROM without being installed with the rest of the application, conserving hard disk space.

However, there are a couple of limitations that govern the use of the Windows Installer. First, for applications to take advantage of the service, the setup routine must be packaged in a certain file extension, as outlined next. Second, it relies on the application of Group Policies, which can be applied only to Windows XP or 2000 computers. Third, in order to use Installer packages, you must be a part of a Windows 2000 or .NET domain.

There are three types of setup files that Windows Installer can use to set up Installer packages. Listed next, along with their respective file extensions, they are:

- **Microsoft Installer (.msi)**   This setup file is created by software vendors like Microsoft as an alternative to the setup routine that has been used for years to install application packages, the setup.exe file. The .msi file used by the Windows Installer Service is a little database that defines all of the installation options available. One of the first places it showed up was in the Office 2000 suite of applications, which were installed using an .msi file. If you have ever done a custom setup of Office 2000, you have been exposed to the installation options that are available through an .msi file.

- **Repackaged applications (.msi)**   Repackaged applications are used to provide users with applications that can be deployed, modified, and uninstalled cleanly with ease.

- **ZAP files (.zap)**   These are used to package an application if you do not or cannot create an .msi file. They are created with text editors such as Notepad, and can only be published, not assigned. These ZAP files allow applications to be installed by pointing to their native setup (setup.exe) routines.

If your application supports it, you can modify the installation further through the use of a *modification (.mst) file*, which can be used in conjunction with Repackaged application or ZAP files to include certain installation specifics.

Know the purpose of the .mst file for the test, not the specifics on how to configure one.

Travel Assistance

For more detailed information about creating and configuring .msi, .zap, and .mst files, please see *Mike Meyers' MCSE Windows 2000 Directory Services Administration Certification Passport*, by Steve D. Kaczmarek (McGraw-Hill/Osborne; ISBN 0072194715).

The Windows Installer becomes a more powerful operating system feature when combined with Windows XP Servers running Active Directory. You'll be able to give an exhaustive definition of this later, but to summarize: Active Directory is the database of users and computers that resides on the Windows 2000/.NET Servers that are domain controllers. There are three steps in the process of configuring a Windows installer package, as outlined here.

1. First, copy the .msi file to a network share.

2. Create a Group Policy Object that will be used to facilitate the package's installation. This is where the Windows 2000 or .NET domain controller comes in. You will create the GPO under one of the two locations. For users, it will be User Configuration | Software Settings | Software installation. For computers, it will be Computer Configuration | Software Settings | Software installation.

3. Finally, add the package to the Group Policy Object and optionally filter that object to apply to just the domain users or computers that you target for application distribution.

Sound easy? It is, after you have done it a few times. (I suppose the same could be said about elective surgery.) There is really no shortcut that will get you familiar with Group Policy Objects other than practice, practice, and practice. You will have to get your hands dirty with this one. We will be fleshing out the concepts and technologies of Group Policy throughout this book and, indeed, throughout the entire MCSE track. Only a limited knowledge of Group Policy, enough to get a Windows Installer package to a user or computer, is needed at this time.

Installation Options: Publishing vs. Assigning

Once you configure a Windows Installer package, it can then be distributed to target computers via one of two mechanisms: as a published application or as an assigned application. You will need to have a clear understanding about the distinction between the two for the exam, so let's spend a little time discussing each here.

Publishing Applications

When you *publish* an application, users will be able to choose whether or not they will install the application. A published application will appear in the Add/Remove Programs applet in the Control Panel and will typically be installed from there—simply a matter of choosing the application and clicking Add. One rule of publishing you have to keep in mind is that packages cannot be published to computers. You only publish to users.

Assigning Applications

When an application is *assigned*, the package is automatically installed, no matter what the user's feelings about the matter. Further, packages can be assigned to either users or computers.

When you assign an application to a *user*, the application is installed when the user launches the program through the Start menu for the first time, or when the user opens a file that was created in that application, using a process called *document invocation*. As an example of document invocation, consider that opening a .doc file would cause the installation of Word.

When an application is assigned to a *computer*, it is installed the next time *any* user logs on, before the desktop is ever presented.

CHECKPOINT

✔**Objective 4.01: Configure and Manage Desktop Settings and User Profiles**
We discussed the purpose and process of user profile creation. We looked at the differences between a local profile and a roaming profile. We also discussed how to make user profiles mandatory.

We focused largely in this section on the options available in the Control Panel, including an understanding of how the Control Panel is really a graphical interface to the Registry. We examined a couple of tools that can make direct edits to the Registry. Also, we started to get familiar with Group Policy and how it can be used to manage the desktop environment.

We looked at how to set up a fax print device in Windows XP. We also looked at some of the considerations for directing the output of a received fax.

Finally, we looked at the Windows XP Accessibility services, including situations when certain Accessibility options would be most appropriate. We also investigated how many of these Accessibility services could be configured at one time by using the Accessibility Wizard.

✔**Objective 4.02: Configure Support for Multiple Languages and Multiple Locations** In this section, we reviewed the options available to configure Windows XP Professional to operate in multilingual environments.

✔**Objective 4.03: Manage Applications by Using Windows Installer Packages** We discussed the technologies behind automatic software distribution and its role in lowering the TCO of Windows XP. We also looked at the different installation options available for applications distributed with Windows Installer Packages.

REVIEW QUESTIONS

1. Nigel Tufnel, tired of life on tour and a dwindling fan base, has become administrator of a Windows XP network. Nigel wants to set up a computing environment where his users can log on to any computer and have their desktop settings follow them. What does Nigel need to do?

    A. Configure all Windows XP Professional computers to join an Active Directory domain, then create a profile pointing to the Active Directory.

    B. Configure all Windows XP Professional computers to join the domain, then configure a roaming profile for each user.

    C. Configure all Windows XP Professional computers to join a workgroup, then set their domain user accounts to point to a shared location.

    D. Nigel can't do this without third-party tools.

2. Your goal as a new network administrator is to keep profile administration to a minimum. Each user has his or her own desk and uses the same computer every day. Another goal is a happy workforce. As a means to this end, you further want to let users configure their desktops as they wish. What's the best kind of user profile to use to meet your two objectives?

    A. Local

    B. Mandatory

    C. Roaming

    D. Active Directory-Integrated

3. You receive a call from a user who is trying to configure the fax settings from the Control Panel, and he reports that he does not have an Advanced Options tab as he does on his home system. He tells you that the driver must be corrupt. What should you do to fix this situation?

    A. Tell the user to update the driver using the Device Manager Update Device Driver Wizard.

    B. The user is using the wrong utility to do this. The fax settings are specific to the application he is faxing from.

    C. Have the user check the resource settings for any possible conflicts in the Device Manager.

    D. Nothing. It is working as designed.

4. Lloyd Dobler is the administrator of a large network and is using Windows Installer to deploy a software application called, cryptically, the K2 on computers running a mixture of Windows 2000 and XP Professional. Lloyd does not want to force users to install by having an icon appear on the Start menu, but rather would like to just make it available to users who want it and who could install it through the Control Panel's Add/Remove Programs applet. How should Lloyd deploy the network's software package?

    A. Assign applications to users.

    B. Assign applications to computers.

    C. Publish applications to users.

    D. Publish applications to computers.

5. You want to use Windows Installer to deploy an application to computers running Windows XP Professional. You want to configure the install to take place only when the users first try to use the application to cut down on network bandwidth usage during the install procedure. You would also like to configure the installer so that only authorized users can perform the install. Choose from the following list all steps you would need to take.

   A. Assign the application to computers.

   B. Assign the application to users.

   C. Set the Deny check box on the Apply Group Policy permission for the Authenticated Users group. Create a new group containing the authorized users and grant the group Allow permission for Apply Group Policy.

   D. Clear the Allow check box on the Assign Group Policy permission for the Authenticated Users group. Create a new group containing the authorized users and grant the group Allow permission for Apply Group Policy.

6. In order to use a roaming profile, the user's account must be configured to do so. What utility is used to direct a user to a roaming profile?

   A. User Profile Editor

   B. Control Panel | System Program | Advanced tab | User Profiles dialog box

   C. Local Users and Groups in Computer Management

   D. User Manager

7. While working on a Windows XP Professional computer that is part of a workgroup, you try to open up an administrative tool from the Start menu. You notice, however, that there is no Start menu choice for the Administrative tools. You check the membership of the user account and confirm that the account is in the local Administrators group. What can you do to access the Administrative tools from the Start menu?

   A. Log on as the Administrator account, not the user account.

   B. Right-click the Start menu and add the Administrative tools through the General tab of the Start Menu Properties dialog box.

   C. Right-click the Start menu and add the Administrative tools through the Advanced tab of the Start Menu Properties dialog box.

   D. Right-click the Start Menu and add the Administrative tools through the Management tab of the Start Menu Properties dialog box.

8. You work for a company that has a distribution center located in Barcelona, and letters need to be viewed and edited in *Español* as part of regular correspondence. You have the bilingual staff needed to accomplish this, and the computers at your office in Santa Rosa are running the Windows XP Professional localized English versions. How will you, as the administrator, configure these machines so that documents can be created and edited in Spanish?

   A. In the Control Panel, use the Regional and Language Options icon.

   B. In the Control Panel, use the Additional Languages icon.

   C. Upgrade the OS to the MultiLanguage version.

   D. In the Control Panel, configure the Locale settings for two locales.

9. One morning, you configure the use of a High Contrast display on a Windows XP Professional computer for a user who needs this option to more easily see the content of the screen. He gives it a try, and everything is working properly when you leave. That afternoon, the user calls to report that the High Contrast display has reverted back to the old desktop when he returned from lunch. What do you suspect is the most likely cause of the problem?

   A. The user has logged on using a different user account.

   B. The user's Accessibility Options were deleted during a Group Policy refresh.

   C. The Accessibility Options are, by default, only configured to work in 30-minute intervals.

   D. The Accessibility Options have been configured to reset automatically if the computer is idle for a period of time.

10. Pete is administering a Windows .NET domain and will be using a Group Policy to deploy several applications to the network's Windows XP Professional computers. Pete knows that there are certain files involved in this process that will help perform the application installation. He also understands that there are files that can customize an application through a transform. Which of the following types of files can Pete be assured will never be used with software distribution through a Group Policy?

   A. .map files

   B. .msi files

   C. .mst files

   D. .zap files

REVIEW ANSWERS

1. **B**   After joining computers to a domain, you can configure roaming profiles for the accounts by modifying the properties of the domain accounts. The path specified must be a network share that the user has Read and Change permissions to. Profiles work best in domains. It's possible to configure roaming profiles in workgroups, but it's not really worth the administrative overhead and security holes involved.

2. **A**   A local profile would be sufficient in this small network because the profiles are created automatically when users log on for the first time, and they are able to make changes to the desktop environment that will be saved for the next time they log on. In other words, there really isn't anything you have to do, just let Windows XP behave the way it's configured by default. B is incorrect because a mandatory profile would not let users make changes to the desktop. C is not a necessary step because a local profile would require less administrative overhead, and the users are not switching computers often, if at all. D is incorrect because Active Directory-Integrated is a description of DNS zones, not user profiles.

3. **D**   For the Advanced Options tab to be displayed, the user must be logged on as an Administrator or have Administrator privileges assigned. Since the question assumes a regular user, the fax settings are working as designed. When the regular user is using his home system, he is using an account with Administrator privileges. A will not work because there is no mention of the fax device not working, just that the Advanced Options tab is not available. C is wrong for the same reason. Resource conflicts would cause problems with the operation of the device. B is incorrect because there is an Advanced Options tab in Windows XP where you can configure fax settings.

4. **C**   Publishing an application to users makes the Windows Installer package available for installation. To install a published application, the application can be clicked in the Add/Remove Programs applet in the Control Panel, or the application installation can be invoked by opening a file associated with the application. Published programs appear in the Add/Remove Programs dialog box. Publishing an application to users does not create a shortcut to the application on the users' desktops when targeted users log on. A and B are incorrect because an application assignment would either install the application automatically (computer

assignment) or place a shortcut in the users' Start menu. D is incorrect because applications cannot be published to computers.

5. **B D** Assigning an application to a user advertises the application to all targeted users at their next logon. The assigned application is installed the first time the user attempts to launch the program via the Start menu or by activating the Installer through document invocation.

6. **C** The Local Users and Groups utility is used to point the user's profile to a network share, making it a roaming profile. A is incorrect because there is no such tool. B is also not right because while a list of profiles is displayed here, it is used to copy profiles, not to specify what type of profile is used. D is the local user management tool in NT 4 and does not apply to Windows XP Professional.

7. **C** From the Advanced tab of the Start Menu Properties dialog box, you can configure such settings as the display of Administrative tools, Logoff, and Favorites. A is incorrect because the user is already part of the local Administrators group, so that won't help matters. B and D are wrong because you won't find the configuration help you need from those tabs. (The Management tab, in fact, does not exist.)

8. **A** Localized versions of Windows XP Professional support localized user interfaces for the language selected. In addition, they have the ability to view, edit, and print documents in more than 60 different languages. You will enable multilingual editing and viewing through the Regional and Language Options icon in the Control Panel. B is incorrect because no such icon exists in the Control Panel. C is incorrect because it is not a necessary step in this case. D is unnecessary because the locale settings would configure such things as time, currency, and the input language used.

9. **D** With the Accessibility Options icon in the Control Panel, you can set how long the accessibility features will be active if the computer is idle. In the example, someone has probably set the Automatic Reset feature from the General tab. You should first check this dialog box to see if Automatic reset settings have been configured to take effect after a given idle period, such as a lunch break. A is wrong because the Accessibility settings will be computerwide. B is incorrect because a Group Policy refresh is unlikely to reset the Accessibility settings. C is incorrect because Accessibility Options, by default, aren't configured to expire after any period of time.

10. **A** .map files have nothing whatsoever to do with Group Policy application deployment. Choices B, C, and D are all incorrect because they are used with software installation. A Windows Installer package (.msi file) contains all the information necessary to describe to the Group Policy how to set up an application. A .zap file is a text file that provides information about how to install a program, along with optional application properties, in the event that an .msi file is not available. It points to the application's setup.exe. An .mst file is a transform file that can be used to customize the application installations.

Implementing, Managing, Monitoring, and Troubleshooting Hardware Devices and Drivers

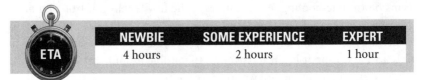

	NEWBIE	SOME EXPERIENCE	EXPERT
ETA	4 hours	2 hours	1 hour

Windows XP behaves in relation to hardware much as its earlier Windows cousins did. That is, not every piece of hardware ever produced will work as advertised. However, the list of what XP will work with is extensive. In fact, it would be a rare instance today if a new component or peripheral did not work with XP.

Before a piece of hardware actually does what it's supposed to do, Windows XP requires a compatible, properly installed and configured driver. The driver is a small, concise piece of code with the job of acting as a communications conduit between a hardware component and the operating system. It takes instructions either from you or from the operating system and then relays these instructions to the hardware, and then back again. In other words, a piece of hardware *is* the software driver as far as Windows is concerned. Without the proper drivers in place, your system's hardware will be little more than an expensive paperweight.

Windows XP provides a vast library of drivers in a compressed file called driver.cab and keeps this file handy in the *systemroot*\Driver Cache\I386 directory. This file is about 75MB at its compressed size. All necessary drivers for most systems that check out okay for Windows XP installation will be included in the driver.cab file. Further, you won't have to worry about whether any of these drivers will behave themselves with XP—all drivers in this file have been tested for reliability and are digitally signed by Microsoft (I'll talk about the whole driver signing thing in a bit). When a new Plug and Play device is installed, XP first consults the driver.cab file for a matching driver and performs installation automatically.

In fact, if you have a system whose hardware components are fully Plug and Play-compatible, it is likely that you won't be prompted for any drivers as you are performing XP installation. All necessary drivers will be loaded automatically, making for a much better experience "out of the box."

As an added benefit, Microsoft makes updated, certified hardware drivers available through Windows Update.

Troubleshooting is the process of isolating the source of a system error and taking corrective measures as needed. Almost all computer books include sections on troubleshooting. Almost none of them will help you troubleshoot a fraction as well as old-fashioned field experience. And as the aim of this book is to get you prepared for an exam, I can only give you a few heads-up warnings in this area and cannot begin to cover all the problems and challenges you are likely to encounter in the real world. Here goes.

Don't underestimate the importance of well-written, properly installed drivers. Or, conversely, don't underestimate the havoc caused by one that isn't. Because drivers access and control some of the most vital computer operations, like displaying pictures on a screen or reading files from a disk, a poorly written or faulty driver is very likely to leave your system in an inoperable state. When compared to programs that run amok, a driver is much more likely to cause a system crash where you experience a loss of data.

The management interface used to perform the vast majority of administrative tasks is pretty much the same as it was in previous Windows versions. If you've used the Device Manager before, there shouldn't be much here to throw you off. But, you will notice that while the core functionality remains the same, Windows XP's iteration of the Device Manager is more versatile.

Implement, Manage, and Troubleshoot Display Devices

Consider a display adapter device: it's an inanimate object made of silicon and aluminum wire that takes pulses of electricity and sends them to a monitor, which in turn shoots electrons through a gun at one end of a tube so that the electrons, in a very precise pattern, light up an array of red, green, and blue phosphorus dots at the other end of the tube. The dots glow because they've been hit with an electron for all of about 1/60 of a second or so. Each phosphorous dot that's hit glows in harmony with its neighbors to paint a picture on your monitor. That picture will be repainted again about 30 times a second, sometimes much more often, each picture slightly different from the last picture that is being drawn as you are trying to keep Tomb Raider's Lara Croft from harm's way at 2 A.M. Slacker.

Fortunately, you don't have to spend much time dwelling on all this complexity. As far as administrators are concerned, implementing a display adapter is a two-step dance. First, the device is *physically* connected to the computer's bus; it has to have a way to transport data to the processor. Then the device needs to be *logically* connected to the operating system, so that the OS and the device can successfully communicate when the device has something to say. We logically connect display adapters, and indeed all hardware devices, to the OS through the installation of drivers.

Install, Configure, and Troubleshoot a Display Adapter

Even though this initial objective dwells primarily on video adapters, most of the concepts and instructions are applicable no matter what piece of hardware you are installing. Let's start by discussing how to install both Plug and Play and non-PnP hardware. What follows will be relevant throughout the discussion of hardware installation.

Installing a Plug-and-Play Device

As you are likely aware, Plug and Play was first introduced with Windows 95, to which many would add: "In theory only." To put it diplomatically, Plug and Play was an evolving technology in the late '90s, still finding it legs. This led some computer aficionados to bestow upon this new technology, between epithets, the moniker Plug and *Pray*. (Not by *me*, I can assure you. Publicly, anyway.) In recent years, however, and especially with the advent of Windows 2000, Plug and Play has begun to live up to its billing. This is not because it's taken Microsoft all these years to get it right. Plug and Play relies on the successful co-operation of hardware and software standards, so there are more entities than just Microsoft at work in getting this thing to work successfully. And, for the most part, hardware manufacturers, driver writers, and Microsoft operating systems coders have all gotten on the same page, and Plug and Play is now more than just a name.

In this first objective, we will look at how Plug-and-Play technology works as we set up and configure a video adapter, and we will also look at what happens when our video card of choice does not conform to this standard.

A video adapter is an output device—usually a card that's attached to the motherboard, although some computers come with integrated video adapters that send information, and lots of it, to your monitor. You will set up your video adapter the same way you set up other hardware devices on your computer, either through the magic of Plug and Play or by using the Add/Remove Hardware Wizard in the Control Panel if the device is non-Plug and Play.

If the video adapter is a Plug and Play device, you simply need to shut down your computer and install the card. When you reboot, Windows XP Professional will automatically detect and install drivers for this new card if they exist in the driver.cab file.

Travel Advisory

Often times, Plug and Play devices will come with their own setup files, usually distributed on a CD. The best time to run this CD is often *before* you physically install the device. When this is done, driver files and the setup information file are copied to your hard drive, so they are handy when the device is physically installed, and Plug and Play will work automatically, as it should, when the system is restarted with the new hardware.

Upon physical installation and subsequent reboot, Windows will examine the Plug and Play signature contained in the hardware's BIOS. Upon identifying the device as PnP-compatible, Windows will then search for a matching signed driver, looking first in the driver.cab file. If successful, the signed driver is installed and all necessary modifications are made to your system without intervention. The only way a user would be aware of this process is through a bubble dialog box in the System Tray saying that a new piece of hardware has been found and installed and is now ready for use.

If the device is Plug and Play, but Windows cannot find a suitable driver during its search, it will launch the Add New Hardware Wizard, and the steps from there will mimic the process for installing a non-PnP component. Usually this step can be avoided by heeding the advice of the earlier Travel Advisory. The Add New Hardware Wizard will ask you what device is being installed and where to find the drivers for the new device. As with many administrative tasks in Windows XP, the process is completed by providing answers to a series of queries.

Configuring a non–Plug-and-Play Device

If a device is *not* Plug and Play, it doesn't take the rocket scientists among us to infer that Windows XP will not automatically install the drivers. In such a case, you will have to manually install the required drivers. So, then, your first job is to make sure you have them handy. You have several options for obtaining drivers for your non-PnP device. These include locating the Setup CD that the device shipped with and, if applicable, downloading drivers from the manufacturers web site. You can even sometimes use Windows 2000 drivers that are compatible with Windows XP.

Travel Advisory

These steps look pretty much the same when using the Add/Remove Hardware applet to install any type of device. We will not go through the wizard every time a new device is mentioned in this chapter, because the skills used to install a display adapter will port well to other device installs as explored later in this chapter.

Once you have the driver files for your non-PnP device at hand, you will take the following steps to complete setup of a video adapter that is not Plug and Play. Remember, the example is for the install of a video card, but the steps that follow look similar no matter what non-PnP device is being installed.

1. If your device came with a setup CD, you should first run its setup program. This will place the driver files on your hard disk prior to device setup and will ease later steps.

2. Shut down your system and install the video adapter. (In the case of a hot-swappable device, like anything USB, you would just connect the device to the computer) Restart the computer when the device is physically connected.

3. After reboot, open the Control Panel and either:
   - With the Control Panel in Classic view, double-click the Add Hardware icon, or
   - Open the System applet and from the Hardware tab choose the Add Hardware button.

4. Either step (and yes, there are still other ways to get here) will launch the Add Hardware Wizard Welcome screen, shown in Figure 5-1. Note that the Welcome screen recommends that you run the setup program from the CD if one shipped with the device (just as I did!).

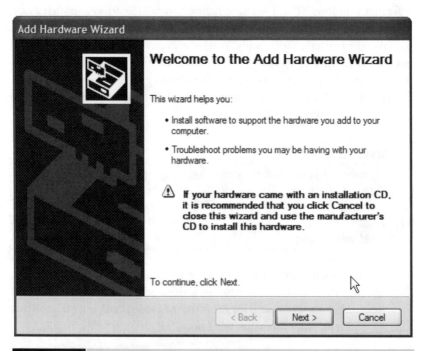

FIGURE 5.1   The Welcome screen of the Add Hardware Wizard

5. Click Next, and the Wizard will begin scanning your system for new hardware. With a non-Plug and Play device, Windows will not find the hardware, and you will be shown a dialog box asking you whether or not the device is physically connected. (Remember that certain computers have hot-swappable capability, which means that devices can be added while the machine is on. In such cases, Windows wouldn't know to do a bus rescan to determine what devices were there, so it is told to do so by the Add Hardware Wizard.)

6. In our case, we are assuming that a video adapter has been installed, so click "Yes, I have already connected the hardware," to proceed.

7. The Wizard will then display a list of currently installed devices, as shown in Figure 5-2. If the device you wish to install appears on the list, you should select it and click Next. It probably won't be, so you will have to scroll all the way to the bottom of the list to the Add a New Hardware Device selection and click Next.

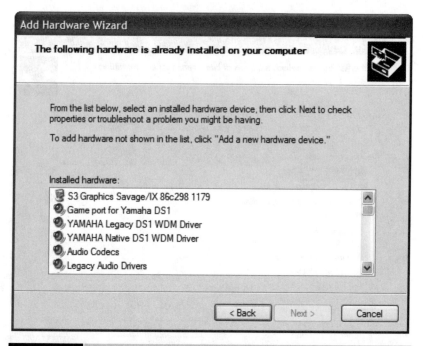

FIGURE 5.2   Adding a new, non-PnP device

8. The Wizard then asks if it can help install the new device, offering to do one of two things:

- *Search for and install the new hardware automatically.* This can be a good choice for devices such as network cards, modems, and printers that can be detected mechanically. After this selection, the Add Hardware program will run a routine that searches for any non-Plug and Play hardware on its list of devices. If it finds the device, it installs the correct drivers, and your work is finished.

- *Install the hardware that I manually select from a list.* You can skip the detection process with this option, which will actually be the more common choice for non-PnP devices.

The example assumes you have chosen the more common option, the manual selection. This dialog box asks you that first vital piece of information: what to install, as shown in Figure 5-3. Make your selection and click Next. We will be selecting the display adapter type from the list.

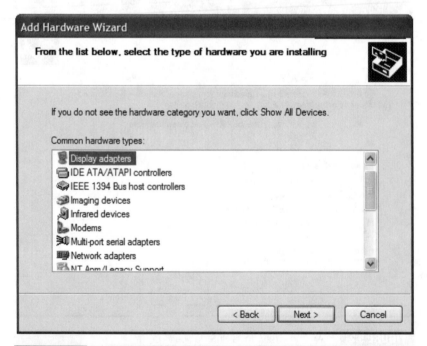

| **FIGURE 5.3** | The list shows you a range of hardware devices, categorized by type. |

9. Which dialog box you see next will depend on what device you just told the wizard you wanted to install. The Select a Device Driver dialog box presents you with a list of devices for which Windows XP already has a driver. Most of the time, these devices would have been detected, so the list isn't all that helpful. The choice for many non-Plug and Play installations with the Add Hardware Wizard is the Have Disk button. Figure 5-4 shows you this dialog box.

10. Once you have selected Have Disk, you are supplying the second vital piece of information to the wizard: where to find the drivers. To Windows, the hardware devices are the drivers, so when you locate and specify the drivers used, you are setting up the device. The first file the wizard looks for will be an .inf file that will help guide the wizard through the installation.

Local Lingo

Inf file   A small text file that contains setup information about the hardware device being set up, like the names of its driver files and the locations where the drivers are to be installed.

---

11. After you have pointed Windows XP to the appropriate device drivers, follow the prompts to complete the device installation. After the drivers have been installed, the Completing the Add Hardware Wizard dialog box will summarize what has just been done. Click the Finish button to exit the Add/Remove Hardware Wizard.

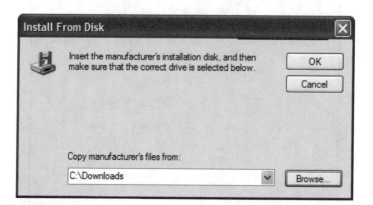

FIGURE 5.4   Make the driver selection

Managing an Installed Video Adapter

After you've installed the video card, you will configure the options of the adapter through the Display Properties dialog box. To get there, you can right-click any free space on the desktop and choose Properties. Keep in mind that you are looking at the Display applet in the Control Panel (using the Classic view) when you do so. From this dialog box, many of the options for configuring the video adapter will be on the Settings tab, shown in Figure 5-5.

You will be able to set the following options directly on this tab:

- **Color Quality** Lets you set the color depth for your adapter. The choices available on this drop-down list will be determined by the capabilities of the adapter. Most video cards today can display 16 million colors without breaking a sweat.
- **Screen Resolution** Configures the resolution of the video adapter. Be aware that not all monitors support all screen resolutions, so just because you are able to configure a given screen area here doesn't

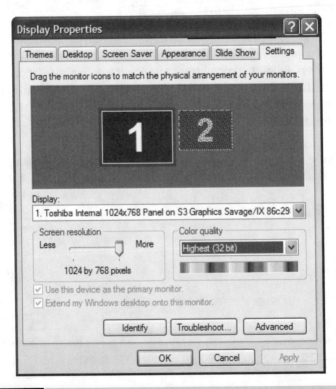

FIGURE 5.5 The Settings tab of the Display Properties dialog box

mean that you should. This is discussed further in the "Troubleshooting the Display" section later in this chapter.

When you change either of these settings, you will be shown an informational dialog box, which informs you that the settings are about to be changed temporarily. If you configure a setting that is not supported by the monitor, the monitor will return to its original settings in 15 seconds. You can accept the new settings by clicking the OK button.

To configure advanced settings for the video adapter, click the Advanced button on the Settings tab, and up pops the Monitor And Video Adapter Properties dialog box, as shown in Figure 5-6, with the General tab selected by default.

You will see at least five tabs, sometimes more, in the Advanced Properties dialog box that will let you further configure how the screen looks on your computer, as Table 5-1 indicates. Figure 5-7 is a peek at what you might expect to see on the monitor tab.

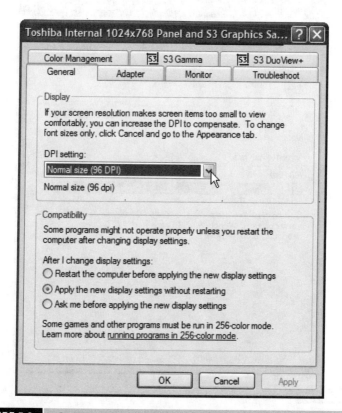

FIGURE 5.6 Setting the advanced properties of your display

TABLE 5.1	The Tabs of the Advanced Properties Dialog Box
Tab	**Lets You Configure...**
General	Font size for the display and what action Windows will take when you change the settings.
Adapter	Properties of your video adapter; the Properties button here will provide you with the Device Manager interface to the device.
Monitor	Properties of your monitor, including the refresh frequency; as a safeguard to the blank monitor situation described next, you can hide all unsupported refresh rates with the check box.
Troubleshoot	How Windows XP uses your graphics hardware.
Color Management	The color profiles used on the computer.

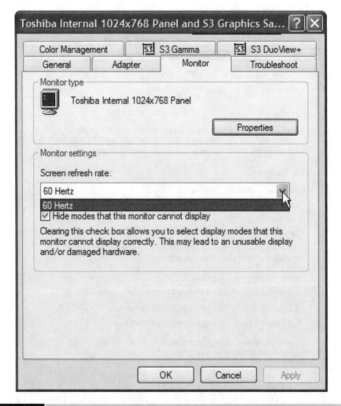

| FIGURE 5.7 | The Monitor tab |

> **Travel Advisory**
>
> Some video adapter manufacturers will write device drivers that will add a few more tabs—or even a *lot* more—on the Advanced Monitor Properties dialog box. So if you see more tabs than are mentioned here, you have one of these adapters.

You will also be able to manage the display adapter, through use of the Device Manager, a centralized hardware management interface. Because so many hardware devices can be managed with this interface, we will discuss it in the next objective when we talk about managing I/O devices as a whole.

Configure Multiple Display Support

For many Windows veterans, the display properties will look familiar. Although Windows XP sports a few display items not shown in previous Windows versions, nothing should be confusing here. What may be a new feature to some, especially if you have been using NT 4 for years, is multiple monitor support. When Windows XP multiple monitor support is configured, you can extend the working desktop to as many as ten monitors.

To support this feature, however, a motherboard must contain a Peripheral Components Interconnect (PCI) or Accelerated Graphics Port (AGP) video adapter for each monitor that will show the desktop. Most computers that run Windows XP Professional (like the one you are likely using) will have only three to five free PCI slots, and motherboards with multiple AGP slots are rare indeed.

> **Travel Assistance**
>
> PCI and AGP are technologies that define how expansion cards attach and send information to motherboards. The AGP bus was developed specifically for video cards and is a faster expansion bus compared to PCI, but current standards only allow for one AGP slot. If you have a choice, go for the AGP card as the primary adapter and then add PCI video cards. For further information about AGP, PCI, and buses in general, please refer to the Webopedia at http://www.webopedia.com.

You should be aware of a few gotchas when configuring multiple monitors on systems that have an integrated video adapter. As always, it is crucial to recognize default behavior: by default, Windows XP recognizes the first detected video adapter as the primary display adapter. The primary display adapter is the display adapter that is responsible for showing the Windows XP logon screen. It is also the default screen space responsible for displaying an application when the application is started up. You may then extend the application to the other displays. When you are using only one monitor, it is the primary display adapter.

However, if your system has a video card and an integrated adapter *before* the setup of the operating system, Windows XP will disable the integrated adapter; it changes your primary adapter, still assuming that you are going to use only one of those adapters (you haven't told it to use two adapters yet).

And when you add a second adapter *after* Windows XP is installed, the newly installed video adapter becomes the primary and the integrated adapter becomes the secondary.

Exam Tip

If your computer has an on-board video adapter and you plan to implement multiple monitors, you should *always* install Windows XP Professional on that system before you install the second video adapter.

Windows XP multiple monitor support lets you configure different settings, such as resolution and color depth, for the different monitors. You will configure multiple monitor support from the same place you already used to configure the properties of the display: the Settings tab of the Display Properties dialog box. This time, however, you should see a box on the Settings tab for every video adapter you have installed. To extend your desktop, click the number of the monitor that will be your additional display and choose the check box that says Extend My Windows Desktop Onto This Monitor, as shown in Figure 5-8.

Once you have it set up, the additional display becomes part of the Windows XP desktop, allowing you to drag and place windows back and forth between the many displays. Further, the desktop display will correspond to the arrangement of monitors you have in the Settings tab of the Display Properties. You can drag and drop to change any display's relative position. In other words, the physical arrangement of your monitors should reflect the arrangement on the Settings tab.

You can also extend a single window across multiple displays if needed.

Because your system is virtually unusable without the display adapter working properly, it is vital that you be able to troubleshoot some common problems. The next section looks at some of these everyday display difficulties and what can be done to correct them.

Troubleshooting the Display

An unreadable display or no video output is often caused by a video adapter and monitor mismatch. This commonly occurs when a new video card is placed in a system that has an older monitor. The new video card, which may have about

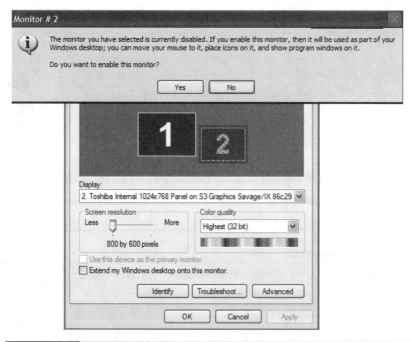

FIGURE 5.8 Multiple monitor support is a matter of a few clicks on the Settings tab.

three times as much memory as your first computer, might easily handle a 1280×1024 resolution at 80Hz, but your monitor has nowhere near the capabilities to paint a picture that detailed that fast. It's like asking the World's Fastest Man (and Kansas City's own) Maurice Green to run a race in a three-piece suit and a pair of wing tips. You aren't quite going to get the performance you expected.

I have seen just this scenario many times, and the result is that a monitor won't display anything. Sometimes the monitor will help with a message like "Outside Scan Range," but other times, nothing works. (It will usually be reported as "My monitor is broken," or "The computer has crashed.") To troubleshoot this situation, you will need to restart the computer in Safe Mode or try booting to the Last Known Good Configuration, although chances are that the former solution will be necessary to resolve the problem. Safe Mode starts Windows XP with a minimal set of drivers, including a VGA video adapter with a limited number of colors and low resolution and refresh rates. Using these Safe Mode settings, Windows XP should display a picture on any color monitor. From within Safe Mode, you can reset the display settings so that the monitor can paint a picture on the screen once again.

Travel Advisory

You must be a member of the local Administrators group to perform a hardware installation. If you are logged on to an account without administrative rights, you will be prompted for the administrator's account and password as the hardware is being set up.

Sometimes, non–Plug-and-Play capable devices will require that you configure available resources and dedicate them to that device. This will be a rare instance on a Windows XP box but one you should be aware of nonetheless. System resources needed to support such expansion devices include I/O and memory addresses, direct memory access (DMA) channels, and interrupt request (IRQ) lines.

Travel Assistance

For more information on the resources that are assigned to devices, please see *Mike Meyers' A+ Certification Passport* (McGraw-Hill/ Osborne, 2002; ISBN 007219363-8).

Objective 5.02 Configure Advanced Configuration Power Interface

If you have ever used a laptop computer, you have at some point been concerned with conserving that computer's temporary energy source, its battery pack. To help in this endeavor, most laptops have the ability to take advantage of a set of power configuration specifications called Advanced Configuration and Power Interface (ACPI). These specifications let a mobile computer put the system in Standby and Hibernate modes, reducing battery consumption when the system is not being actively used. And, although the discussion of ACPI centers mostly around laptop computers, desktop computers can take advantage of these energy saving abilities as well and significantly reduce the energy costs of large corporations. Additionally, the ACPI specifications supported under Windows XP represent a quantum leap forward from NT 4's power conservation abilities.

Windows XP Professional actually supports two power-management specifications: Advanced Power Management (APM) and the aforementioned ACPI. ACPI-compliant computers can take full advantage of reduced power consumption by controlling power requirements for Plug and Play hardware devices. ACPI is a more advanced form of power management that needs the support of both the operating system and the computer hardware. In an ACPI machine, the operating system manages all of the power requirements for your computer subsystems and peripherals. ACPI lets the operating system direct power to devices as they need it, preventing unnecessary power demands on your system.

One way to determine if a computer is ACPI-compliant is by looking in the Device Manager under the Computer node. Look under the System Devices to see if any ACPI devices are listed. If your computer supports APM, you should see an APM tab in the Power Options applet in the Control Panel.

As mentioned, with ACPI systems, the operating system is tasked with the management of power consumption. This is accomplished mostly by having things turned off when they are not in use. The monitor and hard disk are the two components that will result in the most power conservation by being shut down.

You will enable and configure APM and ACPI power options from the Power Options program in the Control Panel, as shown in Figure 5-9. The

FIGURE 5.9   Setting power options

Power Options dialog box has five tabs: Power Schemes, Alarms, Power Meter, Advanced, and Hibernate. The program will let you configure only the features that match your system's hardware capabilities. From this dialog box, you can configure the following power conservation behavior:

- Create a new power scheme or edit one that already exists
- Enable or disable Hibernation mode
- Configure power alarms and Standby mode
- Specify a UPS device and how it will behave
- Configure APM on non-ACPI computers that support APM

Travel Advisory

The Power Options dialog box automatically detects what is available on your computer and shows you only the options that you can control. If APM is not available on your system, for example, you will not see an APM tab. Likewise, you may not see a UPS tab if you don't have a UPS device installed on your machine.

Standby Mode

Putting a computer in Standby mode causes the hard drive and monitor to be shut down, and the power remains on just enough to supply the RAM with power to hold its contents. Most laptops today support, at a minimum, Standby. You usually get out of Standby with a key sequence or by pressing the CPU's power button, and one of the main advantages is that restoration of your working environment is very rapid. The drawback to Standby is that (battery) power is still used, albeit at a significantly reduced rate, but this can still cause a battery to empty if Standby is used for long periods of time.

Hibernation Mode

When a computer hibernates, it writes all of the contents of memory to a file on the hard disk and then turns the power off. Upon restart, the computer grabs the contents of the hibernation file, called hiberfil.sys, and copies it back into memory. It takes a little longer than Standby, but you can still come right back to your working space just as you left it, even though the computer has been shut off and is not consuming power. Hibernation will be available as one of the Shut Down options after you enable it in the Control Panel. Again, every computer is different, but most computers can be restored from Hibernation by hitting the power switch.

Travel Advisory

Lots of third-party tools manage power consumption, and almost every laptop manufacturer supplies its own. These third-party utilities can sometimes conflict with Windows XP's power management. Some laptops will not even let you in the Power Options dialog box, directing you instead to their own power-management software. If you are upgrading a computer that has one of these tools running, you might want to disable it so that Windows XP power support is installed, even if it is not used.

Uninterruptible Power Supply (UPS)

A UPS protects your computer from a sudden loss of electrical power (and subsequent sudden loss of your screenplay, to which you've just added a showstopper scene) by supplying backup battery power. This battery power is intended to run long enough to let you perform a safe shutdown that will save all of your current work (thus ensuring your Oscar nomination). The UPS is a safeguard; you are not meant to run your system on UPS power all the time.

Most UPS devices will be connected to a computer's serial port, although you should follow manufacturer's instructions for installation, of course. After it is physically installed, the UPS status appears on the UPS tab of the Power Options dialog box. From the UPS tab, you can configure how the computer will behave in the event of a power loss. For example, with some UPS types, you can have the system page you if the power goes off.

As with backup devices, many UPS manufacturers will ship their own proprietary configurations, which in many cases are more robust than what is offered with the Windows XP Control Panel, so you may be using a totally different interface to your UPS in the production environment.

Exam Tip

As a final note on this topic, remember that the contents of the Power Options can vary from computer to computer, especially on laptops. If you know the purpose and configuration options of the tabs discussed here, you should be able to answer any questions that will be thrown at you on the 70-270 exam.

Configuring Card Services

Another common component used with laptop computers are Personal Computer Memory Card Industry Association (PCMCIA) card devices. These cards allow laptops to change their configurations easily. The nice thing about PCMCIA cards is that they support hot swapping, which lets you exchange your cards while the computer is running. There are three types of PCMCIA card standards, and Microsoft expects you to know the differences between them:

- **Type I**   Cards can be up to 3.3 millimeters (mm) thick. Type I cards are typically used to add memory to a laptop.

- **Type II**   Cards can be up to 5 mm thick. These are the most common type of card and are typically used to add a network card or modem to a computer.

- **Type III**   Cards can be up to 10.5 mm thick. Type III cards are usually used to connect a portable hard drive.

PCMCIA card devices fully support Plug and Play and work just like any other Plug and Play device. The difference here is that you will not need to shut down the computer to add the device.

Objective 5.03 Implement, Manage, and Troubleshoot Input and Output Devices

Windows XP supports a wide variety of input/output (I/O) devices, each requiring driver installation, configuration, and (occasional, hopefully) troubleshooting to achieve proper operation. We've already taken a look at some of the most common of these I/O devices in the display adapter and disk devices. Again, the job of these I/O devices is simply to transport data in the form of electrical pulses from one place to another—or more specifically from one device to the CPU, and then from the CPU to a device.

The Device Manager

To implement and manage hardware devices successfully, you must be familiar with the use and purpose of one very important tool: the Device Manager, as shown in Figure 5-10. Fortunately, many people are already familiar with this tool, as it is pretty much the same as is has been for several years, starting with Windows 95. If you are familiar with the Device Manager and take the scenic tour of the Windows XP version, there shouldn't be too much in this Objective that will trip you up.

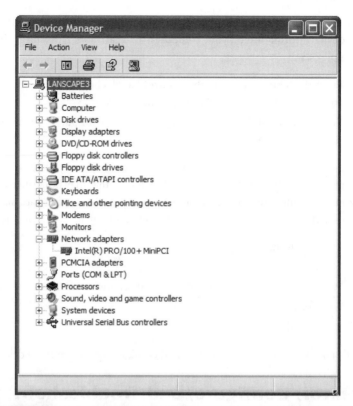

FIGURE 5.10 The Device Manager provides a "Grand Central Station" for hardware management.

The job of the Device Manager is to gather information about all the devices that have been recognized by Windows XP. It also provides an interface from which you can manage and configure these devices. We have already seen examples of Device Manager at work, and we will see more of Device Manager in Chapter 6 when we configure hardware profiles.

For each device discovered by Device Manager, the following information can be gathered:

- Whether the device is working properly
- The settings for the device
- The resources used by the device

The Device Manager also lets you update drivers and print out a report about all the device information on your computer. You can launch this utility in one of a couple of ways:

- From the System applet in the Control Panel, choose the Hardware tab and then click the Device Manager button.
- You can also run the Device Manager from the Computer Management snap-in under the System Tools node.

And while Microsoft thinks enough of the aforementioned I/O devices to devote an exam objective to each, the rest of the devices that may be connected to a particular computer are lumped into one objective. The following hardware I/O devices are also important in the day-to-day operation of any modern machine:

- Multimedia hardware
- Modems
- Wireless devices, especially Infrared Data Association (IrDA) devices
- Universal serial bus (USB) devices
- Smart cards

Let's take a closer look at installing and configuring each of these devices.

Monitor, Configure, and Troubleshoot I/O Devices

Typical multimedia devices include CD-ROM, DVD, digital camera, Musical Instrument Digital Interface (MIDI), and scanner hardware.

You are probably familiar with DVD already, and we have already discussed how to configure these devices back in Chapter 2 when we talked about disk management. You should know that the main difference between a DVD and a CD-ROM is the amount of data it can hold. DVDs are capable of storing anywhere from 8 to 40 times as much data as a standard 650MB CD-ROM. The big problem right now is that there really isn't much everyday use for this kind of static storage other than movies, and who really wants to gather the family around the *laptop* to watch ID4 or MIB? Give me a 42" flat-panel screen and a sound system that can scare off small children any day. (Really. Please give me one. They keep kicking me out of Best Buy.)

Also, as mentioned in Chapter 2, Windows XP Professional supports DVD through the automatic installation of the Universal Disk Format (UDF) file system.

Travel Advisory

UDF in Windows XP does not support write operations for DVD formats that support recording. Third-party software is necessary to record DVD media in Windows XP.

Any installed devices should appear in the Device Manager. As mentioned, you can perform many administrative tasks from here, and Administrative privileges are required to do most of them. One example of this is updating device drivers, which you won't be able to do while logged on as a regular user. If an installed device does not appear in the Device Manager, it might be missing a driver or may have been disabled or otherwise improperly configured in the BIOS.

Just as in Windows 9x, you can use the Add Hardware Wizard to add any drivers for devices that Windows XP Professional doesn't automatically detect. Unlike Windows 9x, Plug and Play usually works as advertised. The requisites are that when the hardware is detected, the drivers must exist in the driver.cab file in the Windows installation (there are thousands of drivers in this file), or the driver must be readily available on disk, usually a CD-ROM. You will also be able to use the Add/Remove Hardware interface to remove, unplug, or trouble-shoot hardware.

Exam Tip

Use the Scanners and Cameras program in the Control Panel to install a digital imaging device that was not detected by Plug and Play.

Drivers for Personal Computer/Smart Card-compliant Plug and Play smart cards and readers are included with the operating system. To use smart cards, the network must support a Public Key Infrastructure (PKI) and an Enterprise Certification Authority (CA). Of course, every computer that uses a smart card requires a smart card reader.

Travel Advisory

Windows XP supports only smart card readers that are Personal Computer/Smart Card-compliant and Plug and Play-compliant.

If a device is controlled by the BIOS and is not functioning properly, you will likely need to update the BIOS. You will be notified of devices that are not working through the Device Manager's warning and failure icons. The most common cause of this will be a resource conflict, such as one involving an IRQ line. However, resource conflicts are rare with Plug and Play devices because PnP eliminates resource conflicts by dynamically assigning resources to devices upon startup. To see which resources are in use by which device, use the Resource by Type and Resources by Connection views.

Monitor, Configure, and Troubleshoot Multimedia Hardware

Scanners and digital cameras fall under the category of imaging devices and are managed with a Control Panel applet named, appropriately enough, Scanners and Cameras. Figure 5-11 shows you the Properties dialog box of the Scanners and Cameras applet.

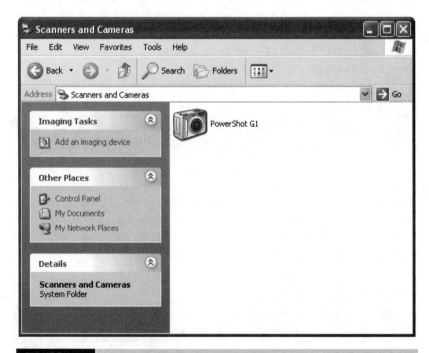

FIGURE 5.11 Manage your imaging devices here.

Scanners and digital cameras both do essentially the same thing: they take an image of something and store it as digital data that can be understood by the computer. Scanners have the capability to scan text as well but are really just working with a picture of the text.

The Scanners and Cameras Properties window only has one dialog box that lists the imaging devices currently installed on your computer. You can click the Add button to add a device, the Remove button to remove one, and the Troubleshoot button to begin using the Troubleshooting Wizard. Clicking the Properties button with the desired device selected displays a device-specific dialog box, where you can configure further options, as shown in Figure 5-12.

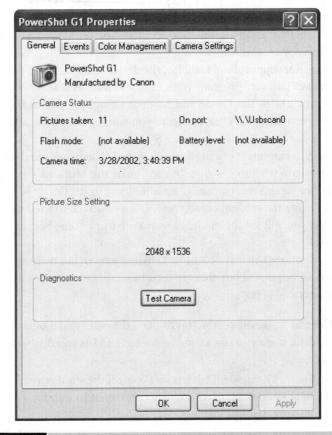

FIGURE 5.12   Configuring additional imaging options

The device-specific Properties dialog box will normally contain three tabs with the following information:

- **General** Lists the make and model of the imaging device as well as its status. You can click a button that will test the device, as you can see from Figure 5-12.
- **Events** Allows you to associate an event with an application, like automatically linking a scanned image to an application for editing.
- **Color Management** Lets you set a color profile with a given scanner or camera.

Install, Configure, and Manage Modems

Installation of modems is no different from the installation of any other device. If it supports Plug and Play, the modem should be recognized automatically and the appropriate driver installed.

If it does not support Plug and Play, the device must be set up through the Add/Remove Hardware program in the Control Panel. You will then configure the modem through the Phone and Modem Options applet in the Control Panel. When you double-click this icon, you will see the Phone and Modem Options dialog box, as shown in Figure 5-13.

To begin management of a modem, select the Modems tab and double-click the modem you wish to manage. In the figure, the Modems tab is already selected. You are also able to manage modems by using the Device Manager and double-clicking the modem object there. Once you have selected the modem to manage, you will see the modem's own Properties dialog box, as shown in Figure 5-14.

Modem options will vary according to manufacturer, but there are generally seven tabs in this dialog box that are used to modify modem behavior. These tabs are described here:

- **General** Like other tabs, this displays the make and model of the modem; it lets you run a troubleshooter, and lets you disable the device.
- **Modem** The modem tab lets you control the speaker volume, the maximum port speed, and whether or not to wait for a dial tone before dialing.
- **Diagnostics** From Diagnostics, you can perform additional troubleshooting and run a test that will check the operating system's ability to communicate with the modem.

FIGURE 5.13   The Phone and Modem Options dialog box

- **Advanced**   This tab allows you to specify additional initialization commands, configure communications port behavior that will be used to transmit and receive buffers, and manage the default call preferences.
- **Driver**   The Driver tab displays information about the currently loaded driver and allows you to update or remove the installed driver.
- **Resources**   This provides a list of the resources used by the modem, including the memory and interrupt request (IRQ) settings. It is useful if conflicts need to be resolved with non-Plug and Play devices on your computer.
- **Power Management**   From here you can set device power consumption options (for example, letting the modem bring the computer out of Standby mode so that the system can still receive an incoming fax while on Standby).

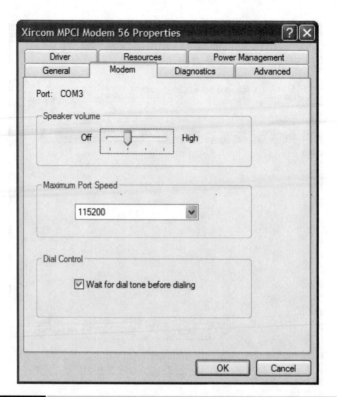

Use this dialog box to configure your modem.

Install, Configure, and Manage Infrared Data Association (IrDA) Devices

Most internal IrDA devices should be discovered and installed by Windows XP Setup automatically, or once you start Windows XP Professional after installing one of these devices. If the IrDA device is not found by either of these methods, you can always do the installation using the Add/Remove Hardware Program, as you will likely do when connecting a wireless device to a serial port. To configure your wireless device, you will use the Wireless Link program in the Control Panel. Then, from the Hardware tab, select the device you want to configure and click Properties.

Install, Configure, and Manage Wireless Devices

When you install a wireless device, you most likely want to set up a wireless LAN. Wireless LANs use radio waves to send data signals between devices, much as radio stations send audio signals between devices. In computing, a wireless network consists of two components:

- An *access point*, which serves as the hub of the wireless LAN
- *Wireless network cards*, which have built in antennas for communicating with the access point

From an installation and configuration standpoint, there's really no difference between setting up a wireless network and one using plain old Ethernet 10/100. The wireless connection will appear as a Local Network Connection in the Network Connections dialog box. You can take a peek at the Network Connections dialog box by right-clicking on My Network Places and choosing Properties.

To configure a wireless LAN connection, right-click its icon and choose Properties. You will follow the same installation guidelines that you do when setting up other hardware devices, as outlined in the previous objective.

Wireless Networks

With a wireless network, it is possible to use a wide range of devices to access data from anywhere in the world. You can transfer data over infrared connections with computers, printers, cameras, and other devices that use IrDA protocols. In addition, you can use an infrared-enabled cellular phone to make a dial-up connection to the Internet or to your corporate network.

This technology is evolving, and there are competing standards being proposed, as the monetary stakes are very high. Imagine a computer without a single cable except for the power connection. You plug it in like a toaster, and it's ready to go. Well, other people have imagined the same thing, although there is no consensus about what the wireless network should look like. Currently, there are several organizations and special interest groups working to develop standards for wireless communications.

For now, XP provides automatic network configuration that supports the IEEE 802.11 standard for networks and minimizes the configuration that is required to access networks. When you enable automatic network configuration on your computer, you can create a list of preferred networks, and you can specify the order in which to attempt connections to these networks. This automatic configuration enables you to roam across different networks without the need to reconfigure network connection settings for each location. As you move from one location to the next, the automatic configuration searches for available networks and notifies you when there are new networks available.

Install, Configure, and Manage USB Devices

The USB is an external bus that allows for the connection of USB devices through a USB port. Support of USB is necessary at both the BIOS and the operating system level, and some previous versions of Windows did not support the USB bus. Windows XP Professional does support this bus, though, and if USB is also enabled in the BIOS, you will see Universal Serial Bus Controllers listed in the Device Manager. You can then configure the USB device by double-clicking the controller to bring up its Properties dialog box, just as with any other device in Device Manager.

One of the advantages of the USB is that most of them are hot-swappable. Another advantage is its scalability. A single USB controller can support up to 127 devices simultaneously, usually with one or more USB hubs. That means that a wide variety of printers, scanners, mice, modems, and other devices can use the same USB roadway to transfer their 1's and 0's to the motherboard, and they can be plugged in and removed as easily as an Atari joystick. The bus is also capable of data transfer rates of 12 Mbps, which may not sound terribly fast today but is still faster than many network cards in use running at 10 Mbps.

Four tabs appear in the USB controller Properties dialog box that let you set the optional behavior about your controller:

- **General**   This lists the device type and the device status and allows you to disable the device with the drop-down box. You can also run a troubleshooter if the device is not working properly by clicking the Troubleshooter button.

- **Advanced**   The Advanced tab lets you play traffic cop on the USB roadway. You can configure how much bandwidth each device connected to the USB controller can use, as shown in Figure 5-15.

- **Driver**   This tab shows the driver properties and lets you remove or update the currently installed drivers.

- **Resources**   Here is a list of all the resources used by the USB controller.

Travel Advisory

Similar configuration options will exist for FireWire devices as for USB devices, although FireWire is not specifically mentioned in Microsoft's exam objectives. FireWire, in essence, is USB's next evolutionary step, another serial interface with top speeds much higher than USB's top speeds. FireWire is designed as a conduit to transfer digital video and camera images to the system.

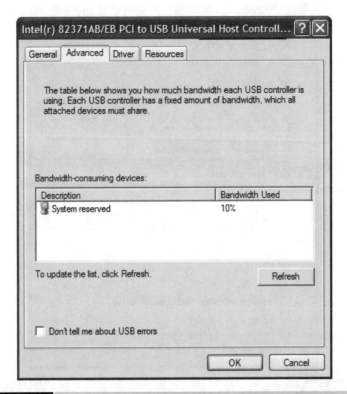

FIGURE 5.15   USB bandwidth is controlled via the Advanced tab.

Install, Configure, and Manage Network Adapters

Windows XP Professional supports many network adapter models as well as protocols and services that use the adapter hardware. As you will see, there is really no difference between installing a network interface card (NIC) and installing any other hardware device, other than a NIC's importance in network communications. A device driver for a Plug and Play network adapter is installed automatically when the operating system detects the device, and the device driver is contained in the driver.cab file on the Windows XP Professional Setup CD-ROM. Installing a device driver for a network adapter that is not Plug and Play-compatible is typically done using the Add/Remove Hardware Wizard, as discussed earlier. After a device driver is installed for a network card, protocols and services are bound to the adapter so that it can communicate on the network.

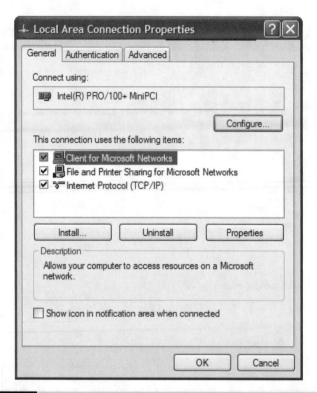

FIGURE 5.16   The Local Area Connection Properties dialog box

Once the network card has been installed, you will manage its behavior through its Local Area Connection Properties dialog box. You can access this dialog box, as shown in Figure 5-16, by right-clicking the Local Area Connection icon in My Network Places and choosing Properties.

If you click the Configure button, you'll see another Properties dialog box, which we will be dealing with here. Figure 5-17 shows you the network card's Properties dialog box, with five tabs displayed: General, Advanced, Driver, Resources, and Power Management. We will talk about each of these in the following section.

Travel Advisory

You should not need to make any changes from the network's Properties dialog box unless instructed to do so by the network card manufacturer.

FIGURE 5.17 The network card's Properties dialog box

As you've seen, there are actually several ways to bring up this dialog box; I have just outlined my personal preference. The same dialog box, for example, can be launched by finding it in Device Manager. Now let's see what is possible from each of these tabs.

- **General** This displays the name and manufacturer of the network card for quick reference. You can also enable or disable the device from here and run a Troubleshooter on a mutinous device.

- **Advanced** The contents of the Advanced tab will be specific to the adapter you are configuring. We have seen this before when configuring UPS devices. To make configuration changes from this tab, choose the property you want to modify in the left column and then the value you want to set from the drop-down box on the right.

- **Driver** The Driver tab should look pretty familiar by now. You can view the driver provider, date of manufacture, and the digital signer (the company that provided the digital signature), and you can upgrade the driver by launching the Update Driver Wizard.

- **Resources**   The Resources tab is most useful in troubleshooting circumstances, when devices are using the same computer resources. Information gathered here includes the IRQ the device is using to get the attention of the processor and the I/O settings. Figure 5-18 shows the Resources tab.

- **Power Management**   As with the Modem's Power Management options, you can configure the network card to be turned off when the computer is in low power mode or to bring the computer out of a standby state to respond to a network event.

FIGURE 5.18   The resources a device is using are displayed here.

Travel Advisory

Microsoft does not expect you to memorize IRQ lines of memory addresses, but you should know that when other devices are trying to use the same resource settings, the devices will not work properly.

Troubleshooting Network Cards

When you look at the General tab and find that the device is not working properly, what should you do? Microsoft expects you to have the answer, at least to a couple of the more common conditions that affect network card performance. Table 5-2 lists some common problems and solutions that will serve as a good starting point when troubleshooting network cards. Some of the solutions here are fairly intuitive once you know the source of the problem, but that's the hitch—the thorny part in most troubleshooting is pinpointing the cause.

TABLE 5.2	Common Problems and Solutions for Troubleshooting Network Cards
Problem	**Solution**
Network adapter not supported by Windows XP	Contact the vendor for advice or buy a new adapter that is supported (you can get one for about $20 today).
Outdated driver	Get the most current driver for the card, usually to be found on the hardware vendor's website (which you might have to access with another computer).
Adapter not recognized by Windows XP	The device might not be Plug and Play, and you will have to set it up through the Add Hardware program in the Control Panel. You should also check for resource conflicts.
Hardware not working properly	Use the diagnostics software that ships with the adapter. Rule out cabling and hub issues by testing with known goods.
Improperly configured	Configure your protocols properly.

Objective 5.04

Manage and Troubleshoot Drivers and Driver Signing

A device driver is software that acts as an intermediary between the Windows XP operating system and a specific piece of hardware. New drivers are being developed and tested all the time that add new functionality, fix bugs, or just get something to work faster. Managing device drivers involves updating these drivers when necessary and deciding how to handle drivers that have not been tested for reliability.

A number of procedures exist for updating installed drivers. Most manufacturers are in a state of constant development with drivers and will typically post new drivers to their websites for download. Further, many manufacturers include a setup routine when they distribute device drivers, and installation is simply a matter of double-clicking the setup executable. Another of the more simple ways is to use the Windows Update tool, which will update many core operating system drivers, as discussed in Chapter 1. This tool also works in reverse. If a driver needs to be removed, you can connect to the Windows Update site and follow the instructions to restore the previous configuration, or you can run the Update Wizard and Uninstall tool. This is a system tool available with the System Information snap-in.

The Upgrade Device Driver Wizard

You can update most other drivers by accessing the properties of the device in Device Manager:

1. Click the Driver tab, then click Update Driver. This will launch the Upgrade Device Driver Wizard, whose interface looks almost exactly like the Add Hardware Wizard did before.

2. Click Next, and you will see the Install Hardware Device Drivers dialog box. These dialog boxes, and almost all of the steps of the Upgrade Device Driver Wizard, look much like the Add New Hardware Wizard. You tell the Wizard where to find the new files by making your selection, as shown in Figure 5-19, and then click Next.

3. The next dialog box asks you where to find the updated drivers. You can have the Wizard look on a floppy or CD-ROM, search the network, or use the Microsoft Update utility. Make your selection based on where the files are and click Next.

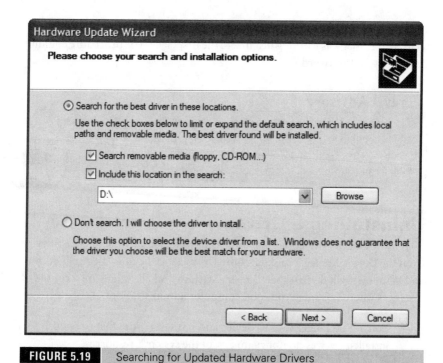

FIGURE 5.19 Searching for Updated Hardware Drivers

4. The Driver Files Search dialog box appears, letting you confirm the location and filename of the driver to be installed. Click Next if the appropriate driver is selected, and the driver installation process will begin. When finished, the Completing the Upgrade Device Driver Wizard dialog box appears.

Rolling Back a Driver to a Previous Version

So that new driver doesn't work *exactly* like you planned. Is there anything you can do short of uninstalling the device drivers and starting over? With XP, there is.

You probably noticed in Figure 5-17 a button on the device's Properties dialog box called Roll Back Driver. This button is new to XP and represents a much easier way to return to a working driver installation than the uninstall/reinstall method mentioned earlier, the only way available with prior versions of Windows.

So with a single-click, you can banish any ill-behaved new driver and go back to the driver that was working just fine in the first place. The procedure couldn't be more straightforward.

Travel Advisory

It is recommended, and sometimes mandatory, that a rollback be performed while booted to Safe Mode. Further, you can only rollback if an update has been performed (otherwise there's nothing to roll back to) and can only roll back one level of driver update.

Uninstalling a Driver

To remove a device driver permanently from your system, double-click a device from the Device Manager and select the Driver tab. Click the Uninstall button, and Windows will do just that, registry settings and all. There are a couple of instances where this might be good computer administration:

- You are no longer using a device and want to ensure that previously installed devices do not claim any of the system's resources.
- You are concerned that the drivers, when installed, cause your system to become unstable.
- You don't feel confident with a rolled-back driver either and want to start over from scratch.

Driver Signing

In the past, Microsoft has blamed operating system issues on poorly written drivers that cause conflicts, usually in the area of memory. These conflicts will prevent a device from working properly and can even cause the operating system to crash. (I'm sure that the writers of the bad drivers have their own view of what's poorly written, but that's another debate.)

One of Microsoft's answers to drivers that cause mischief on a system has been the Hardware Compatibility List (HCL), a list of hardware devices that have earned the Microsoft stamp of approval after being tested by the folks in Redmond. Installing devices that appear on the HCL is discussed in Chapter 1.

One of the other mechanisms that's newly available is driver signing, a signature that's associated with a driver installation file that certifies that it has been tested in Microsoft's Windows Hardware Quality Lab and is therefore safe for installation. It is easy to spot a driver that has been signed, as it will be marked with a little icon that looks like a diploma with a check mark beside it, as shown in Figure 5-20.

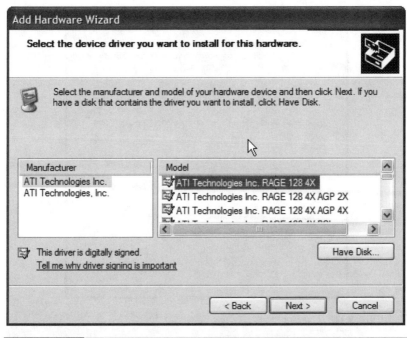

FIGURE 5.20 The signed drivers will be easily identifiable even before installation.

You will be able to specify how Windows XP Professional will respond to unsigned drivers through the Driver Signing Options dialog box, found on the Hardware tab of the System Properties dialog box. When you click the Driver Signing button, you can set three levels of behavior before the driver is installed: Ignore, Warn, and Block, as seen in Figure 5-21. The default is set to warn you when drivers are unsigned, giving you the option of whether on not to perform the install.

There is yet another layer of faulty driver protection offered with Windows XP, and it works like a "bad check" list at a local merchant. It's called Windows Driver Protection, and it prevents the installation of any drivers that are known to cause serious problems. Windows keeps this list of specific problem drivers in a database, and that database is consulted when you launch the Add Hardware Wizard. If the driver you are installing matches one listed in the database, you will see multiple dialog boxes explaining that, in effect, the driver will not be installed because of the stability problems it causes.

FIGURE 5.21   Driver signing options—notice the default

Objective 5.05

Monitor and Configure Multiprocessor Computers

The Windows XP operating system kernel is scalable in that it is able to use multiple processors to execute processes and threads. Windows XP Professional includes support for one or two processors. Even though they are supported in Windows XP Professional, you will typically use multiprocessor machines with installations of .NET or 2000 Server and, more specifically, on application servers like Web or database servers, because of the processor-intensive nature of applications that can be running on a server. Typical Professional front-end applications, like Microsoft Access or Internet Explorer, are not considered processor-intensive when compared to back-end applications like SQL Server or Internet Information Server (IIS). Of course, you won't be running SQL or fully-functional installations of IIS on your XP Professional system, but there are still occasions where two processors are merited. One example would be in the case of a graphics-rendering program.

Local Lingo

Scalable   A catch-all term that simply means adding more without changing how the thing works. Lots of things are described as scalable, like Active Directory or TCP/IP. TCP/IP is scalable because it works just as well for a two-workstation network as it does for a 2 million-workstation network. In this case, the addition of more than one processor makes the Windows kernel scalable.

Support for multiple processors is provided by the hardware abstraction layer (HAL), a hardware-specific operating system component. Different computers will use different HALs. The function of the HAL is to isolate the rest of the Windows XP operating system from the underlying hardware. If you want to implement a system with multiple processors, you typically need to upgrade the HAL. To do this, you must go to the computer device Properties dialog box in the Device Manager. You will then upgrade the HAL with the Upgrade Device Driver Wizard. Upgrading to an incompatible HAL is likely to cause a critical system failure.

Travel Advisory

This procedure upgrades only the driver on your computer. If your system has only one processor, upgrading the HAL isn't going to suddenly make it a multiple processor computer. In fact, if you have a HAL that supports two processors on a computer that only has one processor; the computer will likely be able to process instructions about as well as a doorstop.

Uniprocessor computers contain the simple Programmable Interrupt Controller (PIC) hardware, referred to as Standard PC in Device Manager. The HAL for a computer containing ACPI and PIC hardware is not upgradeable to the HAL for a PIC computer that is not ACPI-compliant.

Managing SMP Computers with the Performance Console

Once you install your second processor, you will use the Performance Console to monitor your new symmetric multiprocessing (SMP) system. Performance monitoring establishes a baseline of satisfactory performance and then continues to monitor the system to identify bottlenecks that impact performance. The following are the primary processor-specific objects to monitor:

- **Processor**   Counters that monitor each processor individually
- **System**   Counters that monitor all processors as a single unit
- **Process**   Counters that monitor each application process running on the processors

The Performance Console will be explored in much greater detail in Chapter 6. Stay tuned.

Local Lingo

Symmetric multiprocessing (SMP)   A description of the methodology involved when multiple processors execute the instructions of an application. With SMP, all processors share the same memory space and work on the same copy of an application. SMP's cousin is *asymmetric multiprocessing* (ASMP), in which each processor can operate on independent tasks. For example, one processor could be dedicated to operating system instructions and the other processor could handle applications. Windows XP supports SMP, not ASMP.

Using Task Manager to Manage SMP

Another important tool for multiprocessor systems is the Task Manager, which will be used to verify that the second processor has been recognized by the operating system. Probably more importantly, you can also configure the use of multiple processors through the Task Manager. On the Processes tab, you will associate each processor with the processes that are running on the computer. This configuration of processes to run across multiple processors is called *processor affinity*, and you won't be able to configure this for just any old application. To take advantage of two or more processors, a process has to be *multithreaded*.

To set processor affinity, right-click the process you want to associate with a specific processor and select the Processor Affinity option. Then, from the Processor Affinity dialog box, select the specific processor that you want the process to execute on and click OK.

Local Lingo

Multithreaded   Multithreaded processes have distinct units of execution, called *threads*, which can be configured to execute at the same time across two or more processors.

CHECKPOINT

✔**Objective 5.01: Implement, Manage, and Troubleshoot Display Devices**   We looked at some ways to manage the display of Windows XP Professional, including the capability to add video adapters and extend the desktop across multiple monitors. Further, this objective was used to examine the hardware installation in general, as many of the lessons here apply no matter what hardware device is installed.

✔**Objective 5.02: Configure Advanced Configuration Power Interface**   In this section, we noted many of the technologies that make Windows XP Professional an excellent choice for laptop computers. Included in this section was a discussion of the various power management options available. The power saving options of Hibernate and Standby were discussed as ways to help mobile computers conserve battery power.

✔**Objective 5.03: Implement, Manage, and Troubleshoot Input and Output Devices**   We looked at ways to install and configure input and output devices that are not covered specifically by other objectives. These I/O devices included wireless and USB devices, cameras and scanners, and even handheld devices. We also looked at how to get network cards and modems up and running so that a Windows XP Professional computer can take advantage of networking.

✔**Objective 5.04: Manage and Troubleshoot Drivers and Driver Signing**   We looked at the process for updating the device drivers for the many hardware components of our system. We defined what a driver does and then walked through the Update Driver Wizard, which helped us make the driver updates.

✔**Objective 5.05: Monitor and Configure Multiprocessor Computers**   Because Windows XP Professional can take advantage of multiple processors, we need to know how this is done should the occasion arise. We looked at issues such as upgrading the HAL and setting processor affinity for currently executing processes.

REVIEW QUESTIONS

1. You have assembled a Pentium 4 system that includes an AGP-slot video adapter. You run Windows XP Professional Setup, and the adapter is detected and driver installation occurs automatically. You are unhappy, however, with the default refresh rate and want to change this to reduce eye strain. What should you do to change this?

   A. Use the Refresh Rate node of the Computer Management MMC snap-in.

   B. Use the Monitor tab in the Display Adapter Advanced Options dialog box.

   C. Open Computer Management and access the Device Manager.

   D. Refresh rates are set by the video card manufacturer and cannot be changed.

2. You have just purchased a new computer that shipped with an installation of Windows XP Professional. The motherboard came with an onboard display adapter, but you have another video adapter and want to use this second adapter to extend your desktop across two monitors. What do you need to do? (Choose all that apply.)

   A. Install Windows XP after installing the second video adapter.

   B. Install Windows XP before installing the second video adapter.

   C. Ensure that the motherboard adapter is multidisplay-compatible.

   D. Ensure that the motherboard adapter is configured as the primary adapter.

3. You have recently upgraded a system from Windows 98 to Windows XP Professional. You want to tweak some of the power options, and you open the Power Options program in the Control Panel. When you do, you notice that no APM tab is displayed. Why might this be? (Choose all that apply.)

   A. APM is disabled in the BIOS.

   B. The computer does not have an APM-compliant system board.

   C. The computer has an ACPI-compliant system board.

   D. The computer does not have a smart UPS device connected to the serial port.

4. There are several ways to install a modem on a computer running Windows XP Professional. From the following list, which ones will work? (Choose three.)

   A. Use Device Manager.

   B. Plug in a Plug and Play modem.

   C. Use the Mail and Fax program in the Control Panel.

   D. Use the Add/Remove Hardware tool in Control Panel.

   E. Use the Add/Remove Modems and Network Devices tool in the Control Panel.

   F. Use the Phone and Modem Options program in the Control Panel.

5. You have a digital camera that you want to hook up to your system to save pictures to the hard drive. Your system is running Windows XP Professional, and the camera supports a USB connection. You connect the two devices together, but Windows does not install the digital camera device. What is the first thing you should investigate?

   A. USB support is disabled in the BIOS.

   B. USB support is disabled by default in Windows XP Professional.

   C. The USB port is damaged.

   D. The device is not supported by Windows XP. You need to get an updated driver from the manufacturer.

6. You attach an IrDA transceiver to a serial port for the transfer of information between your system and a handheld device. The computer is running Windows XP Professional, but you notice that the transceiver is not automatically installed. What should you do to install and enable the IrDA device?

   A. Use the Wireless Link program in the Control Panel.

   B. Use the Add/Remove Hardware program in the Control Panel.

   C. Use the Add/Remove Programs program in the Control Panel.

   D. Windows XP Professional does not support IrDA devices connected to a serial port.

7. You have a system running Windows XP Professional. You have recently noticed an updated driver is available for the video adapter on the manufacturer's website, and have downloaded the new driver. What tool will you now use to update the video driver?

   A. Device Manager

   B. The Add/Remove Hardware Wizard

    C. The Installed Drivers program in the Control Panel

    D. The Devices and Drivers node in Computer Management

8. You have a Windows 98 computer. The hard disk on this system has just failed. You decide that because the disk is unrecoverable, you will just punt and replace the disk and install Windows XP Professional on the new hard drive. As you are performing this task, one of the drivers for the system is not automatically installed by Windows XP. Which conditions might require a manual installation of drivers? (Choose all that apply.)

    A. An error occurs during installation.

    B. The driver package is not digitally signed.

    C. The driver installation process requires a user interface to be displayed.

    D. The driver package does not contain all files needed to complete the installation.

9. You have a system running Windows XP Professional, and the motherboard supports a single processor. Because of the load on this machine, you decide to upgrade to a motherboard that supports two processors a few months later. How will you now configure the new XP Professional machine to evenly distribute the processing load across the two processors?

    A. Recompile the operating system components that you want to use the two processors.

    B. Upgrade the HAL from Device Manager.

    C. Windows XP Professional does not support multiple processors.

    D. Do nothing. Windows XP Professional will automatically start to use the two processors for applications that are multithreaded.

10. Windows XP Professional supports a certain type of multiprocessing on systems with multiple CPUs. What kind of multiprocessing is this?

    A. Symmetric multiprocessing (SMP)

    B. Asymmetric multiprocessing (ASMP)

    C. Both SMP and ASMP

    D. None of the above

REVIEW ANSWERS

1. **B**   You will configure the display settings in the Monitor tab of the Advanced Options dialog box. This tab provides information about the model of monitor detected and the monitor's properties. You configure the refresh frequency from there.

2. **B** **C**   When Windows XP is installed on a computer with a single integrated video adapter, a driver will be loaded for the onboard device. To install a second video adapter, first shut down the computer and physically install the second video card in an AGP or PCI slot. After Windows starts again, the second adapter will be detected and the driver will be installed. As long as the BIOS is not configured to disable the motherboard video adapter, you will now be able to configure multiple displays. Some motherboard video adapters, however, do not support multiple monitor displays. Laptop computers, for example, often have video adapters that are disabled when connected to a docking station that has a video card.

3. **B** **C**   A computer without an APM-compliant BIOS, or a computer that supports ACPI, will not have an APM tab in the Power Options Properties dialog box. Windows XP can still provide limited power management features, like disk and monitor power control, but there will be no APM tab from which to configure this behavior. ACPI functions are fully controlled by the operating system and are automatic. You can change individual power management settings in the Power Options Properties dialog box, but you cannot enable and disable system ACPI support.

4. **B** **D** **F**   After connecting a Plug and Play modem to the computer, the Install New Modem screen appears (it is actually part of the Add/Remove Hardware Wizard) and automatically detects the modem. If a modem cannot be detected, you are prompted to select the appropriate model. You will usually have to point to a driver location, and an .inf (information) file will be read to present the list of devices to set up. From the Add/Remove Hardware Wizard, you can select the Add A New Device option on the Choose A Hardware Device dialog box. After selecting an option and clicking Next, you can either search for new hardware or select one from an existing list. From here, the process will look similar to adding a Plug and Play device. Clicking Add in the Modems tab in the Phone and Modem Options dialog box

opens the Install New Modem screen of the Add/Remove Hardware Wizard.

5. **A** This question is a bit tricky, because it asks the first thing you should suspect. It is possible that the device is not supported by Windows XP or that the USB port is damaged, but it would be best to start with a check of the BIOS here. As USB is a relatively new interface, and Windows XP Professional will support most devices that use it. You are more likely to run into problems with older devices.

6. **B** Serial ports are an older interface developed before the days of Plug and Play, so it's unlikely that devices attached to a serial port will be detected automatically and installed. You are more likely to expect this behavior on a USB-connected device (see question 5). In this case, you should use the Add/Remove Hardware Wizard to locate and install the IrDA device.

7. **A** You can update drivers through a variety of methods, but Device Manager is the only valid choice in this question. The last two are fictional utilities. To update a driver, access the properties of the device from Device Manager and then, from the Driver tab, click Update Driver to begin the driver upgrade process.

8. **A B C D** All these conditions will cause automatic driver installation to be skipped, requiring a manual install of a driver. Some devices use a device driver interface that is separate from the Windows XP Professional Setup routine.

9. **B** You are assuming that the computer here is capable of supporting a second processor. To change the installed HAL, start Device Manager, expand the Computer node, and access the Properties dialog box for the Computer node. From there, click the Update Driver button to start the Upgrade Device Driver Wizard.

10. **A** SMP is a multiprocessor architecture in which all processors share the same memory space, containing a single copy of the operating system and one copy of each running application. The Windows XP Professional kernel divides the instructions that need to be processed into distinct units called threads, and two threads can be sent to each processor simultaneously for execution.

Monitoring and Optimizing System Performance and Reliability

CHAPTER 6

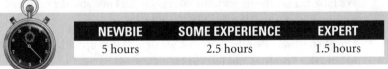

	NEWBIE	SOME EXPERIENCE	EXPERT
	5 hours	2.5 hours	1.5 hours

267

There are several management tasks that fall under the umbrella of keeping your XP installation in good working order, and this chapter focuses on a number of them. These management tasks include:

- **Scheduling Tasks**   To reduce the amount of time spent actually administering a computer, Windows XP, like previous versions of Windows, has included the Scheduled Tasks utility. With this utility, you can leverage the computer's capability to never forget when routine housekeeping tasks need to be performed, allowing you to turn your attention to more pressing jobs.

- **Measuring Performance**   Unless we know what is normal, we can't really say if a machine is being pushed beyond its limits. We will look at the tools and techniques used to quantify just what is happening to a system, and from there determine what adjustments, if any, need to be made.

- **Using Offline Files**   To reduce confusion when using a laptop computer to update files, XP is capable of working with Offline Files. With Offline Files, you can work with files from a central location, whether or not the network connection to that location is actually present. The Offline Files feature reduces the time spent shuffling files from one computer to another and can therefore help make laptop use as efficient as possible. In this section, we also look at how to best configure the Power Options when using laptops on battery power.

- **Backup and Recovery**   You may find this hard to believe, but computers of every ilk have been known to crash. If this occurs, there are a couple of wonderful utilities Microsoft provides to recover your working environment. These tools are examined in this chapter. We look here at the importance of regular backups and the different variety of backups that can be performed.

- **Use of Hardware Profiles**   Finally, we wrap things up with a discussion of hardware profiles and look at how they can be used to enhance problem-free operation. The Hardware Profiles feature tells your system to use certain hardware devices in one configuration and other devices in alternate configurations. It is also best suited for laptop computers.

Monitor, Optimize, and Troubleshoot Performance of the Windows XP Professional Desktop

Objective 6.01

In order to keep your XP Professional installations running in tip-top shape, there are a number of tasks that need to be run on a continuing basis. And, to facilitate this with the least amount of administrative overhead, Windows provides the capability to automate these tasks. To optimize performance, administrators need a mechanism to quantify if a system is running slowly, and XP provides a number of tools that accomplish this goal. This first objective more closely investigates these technologies.

Configure, Manage, and Troubleshoot Scheduled Tasks

Windows XP includes two utilities, the Scheduled Task Wizard and the Schtasks command-line utility, that make use of the Task Scheduler service. As you probably have guessed, the job of the Task Scheduler is to allow you to configure operation of tasks to run at specified intervals. You can have Windows XP Professional run any program, script, or document at a predefined time—which can be every day, week, month, or even when the computer starts up or when a user logs on. Common uses of Scheduled Tasks include regular backups, virus scans, and disk cleanup. You can even use the Scheduled Tasks utility to run tasks at remote computers.

Scheduled Tasks

Starting and configuring a task to run using the Scheduled Task Wizard is straightforward. You launch the program with the applet located in the Control Panel (using the Classic view, as we have most of the time in this book) or choose Start | All Programs | Accessories | System Tools | Scheduled Tasks. The Scheduled Tasks window appears, as shown in Figure 6-1.

1. From the Scheduled Tasks window, you can access a task to configure by double-clicking the Add Scheduled Task icon. The Scheduled Task Wizard will then lead you through the steps to create a scheduled task.

| **FIGURE 6.1** | The Scheduled Tasks window |

2. Click Next to see the tasks that can be run, as shown in Figure 6-2. You can select a job from the list of applications presented here or browse for another, even one stored on a remote computer.

3. In the next couple of dialog boxes, you will be asked to specify exactly when you want the task to run. Depending on the frequency of the task, you will be given the options to further modify the schedule in your time frame.

4. The final dialog box summarizes your Scheduled Task selections. Verify that the information is correct, click Finish, and the task will be saved with a .job file extension and added to your Scheduled Tasks window.

If at any time you change your mind about how and when you want the scheduled task to run, no problem. You can manage the properties of that task whenever you like in the Scheduled Tasks program by right-clicking the task and choosing Properties.

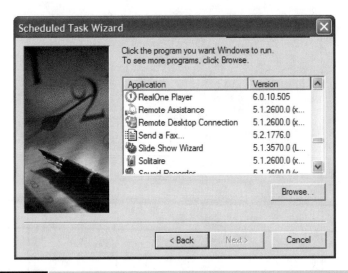

FIGURE 6.2 Choosing which task to run

The task's Properties dialog box has three tabs with an optional Security tab that appears only on an NTFS partition. You can use these tabs for managing and modifying how the task is to run, including a tab that lets you specify who can further manage the task. Let's take a look at these configuration options.

- **Task** Here you configure the command-line program that actually runs the task, enter comments for informational purposes (helpful if other people will be managing the scheduled task), and add the user name and password that will be used to represent this task when the program is run. This information is vital because many common administrative tasks require a higher level of rights than a normal user account typically has. Finally, you can even disable the task without deleting it by clearing a single check box. The task is enabled by default. Figure 6-3 shows the Task tab.

- **Schedule** The Schedule tab, shown in Figure 6-4, is where you can modify when the task is run. When you change the option in the Schedule Task drop-down box, the rest of the options change accordingly.

- **Settings** The Settings tab assists with housekeeping details such as allowing you to delete a task if it is not to be run again or stopping the task if it takes too long to complete. The Idle Time section is useful

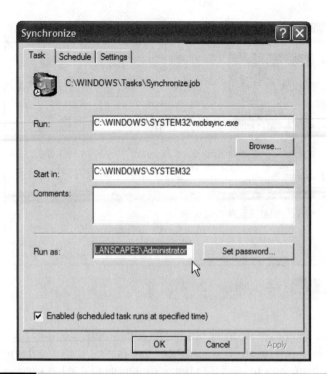

FIGURE 6.3 The Task tab of the Properties dialog box

if the computer must be idle for the task to run. You can specify that the task be stopped if the computer is not idle. The Power Management section comes in handy if the task runs, or may be run, on a computer that is battery-powered. Figure 6-5 shows the options configurable from the Settings tab.

- **Security** The Security tab will appear only if Windows XP is installed on an NTFS partition. Normally, only administrators can manage Scheduled Tasks. You may occasionally want to assign the task to other users, and those users may need permissions to run the task. The Security tab contains an Access Control List (ACL) of who can manage the task, and the management of this list is no different than managing access to folders and files, as discussed in Chapter 3.

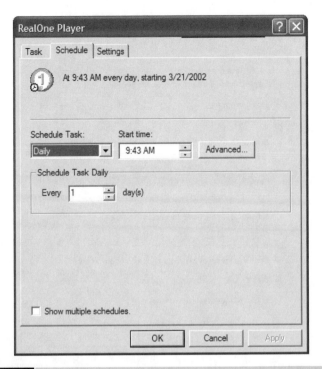

FIGURE 6.4 The Schedule tab

Travel Advisory

If you have scheduled tasks to run for particular accounts, they will not run if the switch to another user is made using Fast User Switching. Logon tasks only run when a user logs on while all other users are logged off.

While the Scheduled Tasks utility provides an easy, intuitive, wizard-based method of setting up tasks, Windows XP offers another way to schedule tasks by using the command line. This method can be especially effective when scheduling a task to run on a remote computer over a slow WAN link. This can be an important administrative task in enterprise environments and therefore makes for "target-rich" test subject matter. The next section looks at the specifics of the Schtasks utility.

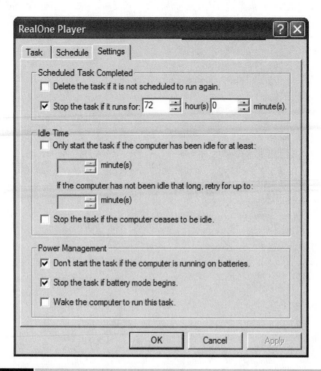

FIGURE 6.5   The Settings tab

Scheduling with the Schtasks Utility

The Schtasks lets you do the same thing that the Scheduled Tasks does: configure, modify, delete, view, and run scheduled tasks, either on your computer or
on others on the network. The main difference is the interface; Schtasks uses the
Command Prompt.

Travel Advisory

You can still use that venerable sawhorse, the AT command, which allows you to
schedule tasks to run, quite literally, at a certain time. Tasks scheduled from the
AT command appear as normal scheduled tasks in the Scheduled Tasks folder.
You can even edit the AT tasks from within the Scheduled Tasks
window, but be aware that when you do, they are "annexed"
by the Scheduled Tasks program and can no longer be deleted
from the command line.

If you've got an extra hour or so on your hands and thrill to the reading of help files, I invite you to perform a search on the Schtasks utility in the Help and Support Center. When you expand the individual commands, the documentation runs to nearly 20 pages of text. However, as with many utilities, you don't have to memorize all the minutiae of syntax in order to use it effectively. There are six main switches used with the Schtasks that you need to be familiar with, which I have summarized in substantially *fewer* than 20 pages here. (Hey, that's what makes this book one of the planet's best bargains, right up there with the postage stamp and the daily newspaper. Please feel free to send your praise to the e-mail address in the front of this book.) All Schtasks commands can, and will, be used with a series of arguments, or switches, that specify exactly what to do. The six main switches are:

- **Schtasks/Create**   This switch creates a new scheduled task. It has an extensive list of arguments that are used in conjunction with it, which gives this command all the scheduling flexibility of the Scheduled Tasks utility.
- **Schtasks /Change**   The Change switch lets you modify an existing task. You can change the program that the scheduled task runs as well as the user account and password under which the task runs.
- **Schtasks /Run**   This starts a task to begin immediately, in total disregard of the schedule.
- **Schtasks /End**   Do I really have to say? It halts a program that's been started by a scheduled task.
- **Schtasks /Delete**   This deletes…well, you've got the hang of it now. In addition to vaporizing a specific task, it can be used to delete all tasks for a given computer.
- **Schtasks /Query**   This switch displays all the scheduled tasks on a computer, including those created by other users. This is the command-line equivalent of looking at the Scheduled Tasks window.

As mentioned, these switches require a series of arguments, or parameters, in order for them to actually do anything. Here's one that you will find *very* helpful when first using the Schtasks command: the /?, the stalwart tour guide through the command environment. The use of the /? parameter with one of the switches will show you proper syntax for the switch, like this:

```
Schtasks /create /?
```

There are several improvements offered by the Schtasks utility over the AT command. These advantages include the following:

- Schtasks lets you specify tasks using a friendly name rather than the serial ID number, as needed by the AT command.
- It offers many more options in configuring schedules than does AT.
- With Schtasks, you can view, modify, or end existing scheduled tasks.

Here's an example of how the Schtasks syntax would work in setting up a task.

```
Schtasks /create /tn "Musical Interlude" /tr \Program Files\Real\
RealOne Player\realplay.exe /sc hourly /mo 2 /st 08:30:00
```

In the preceding command, the /tn parameter specifies the task's name, /tr specifies the executable and the path to it, /sc dictates the schedule to be used (in this case, hourly), /mo is the modifier (here configuring the task to run every two hours), and /st is the start time (specified in the 24-hour clock format). This task is set to begin at 8:30 A.M. and run every two hours.

Travel Advisory

The Schtasks command is only available to members of the local machine's Administrators group. Users who are not among this elite will be scolded, "Access is Denied," when attempting to use Schtasks.

The tasks configured this way will also appear in the Scheduled Tasks window, but they are further managed from the command line. You can modify Schtasks-configured tasks with the Scheduled Tasks applet, but be aware of what happens if you do. If you modify a task with Scheduled Tasks that has been originally scheduled with the Schtasks command, Scheduled Tasks will remove the task from the Schtasks job list and make it a Scheduled Task.

Either interface lets you schedule, reschedule, disable, or remove a task. The Scheduled Tasks interface is just a bit more user friendly. Okay, a *lot* more user friendly.

Travel Advisory

It is possible to configure certain jobs to run on a schedule through other interfaces, like the Windows Backup utility. However, even though the jobs are scheduled with a different program, they still rely on the Task Scheduler service to launch successfully. In other words, when you're scheduling a backup job with the Backup utility, you're still using the Task Scheduler.

Task Management

There are a few methods you should be familiar with to help manage scheduled tasks. One of the most straightforward is to use the Details view of the Scheduled Tasks utility. If you refer back to Figure 6-1, you will see that this is not the view I have chosen. To look at the details of your tasks, choose View | Details (alternatively, you could right-click in the window and do the same). The Details view will provide several items of useful information about a task, such as when the task was last run, when the next time it's scheduled to run, and the user who created the task.

Another way to manage scheduled tasks is by reviewing which tasks the Task Scheduler service has attempted to start. As mentioned, you can manage an individual task by accessing its Properties dialog box. This places a summary of potential management changes at your fingertips.

If a task fails to run, the Details view will report that fact to you, but it cannot tell you the reason why the task failed. In order to review more detailed results, you need to look at the contents of the Task log, which is stored in the *systemroot* directory and is called SCHEDLGU.TXT. When problems are encountered during Scheduled Task operation, the log file can be an important troubleshooting aid. The log file is the best tool to help you pinpoint exactly why a task is not running. View a log file, as shown in Figure 6-6, by choosing Advanced | View Log from the Scheduled Tasks window.

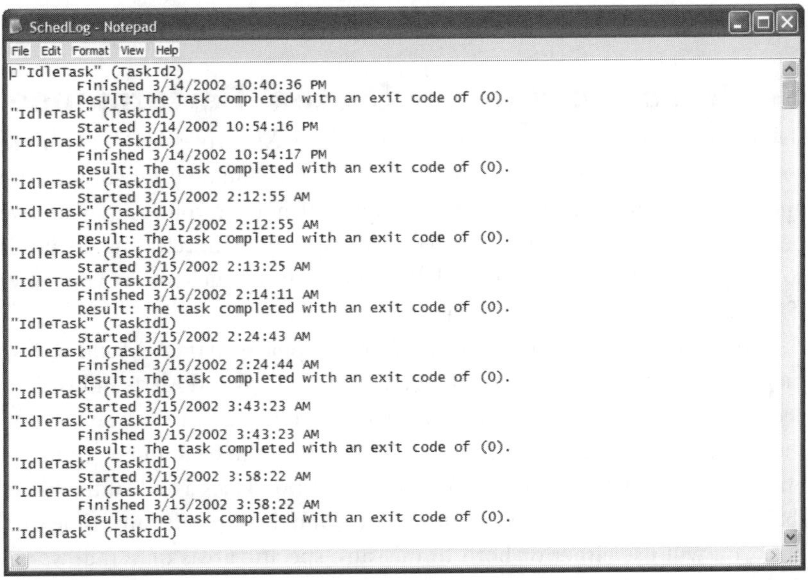

FIGURE 6.6 Viewing the Scheduled Tasks log

Other important management tasks can be configured from the Scheduled Tasks Advanced drop-down menu, including notification options when a task is missed. Further, you can pause and resume the Task Scheduler service and configure the user account context for tasks scheduled with the AT command (remember, tasks set up with the AT command will appear in this window, too). The user context configuration is especially important, because everything that happens in the Windows XP operating system—including scheduled tasks that run without intervention—happens in the context of a user account.

Exam Tip

A task cannot be scheduled, run, or modified if the Task Scheduler service is stopped. (Check under the Services node from Computer Management for the Task Scheduler Service; the service runs automatically in the background, by default.) It must be either running or paused.

One of the mechanisms for optimizing performance is the scheduling of routine tasks, as we have just seen. Scheduling routine administrative tasks to run automatically helps to ensure that our systems are kept in good working order and that our critical data is always backed up. Another important goal of optimizing the performance of XP is to make sure the system components are working at their optimal levels. To do so, we first must determine what is normal for a system; the next section of this objective will describe the tools necessary to accomplish this.

Setting a Baseline for System Performance

Before optimizing the performance of Windows XP Professional, you need some way of measuring current performance. You should be able to measure and quantify your performance observations, if not for your administrative benefit, then at least for the people who are responsible for releasing the funds so that your system can be upgraded. (See, look at how much money you'll *save* if you let me buy that new 2GHz laptop!)

Two tools that ship with Windows XP Professional help track system performance: the System Monitor and the Performance Logs and Alerts utility. You access both of these tools through the preconfigured Performance snap-in on the Microsoft Management Console (MMC), which can be found by choosing Start | Programs | Administrative Tools. This section takes a look at the use of these two tools and what they can be used for, and then spends some time with how you will use either or both to measure specific areas of Windows XP desktop performance.

Before you can accurately quantify *abnormal* use on your system, you have to go about defining *normal* use. This process of appraising normal use is also known as *establishing a baseline*.

> ### Local Lingo
>
> **Benchmarking**   Sometimes establishing a baseline is described as *benchmarking* a system. No matter what you call it, the question answered by the process is the same: what is normal for this machine?

In real-world use, there is probably no great need to establish baselines for each and every one of your enterprise's computers. You should certainly do this, however, on any servers that will form the backbone of your network, because if these machines perform poorly, so will your entire network. You should especially measure baselines at the following times:

- When the computer is first brought online and begins operation—this lets you accurately state what users should expect from a system.
- When any changes are made to the hardware or software configuration— this lets you measure the effect made by any upgrades.

The reason that baselines are useful for the preceding situations is self-evident: when any changes are made to the system, you will have something to which you can compare the changes. Like a weight-loss advertisement, you will create a "before" snapshot that you can compare to the "after." Good administrative practice is to make sure baselines have been created *before* making any changes to your Windows XP Professional computer.

Another way these two tools are used is to identify a *bottleneck*. A bottleneck is any system resource that causes slowdowns to the computer system as a whole. Bottlenecks cause slowdowns by causing other resources to sit around waiting while the source of the bottleneck completes its task. The thing you need to keep in mind about bottlenecks is that there's *always* a bottleneck. The computer won't send its data from component to component at the speed of light. (Not for now; they will someday. I won't go into the Feynman-esque details of this—not that I could articulate it without sounding like a couch potato cartoon character anyway—but scientists in recent experiments have demonstrated the ability to send music from one place to another *faster* than the speed of light. But that is another book, by a different author...)

The point is this: upgrading a component to resolve a bottleneck in one area can shift the focus of a bottleneck to another area. It's just a matter of finding and resolving the ones that are causing a noticeable degradation of performance. Same thing happens when you buy a new pair of shoes: as soon as you throw 'em in your closet, your old ones in there don't look so great anymore.

The other monitoring duty you have is to proactively find *trends* that are occurring on a system. This job goes hand in hand with the creation of baselines and is really nothing more than comparing multiple baselines against one another to determine whether usage patterns emerge. For example, suppose you are taking snapshots of normal usage for one day per month, and the log files show that CPU usage is increasing by about five percent each time you measure. You can then assume that after eight months, your CPU usage will increase by 40 percent—and you're going to have problems. By tracking trends, you can proactively take steps to ensure that certain performance problems never occur.

Using the System Monitor

A picture is worth a thousand words, and the System Monitor helps you create pictures from the data that is collected during monitoring. I cannot overstate the following: a good comprehension of the System Monitor will be crucial to your ability to measure performance baselines and determine where bottlenecks occur. There are other software tools that will assist in this effort, but System Monitor is the one that ships with Windows XP, and it is the one you will be expected to have seen as you sit for the exam.

The System Monitor is part of the Performance Console, which lets you easily display data generated from either real-time activity or log files. When you first open System Monitor, you'll notice that nothing is tracked by default. To start making use of the tool, you must tell the System Monitor exactly what to track. You do this by adding instances of counters of certain objects to the current graph in the Add Counters dialog box, as shown in Figure 6-7. To access this dialog box, either right-click any area in the System Monitor graph and choose Add Counters, or click the plus-sign icon above the System Monitor graph.

Local Lingo

Object The individual system resource that can be monitored.
Counter A unit of performance of that object that can be quantified numerically.
Instance A further subdivision of a counter. For example, on a system with two processors, there can be three instances of the %Processor Time counter: one for processor 1, one for processor 2, and a third instance for Total processor time.

When you start using System Monitor, the options available can be a little overwhelming. Don't worry; nobody outside of Redmond has a thorough

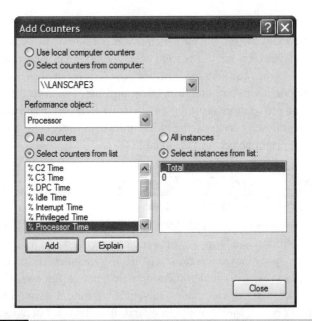

FIGURE 6.7   The Add Counters dialog box

understanding of every single counter that can be tracked with System Monitor. You won't be able to memorize every aspect of the System Monitor, so don't try. The important thing to remember, both for exam purposes and for real-world use, is which counters are most effective for measuring everyday usage of a system. You will have to experiment with the System Monitor, of course, to get comfortable with this tool, but one nice feature is a detailed description of what each counter does that pops up when you click the Explain button from the Add Counters dialog box as you add a counter. You can see what happens when you click this button in Figure 6-8.

To further explain what I mean about getting a handle on the System Monitor, think about the areas that have the greatest impact on the vast majority of

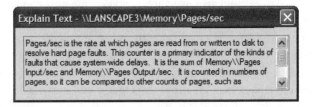

FIGURE 6.8   The contents of an Explain button

systems. What are they? In the order of importance, the resources that have the greatest impact on performance are memory, processor, network, and disk. It's the old 80/20 rule at work (20 percent of your work takes 80 percent of your time), and we've just considerably whittled down our list of objects to which we need to give our day-to-day attention. Of the possible counters for these objects, some are going to be more helpful than others when taking performance snapshots. In the following sections, the most common counters that are used with the most important objects will be noted.

Optimize and Troubleshoot Memory Performance

Consider the metaphor of the desktop as it applies to the computer (in other words, the Windows desktop is *like* the top of a real desk). Windows has been using this metaphor for years because it is an *anchor*, a link to something that we are already familiar with, and something we've had an understanding of for years—a desk—that helps us relate to this entirely new tool, a computer operating system. (Yes, yes, there have been operating systems for decades now, but we're talking about ones that were not configured by punch cards—ones, like XP, that brought this computing power to the desktop.)

You can also extend this office desk metaphor to help you understand most computer hardware. If you think of your brain—that is, you, sitting there at the desk—as the CPU, all the stuff on your office desk—the stuff you have to "process"—is the area of memory. It is the place you first look when you want to work with some information. If the information you are looking for is on your desk (in your memory), that's great, and you can access it quickly. If not, you have to go to the filing cabinet (the hard disk) to retrieve the information you want. The bigger the desk space you have (the better your memory is), the more things will quickly be at your fingertips when you want to work with them.

Memory is the most common cause of system bottlenecks. There is virtually no way for a system to have too much memory, and it is a great starting point as you begin to look for bottlenecks. To find out how much memory your system is using, you need to examine two main areas: physical memory and the page file.

Physical memory is the physical sticks of RAM that hold all the 1's and 0's that make up the instructions of an application, an operating system, or a hardware device. Each location in memory is given a memory address, which is how the CPU keeps track of what application is placing instructions where. So to applications, RAM is simply a long list of numbers that it sees as available. Again, you can't have too much and it's next to free.

Virtual Memory   Not all memory exists on the chips of RAM. Some working data is stored in *virtual memory*, which is hard disk space that looks to the applications like any other area of memory space.

And in order to implement virtual memory, Windows makes use of a *page file*. The page file is logical memory that exists in a file called pagefile.sys located on the root of the Windows installation drive. Like physical RAM, the page file is a list of addressable locations meant for storing data as it waits to be processed. In fact, applications have no idea whether or not the instructions it is sending to memory are kept on the page file or in physical RAM. The one who can tell the difference is you, the user, who will notice a considerable slowdown in performance when the page file is accessed frequently.

When using the System Monitor tool in Performance, there are certain counters that help provide an overall barometer of memory usage. Following are the most important counters for monitoring memory:

- **Memory—Available MBytes**   Measures the amount of available memory that is available to run a process. If this number is less than 4MB, you should add more memory.

- **Memory—Pages/Sec**   Shows the number of times that the processor requested information that was not in physical memory and had to be retrieved from disk. For optimal performance, this counter should be set at around 4 or 5.

- **Paging file—%Usage**   Indicates how much of the allocated page file is currently in use. If this number is consistently larger than 99 percent, you may need to add memory.

Exam Tip

Because of the page file, systems that are short on memory will often report high disk usage. This is because the disk is being asked all the time for instructions that should be living in physical memory. See the Exam Tip in the "Optimize and Troubleshoot Disk Performance" section, later in this chapter. Fix the memory problem, and the high disk usage problem disappears.

Optimize and Troubleshoot Processor Utilization

It's rare that a processor is the source of a bottleneck in an XP Professional system. Most people actually buy much more processor than they really need.

Then again, people buy SUVs and won't drive them over a curb. After all, how fast do you need that e-mail to open anyway?

However, if you suspect that your processor is cause for concern, you should monitor the following counters:

- **Processor—%Processor Time** Measures the time that the processor is busy responding to system requests. If this value is consistently above 80 percent, you may indeed have a processor bottleneck.

- **Processor—Interrupts/Sec** Shows the average number of times each second the processor is interrupted by hardware requests for attention. This number should generally be less than 3,500. However, problems in this area indicate a problem with hardware that may be malfunctioning and sending unnecessary interrupts.

Optimize and Troubleshoot Disk Performance

Disk access is the amount of time it takes your disk subsystem to retrieve data that is requested by the operating system. You can monitor two objects when measuring disk performance. The PhysicalDisk object is a sum of all logical drives on a single hard disk, and the LogicalDisk object represents a single logical disk. The following counters can be tracked for both the PhysicalDisk and LogicalDisk object (the PhysicalDisk is used in this example):

- **PhysicalDisk—%Disk Time** Shows the amount of time a disk is busy responding to read and write requests. If the disk is busy more than 90 percent of the time, you can improve performance by adding another disk channel and splitting the I/O requests between the channels.

- **PhysicalDisk—%Current Disk Queue Length** Indicates the number of outstanding disk requests that are waiting to be processed. This value should be less than 2.

Exam Tip
High disk counter measurements can result from high usage of your paging file, which is an indicator of low memory, not of a disk that needs to be upgraded. Just wanted to remind you.

Optimize and Troubleshoot Application Performance

If you are consistently running multiple applications concurrently on your Windows XP Professional system, there are a couple of ways to optimize performance. To access the location where these settings are tweaked, open the System Properties dialog box (right-click My Computer and choose Properties), select the Advanced tab, and then click the Settings button under the Performance section. The Performance Options dialog box appears, with the Visual Settings tab selected, as shown in Figure 6-9.

As you can see in this Visual Settings tab, there are several configurable items that affect either the speed or the appearance of a system. It is not worth explaining each and every configurable item here, as most of them are self-explanatory,

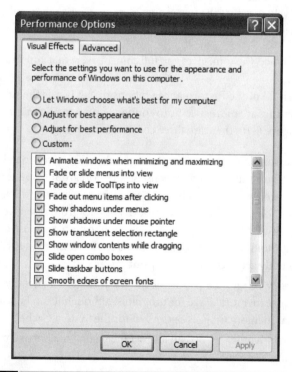

FIGURE 6.9 The Performance Options Visual Effects tab

and you probably will not be required to memorize specifics from this dialog box for the exam. Take the options out for a test drive if you like; you won't harm your computer by doing so. Usually, you'll find that there's an inversely proportional tradeoff between speed and appearance: the better XP looks, the more resources it will need. You'll also likely find that some of the options will have a negligible effect on performance, either on or off.

You will also notice in Figure 6-9 three preconfigured templates that apply settings automatically:

- **Let Windows choose what's best for my computer** Lets Microsoft decide what beauty/speed tradeoffs are appropriate.
- **Adjust for best appearance** For poets; it selects all of the appearance-related settings.
- **Adjust for best performance** For NASCAR speed freaks (I am relatively sure that the two groups share no common members), it chooses none of the aesthetic enhancements.

The last choice, Custom, gives you full control over what appearance options are enabled.

The other tab of the Performance Options dialog box is the Advanced tab. This tab's settings are more specific to configuring application performance. As shown in Figure 6-10, there are three configurable settings.

- **Processor Scheduling** The Processor Scheduling section allows you to configure application response so that foreground applications either are always given a higher performance priority, which is the default, or are given the same priority as background services. You might want to consider changing the application response option to background services if your Windows XP Professional system is frequently accessed as a file or print server.
- **Memory Usage** Same for the memory usage. The default is to optimize memory usage for programs, although it can be configured so that memory usage is optimized for the System Cache.
- **Virtual Memory** You can also set the paging file (virtual memory) size and location.

To review virtual memory issues, the paging file is the physical location of logical memory—memory that exists on the hard drive. Windows does a pretty good job of managing virtual memory, and it would be rare for an administrator to change any of the virtual memory settings on a Windows XP Professional

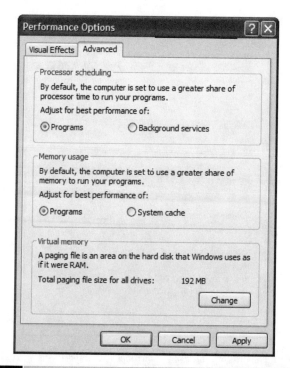

FIGURE 6.10   The Advanced tab of the Performance Options

computer. It is possible to improve virtual memory slightly by moving the paging file, pagefile.sys, to a faster hard drive. You can configure this by clicking the Change button on the Performance Options dialog box. Then, from the Virtual Memory dialog box, as seen in Figure 6-11, you can change the location of the page file by selecting the desired drive, choosing the Initial Size and the Maximum Size settings, and clicking Set. You can also improve virtual memory performance by setting the paging file's initial size and maximum size to be the same. This step will greatly reduce fragmentation of the swap file, thus making virtual memory access more efficient. Keep in mind, however, that these steps will produce only incremental increases in memory performance.

Travel Advisory

Of course, the best way to optimize the use of virtual memory is not to use it—install more physical memory instead, which is, conservatively, about 1,000 times faster than virtual memory.

| FIGURE 6.11 | Altering the default virtual memory settings |

Optimize and Troubleshoot Network Performance

The measurement of network performance is usually done by looking at the network as a whole, not the performance of an individual computer. Windows XP Professional does not include a tool for monitoring the entire network, but you can monitor the traffic that is being sent and received on the local network card, as well as the performance of any protocols bound to that card. Here are the network counters that you will find most useful:

- **Network Interface—Bytes Total/Sec** Measures the total number of bytes sent and received from the network interface card (NIC). It does not specify which protocol, but instead looks at total traffic. You can compare this number against the total bandwidth capacity of your card. You should not exceed 30 percent of your card's total Megabits per second (Mbps) rating for extended periods.
- **TCP—Segments/Sec** Filters and measures the number of bytes that are sent or received from the network interface that are TCP-specific.

By the way, how does one go about fixing these problems when bottlenecks are detected? In a word, *upgrade*. In other words, add more memory, swap out to a better processor if the motherboard allows, use faster drives or a striping array, and get a faster NIC of at least 100 Mbps.

Other System Management Tools

You use the Performance Logs And Alerts node of the Performance Console to collect performance data over time and to configure notification of exceeded activity thresholds. The Performance Console is a preconfigured MMC snap-in that can be found under the Administrative Tools menu. The Performance Logs and Alerts utility is capable of creating two types of logs—Counter logs and Trace logs—and is capable of generating alerts.

Counter Logs

Counter logs let you record data about system resource usage over time and are a useful tool to help you establish a baseline of system use. Counter logs are configured to collect data at specific time intervals. We have already seen an explanation of just what a counter is, so it can be used as a reference point here in our discussion of counter logs.

1. To create a counter log, right-click the Counter Logs node in the Performance Console and select New Log Settings from the pop-up menu. Then give your log file a name. Click OK.

2. The counter log Properties dialog box appears. Click the Add button to begin specifying the counters to be tracked by the log file and how often to track them, as shown in Figure 6-12. When you are finished adding counters that will be monitored in your log, click Close and then OK from the log Properties dialog box.

3. You will add counters to track from the Properties dialog box's General tab by clicking the Add button and choosing the specific counters.

4. The Schedule tab lets you specify when the log will start and lets you set logging with a minimum of administrative overhead.

5. The Log Files tab lets you set the log file location, type, and size.

Once you have configured the counters, duration, and schedule, the counter log will begin to track data, as will be indicated by a green icon in the details pane of Counter Logs. (Notice that there is a System Overview log—which tracks just that—already configured but not running. You can start this log file capturing data by right-clicking the icon and choosing Start from the context menu.)

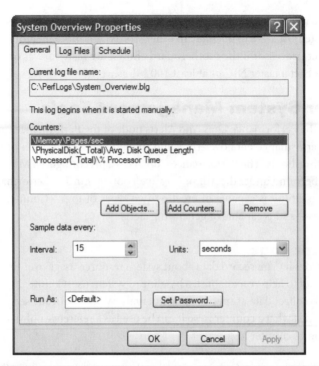

FIGURE 6.12 Set the counters to track from the Properties dialog box's General tab

Trace Logs

Trace logs measure data continuously rather than through specific timed intervals, as is the case with counter logs. Trace logs are used mainly to track the behavior of the operating system or applications, such as when an application creates or deletes a process or thread.

Trace logs are created using almost the same procedure as described previously when configuring counter logs.

1. Create a New Log Setting, and then give the trace log a name.

2. Configure the events to trace from the Properties dialog box that will be presented next. The General tab is the only one that will differ from that of the counter logs process—you will be selecting the system events to trace from here. For example, you can select the Disk Input/Output And Process Creations/Deletions by clicking the appropriate check box.

Alerts

Alerts are used to generate an event when preconfigured thresholds are tripped. For example, you can create a trace log that will record an event every time processor activity is greater than 80 percent capacity. You can configure alerts so that a message is sent, a program is run, or a detailed log is written when these values are exceeded.

The process for creating an alert is also similar to that for setting counter logs. But rather than just gathering data, you will be instructing the utility to take a specific action or actions. What action is performed will be configured from the Action tab after you have created a New Alert Setting by the same method as outlined previously. In the Action tab, you can specify that a message be sent, as shown in Figure 6-13.

Task Manager

XP also provides a new update of an old monitoring tool, a tool that most Windows NT and 2000 users have already put through its paces many times by now. I'm talking, of course, about the Task Manager.

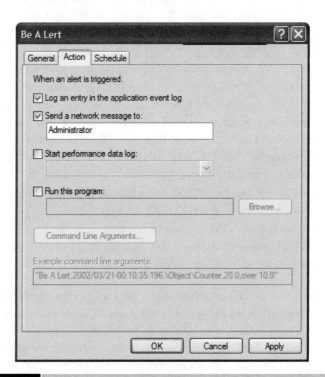

FIGURE 6.13   Setting alerts

Of the monitoring tools discussed here, the Task Manager provides the quickest way to get a "snapshot" of system performance and also provides a way to close cranky programs that otherwise will not go away when you tell them to. There are four (possibly five) tabs of the Task Manager:

- **Applications** When Task Manager opens, it defaults to this tab. Just as in previous versions, you will see a list of open applications and can choose to end them if you want.
- **Processes** Also the same as before. The Processes tab, as shown in Figure 6-14, lists all the currently running processes on your computer. You can sort these by CPU utilization (just click the heading) and kill a process, which in turn will end the application that depends on this process.

Travel Advisory

You can really foul up your system by killing the wrong process, so be careful. One neat little trick is to use the right-click from the Applications tab and choose the Go To Process option. You will then be taken to the Processes tab, and the process running the just-selected application will be highlighted. Kill that process, and you safely kill the app.

- **Performance** This tab, as seen in Figure 6-14, lets you see at a glance if any of the two main predictors of system performance—processor and memory utilization—need further investigation. The two graphs here show CPU utilization and Page File (virtual memory) use. Neither of these graphs should be high and remain high (75 percent or higher) for extended periods of time.
- **Networking** This tab will display information about your current network connection, if you have one configured. You can see if the network card is busy processing traffic here.
- **Users** Only available if Fast User Switching is enabled, this tab quickly shows what user accounts are in use.

Also new to the Windows XP version of Task Manager is a Shut Down menu, which will let you turn off the system, Lock, Log Off, Standby, or Hibernate as appropriate.

You can launch the Task Manager with the keyboard shortcut CTRL-ALT-DELETE, or you can right-click an empty area of the Taskbar and choose Task Manager from the context menu. When loaded, the Task Manager will place an icon in the System Tray, which will remain there until the utility is closed.

```
┌─────────────────────────────────────────────────────┐
│ ⬚ Windows Task Manager                    [_][□][X]   │
├─────────────────────────────────────────────────────┤
│ File  Options  View  Shut Down  Help                 │
│ ┌──────────┬──────────┬─────────────┬─────────────┐  │
│ │Applications│ Processes │ Performance │ Networking │  │
│ │ ┌─────────────────────────────────────────────┐ │  │
│ │ │ Image Name      User Name      CPU  Mem Usage│▲│  │
│ │ │ System Idle Process  SYSTEM      84     20 K │ │  │
│ │ │ FullShot99.exe   Administrator  08   6,336 K │ │  │
│ │ │ taskmgr.exe      Administrator  05   2,420 K │ │  │
│ │ │ EXPLORER.EXE     Administrator  02  13,660 K │ │  │
│ │ │ SERVICES.EXE     SYSTEM         01   1,004 K │ │  │
│ │ │ QW.EXE           Administrator  00  15,500 K │ │  │
│ │ │ HelpHost.exe     Administrator  00   3,828 K │ │  │
│ │ │ Fast.exe         SYSTEM         00      28 K │ │  │
│ │ │ OWSTIMER.EXE     SYSTEM         00     996 K │ │  │
│ │ │ INETINFO.EXE     SYSTEM         00   1,004 K │ │  │
│ │ │ SPOOLSV.EXE      SYSTEM         00   1,168 K │ │  │
│ │ │ HelpCtr.exe      Administrator  00  10,288 K │ │  │
│ │ │ SVCHOST.EXE      LOCAL SERVICE  00     700 K │ │  │
│ │ │ SVCHOST.EXE      NETWORK SERVICE 00    616 K │ │  │
│ │ │ iexplore.exe     Administrator  00   1,468 K │ │  │
│ │ │ DownloadWizard...  Administrator 00    464 K │ │  │
│ │ │ SVCHOST.EXE      SYSTEM         00   6,540 K │ │  │
│ │ │ SVCHOST.EXE      SYSTEM         00   1,148 K │ │  │
│ │ │ OWDLLS.EXE       Administrator  00     168 K │▼│  │
│ │ └─────────────────────────────────────────────┘ │  │
│ │ ☐ Show processes from all users    [End Process]│  │
│ └─────────────────────────────────────────────────┘  │
│ Processes: 31   CPU Usage: 17%   Commit Charge: 162020K / 3152 │
└─────────────────────────────────────────────────────┘
```

FIGURE 6.14   Task Manager with the Processes tab selected

This icon appears as a tiny graph and will report on CPU utilization percentage as the system continues operation.

There are a few other areas of performance management that are more specific to the management of laptop systems. These performance-related items include the use of Offline Files and the optimization of battery power. The next test objective investigates both of these in further detail to prepare you for the test.

Objective 6.02 Manage, Monitor, and Optimize System Performance for Mobile Users

A s recently as a few years ago, it was difficult to bring the stability and security of the NT platform to the laptop computer. This is no longer the case. One of the great features of XP Professional is that it supplies the stability of NT

4 to a laptop computer, while at the same time integrating all the best features of the Windows 9x platform. This initiative of bridging the gap between the two operating system families met with success in Windows 2000, and now has been improved upon with Windows XP. Laptop computing is one of the areas of Windows NT 4 and 9x integration is most apparent.

We have already spent time talking about some of the security and stability features of the XP Professional operating system. Now we'll turn our attention to a couple of features that help make XP ideally suited for use on laptops.

Manage and Troubleshoot the Use of Offline Files

Offline Files is one of the tools that help achieve this goal, and it's a welcome departure from the previous iteration of Offline Files, an albatross you may remember called My Briefcase.

The Offline Files feature in Windows XP Professional synchronizes files from a network to a local hard disk, ensuring that the files are always available, even if either server or client computer is disconnected from the network. It is especially useful for mobile computers for obvious reasons, but it's also well-suited for networked desktop computers for less obvious ones. For example, Offline Files can increase the performance of the network because users work on a local copy of the file instead of accessing files over the network.

Offline Files are made available the same way that other file resources are made available, through folder sharing. Because the Offline Files mechanism is built on the technologies of sharing, it is probably useful here to jog your memory about some of these fundamental concepts:

- On a Microsoft Windows XP network, the computer that hosts the share does so because it runs the Server service (called *File and Print Sharing for Microsoft Networks* on Windows 9x).

- The computer that accesses the share is the client, running the Workstation service, which is the client redirector on XP machines. (It's called *Client for Microsoft Networks* on Windows 9x computers.)

- Now here's the really important part, because it has to do with how computers in a Microsoft network exchange files. Both the Server service and the Workstation client redirector are using the same file sharing protocol, Server Message Blocks (SMB), for network communication. This combination of Microsoft networking components is worth mentioning again because it is the only one that supports the use of

Offline Files. You cannot set up Offline Files with a Novell NetWare Network, although you can synchronize folders that are shared from Windows NT 4 or 9x computers. Novell computers use NetWare Core Protocol (NCP) as their file and print sharing protocol.

After sharing a resource, the Offline Files feature is either enabled and configured centrally using Group Policies or is configured independently on each computer that needs the ability to access files when not connected to the network.

Setting Up Offline Files

Configuring Offline Files is a two-step process. The first step is done through the Offline Files tab of the Folder Options dialog box, as shown in Figure 6-15. Once you locate this tab, verify that the Enable Offline Files box is checked. This single check box gives your computer the capability to connect to and use offline files. Note also that this check box is enabled by default on XP Professional computers, as was the case on 2000 Professional.

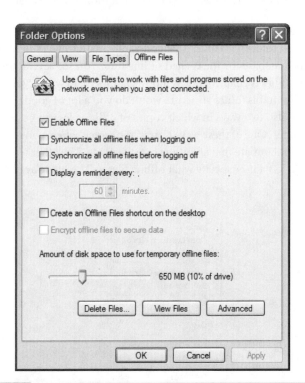

FIGURE 6.15   The Folder Options dialog box

The second step in this process is telling your computer exactly what shares you want available offline. This can be done one of two ways: on the server or the client side. Client side configuration is the more common practice, so we'll explain it here.

1. Right-click a network share, and choose Make Available Offline, as shown in Figure 6-16. This launches the Offline Files Wizard, which runs the first time you create an offline file or folder.

2. The Wizard asks you questions about how you want the synchronization of the offline files to behave and whether you want a shortcut placed on your desktop.

3. When you are done answering these questions, the offline files are copied to your local machine, and you see that the share has been enabled for offline access by the new double-arrow icon (it looks like a Yin/Yang symbol, sort of). From now on, you won't be led through the Offline Files Wizard when you make additional files available offline.

Enabling and configuring Offline Files initiates an upgrade of the *systemroot*\Csc folder with offline file cache information. The Client Side Cache (CSC) is the database for the cached offline files. You see several folders there when Offline Files is enabled, but Windows names them with cryptic names, so looking through this folder structure won't do you a lot of good.

There are also two ways in which copies of offline files can be created at the client computer. One of these ways is from the server, where connections made to the share will initiate that an offline copy be made. The other way is from the client, which lets a user specify what offline files will be made available.

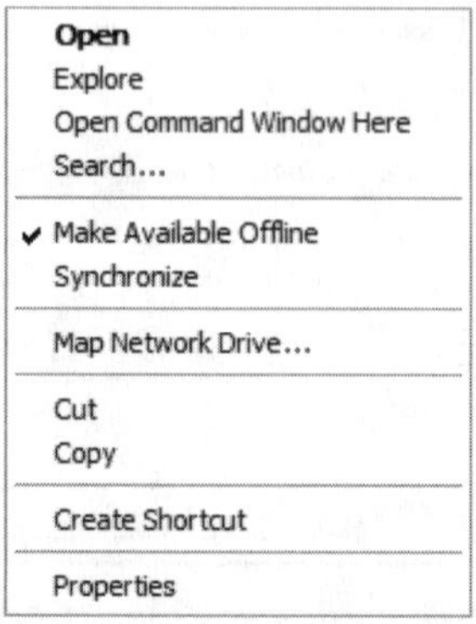

| **Open** |
| Explore |
| Open Command Window Here |
| Search... |
| ✔ Make Available Offline |
| Synchronize |
| Map Network Drive... |
| Cut |
| Copy |
| Create Shortcut |
| Properties |

FIGURE 6.16   Making a share available offline

Automatic Caching

Files are not automatically synchronized as a result of enabling and configuring Offline Files. Instead, files are made available offline through either automatic file caching or manual file caching. Automatic file caching copies any files selected or opened to the client cache. Automatic file caching is configured from the server side, at the share level, so that files below the share are also configured for automatic file caching. This is a bit of a fascist take on offline files, as you are not giving any choice to the clients about the files available offline. The files will be available whether the client likes it or not.

In the Caching Settings dialog box, which you access from the Sharing tab of the folder (refer to Chapter 2 for how to access this dialog box), the default setting on the share is for Manual Caching of Documents. This must be changed to support automatic caching, as shown in Figure 6-17. The cache size on the client is set, by default, to be 10 percent of the total logical disk capacity on the drive holding the \Csc folder, but this parameter is adjustable. Files automatically cached are not guaranteed to be available on the cache for this reason, as cached files are automatically deleted on a First In, First Out (FIFO) basis when the cache approaches the maximum configured size.

Manual Caching

Files are made permanently available offline through manual file caching, which is done from the client side of things and is a little bit more of a democratic approach. It lets users choose what they want offline. Use the Offline Files Wizard

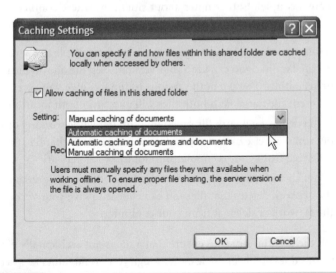

FIGURE 6.17   Setting automatic caching in the Caching Settings dialog box

to make files permanently available offline. Launch the Offline Files Wizard by selecting a share and then choosing Make Available Offline from the File menu (or right-click to access the context menu and choose the command from there). The share must be located on a remote computer, and unless it's configured for caching, the Make Available Offline option will not appear on the menu.

Certain file types cannot be cached, such as .pst (Microsoft Outlook personal store files) and .mdb (Microsoft Access database files). You can modify this, however, by changing the exclusion list through the Files Not Cached Group Policy setting.

No matter what type of file synchronization you have configured, it will be carried out according to one of the following events: logon, logoff, idle time, or a fixed schedule. To accomplish manual synchronization, in Windows Explorer, choose Tools | Synchronize to open the Items To Synchronize dialog box. Then click the Synchronize button. To configure synchronization settings, click the Setup button in the Items To Synchronize dialog box.

Travel Advisory

I always get the same questions in class: What happens if more than one user is synchronizing a file? Whose copy gets saved? The answer is that the last one to make the sync wins. Preventing this really has nothing to do with Offline Files, however. If you don't want users overwriting each other's files, don't give them all change permission to the same file.

Here are a couple of other notes about situations where conflicts can arise between the network version of a file and the copy you are working with offline:

- If someone else makes changes to the same network file that you have updated offline, you can keep your version, keep the one on the network, or keep both. To save both versions of the file, give your version a different file name, and both files will appear in both locations.
- If you delete a network file on your computer while working offline but someone else on the network makes changes to that file, the file is deleted from your computer but not from the network.
- If you change a network file while working offline but someone else on the network deletes that file, you can choose to save your version onto the network or delete it from your computer.

As you can see, the aim is to ensure that a file is not accidentally deleted or that someone does not delete a file even though you would rather keep a copy.

Configure Advanced Configuration Power Interface

There is another technology supported by Windows XP that is especially important for mobile users: the Advanced Configuration Power Interface (ACPI). While most essential for laptop users who are concerned with extending battery life as long as possible, the technology's use is not confined to mobile computing. It can be used on a variety of systems. For this reason, I have decided to include its discussion in Chapter 5, in the "Implementing, Managing, Monitoring, and Troubleshooting Hardware Devices and Drivers" section, rather than here. So, if you are not reading this book in sequence, please flip back to Chapter 5, and look at Objective 5.02, for a review of the ACPI technologies and configuration requirements.

Objective 6.03

Restore and Back Up the Operating System, System State Data, and User Data

Windows XP Professional includes a powerful set of tools and utilities that can help you recover a failed system and the data contained therein. These tools include

- Windows Backup
- Automated System Recovery
- System Restore
- Recovery Console

If you use computers long enough, you'll eventually need one, if not all, of these tools. This test objective will devote a section to each of these technologies so that we can examine them more closely.

Recover System State Data and User Data Using Windows Backup

The Backup utility is the one tool you should be familiar with right from the start. You've no doubt heard the admonishment by now, so why not one more time from me: if it's important, or even if you just think it will be, back it up.

The hard disk on your system is arguably the most important piece of your computer; without it, your computer would be little more than a calculator or a video game console. People buy computers so that they can work with a set of information day after day, and that data needs to be stored on a hard drive if it is to be available. Think about it another way: which is more valuable to you, your computer's processor or the data on your hard drive? Which would be harder to replace? You can easily snap in another processor, but getting data back is another story. Yet the hard disk is also one of the more fragile devices of your system, failing on average more times then any other computer component. In the event of a disk crash, your data can be impossible to retrieve without forking over the GNP of New Zealand for a data recovery service.

And, along with being at risk because of mechanical failure, your data is also vulnerable, as you may have experienced by now, to the vagaries of human error. People (not me, mind you) have been known to make typos, and they have also clicked the wrong button a time or two, sending critical data into the ether. Also, people have been known to "try out" the format and fdisk utilities for (their own) entertainment.

There are two things you will need to back up and restore to bring a crashed system back to its original state. These two data components are (in case you missed the tip-off in the section's title) the user data and the System State.

User Data

The definition of what comprises user data is very straightforward and one which you could probably guess. It's the data that has been saved by users of a system. That data can come in many forms: customer lists stored as database files, cash flow reports in spreadsheet formats, or chapters of test preparation books stored in word processor document formats. In short, it's anything you work on, anything you would be loathe to see destroyed or lost. The reason why regularly backing up user data is important is beyond obvious.

System State

The System State of a computer is something that you are less likely to be familiar with. It is generally defined as all the files that are critical to the operating system environment. In plain English, the System State includes information about user accounts, hardware and software settings, and files required for startup. However, what exactly is included in the System State differs from operating system to operating system and depends on which services are running on a computer.

Backing up the System State is critical when many changes have been made to the computer. For example, if you have a system that includes several accounts in the local Security Accounts manager (SAM) database (we will discuss the SAM in Chapter 8) and the hard disk crashes, you will most likely immediately reinstall the operating system to a new disk. However, this step does not restore the contents of the SAM, a function that is critical to recovering your original environment. You would have to re-create all user accounts—that is, unless you had backed up the System State. When you back up the System State, you ensure that the computer can be returned to its original condition.

Now that we know what we are going to back up, and why this backed up data is important, let's take a look at the tools XP provides to back up and restore this vital information. We'll start by examining the Windows Backup utility.

Using Windows Backup

The Windows Backup utility, as first introduced in Chapter 2, backs up all selected data to a single file that is named with a file extension of .bkf. The utility can make use of tape devices just like its predecessor backup utility used in NT 4. But unlike NT 4's Backup utility, the Windows XP version can also back up to other media, such as hard drives or even writeable CD-ROMs. The Backup utility's executable is called ntbackup.exe. For help using ntbackup from the command line, don't forget the /? switch, which will guide you in the use of the command-line version of this tool.

The more common way to launch the XP Backup is through the Start menu, and the first time you do, you launch the Backup or Restore Wizard. To launch the wizard from the Start menu, choose Start | All Programs | Accessories | System Tools | Backup. As Figure 6-18 shows, the Backup utility always starts with the Welcome screen, unless you clear the Always Start In Wizard Mode check box.

By this point in the book, and by this point in your Windows experience, I am confident that you have used wizards, and I won't waste precious pages describing each and every screen of this utility. If you have backed up *anything* before, you'll find this tool easy to use. To summarize: you simply tell the wizard which files to backup with a series of check marks, then where to store the backed-up data. When the backup is done, you can click the Report button to view a log file generated as the files were copied and verify that the backup was a success.

Instead of using the wizard, you can back up manually using the Advanced Mode, as shown in Figure 6-19, by clicking the Advanced Mode link in the Welcome dialog box. When you back up manually, you have essentially the same options; you just don't have a wizard prodding you along. You can specify whether to verify the data after the backup, whether to replace the backup files or append them to exiting backups, and specify (from the Schedule Jobs tab) when to run the backup.

FIGURE 6.18 The Backup or Restore Wizard opens at the Welcome screen.

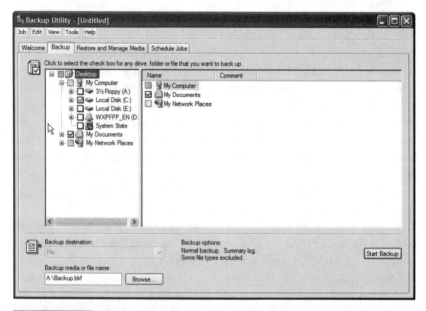

FIGURE 6.19 You can use Advanced Mode to back up manually.

Click the Backup tab, and select the files and folders you want to back up. At the bottom of the Backup tab, use the Backup Destination list to choose the location for the backup.

You use the Restore And Manage Media tab to specify what you want to restore and where you want it restored to. Again, it's just a matter of a few clicks. You use the Schedule Jobs tab to schedule backups. (I'll show you how to do this later in this chapter.)

Exam Tip

Users with Administrator or Backup Operator-level privileges can back up and restore any files on the system, even those they cannot otherwise access. Individual users can back up files that they own.

Backing Up the System State

The Windows Backup utility also provides a System State backup option that's used to restore the operating system back to its original state in the case of a catastrophic system failure. (This would usually be applied to a clean OS install to retrieve all configuration changes quickly.) This option appears in Windows Backup as a selection on the Backup tab and backs up the following on a Windows XP Professional installation:

- Registry
- Windows XP boot files
- System files on the boot partition
- COM+ Class Registration database

When you choose to back up or restore the System State data, all the System State data that is relevant to your computer is backed up or restored; that is, you cannot choose to back up or restore individual components, because of dependencies among the components. However, you can restore the System State data to an alternate location.

As might be obvious, backing up the System State is a more critical task for most of your servers on the network. It is not quite as crucial on Windows XP Professional systems. On these computers, the System State data is composed of only the registry, the COM+ Class Registration database, files under Windows File Protection, and boot files. In other words, not much that can't be (relatively) quickly restored after a reinstall of the OS.

While it is crucial in a real-world environment to configure regular backups of the appropriate data and system state, what is more important from a testing perspective is the different kind of backups available through the Backup utility. Knowledge of these backup types can make your backup strategy more effective, and the next section describes the different backup types in further detail.

Backup Types

Earlier in the chapter, we looked at use of the Backup Wizard, telling the utility exactly what to back up. If you stepped through the wizard, you no doubt noticed that on the final screen you can click the Advanced Options button to open the Options dialog box. From this dialog box, click the Backup Type tab to specify the type of backup you want to make. (You can also open the Options dialog box by choosing Tools | Options in the Backup Utility's Advanced Mode.)

To make an informed choice from the Backup Type tab of the Options dialog box, it is important that you understand the differences between the backup types. Further, an understanding of the different backup types requires that you know the significance of the archive bit, or backup marker, and how different backup types treat this marker. You will set the default backup type from the Backup Type tab, as shown in Figure 6-20.

> ### Local Lingo
>
> **Archive bit**   A bit that is set on a file when the file has changed and is removed by certain backup types to "flag" the file as having been backed up. Some backup types "care" about this flag and some don't.

So which backup type is best? As is the case with so many computing scenarios, it all depends. The best backup type for your situation depends on how much data you are backing up, how often, how quickly you want the backup to be performed, and how many backups you are willing to apply in the event of a restore. Your choices will be described next.

Normal   Backs up all selected files and marks each file as having been backed up; that is, it clears the archive bit. This type of backup is often used as a benchmark that other backup types can use to determine what needs backing up. Because it backs up everything you select, the normal backup takes the longest, but is the easiest to restore. Many companies that shut down operation for the night perform a full nightly backup, because, time is not a concern.

Copy   Backs up all selected files and does not mark them as being backed up. A copy is useful as a quick way to archive working data without impacting your overall backup strategy.

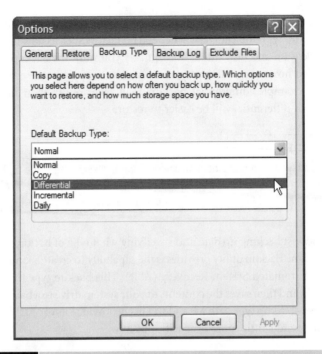

FIGURE 6.20   The Backup Type tab

Differential   Backs up only the selected files that have changed since the last normal or incremental backup and does not clear the archive bit, which would mark them as having been backed up. Because it does not clear the archive bit, a differential backup always uses as a point of reference the last time the archive bit was cleared. These backups take longer, but are quicker to restore. You can restore all data by using the last full backup and then applying only the most recent differential backup.

Incremental   Backs up selected files that have not been marked as archived and marks the files as having been backed up. These backup types perform a backup much more quickly, but take longer to restore because more backups must be applied to the last normal backup. To perform a restore, this strategy requires that the last normal backup and all the incremental backups be applied.

Daily   Backs up only the selected files that have changed on the current day and does not clear the archive bit. Each daily backup and the last normal backup are required for a successful restore. The daily backup is a way to back up a day's work without affecting the overall backup strategy.

As you can see, backup types differ mainly in how they treat the archive bit. Which backup type you choose will depend on factors such as how much data is being backed up and how often, how quickly you want the backup to be performed, and how many backups you are willing to apply in the event of a restore. For example, differential backups will take longer than incremental backups, but differential will be easier to restore.

> ### Exam Tip
> You probably will not see a lot of questions about the actual use of the Backup utility, but you will likely see a question or two that requires that you understand the significance between the different backup types.

Beyond just backing up data and specifying what type of backup to use, another thing the Backup utility provides is the capability to create a kind of backup called an Automated System Recovery (ASR). This backup type first creates a floppy disk, and then saves the contents of your system drive to a backup device. This is a new backup type with XP and will likely provide lots of testable material, so we will spend a little more time with this now.

Creating an Automated System Recovery

An ASR is a backup configuration whose purpose is to get your system partition up and running again in as short a time as possible. It saves the entire contents of your system drive to a backup media of your choice. Moreover, it saves information about your current location of system files, list of detected hardware, and partition (or volume) information to a floppy disk. It's good administrative practice to create an ASR right after a successful installation of Windows XP and then update it any time you significantly change the system—for example, when you change or upgrade any vital device drivers. However, one of the drawbacks of the ASR is that is backs up (and restores) only data that exists on the system volume. If you want to be able to restore other disks on your computer, run the Backup Wizard and choose the option to back up everything on the computer.

To create an ASR, click the Automated System Recovery Wizard option on the Welcome To The Backup Utility Advanced Mode dialog box to start the Automated System Recovery Preparation Wizard. Again, I will not walk you though each step of this wizard; it's much more important that you know the *purpose* of the ASR. You will be asked for the location of the system partition backup; when prompted, insert the floppy disk to save the system recovery information. Keep this disk in a safe place when you are finished.

Again, you use the ASR to quickly repair and restart Windows XP if your computer will not start or if system files become corrupt. But remember: the ASR floppy disk is not a bootable disk. To access the ASR floppy, you must first boot the computer using either the Windows XP Professional installation CD-ROM or the setup floppies that can be created from the XP Professional CD. Follow these steps:

1. Set your computer's BIOS to boot from the CD-ROM, and then restart the computer. Alternatively, you could use bootable floppies, although making them is only slightly easier than memorizing the first 15 numbers of Pi (see the Travel Assistance that follows).

2. When prompted to do so, press F2.

3. When prompted to insert the ASR floppy, do so and follow the onscreen instructions to restore your system files.

Travel Advisory

The ASR is available in Windows XP Professional, but not in XP Home Edition. Although the Backup utility in the Home Edition may appear to make an ASR disk, you can't use this disk to restore because XP Home Edition doesn't support setups from ASR disks.

Travel Assistance

You used to be able to make bootable floppy disks on Windows 2000 machines with a utility called makeboot.exe. No more. Now, the only way you can make them is to download them from www.microsoft.com/xp. You will need *six* disks to make the bootable floppy set for XP machines.

Performing a Restore

A carefully planned backup policy, a thorough understanding of the backup types, and all the backups in the world are useless if you are unable to restore your data to its original state. Your most important line of defense in this effort is a consistent testing of the restoration process. To ease the restoration procedure, you can use the Restore Wizard to guide you along the way to a successful restore.

To use the Restore Wizard, you should take the following steps.

1. From the Welcome tab of the Backup utility, click the Restore Wizard button.

2. Click the Next button from the wizard's Welcome screen, which will bring up the What to Restore dialog box, as shown in Figure 6-21. This is the heart of this wizard. Click the filename of the backup job you want to restore and click the Next button.

3. After you have selected the backup you want to restore, you can choose to restore the entire session or selectively restore individual drives, folders, or files.

4. The Completing the Restore Wizard dialog box then appears, summarizing your chosen restore options. When you are certain of your selection, click the Finish button to proceed with the restore.

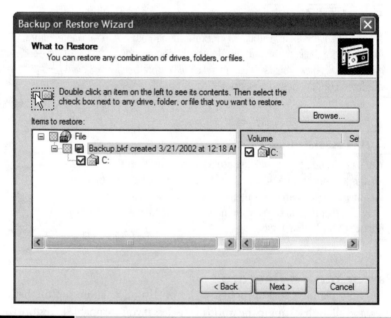

FIGURE 6.21 The What to Restore dialog box

Troubleshoot System Restoration by Starting in Safe Mode

When you press the F8 key during startup, you will see the Advanced Startup Options menu. From this menu, you can select from three different versions of Safe Mode: with networking support, without networking support, and command prompt only. You can use the Safe Mode startup commands to resolve device driver conflicts, system service failures, and even application autostart problems. When the computer is started in Safe Mode, boot logging is automatic. Boot logging can also be configured to occur during normal startups from this Advanced Options menu. You will be able to resolve incompatible display settings using the Enable VGA Mode command. You can also solve system configuration changes that have prevented the operating system from starting by selecting the Last Known Good Configuration. Troubleshooting the system with a kernel debugger starts by choosing Debugging Mode from the Advanced Options menu.

Safe Mode will give you several startup choices, as seen in Figure 6-22.

In Safe Mode, Windows will not load any support for audio devices and all nonessential peripherals, including most devices connected through a USB port. It will also ignore all programs configured to load at startup time as well.

If Windows will load and operate in Safe Mode, the problem is usually resolvable. You can be relatively certain if a Safe Mode boot up is successful, there is no problem with basic operating system services. You can use the Device Manager or Event Viewer to try to determine the source of your trouble.

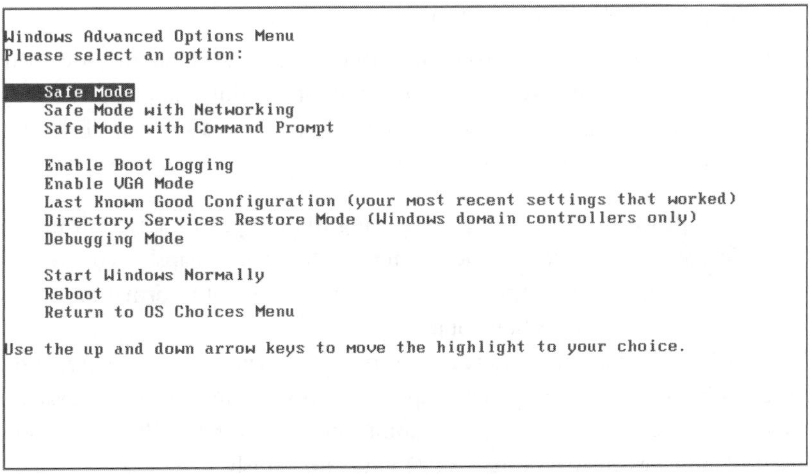

```
Windows Advanced Options Menu
Please select an option:

    Safe Mode
    Safe Mode with Networking
    Safe Mode with Command Prompt

    Enable Boot Logging
    Enable VGA Mode
    Last Known Good Configuration (your most recent settings that worked)
    Directory Services Restore Mode (Windows domain controllers only)
    Debugging Mode

    Start Windows Normally
    Reboot
    Return to OS Choices Menu

Use the up and down arrow keys to move the highlight to your choice.
```

FIGURE 6.22   The Startup options provided by Safe Mode

With the Device Manager, you can further remove or disable suspected device driver offenders. You can also do the same with any applications you are suspicious of with the Control Panel's Add or Remove Programs applet.

After you have done your tinkering in Safe Mode, restart the system to see whether or not the problem was resolved.

Another task that can be completed from Safe Mode is the System Restore. In fact, when you start the computer in Safe Mode, XP will ask you if you want to run System Restore. You don't have to be in Safe Mode to perform a Restore; XP just assumes, correctly I should add, that you wouldn't be booting into Safe Mode unless something was running afoul.

The System Restore

The System Restore utility was first introduced with Windows Me and works by taking "snapshots" of your computer's state as you work with and configure your system. The utility lets you use these snapshots as restore points if you encounter problems, like an accidentally deleted program, a virus, or a driver that causes the system to act strangely. To restore your system to a given point in time using the System Restore, follow these steps:

1. Choose Start | All Programs | Accessories | System Tools | System Restore.

2. Select Restore My Computer to An Earlier Time and click Next.

3. You will see a calendar, with days highlighted on which restore points exist. Choose a highlighted day to see a list of Restore Points for that day. Select the desired Restore Point.

4. Follow the onscreen instructions, which might direct you to close open programs. System Restore will then reboot Windows, and you will see a report telling you whether or not the restore was a success. Click OK to exit the System Restore Wizard.

System Restore works by keeping a log of changes to a system in the *systemroot*\system32\Restore folder. System Restore takes snapshots of the System State at regular intervals, looking at the same type of information that is saved when you back up System State data.

By default, System Restore creates restore points without user intervention every 24 hours if you leave your computer on. If you shut down your system, System Restore creates a new restore point when you restart if the most recent restore point was created more than 24 hours previously.

Using System Restore is especially effective in the following situations:

- You install a program that conflicts with other software drivers on your system. If uninstalling the program doesn't fix the situation, you can restore to a point before the program was installed.
- You install one or more updated drivers that cause system instability. You can use System Restore to restore all previously installed derivers instead of using the Driver Rollback feature from the Device Manager.
- Your system develops performance or stability problems for no apparent reason. This situation may not seem plausible at first glance; after all, problems always occur for a reason right? But consider a situation in which a computer is shared by many people—family members or coworkers who may or may not document changes they make or install untested or unsupported software or devices without compatible drivers. You can restore to a point where you are reasonably sure that the system was functioning properly (that is, the last time *you* were using it).

Travel Advisory

Don't count on System Restore to replace a good antivirus program. A system can become infected and not exhibit any symptoms. Thus, files stored in restore points can be infected without your knowledge, even if the computer was functioning properly at the restore point.

In addition to creating restore points at 24-hour intervals, System Restore creates restore points when you do the following:

- Install an unsigned third-party driver. As you recall, when you install an unsigned driver, Windows displays a warning message. If you continue anyway (who doesn't?), the system creates a restore point before completing the installation.
- Install an application using an installer that's compatible with System Restore.
- Install a Windows update or a patch. Windows creates a restore point automatically when you download and install an update using Windows Update.
- Restore a prior configuration using the System Restore. Each time you run System Restore, System Restore creates a new restore point so that you can undo the restore.

- Restore data from a backup set created with the Windows XP Backup Utility program. If the restoration of the backed-up files creates problems, you can reverse the effects using System Restore.

There are times when the system is in such a state of disrepair that you cannot start it either in Normal *or* Safe Mode, rendering any of the restore options previously outlined useless. (If you can't boot, you can't run System Restore.) In such an instance, all might not be lost. You just might be able to get the system up and running again by using the Recovery Console, a command-based interface that provides a number of tools that can help get a Windows XP up and on its feet again. The next section examines this recovery tool and how it is used.

Recover System State Data and User Data with the Recovery Console

The Recovery Console will start even when the Windows system files are corrupted, unlike a Safe Mode or Normal startup. This gives the Recovery Console its chief advantage and allows it to act as a last line of defense before complete OS reinstallation. The Recovery Console's function is to run a Windows XP command interpreter to provide access to the local disk.

You start the Recovery Console in one of two ways: either from the Windows XP Setup routine or from the local disk. To start from the Setup routine, press R when prompted by the appropriate installation screen; doing so will display the Repair Options screen. From the Repair Options screen, press C to start the Recovery Console.

It will allow you to do the following tasks:

- Copy or replace Windows system files and folders
- Enable or disable services or device drivers
- Repair the file system boot sector or the Master Boot Record (MBR)
- Rebuild or repair the Windows boot menu
- Create and format partitions or volumes

All file systems that Windows XP Professional uses are accessible from the Recovery Console. This console includes a number of disk utilities, such as ChkDisk, DiskPart, Fixboot, and Fixmbr. You can also run several file manipulation utilities, such as Expand, Md, Rd, and Ren. If you are familiar with working in a command environment, like MS-DOS (many of the commands are the same), you will probably find the Recovery Console second nature. And if you need help using the Recovery Console, simply type **help** for a list of available commands. To learn about a specific utility, type the utility name and then **/?**.

Using the Recovery Console is a better way to restore a damaged Registry than running an Emergency Repair. This is because the Registry files in the *systemroot*\Repair folder are from the original installation of Windows XP Professional, so any changes made after the initial operating system installation are lost when you use the Emergency Repair. Conversely, the Registry data from the *systemroot*\Repair\Regbak folder will be current.

If you would like to select the Recovery Console from the Advanced Startup menu, you must keep in mind that the Recovery Console is not installed by default. To install the Recovery Console, open a Command Prompt window and locate the \i386 folder on the Setup CD-ROM and type **winnt32 /cmdcons**. This local hard disk installation requires about 7MB of free space and will be an easy way to launch the Recovery Console. However, it is often needed when local disk access is impossible. In this case, running it from the Setup CD-ROM is the only viable option.

To run the Recovery Console from the Windows XP CD, first boot to the CD and, from the Welcome to Setup screen, press R to choose to Repair a Windows installation, and then C to start the Recovery Console.

Objective 6.04 ## Manage Hardware Profiles

W hen you set up hardware profiles, you specify different hardware configurations to be used when Windows XP Professional is started. You manage hardware profiles through the Hardware Profiles dialog box, which is accessed by launching the System program in the Control Panel. In the System Properties dialog box, click the Hardware tab and then click the Hardware Profiles button. You see the dialog box shown in Figure 6-23.

The default hardware profile is created when you install Windows XP and is made up from the devices that are attached to your computer at the time. The name of this first profile will always be Original Configuration, but this can be changed if you feel the need. (Renaming might make the profile a little more user friendly if you plan to configure additional hardware profiles in the future; otherwise, it won't make any difference because you won't be presented with the option to choose a profile.)

FIGURE 6.23 The Hardware Profiles dialog box

The actual contents of a hardware profile can be set and edited using Device Manager. You can use Device Manager to either enable or disable the use of certain hardware devices. On the General tab of the device's Properties dialog box, select the Device Usage drop-down box to specify whether the device is enabled for all profiles, disabled for the current profile, or disabled for all profiles, as shown in Figure 6-24.

What's more, you can also configure the behavior of certain services as part of the hardware profile. For example, you might not want the Messenger Service to run as a part of an offline profile.

You can open the Services MMC snap-in from the Administrative Tools section in the Start menu. To access the Properties of a particular service, simply double-click the services name in the details pane. From the Services program, access the properties of the Messenger Service. Then, on the Log On tab in the Services Properties dialog box, select the hardware profile appearing in the You Can Enable Or Disable This Service For The Hardware Profiles Listed Below list box, as shown in Figure 6-25. Then click Enable or Disable to change the state of the service for the selected profile.

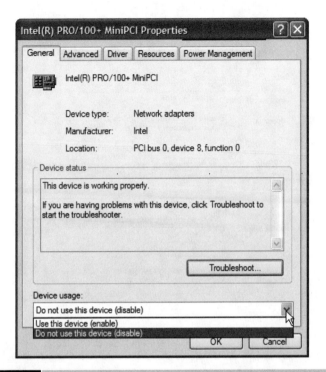

FIGURE 6.24   Disabling a device in Device Manager

The results of the changes made in either Device Manager or the Services applet are saved to the current hardware profile upon shutdown and are used again the next time the hardware profile is selected. For example, suppose you disable the network card on your laptop and shut down. The next time you boot up, your network card will be disabled. Why? Because you're using a hardware profile that has the network card disabled.

As mentioned, most users will never need a second hardware profile, because on a desktop computer there is little need for a device to be enabled one day and disabled the next. A common use for hardware profiles is on laptop computers, especially those with a network card that will not be needed when the computer is used without network connectivity.

To create a second hardware profile, access the Hardware Profiles dialog box (shown in Figure 6-26) and click Copy to copy an existing profile. Once you have the second hardware profile configured, the bottom half of the Hardware Profiles dialog box comes into play. From the Hardware Profiles Selection

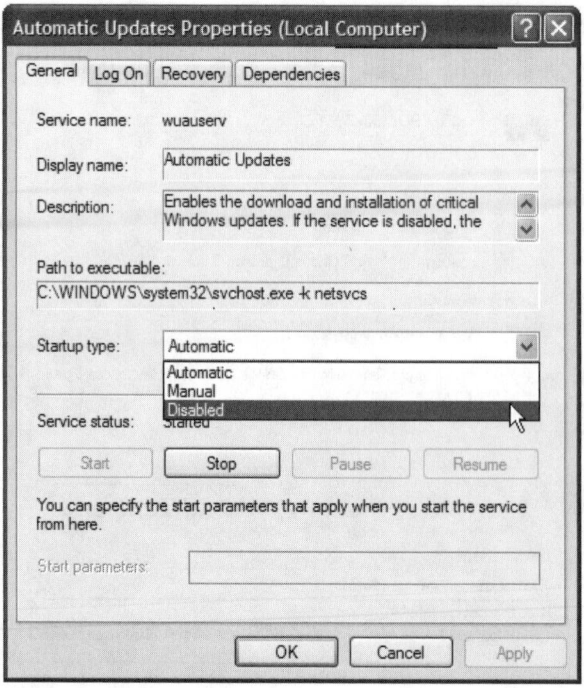

FIGURE 6.25   Disabling a service as a part of a hardware profile

section, you can tell Windows to either wait until you specify a hardware profile or select the first profile after a given time interval, which is 30 seconds by default. The first profile in the list is what Windows XP considers the default profile.

You can then choose either profile at startup time and configure away with the Device Manager and the Services applet. Additionally, you can specify whether or not the computer is portable and whether or not a docking station is used by looking at the Properties dialog box of a profile. To open this dialog box, simply double-click a Profile name in the Hardware Profiles dialog box.

Travel Advisory

Windows XP Professional automatically creates a Docked Profile and an Undocked Profile for a laptop computer if the following conditions are met: it must be fully ACPI compliant, and it must run only Plug and Play-compatible device drivers. If these two conditions are met, you should not manually tamper with these two hardware profiles. Also, it's recommended that you install and configure the machine undocked first, then dock and let XP create the profile. You probably won't be tested on this information, but you should be aware of this for real-world laptop use.

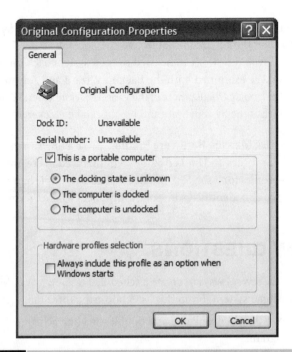

FIGURE 6.26 The individual profile Properties dialog box

CHECKPOINT

✔**Objective 6.01: Monitor, Optimize, and Troubleshoot Performance of the Windows XP Professional Desktop** In this objective, we looked at the two tools used to automate certain tasks: the Task Scheduler and the Schtasks command-line utility. This automation will ease the overhead of day-to-day administration, especially on larger networks. Also in this objective, we examined ways that we can monitor system performance, assisting the administrator in the vital tasks of benchmarking and bottleneck detection.

✔**Objective 6.02: Manage, Monitor, and Optimize System Performance for Mobile Users** This objective looked at the use of Offline Files, which are most often used to keep files synchronized between laptop computers and network servers. We looked at the steps needed to configure a client for Offline Files and ways to automate offline file usage by changing the server's configuration.

✔**Objective 6.03: Restore and Back Up the Operating System, System State Data, and User Data** In this objective, we looked at the Windows XP Backup utility and how it can be used to get a system back on its feet after loss of data. We examined both the Backup Wizard and Advanced Backup interfaces and took particular note of the various backup types. We also defined what comprises the System State and how it can be recovered.

✔**Objective 6.04: Manage Hardware Profiles** We gained an understanding of hardware profiles and looked at the steps involved in creating additional hardware profiles for a single computer that uses multiple hardware configurations. We also identified some of the instances where this might be most beneficial.

REVIEW QUESTIONS

1. There are several ways to create a scheduled task on a Windows XP Professional system. From this list, choose the three that are possible.

    A. Open the Control Panel and double-click the Scheduled Tasks program.

    B. Open the Control Panel and double-click the Administrative Tools folder.

    C. On the Start menu, choose Programs | Administrative Tools and click Scheduled Tasks.

    D. On the Start menu, choose Programs | Accessories | System Tools and then click Scheduled Tasks.

    E. Use the Schtasks command-line utility.

2. You are administering a small network of computers running Windows XP Professional. You want to automate several utilities, such as Disk Defragmenter, so that you will not have to remember to walk over to every computer to run them each time. Which of these properties will you not be able to configure as you manage your routine tasks?

    A. That the user account will be used to run the task

    B. That the task will not run if the computer is running on batteries

    C. That the task will be run only one time

    D. That another task will be run if certain conditions trigger the secondary task

3. Marion is the administrator of the corporate network, and the infrastructure includes a file server running Windows 2000 Server. There are several folders shared out from this server that most users

access regularly. All of the client machines, including the laptop computers of the outside sales department, have recently been upgraded to Windows XP Professional. She wants to use Offline Files to synchronize changes made to network files on the laptops while the sales staff is away from the office. Which computer(s) do you need to configure?

A. Both server and laptop

B. The server

C. The laptop

D. Neither server nor laptop. When Windows XP Professional is installed on a laptop, default behavior for the laptop is to enable caching on all shares accessed.

4. Which of the following statements is true about Offline Files?

A. From the XP client, you can make files available offline on any computer that is sharing out a folder by using the SMB protocol.

B. Offline files are available only between computers running a version of Windows XP.

C. You can access files offline when the sharing computer is on the local network, but not when traffic must cross a WAN connection.

D. Once the Enable Offline Files option is set on the client, any connection to a share is automatically cached.

5. Crystal is administering a peer-to-peer network of Windows XP Professional computers. The users of this network access her machine for client lists that are kept in a shared folder on her system. To reduce the amount of network traffic to her machine, Crystal wants to configure it so that users are always working with cached copies of the lists, and she decides to set things up so that any opened files in this folder are automatically downloaded each time a user connects to the folder. The clients have already configured Offline Files from the Folder Options dialog box. How should Crystal configure the share for automatic download?

A. From the Shares node of Computer Management, set the Share Properties to Automatically Cache Accessed Files.

B. On the Sharing tab of the folder's Properties dialog box, click the Caching button and select the Automatic Caching for Documents setting.

C. On the Sharing tab of the folder's Properties dialog box, click the Caching button and select the Automatic Caching for Accessed Files setting.

    D. On the Sharing tab of the folder's Properties dialog box, click the Caching button and select the Manual Caching for Documents setting.

6. Natasha has just purchased a new laptop computer, and has finished configuring two hardware profiles—one docked and one undocked. She will use the docked profile when she is at the office and connected to the network and use the undocked profile while telecommuting. One day at the office she reboots the computer and then checks her voice mail for the next five minutes. Upon returning to the laptop, Natasha notices that she cannot use the company network. What is probably going on?

    A. The network card has just gone out.

    B. She has been disconnected by a failure at the hub.

    C. The undocked profile has been set as the default hardware profile.

    D. The DHCP scope has run out of IP addresses.

7. Jonathon has recently checked out a company laptop for out of town meetings. The laptop has a fresh install of Windows XP Professional, and Jonathon wants to configure a separate profile that will apply when the computer is used for these meetings. What steps should he take before configuring this second hardware profile?

    A. Back up the System State data and reboot the computer.

    B. Make a copy of the default profile, reboot the computer, select the copied profile, and make changes.

    C. Make a copy of the default profile, switch your Current Configuration to the copied profile, and make changes.

    D. No preparation is necessary. Two profiles will be created automatically for a Windows XP Professional laptop.

8. You are sitting down and installing Windows XP Professional on a brand new computer. How many hardware profiles will be created during this install?

    A. None

    B. One

    C. Two: one for networked and one for standalone

    D. Two: one for the Guest account and one for Administrator

9. Matt's XP system is not starting, and he wants to try to repair it without blowing out the current operating system installation. What possible methods does Matt have at his disposal to repair this installation? (Choose all that apply.)

A. Use the Recovery Console.

B. Use the Emergency Repair process.

C. Use Directory Services Restore mode.

D. Use the Local System Restore option from the Advanced Options startup menu.

10. You want to use the Recovery Console from the Advanced Startup menu, but do not see it. What utility should you run to install the Recovery Console as a startup option?

A. Winnt32 /cmdcons

B. Winnt32 /console

C. Setup.exe /cmdcons

D. Setup.exe /console

11. Angelique is busy planning a backup strategy for a Windows XP Professional computer at a web design firm. There are several sites that are maintained from her machine. Each site's contents, with the subfolders, can be several gigabytes in size. She wants the backups to be done every day in the least amount of time possible, but she wants the restores to be performed quickly as well. What should Angelique's strategy be?

A. Normal backups

B. Incremental

C. Differential

D. Normal and Differential

E. Normal and Incremental

REVIEW ANSWERS

1. **A D E** Double-clicking the Scheduled Tasks in the Control Panel opens the Scheduled Tasks window, where you can create or modify scheduled tasks. This Scheduled Tasks window can also be launched from the System Tools program group. Alternatively, you can create scheduled tasks from the Command Prompt with the Schtasks utility. B and C are not correct because they are not valid paths to the Scheduled Tasks utility.

2. **D** This question requires you to have explored a bit beyond the text of the book and taken a peek at the Scheduled Tasks Properties tabs. This option cannot be specified from the task management tools. A, B, and C are incorrect because all of these things can be configured about a given task.

3. **D** Both the server and the laptop. A share must be configured at the server. Caching is automatically enabled and set to Manual Caching For Documents. The client then accesses the share and makes the data available offline by choosing Make Available Offline from the context menu.

4. **A** You can make files available Offline from an XP client on any computers that are running the SMB protocol, the Microsoft file sharing protocol. Therefore, B is wrong; the Offline Files feature is not limited to the XP operating system. C is wrong because the physical connectivity component is not a concern, just as it is not a concern with sharing. D is also incorrect because the client usually has to specify exactly what resources will be available offline by running the Offline Files Wizard.

5. **B** After a folder is shared, it is enabled for manual caching only. Clicking the Caching button opens the Caching Settings dialog box. From there, in the Setting drop-down box, select Automatic Caching For Documents. After a client computer is configured for Offline Files access to this share, opening any file automatically downloads it and makes it available offline.

6. **C** The question asks what is most likely, and C is the troubleshooting step you should take first. The default hardware profile will be used after a countdown, which is, by default, 30 seconds. Answers A, B, and D could all be the cause of lost network function, but none is as likely as the profile problem mentioned here.

7. **B** These are the necessary steps to create and modify a second profile. A is incorrect because, while necessary sometimes, backing up the System State will not help in this matter. C is incorrect because you cannot switch to the second hardware profile unless you reboot the computer. D might be correct if the laptop devices fully supported Plug and Play and are ACPI-compliant and a docking station was used, but no mention of such a configuration is made, so you can't assume this in the question. Good Microsoft test practice is to take the questions at face value and not to outwit yourself reading too much into the question. (And, you *know* what happens when we assume.)

8. **B** One hardware profile is created, called Profile 1, containing all of the hardware detected at setup time. Any changes are made to that default profile until a second hardware profile is created. A is incorrect because a profile is needed for the computer to start. C is incorrect because only one profile is created. D is something that would apply to user profiles, not hardware profiles.

9. **A B** The Recovery Console provides access so that recovery commands and utilities can be run—for example, copying a known good copy of a boot.ini file. The Recovery Console is also the preferred method of restoring a damaged Registry. The Emergency Repair process returns the computer to the state it was in when the operating system was first installed. This is not to say that data is harmed, but any configuration changes that were made to the Registry will be reset. C is a valid option from the Advanced Options Start menu, but only on domain controllers, and the Windows XP Professional computer is *not* one. D is incorrect because this is not a valid recovery option.

10. **A** This is the command to install the Recovery Console, which is not installed by default. Choices B, C, and D do not exist, except in my imagination.

11. **D** There's some room for argument here, but combining these two backup types is the best way to balance these two goals. A nightly differential backup would back up any changes to the share and could be applied quickly to the last normal backup in the event of a restore. A is wrong because the normal backup would back up the whole share, taking too much time. B is wrong because there would never be a reference point for the incremental backup to look for. C is wrong for the same reason. These backup types need to be combined with a normal backup. E is wrong because while backups would be a breeze, you would potentially have many incremental backups to apply in the event of a restore, taking up too much time.

CHAPTER 7

Implementing, Managing, and Troubleshooting Network Protocols and Services

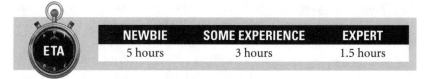

	NEWBIE	SOME EXPERIENCE	EXPERT
ETA	5 hours	3 hours	1.5 hours

XP Professional is an operating system that is built to talk to other computers and to be a good network citizen— this chapter looks at the mechanisms that allow this to happen. What follows is an explanation of the languages spoken and rules followed when computers are exchanging information. We also examine how computers establish connections to one another and share information.

We explore the Transmission Control Protocol/Internet Protocol (TCP/IP) and how it relates to networked computing. Ages ago, when Microsoft was certifying folks for a mastery of the Windows NT 4 operating system, the information about the TCP/IP protocol was covered in an elective exam. Now, however, make no mistake: the material presented in this chapter is "elective" no more. Because of the central role TCP/IP plays in allowing networks from vendors of all types to communicate with each other, you need to have a complete understanding of how it works, no matter where your next step in the computer field takes you.

The services of TCP/IP have evolved with the explosion of computer networks and, more specifically, with the development of the largest computer network on the planet, the Internet. Despite the one-time claims of former presidential candidates (and election winners), TCP/IP was originally developed during the 1970s by the Department of Defense for the same reason that the interstate highway system was developed: to get things across the country quickly using many possible routes in case one of those routes was bombed. And, like the highway system, business and individuals quickly recognized the computing system as a means to transform the way we conduct commerce and pursue leisure activities. Since those early days, TCP/IP has been evolving and has been improved and added to by the open standards community.

This last point has been one of the keys to TCP/IP's success and survival: because no one really *owns* the protocol, and because hundreds of programmers are constantly looking at ways to improve its performance and flexibility, it has become an excellent way to connect dissimilar networks, as in the case of the Internet.

The design of Windows XP tightly integrates with these dependable, time-tested, and open-standard Internet technologies. As a result, when you understand how to configure and maintain a TCP/IP network, you understand how Windows XP operates in a network computing environment.

Along with an overview of the TCP/IP protocol stack, we will focus in this chapter on some of the additional services that take advantage of the wide availability of the TCP/IP infrastructure. Services like dial-up networking and virtual private networks (VPNs) allow us to extend a local TCP/IP network across wide geographic boundaries, without any change in network functionality.

Dial-up networking and VPN support are key technologies to operating Windows XP Professional in a wide area network (WAN) computing environment.

Microsoft also wants you to be familiar with some of the technologies that are used to take advantage of TCP/IP networks. One such technology is Internet Explorer, an operating system component (if you buy the argument) that allows you to easily connect to and request resources on TCP/IP networks. Another is Internet Information Services, which lets you set up a website, so that people using browsers, um operating systems, um...well now I'm confused...can request resources made available through this sharing service.

Finally, this chapter will look at the Remote Desktop and Remote Assistance. Again taking advantage of the connectivity provided by TCP/IP, these new tools will let you take control of your uncle Elwin's machine from hundreds or thousands of miles away, so that problems can be fixed or you can show him how to get that copy of Flight Simulator up and running. Microsoft has offered similar versions of this before—NetMeeting comes to mind—but never quite like this.

Objective 7.01 Configure and Troubleshoot the TCP/IP Protocol

A *protocol* is the "language" a network interface card (NIC) uses to communicate with other NICs on the network. The principle used is much like human-to-human spoken communication: network cards that want to exchange information must adhere to one of the two following rules:

- They must both "speak" the same language.
- There must be a language translator between the two.

Windows XP Professional supports several network protocols, including TCP/IP, NWLink (Microsoft's version of Novell's proprietary network protocol, Internetwork Packet Exchange/Sequenced Packet Exchange, or IPX/SPX). However, TCP/IP has become the *de facto* standard of network communications, so don't be surprised to see the other network protocols phased out altogether over the next few years. In other words, you won't have to know that much about protocols besides TCP/IP unless you really have to for some special situation.

Because it is the core protocol used to transport packets of information back and forth across the Internet, by a wide margin the most widely used protocol today is TCP/IP. In addition to the advantage of enjoying the support of almost all network operating systems, it also offers the following advantages:

- It is *scalable* for use in networks large and small.
- It is *routable*, which means that the data being delivered may leave the physical network using this protocol. The network device that sends information from one network to another is called a *router*, and a routable protocol has the ability to cross that router.
- It works with companion services like Dynamic Host Configuration Protocol (DHCP) and Domain Name System (DNS) to offer additional functionality and ease of use. These companion services can further be developed and improved independently of the TCP/IP protocol.

All networking protocols, however, share the following characteristic: they are designed to communicate with other network-accessible devices that are running the same protocol. The protocols accomplish this by first breaking up data to be sent—documents, pictures, executables, and the like—into packets, which are then affixed with information so they can reach their destination. At its very essence, the protocols job is to define what information is written on these packets and where that information is written in the packet.

The Role of the Packet

First, understand that information sent over a network—this chapter on its way to the editor, say—is placed on the network wire as a single entity. It is broken up into pieces, and then those individual chunks of data are packaged and sent over the network in something called a *packet* (or *frame* or *datagram*). The terms are really interchangeable, but I'll stick with *packet* for the discussion here. The role of the packet is to make network communication more diplomatic and efficient. If sent as one huge chunk, this chapter would tie up the wire for a considerable amount of time, not letting other computers send data until the entire chunk had been transmitted. Further, if the chunk were corrupted, it would need to be re-sent, doubling the amount of time the data transmission would take.

Through the use of packets, these problems are addressed. Using packets, a smaller portion of the chapter can be placed on the wire, tying it up for a much shorter period of time. This allows other computers to send their own packets when my system is not sending. Network communication is more diplomatic. Also, suppose a piece of data becomes corrupted as it reaches its destination. With packet transmission, only the packet with the corrupted data need be retransmitted, instead of the entire chapter. Communication is more efficient.

You can think of a packet the same way you think about a piece of mail, where the envelope is analogous to a data packet. When you drop a piece of mail into the old mailbox, it contains a destination address and a sender address, and inside the envelope is the "data" meant to get to the recipient—likewise the packet. It, too, contains a sender and destination address, plus the information meant for the target application.

In certain parts of the mail system, mail sorting components look only at the ZIP code. They don't care about the street address or about the name on the envelope, and to look at the "data" would constitute a felony. In certain parts of the TCP/IP suite, the only thing looked at is the destination network address. These components don't care what application is going to pick up the data and don't care what that data says.

As might be inferred from the preceding paragraph, today's networking protocols are implemented as protocol *suites*, or *stacks*, which represent a combination of several pieces of networking software and services working in tandem to provide network functionality. Protocol suites precisely define the series of steps that are applied to a piece of data—the preparation of a packet—that is to be sent over the network wire.

For example, let's take a look at website browsing and the protocols involved: the TCP/IP suite contains Hypertext Transfer Protocol (HTTP) services to support TCP/IP file transfer, which can be sent over an Ethernet network. If you were to diagram it schematically, the HTTP protocol lives on top of the transport services of the TCP and IP protocols. As represented in Figure 7-1, below TCP/IP lives the Ethernet protocol, which defines how the network wire is accessed. Each layer of the protocol suite performs specific actions to a packet of information before the data is either sent from a web server or received by a web browser.

Protocols must be configured on each computer for each computer to operate on the network properly. In fact, most troubleshooting of network protocols comes down to fixing improper configuration of a particular protocol. For example, for TCP/IP to work, a network card must be configured with an IP address. There are a couple of ways that this address can be configured: manually, by typing a number into dialog boxes, or dynamically, through the services of either DHCP or Automatic Private IP Addressing (APIPA). (Both DHCP and APIPA are discussed later in this chapter in the "Configuring TCP/IP" section.)

In addition to the networking protocols, there are operating system components that must also support networking for this all to work, and the next section gives you a better understanding of what these components are.

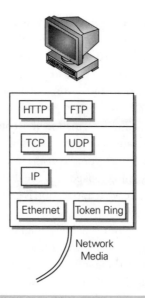

Representation of the TCP/IP stack

Operating System Components of Network Communication

Another critical software component that runs on client computers that access file and print services from server computers is the *redirector*. The job of the redirector is to play traffic cop: it decides whether a request for a resource is to be serviced *locally* by one of the disk device drivers or *remotely* on a network server. Just like transport protocols, the redirectors and server components in a network must also be compatible.

For example, the Microsoft redirector in Windows XP is called the Client for Microsoft Networks (and, just to confuse matters, it's listed as the Workstation Service when you investigate the Services MMC on your system), and it's used to request file and print resources from the Microsoft operating systems running File and Print Sharing for Microsoft networks. (To further confuse, this service goes by the alias Server service when examined under the Services MMC.) You can look at and modify the startup behavior of both these services when you look in the Services MMC Console under the Administrative tools.

If, on the other hand, you want a Microsoft client to access a NetWare server, you must install another redirector that is compatible with NetWare. The redirector for accessing a NetWare server is called Client Services for NetWare (CSNW), which also relies on the installation of the NWLink transport protocol. It is important to know that these two redirectors (client software) can live happily side by side; this is practical, because a lot of organizations are still running both Windows XP and NetWare servers to provide network resources. The Workstation service will be used to access the Microsoft servers, and the NetWare client will be used to access resources from the Novell servers.

Exam Tip

Since the exam focuses on Windows XP Professional, it is best to focus on the redirector's (client's) role in network interoperability as opposed to server interoperability components.

Just as Microsoft clients cannot talk to a NetWare server by default, a NetWare client cannot talk to the Microsoft Server service. Neither can the Macintosh client software. For these clients to interact with a Microsoft Server service, additional software components must be installed on the Windows XP server. These components include File and Print Services for NetWare and File and Print Services for Macintosh. They exist to "fool" non-Microsoft clients into thinking they are talking to non-Microsoft servers, as illustrated in Figure 7-2.

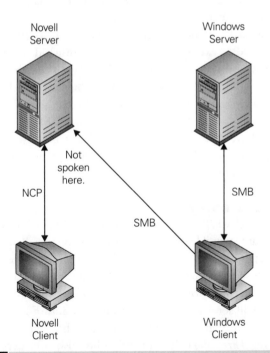

FIGURE 7.2   Clients and servers must speak the same language to exchange data.

TCP/IP Fundamentals

To help you understand TCP/IP, let's start by illustrating a more simplified protocol, one that people already use every day: the telephone system. When you place a phone call, you must dial the area code first (well, you *almost* always have to dial the area code; there are exceptions of course but for Pete's sake it's just an illustration, so stay with me). Your call won't connect with the desired recipient if you decide to dial the area code *after* you dial the seven-digit number. Why? Because dialing the area code first, not last, is part of the set of rules, or the *protocol*, of telephone communications. The area code must be dialed first and be three digits in length, and everyone who uses the Public Switched Telephone Network (PSTN) follows this standard. If you were to dial an imaginary four-digit area code, the phone system would get confused about your request, and communication would fail. These same concepts hold true for the protocols used in computer communication.

We also use a protocol when sending data along a computer network, and as mentioned, TCP/IP is the most commonly used network protocol today. It, too, defines the steps that are taken when computers communicate with one another. On a clean installation of Windows XP Professional, TCP/IP is the default networking protocol installed.

What follows is the condensed version of a lesson in TCP/IP. Entire books have been devoted to exploring TCP/IP, and with good reason. Microsoft, back when they were certifying folks on NT 4, used to teach it in a five-day class. With this in mind, be forewarned: there is *no way* that this chapter can do anything other than present an overview of what is needed to acquire a thorough understanding of TCP/IP. As mentioned, Microsoft assumes by now that you have already gained much of this understanding through real-world TCP/IP networking experience, or through preparation certifications like Network Plus.

TCP/IP's Big Three

When configuring TCP/IP, an IP address and a subnet mask are absolutely required. In a minute you'll learn why. You can, and often will, configure many other optional parameters, such as the default gateway and the preferred and secondary DNS server addresses. One of these optional parameters, the default gateway, is essential for communicating on larger networks, such as the Internet, as we will soon see. For this reason, your author has christened the following TCP/IP configuration settings, in classes he teaches and here in this book, as the *Big Three of TCP/IP*. (Your author also considers it somewhat awkward to refer to himself in the third person. Just thought you would want to know.)

Travel Assistance

If you don't have a fairly good idea of what an IP address is already, you need to begin your studies elsewhere, such as *Networking: A Beginners Guide, Second Edition* by Bruce Hallberg (McGraw-Hill/Osborne; ISBN 0072132310), or in *Mike Meyers' A+ Certification Passport* (McGraw-Hill/Osborne; ISBN 0072193638), and then come back to this chapter. As I said, this should mostly be review.

The IP Address   Computers speak to each other using numbers, and the *IP address* is the number that uniquely identifies your computer on the network. Further, the IP address identifies what network your computer is living on. The IP address is a 32-bit binary address—a string of 32 1's and 0's—that humans work with by breaking up into four octets (each octet being made up of 8 bits) that are then converted into decimal equivalents and separated by periods. In other words, the IP address to a human is going to look something like this:

```
192.168.2.200
```

but to the computer, it's just a string of 32 1's and 0's:

```
11000000101010000000001011001000
```

Every IP address is composed of two parts: the *network* ID and the *host* ID. The network ID represents the network the computer belongs to, while the host ID uniquely identifies the computer on that network. Every network ID on a TCP/IP internetwork (like the Internet) must be unique—kind of like every ZIP code in the U.S. must be unique. Further, every host ID on each network must also be unique—kind of like every house on a street must have a different number. So there must be a way to separate the IP address into a network portion and a host portion. But how does IP do this? How does the computer know which part of the IP address is the network identifier and what part is the host identifier? Read on.

The Subnet Mask   The *subnet mask* is used to divide the IP address into the network portion and the host portion. It is a required TCP/IP setting. Without the subnet mask, the computer has no idea what network it belongs to. The subnet mask is also a 32-bit binary number broken into four octets for easy human consumption. A subnet mask might look like this to us:

```
255.255.0.0
```

The interesting thing to note about the subnet mask is how it looks to the computer, as shown in Figure 7-3.

4 decimal octets

To You: 2 5 5 . 2 5 5 . 0 . 0

Subnet
Mask

To Your
Computer: 11111111   11111111   0000000000000000

4 binary octets

| FIGURE 7.3 | The subnet mask displayed in decimal and in binary |

Notice anything about the binary number shown in Figure 7-3? That's right; it's a string of *contiguous* 1's followed by another string of *contiguous* 0's. Note also that the decimal number 255 octet is a string of eight binary 1's. The decimal 0 octet is a string of eight binary 0's. The job of the 1's, then, is to *mask* out the network number—they identify which of the 32 1's and 0's in the IP address are used as the network ID. Everything else—everything that lines up with the 0's in the subnet mask—denotes the host ID.

If we use the IP address with the subnet mask here, we are able to determine which 1's and 0's of the IP address are the network ID, and which 1's and 0's are the host ID. The subnet mask tells us that the first 16 binary numbers are the network number, which when we convert back to decimal is 192.168. The next 16 binary numbers are the host ID, which translate into 2.200.

If any of this is confusing, think back to the example of the telephone protocol. Part of the telephone number you dial represents a big grouping of phone lines (the first three numbers), and part represents an individual line within that larger grouping (the last four numbers). You can think of this as the network ID and the host ID in IP communications.

So why is this determination of network ID and host ID important? Why is a subnet mask *required* for a valid IP address? It is needed for the successful delivery of information to the proper network, and it helps make TCP/IP a *routable* protocol.

Each and every packet of TCP/IP communications has a *source* address and a *destination* address. And once TCP/IP determines the network ID of the source and destination computers, an important decision is made about how to deliver the packet to its destination. If the network IDs match, the packet is delivered to the local segment of computers. But if the network IDs of source and destination do not match, the packet must be *routed* to a remote network via a default gateway.

The Default Gateway   Here's another key ingredient in IP configuration, the last component in the Big Three. Although it is not technically required, your network communication would be very limited without a default gateway.

A default gateway is the IP address of the *router*, which is the pathway to any and all remote networks. To get a packet of information from one network to another, the packet is sent to the default gateway, which helps forward the packet to its destination network. In fact, computers that live on the other side of routers are said to be on *remote* networks. Without default gateways, Internet communication is not possible, because your computer doesn't have a way to send a packet destined for any other network. On the workstation, it is common for the default gateway option to be configured automatically through DHCP configuration (We'll discuss DHCP in a bit).

> **Local Lingo**
>
> **Router**   We tend to think of a router as a big box with the letters C-I-S-C-O etched on the front, but it can be any device that simply passes information from one network to another. Almost any Windows machine with multiple network cards can be configured to act as a router.

CIDR Notation

There is another way of expressing the IP address without having to spell out the subnet mask in octets of 255's and 0's. Instead, you can count out the number of 1's in the subnet mask and then represent the IP address and subnet mask with a forward slash followed by the number of 1 bits in the subnet mask, like this:

```
192.168.2.200/16
```

This notation is called Classless Inter Domain Routing, or CIDR (pronounced "cedar") notation, for short. The notation here specifies the same IP address as used in the preceding example. To wit: the IP address part is very straightforward. The same one as just mentioned. The "forward slash 16" (/16) tells you that this IP address has a subnet mask with the first 16 bits set to 1. And 16 1's gives you a subnet mask of: 255.255.0.0. Same as in the example.

CIDR notation is used to simplify entries on routing tables and is the notation used by a majority of backbone Internet routers. It is also used to cut down on the number of wasted IP addresses in the class B address space. You should know how to recognize the CIDR notation when you see it and to convert the CIDR subnet mask notation into an octeted decimal equivalent.

Travel Assistance

I wish I had the space to explain every concept in painstaking detail, but that's not why you have obtained this book. Much of the reasons why CIDR was developed is beyond the scope of this book and the 70-270 test. For further information on CIDR and IP address classes, please see the *Microsoft Windows 2000 TCP/IP Protocols and Services Technical Reference*, by Thomas Lee and Joseph Davies, Microsoft Press.

Configuring TCP/IP

After you install and bind TCP/IP to a LAN or a WAN adapter (remember that this will be done automatically by Windows XP Setup), the core tasks for configuring TCP/IP include the assignment of an IP address, the configuration of name resolution, and the configuration of TCP/IP security.

A client can get an IP address *statically* or *dynamically*. Static addressing is accomplished through the Internet Protocol TCP/IP Properties dialog box by an administrator who manually types in the IP address, the subnet mask, and the default gateway, as shown in Figure 7-4.

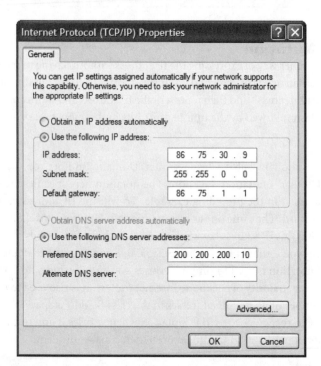

FIGURE 7.4 Configuring TCP/IP

To open the Internet Protocol TCIP/IP Properties dialog box:

1. Right-click My Network Places and choose Properties.

2. Right-click Local Area Connection and choose Properties.

3. Select Internet Protocol (TCP/IP) and click the Properties button.

Rather than typing all this information on hundreds or thousands of computers in your network, you can let DHCP do it for you by selecting Obtain an IP Address Automatically. As one of the companion services of TCP/IP that can run on a Windows 2000 or .NET Server, DHCP's job is to hand out valid IP addresses to computers on the network at boot-up time. It must always be configured to assign the two required IP address components—the IP address and the subnet mask. It can be, and usually is, configured to assign configuration information about the default gateway and name resolution servers. By using this vital component of modern TCP/IP networks, you can automate the IP address allocation to network computers to reduce confusion, administrative overhead, and problems related to human error.

> **Travel Advisory**
>
> You will be tested heavily on the DHCP server topic—but not on the Windows 70-270 Exam. You cannot set up a Windows XP Professional computer as a DHCP server, although, as explored next, XP can be configured to behave *like* a DHCP server.

By default, when TCP/IP is installed on a Windows XP Professional computer (which is always the case with a default installation), the computer is configured as a DHCP client. This configuration can be done at any time from the Internet Protocol TCP/IP Properties dialog box.

And, although it's counterintuitive, a DHCP client does not even need a DHCP server to get an IP address. A DHCP client that cannot locate a DHCP server will assign an IP address to itself through a mechanism called *automatic private IP addressing* (APIPA). APIPA is not new to Windows, as it was used beginning with Windows 98. It was first introduced to the NT product family with Windows 2000. The following section explains how it works.

Automatic Private Internet Protocol Addressing

When a DHCP client is unable to locate a DHCP server, the client picks out a random IP address from the private APIPA address range of 169.254.*x.y*, with a subnet mask of 255.255.0.0. The 169.254.x.y IP range is *private* because that network number is not in use on the Internet; it is *random* because the client generates an arbitrary host number (the *x.y*) for that network. Let's say the client picks the host ID of 100.23. The client will then announce to the network that it wants to use the IP address of 169.254.100.23. If no other computer announces, "You'll get this IP address when you pry it out of my cold, dead, silicon chipset," or a bunch of 1's and 0's to that effect, the client registers that IP address and binds it to the network card.

The significance of APIPA is that DHCP client computers that cannot find a DHCP server can still be assigned an IP address and communicate with other computers on the same subnet that also cannot find a DHCP server. It allows communication when the DHCP server is down, or just plain not there. Note, however, that APIPA does not assign a default gateway, and therefore it cannot communicate with any computers that live on the other side of a router.

At times you might prefer this behavior, as it can be an effective method for easily administering TCP/IP in a small network. Keep in mind, however, that the addresses assigned will not be able to communicate with Internet hosts or with a host that exists on any other network, because APIPA assigns an IP address and subnet mask but not a default gateway.

Exam Tip

APIPA, because of its relative newness in the NT world, is an exam topic you can expect to see covered. I would especially be prepared to identify the indicators of an APIPA-configured machine (an IP address of 169.254.x.y), what its significance is (the DHCP server is down or nonexistent), and what its symptoms are (computers on a segment can communicate with one another, but not with remote computers).

Name Resolution

Computers identify each other using numbers, because that's what computers do—they crunch numbers. Humans, however, like to give computers names, because that's what people do. After all, humans invented computers so that we wouldn't have to work with the numbers. The upshot of these anthropological considerations is that computer communication, at least when humans are involved, usually relies on name resolution to translate names to IP addresses.

A quick example to illustrate. When you log on to a domain, you use a domain name, not a number. That request is sent to another computer, in this case a domain controller. But how does your client computer know to which domain controller to send the request? And how does it actually send your logon request to a domain controller? It does this through a name resolution mechanism that resolves the *name* of the domain into a *number* for the domain controller(s) that can answer your logon request. Which name resolution mechanism is used depends on how the network is configured. Again, there are several mechanisms whose entire *raison d'être* is to resolve names to IPs. These methods include using files such as HOSTS and LMHOSTS, and services like DNS and WINS (Windows Internet Naming Service) servers, all of which we'll discuss next.

Old School: HOSTS and LMHOSTS Files   HOSTS and LMHOSTS files are simple text (ASCII) files that contain name-to-IP address mappings. The HOSTS file maps either host names or fully qualified domain names (FQDN) to IP addresses. It was the original name resolution method used on the Internet, and there are still some situations where its use is merited, but these situations are few and far between (more on that in a moment). A sample HOSTS file is shown in Figure 7-5.

So how do you know what your host name is? Look at the System Properties dialog box, and then check out the Computer Name tab. You will see an entry that specifies the Full Computer Name. The host name is the left-most portion of that Computer Name if your system lives in a domain. If you are in a workgroup, you will see only the Host name listed. To change the Host name for a system, click the Change button from This Computer Name dialog box.

Your system also has a NetBIOS name assigned to it. This name is kept for backward compatibility with NetBIOS applications and services, and it will always match the Host name assigned to your machine. To examine the NetBIOS name for your machine, click the Change button from the Computer Name tab,

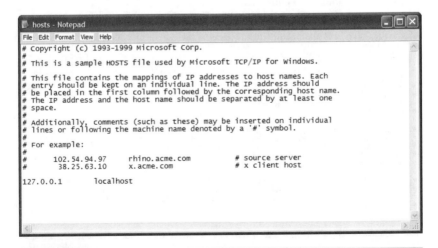

FIGURE 7.5   The sample HOSTS file

then click the More button. Notice that this NetBIOS name will match the host name and that you cannot configure an alternate NetBIOS name.

The LMHOSTS file does for NetBIOS names what the HOSTS file does for host names, again simply mapping names to IP addresses, as shown in Figure 7-6. This figure shows you just a section of the LMHOSTS file, as the entire file includes extensive instructions about how to use the file. What's important is to note the difference in syntax between the HOSTS and LMHOSTS files.

Oh, and where do you find these two files? They can be examined and edited from this location: *systemroot*\system32\drivers\etc.

As mentioned, you won't be using these files too often because of their limitations. One of the drawbacks of using the HOSTS file or the LMHOSTS file for name resolution is that they are created manually, which can be a pain and is prone to human error. The other big drawback of the HOSTS and LMHOSTS files is that they are static and do not adapt well to an environment in which the IP addresses of machines is changing constantly. Where do IP addresses change constantly? In any environment that uses DHCP, and that pretty much means every single network out there today.

To illustrate, consider what happens if a client grabs one IP address one day and you manually update the HOSTS file to reflect this. The next day, however,

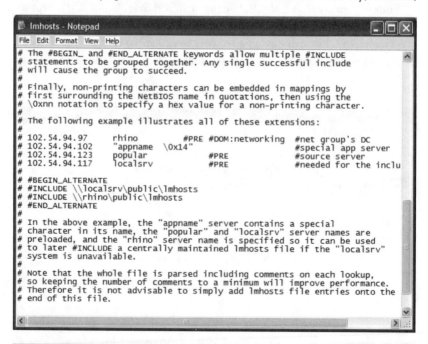

FIGURE 7.6   A sample LMHOSTS file

the client grabs another IP address from the DHCP Server. What happens then? The HOSTS file would then contain an incorrect address mapping, that's what, and you would have to edit the HOSTS file again. In such a case, you should consider using a name resolution server solution where the entries are updated automatically. Enter DNS and WINS.

The King of Name Resolution: Domain Name System Servers   Domain Name System (DNS) Servers are used to resolve host names, or FQDNs, to IP addresses. They perform the same function as the HOSTS file, but the database of DNS name-to-IP address mappings can be updated automatically. As clients obtain new IP addresses, their mapping information is updated so that name resolution to IP addresses is always current.

Local Lingo

Fully Qualified Domain Name (FQDN)   The name assigned to a TCP/IP host combined in the domain parent containers. For example, an FQDN of brian.techking.net would identify the host called brian, which lives in the .techking parent domain, which in turn exists in the .net parent domain container, which in turn lives in the root (.) DNS domain.

DNS serves as the *core* name resolution service for Windows XP; as you will learn, Windows 2000 and .NET Active Directory domains are not even possible without a DNS server. In other words, everything Windows 2000 and beyond relies on DNS for name resolution, so the sooner you learn DNS inside and out, the better.

You configure a Windows XP Professional client to use a DNS server for name resolution in one of two ways: by setting it as optional configuration information in DHCP, or by manually pointing the client to the IP address of a DNS server in the Internet Protocol TCP/IP Properties dialog box (either from the General tab or the Advanced Properties dialog box, DNS tab), as shown in Figure 7-7.

A Four Letter Word: WINS   WINS servers are to DNS servers as LMHOSTS files are to HOSTS files. (Was that an SAT test question? Can't remember.) They are used to resolve NetBIOS names to IP addresses, which can be an important function for backward compatibility with Windows NT 4. NT 4's default networking protocol and naming scheme was NetBIOS. The WINS database of computer name-to-IP-address mappings is also capable of being updated dynamically, just like Windows 2000's and .NET's version of DNS. This makes WINS another excellent choice for clients when DHCP is used in a network.

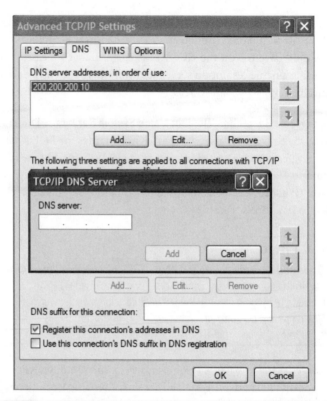

FIGURE 7.7   Configuring the DNS server addresses for a Windows XP Professional client

You may configure a Windows XP Professional system as a WINS client by having DHCP hand out the address of a WINS server as part of automatic IP address configuration, or you can configure the Windows XP Professional computers with a WINS Server address manually. To configure this manually, access the WINS tab after clicking the Advanced button from the Internet Protocol TCP/IP Properties dialog box. The Advanced TCP/IP Settings dialog box is shown in Figure 7-8.

Other Networking Protocols

Earlier in this chapter, we discussed how multiple client redirectors can be installed on the same Windows XP Professional computer. Doing this lets a client access resources kept on different types of servers. Likewise, multiple networking protocols can be installed on the same computer, which is also a necessary

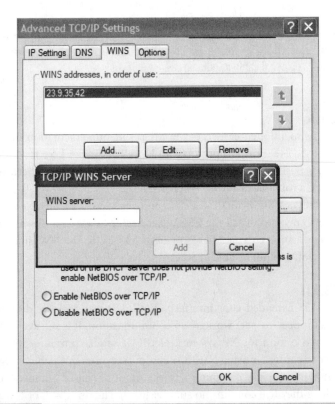

FIGURE 7.8 Configuring Windows XP Professional for WINS

step in enabling communication between different networks. In fact, when you install certain client components, such as Client Services for NetWare (CSNW), you also install the networking protocol needed for communication, such as NWLink.

Keep in mind, however, that due to the popularity of the Internet, there is only one protocol you really need to understand: TCP/IP. Several years ago, it was not uncommon for a Windows computer to require many networking protocols in order to communicate on a large network. (Most small business and home users found these protocols useless.) Because TCP/IP is now the networking protocol standard, though, these additional protocols have become more and more irrelevant, and I would not be surprised if you *never* have to install or configure either of these two protocols in your life, outside of preparing for these exams. However, this is precisely why I have included a small section on them here.

Travel Advisory

You can't remove TCP/IP from a Windows XP machine. It's that essential. You can disable it, but you cannot uninstall it.

NWLink

NWLink, as mentioned earlier, is the Microsoft implementation of Novell's IPX/SPX, used as a transport protocol for Novell networks. Like TCP/IP, its job is to deliver packets of information from one computer to another. Also like TCP/IP, it is a routable protocol. When installed by itself, however, the NWLink protocol does not allow you to access file and print resources on a Novell server; you will also need to install the CSNW redirector to access a file on NetWare servers. You can even run Microsoft networks using the NWLink protocol alone, but you will not be able to access Internet resources.

NetBEUI

The NetBIOS Extended User Interface (NetBEUI) protocol was developed in the 1980s for peer-to-peer workgroup communication. It is still available as an unsupported option for XP systems. NetBEUI sends communications from computer to computer using NetBIOS computer names in a *flat naming* space. (In a flat naming space, computer names cannot be reused because the name space where they live contains no subdivisions.) The drawback of NetBEUI is that it is not routable and is therefore not a solution for routed networks, like the Internet. It can cause performance problems on some networks, and should only be used if an existing network absolutely requires it.

To install either of these alternates to TCP/IP, follow these steps.

1. Click the Install button on the Local Area Connection Properties dialog box. (The procedure for opening this dialog box is described earlier in the "Configuring TCP/IP" section.)

2. The Select Network Component Type dialog box appears, as shown in Figure 7-9. Specify that a Protocol component will be installed (as opposed to a Client or Service component), and then click Add.

3. In the Select Network Protocol dialog box, choose the protocol you want to add.

   • To install IPX/SPX, select the NWLink IPX/SPX Compatible Transport Protocol and click Add.

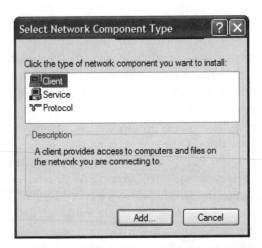

FIGURE 7.9 Selecting the network component type

- To install NetBEUI, you must insert the Windows XP CD, click the Have Disk button, and then browse to the Valueadd\Msft\Net\ NetBEUI folder. Click Open and then click OK.

4. You can start using IPX/SPX immediately. A reboot is required before you can use NetBEUI.

Travel Advisory

Notice that if you install NetBEUI, you will get a warning that the driver is unsigned. Told you it was unsupported. Also, XP will preserve a NetBEUI installation and settings if the computer is upgraded from a previous version of Windows, you'll just never see it as an option on new installations.

Binding Order

In the unlikely event that you are using multiple protocols on your XP Professional client computer, an important performance setting for your computer is the *binding order* of the protocols. On a system with only one protocol (as is the default, TCP/IP), you can't set a binding order. When a system is running multiple protocols, though, the binding order determines what protocol is used first when establishing network communications. What's important to understand when setting binding order is that the *client* determines the protocol used in information transfer, not the server. Therefore, setting binding order on the server does not have a significant impact on network performance, but setting it on the workstation can have considerable effects. You will set the binding order from the Advanced Setting dialog box shown in Figure 7-10, which you access from the Network and Dial-Up connections window by choosing Advanced | Advanced Settings.

How will the binding order of protocols make a difference when networking computers together? Let's say, for example, that your network connection has both IPX/SPX and TCP/IP installed and bound, but you rarely use the IPX/SPX protocol because you rarely access NetWare servers. In this case, you would make sure that the TCP/IP protocol was at the top of the list of bound protocols to ensure best performance. This would tell the computer to try TCP/IP first when establishing a network connection. Again, because the client, not the server, is initiating the conversation, the binding order on the client is of greatest import.

FIGURE 7.10   Setting the binding order for network protocols

Troubleshooting TCP/IP

Many things can go wrong in network communication, and you will spend a great deal of your administrative time making sure computers can get information back and forth. As with all troubleshooting, you will gain more expertise by doing rather than by reading. However, you should be familiar with a few tools and techniques ahead of time.

The first line of any communications effort should be to check the physical connections. Is everything turned on and attached? One of the old saws of network troubleshooting is that the top ten reasons that networks break are at the ends of your arms. People mess with things, sometimes unknowingly, and they break. Cables get kicked, tripped over, cut by construction crews, and just generally moved, and cleaning crews have been known to unplug devices to plug in their vacuum cleaners. Companies have exposed cable close to radio transmitters, acting as antennas that attract excess network noise. The more time you spend in the field, the more things you will see that can interrupt network communication, none of which call on your actual knowledge of operating systems or network protocols.

If, however, you determine that everything is attached properly, but a network adapter is not able to communicate on the network, check the Device Manager to verify that the driver is installed and operational. If everything then checks out, you can get down to the business of checking and testing your network protocols.

TCP/IP is a complex and mature protocol suite, and it includes as a part of the protocol stack a robust set of utilities for troubleshooting and diagnostic purposes. These are the utilities that you need to be familiar with for the exam. To diagnose whether the TCP/IP stack is loaded properly, you can use tools such as IPCONFIG.EXE, PING.EXE, and TRACERT.EXE.

IPCONFIG.EXE   The IPCONFIG.EXE command-line utility displays IP configuration information. When it is run without any switches, it will show the configured IP address, subnet mask, and default gateway. It can also be used with one of several switches that can be listed by running IPCONFIG with the / ? (help) switch. Table 7-1 shows a few of the more common IPCONFIG switches you will use.

PING.EXE   The Packet Internet Groper (PING) command-line utility is used to send a packet of information that is used to verify that a computer can communicate with other devices on the network. You can think of it as sonar for computer communication. If a PING is successful, the computer is on and can send and receive TCP/IP packets with a remote host. Therefore, other types of communication should work as well.

TABLE 7.1	Common IPCONFIG Switches
Switch	**What It Does**
/all	Shows information about your IP connection, including any DNS and WINS servers used and whether the address is dynamic or static, and shows the host name.
/release	Releases the IP address that has been assigned through DHCP. You cannot release a leased IP address through the TCP/IP Properties dialog box.
/renew	Renews a DHCP address. Not possible through the TCP/IP Properties dialog box.
/registerdns	Re-registers the DNS name with the configured DNS server. Can be useful for troubleshooting name resolution problems.
/flushdns	Clears the contents of the DNS resolver cache located on the workstation. A client will check its DNS resolver cache before checking a DNS server. This will clear out an incorrect entry made by an improperly configured DNS server.

The syntax of the PING command is this:

```
ping IP Address or computername
```

The PING command can be used with a series of modifiers, such as changing the size of the PING packet. Use the /? (help) switch to see a list of these modifiers. You won't see test questions on any of these modifiers, though.

When communication is failing, the general flow of PINGing to verify TCP/IP connectivity from a computer is as follows:

1. PING the loopback address of 127.0.0.1.
2. PING the local computer's IP address.
3. PING the default gateway.
4. PING the remote computer you are trying to reach.

This can also be done in reverse order to try to isolate the cause of broken network communication.

Further, you can PING other computers by using IP addresses or by using host names. This is a good way to troubleshoot name resolution problems. If a PING is successful using the IP address of a computer but not its host name, you should check your name resolution methods for problems. (This might be a good time to run ipconfig /flushdns.)

If PING is unable to resolve an IP address on the network but PINGing the local loopback adapter address of 127.0.0.1 works, type **ipconfig** to verify that an address has been assigned to the network adapter. Configuration and protocol testing varies from one protocol to the next.

TRACERT.EXE The TRACERT.EXE utility is used to follow the path a packet takes as it tries to reach its final destination. This utility uses PING packets with progressive time-to-live (TTL) values, starting with a TTL of 1. Each time a packet hits a router, the TTL value is decremented by at least 1. When the TTL value reaches 0, the packet is dropped. This prevents all undelivered traffic on the Internet from still being out there, passing from one router to another in a never-ending attempt to reach its destination.

In the case of TRACERT, a TTL of 1 means that the packet will die at its first stop. When it dies, another companion protocol will report back that the packed has, indeed, expired and will also report the IP address of the device that dropped the packet. The next PING packet sent to the destination has a TTL value of 2. It dies two hops away from its source. The TTL keeps incrementing until the PING reaches its destination, at which time the route from sender to receiver has been reconstructed.

The TRACERT utility, because it steps through the path a packet takes, is useful for identifying slow or broken links in the information chain from point A to point B. The syntax of the command is similar to PING:

```
tracert IP Address or computername
```

The TRACERT utility should begin reporting the route taken by the packet, along with performance indicators for each stop along the way. You will be able to see where the slow links are in the network.

Travel Advisory

It is possible that you will be able to browse a website even though you cannot PING the web server, because many firewalls on the Internet filter out the type of packets used for PINGing (Internet Control Message Protocol, or ICMP, traffic). This is a security measure— one easy and effective hack is to flood a web server with continuous "fat packet" PINGs from one or more computers, which try to overwhelm a server with repeated, large PING packets. One way to combat this is to have a firewall block all ICMP traffic. You can experience this firsthand by surfing to a site like www.microsoft.com and then opening a command prompt and trying to PING the same site.

NSLOOKUP The NSLOOKUP utility displays information that you can use to diagnose Domain Name System (DNS) infrastructure and is available only if you have installed the TCP/IP protocol. There are two modes of NSLOOKUP:

interactive and *noninteractive*. Which one is appropriate depends on the kind of information you want. As always, use the /? switch to retrieve exact syntax. For test purposes, you need to know what this tool does, not necessarily how to use it.

If you need to look up only a single piece of data, use the noninteractive mode. For the first parameter, type the name or IP address of the computer that you want to look up. For the second parameter, type the name or IP address of a DNS name server. If you omit the second argument, NSLOOKUP uses the default DNS name server. For example, to find out what IP address mapping a DNS server called SERVER1 has for a computer called GRIFFIN, the NSLOOKUP syntax will look like this:

```
nslookup griffin -server1
```

If, however, you need to look up more than one piece of data, you should use interactive mode. Type a hyphen (-) for the first parameter and the name or IP address of a DNS name server for the second parameter. Or, omit both parameters and NSLOOKUP will use the default DNS name server; that is, just type **nslookup** at the Command Prompt, and you will be in interactive mode at your default DNS server.

Travel Advisory

A Reverse Lookup zone must be properly configured at the DNS server for this to work, because you are looking up the name of the DNS server based on the IP address gathered from your client's TCP/IP properties information. For additional information on Reverse Lookup zones, please see *Mike Meyers' MCSE Windows 2000 Network Infrastructure Administration Certification Passport (Exam 70-216)* from McGraw-Hill/Osborne (ISBN 007219568-1).

PATHPING This utility combines the functionality of the TRACERT and the PING utilities to provide information about problems at a router or a network link. It does so by providing information about network latency (slowness) and network loss (dropped packets) at all points between a source computer and a destination computer. Because PATHPING displays the degree of packet loss at any given router or link, you can determine which routers or subnets might be having network problems. There are several parameters that govern PATHPING's use, and when used without parameters, PATHPING displays help.

When PATHPING is run, it generates a report that will take some time to create. The first results you see will list the route taken from source to destination.

This is the same path that is shown using the TRACERT command. However, next you will see a busy message displayed for approximately 90 seconds. During this time, information is gathered from all routers previously listed and from the links between them. At the end of this period, the test results are displayed, and you will be able to use this information to determine where problems lie in the network infrastructure.

Troubleshooting Tips

Much of your troubleshooting effectiveness is predicated on a thorough understanding of the technologies that let computers communicate with one another. For example, if clients are set up as DHCP clients, check to ensure that the DHCP server is available. Remember that Windows XP Professional DHCP clients who cannot locate a DHCP server will choose an IP on their own using APIPA. What would be the result of an IP address chosen from APIPA? Your ability to recognize this problem will depend on your understanding of this technology. One of the common symptoms of such a condition is that these computers will all be able to talk to each other on their own subnet (because they *will* be on the same 169.254.*x*.*y* IP subnet), but they will be unable to communicate anywhere else, such as the Internet. When troubleshooting, remember that APIPA does not assign a default gateway.

As was mentioned, every IP address must be unique. If a computer tries to use an IP address that is already in use on the network, the IP address will not bind to the network adapter. This arrangement prevents disruption of network communications. Fortunately, Windows XP is kind enough to inform you when a duplicate address is detected. You will see a dialog box explaining that an IP address conflict has been detected, usually before you are able to log in. If you run the IPCONFIG utility, the subnet mask will be 0.0.0.0.

To troubleshoot name resolution problems, determine whether the problem is related to NetBIOS name resolution or host name resolution and check the corresponding files and/or services. If NetBIOS name resolution is the problem, review the LMHOSTS file and conduct a check of WINS. If host name resolution seems to be the trouble, check the HOSTS file and the DNS service. You can also generate a summary status report of network activity with the Network Diagnostics utility (NETDIAG.EXE).

Using Repair   If you are used to Windows 98 or Me, you are probably familiar with the Winipcfg command to help you diagnose and troubleshoot IP configuration problems. This command is no longer available with Windows XP, and you will have to use the IPCONFIG utility, as described previously.

There is however, a simplified way to graphically look at network configuration called Status, and from the Status window you can use Repair. To view the Status of your network connection, follow these steps:

1. Open the Network Connections dialog box, as described earlier, and then double-click a connection for which you want to see more information.

2. There are two tabs here, the General and the Support tabs, as shown in Figure 7-11. Choose the Support tab to see the currently assigned Big Three: IP address, subnet mask, and default gateway.

3. If there is a problem with connectivity, you can use the Repair button to use the automated repair. Clicking this button will run the following commands in the background, all usually a part of normal troubleshooting resolution:

   - **ipconfig /renew** Automatically renews your IP address from a DHCP server.

   - **arp –d** Flushes the Address Resolution Protocol cache. Incorrect cached entries can cause resolution to the wrong IP address, even if the other name resolution services in the network are working properly.

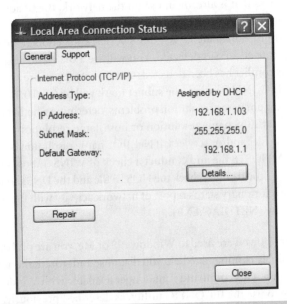

FIGURE 7.11 The Status window, showing an IP address assigned by a DCHP server

- **Nbtstat –r**   Reloads the NetBIOS cache.
- **Ipconfig /flushdns**   Does the same for the DNS cache.
- **Ipconfig /registerdns**   Registers the computer name at the configured DNS server.

Connect to Computers Using Dial-Up Networking

Objective 7.02

So far, the focus of networking has been on a LAN—computers in a room or office building that communicate with one another using networking components such as network interface cards (NICs), CAT 5 cabling, and switches (or hubs), with maybe a router separating floors of an office. But what if you want to extend that network to include computers in other cities, in other countries even. Well, you can't very well string cable between computers from, for example, Athens, Georgia, to Atchison, Kansas. Fortunately, however, other companies do lay this wire so that information can be carried over long distances. One of those networks of wire is the Publicly Switched Telephone Network (PSTN), built by companies like Ma Bell for the express purpose of enabling telephone communications. With different equipment and different communication protocols, computers, too, can take advantage of this existing infrastructure to get data from point A to point B.

Connect to the Internet Using Dial-Up Networking

So while it may seem difficult, complex, and even mysterious, at its heart, dial-up networking behaves exactly the same as a local network set up in your office: computers send information to one another in the form of an electrical signal, which is carried over a wire connecting the two computers. It's incredible to think about, but every web page you view as you are surfing is a result of a physical connection (there are a few wireless exceptions) of wire between the sender and recipient. All that's different with dial-up networking are the wires and the protocols. When we dial-up, we are connected to every other computer on the Internet. We have become the Borg.

The purpose of dial-up networking is to allow you to connect to and access remote network resources, such as an Internet service provider (ISP) or your corporate network. You will accomplish this by creating a connection in the Networking And Dial-Up Connections window. Each connection object in this window is a logical object and can contain settings unique to that connection.

One of the places you are likely at some point to dial up and connect to, even as broadband Internet access becomes more readily available, is an Internet service provider. The steps to creating a dial-up Internet connection are very straightforward and are as follows:

1. On the left side of the Network Connections dialog box, under the list of Network Tasks, is the Create New Connection task. Click this task.

2. The New Connection Wizard will launch, and you will then click Next to proceed.

3. Here's about the hardest part: the next window, as shown in Figure 7-12, will ask you what type of connection you want to create. There are five choices here; for this example, we will select the first choice, Connect to the Internet. (We will be looking at some of the others later in this chapter.)

4. You will have three choices in the next window—under the assumption that we already have our ISP picked out, we will choose Set Up My Connection Manually.

5. The next window offers you the choice of what hardware is going to make the connection. We are configuring a dial-up connection, so we will choose to Connect Using a Dial-up Modem.

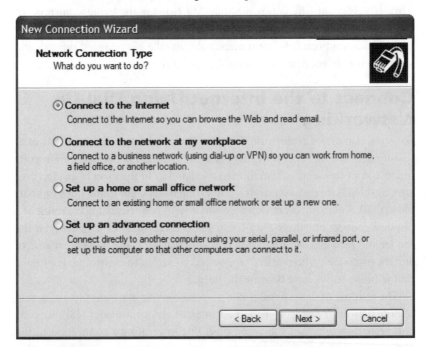

FIGURE 7.12   Setting up the network connection

6. The next dialog box will prompt you for the name and phone number of the ISP, and then the user name and password for the connection. When you have supplied the necessary information, click Finish to complete the wizard.

The dial-up connection will now be represented with an icon in the Network Connections window. As you will see, the dial-up Internet connection can be leveraged to access a remote corporate network through the use of a VPN. However, there are other times when you want to dial directly to a corporate network, bypassing the Internet altogether. For this objective, you will create a connection that dials to a remote access server, as described later.

Create a Dial-Up Connection to Connect to a Remote Access Server

When you dial-in to a remote access service (RAS) server, you are making a direct connection to your private network, as illustrated in Figure 7-13. RAS is a technology that allows remote users to connect to the network by using a modem and dialing the phone number of the RAS server. Once the RAS server answers, the remote user has a connection to that server and can access the network resources as if the user were on the network. The RAS server takes data it receives from one network interface (the modem), and routes it to the LAN using another network interface (the network card). The RAS server acts as the outside boundary between the mobile user and the corporate network, enabling the LAN to be extended over other wires. The RAS client can connect using several dial-up technologies, but a plain old modem is, by far, the most common way.

Note that the RAS server and the dial-up client must be using the same connectivity option; the client can't dial-up with a regular modem if the server has an Integrated Services Digital Network (ISDN) modem installed.

You will configure a dial-up connection from the Network Connections window by taking the following steps:

1. Start by choosing the Create New Connection task. This time, you will select the Connect to the Network at My Workplace option (refer to Figure 7-13).

2. You will then be asked to create either a dial-up connection or a virtual private network connection. For our new objective, we will select the first option, Create a Dial-Up Connection, and click Next.

3. The next few dialog boxes will look familiar. Supply the company name and the phone number of the RAS Server, and you are done.

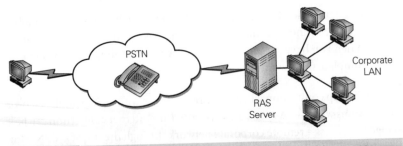

FIGURE 7.13 The RAS server receives your remote request to access the LAN.

Dial-Up Protocols

Because different wires are used in dial-up networking for carrying data across long distances, different protocols are used to help the packets along their way. The Windows XP Professional dial-up client can use two protocols to transmit information over long-distance serial (phone) lines. The Serial Line Internet Protocol (SLIP) can be used to connect to legacy dial-up servers, such as UNIX servers running SLIP. You cannot use SLIP to dial up to a Microsoft Windows NT or Windows XP server, because the SLIP protocol is not supported on the Microsoft RAS server side. The dial-up client can also use the Point-to-Point Protocol (PPP) for dial-up connections, which is the preferred method for establishing serial connections. Most modern dial-up servers support PPP, and, as mentioned, Microsoft servers support *only* this protocol for incoming connections. It is recommended that PPP always be used when you have a choice.

Why not SLIP? In a word, because it's unsafe. Unlike PPP, the SLIP protocol (yes, that's redundant) transmits passwords in clear text. PPP, on the other hand, encrypts passwords before sending them over the wire. Additionally, PPP supports other security features such as mutual authentication, data encryption, and callback, which are not supported by SLIP.

Configure and Troubleshoot Internet Connection Sharing (ICS)

The Internet Connection Sharing (ICS) feature makes a dial-up Internet connection available to other computers on the network, and it functionally behaves the same way as folder sharing. It allows a small office to connect to the Internet through a single connection, as illustrated in Figure 7-14.

To configure ICS, you need to share out the logical connection object from the Advanced tab of the Properties dialog box of that connection, as shown in

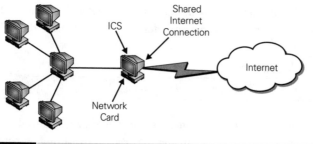

Internet Connection Sharing

Figure 7-15. The other network computers who will be using this shared connection for Internet access need to configure their ICS through a LAN as they step through the Internet Connection Wizard.

Much like the services of DCHP, ICS allocates IP addresses and subnet masks to computers in the network. Also, the ICS computer sets a default gateway on these computers that is the same IP address as the computer performing ICS. That way, any packets destined outside the local network are routed to the ICS

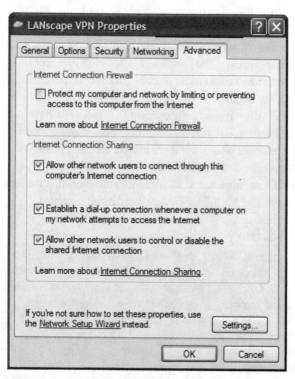

FIGURE 7.15   Sharing the Internet connection

computer. The default gateway in this case is the network adapter of the computer configured for ICS, which now performs the services of a dedicated router.

Travel Advisory
To set up ICS, you must be in the Administrators group.

Demand dialing is an enhancement of ICS that will automatically dial a connection when required. This eliminates the need for the computer running ICS to maintain an open connection, and it can be an ideal solution when WAN access is infrequently needed or when the leasing of a dedicated line would be cost prohibitive.

Multilink   Another feature enhancement of dial-up and ICS connections is Multilink, which allows for the bandwidth of multiple dial-up connections to be combined. When a connection is configured for Multilink, the single *logical* connection uses the multiple *physical* connection components (that is, modems and phone lines) to establish the link to the dial-up server. All the connections are combined and load-balanced to improve performance. Multilink is also dynamic. As bandwidth requirements decrease, Multilink can be configured to drop the number of physical connections to save on connection costs. The Multilink feature relies on the Bandwidth Allocation Protocol (BAP), and both the dial-up server and client must be configured to support Multilink. Most of your Multilink configuration will be done at the Remote Access Server. That's because Multilink is automatically enabled in Windows XP Home Edition and Windows XP Professional. Just specify other phone numbers for a connection.

To assign multiple phone numbers to a connection, access the dial-up connection's Properties dialog box and then, from the General tab, click the Alternates button. From this list, add all additional numbers that the Remote Access Server supports, and Multilink will be automatically enabled.

Travel Advisory
For several reasons, Multilink is not a practical real-world solution for connectivity. If you have two modems and use Multilink, but the dial-up server is not configured to support your two inbound connections (for instance, because it has only one modem installed), you are simply wasting a phone line and a modem. Moreover, the reduction in cost and availability of broadband Internet connectivity means that you can get 10 to 20 times more bandwidth for as much as—and maybe less than—the cost of an extra phone line and modem. Increased availability of broadband access means that configuration of virtual private networks is now imperative. Read on.

Connect to Computers Using a Virtual Private Network (VPN) Connection

A VPN extends the scope of a company's private LAN across a non-private WAN—namely, the Internet. It works by having a remote client establish a connection to the public Internet—doesn't matter how: dial-up, cable modem, DSL—and then, using that networking infrastructure, establish a *tunneled* connection to the corporate LAN. Figure 7-16 is a conceptual representation of this tunneled connection. Note that a VPN connection requires a Windows XP Server computer configured as a VPN server to serve as the endpoint of the tunnel.

Because of the tunneling protocols involved, the communication sent to the remote network remains completely confidential, even though the medium used to transmit the data is completely public. In other words, the network communication is *virtually* private. Get it? To the end user, there is no difference between working locally at the private LAN or remotely through a VPN. Everything's the same to the end user—same shares, same permissions, same access to network printers. The VPN connection just uses different protocols and different wires. VPNs have become an ideal choice for companies to implement WAN connectivity at a dramatically reduced cost.

Authentication Protocols

Several protocols used by Windows XP give you many authentication and encryption options. These protocols are used in conjunction with the existing network protocols (TCP/IP, for example) to scramble user names and passwords, encrypt the data that is being transmitted, or both. These additional protocols define the level of security that your dial-up or VPN connections have, and they are configured via the Security tab of the Virtual Private Connection Properties dialog box, as shown in Figure 7-17.

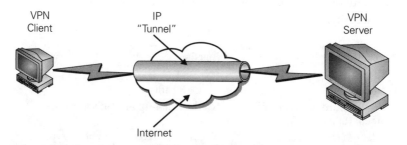

FIGURE 7.16   Representation of a tunneled connection

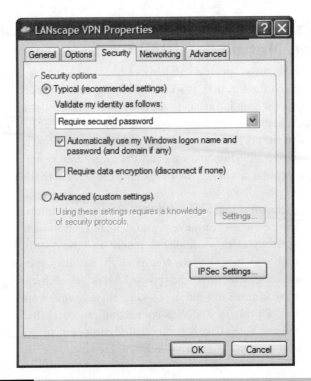

FIGURE 7.17   The Security settings of a dial-up or VPN connection

If you need to configure specific security protocols, select the Advanced radio button on the Security tab and then click the Settings button to open the Advanced Security Settings dialog box, shown in Figure 7-18.

From this dialog box, you can configure the type of encryption that will be used for the VPN connection and whether or not logon security will use the Extensible Authentication Protocol (EAP). As the name suggests, EAP lets you *extend* the functionality of logon security with the use of other devices, such as smart cards or certificates. It also lets you select from the following protocols for logon security:

Protocol	Function
Password Authentication Protocol (PAP)	Uses a plain-text password and is the least secure for this reason
Shiva Password Authentication Protocol (SPAP)	Used for dial-up into Shiva servers
Challenge Handshake Authentication Protocol (CHAP)	Negotiates a secure form of encrypted authentication

Protocol	Function
Microsoft CHAP	Uses one-way encryption with challenge-response method; can be used by XP, NT 4 and 9x clients
Microsoft CHAP version 2	A more secure form of Microsoft-CHAP

Exam Tip

One authentication method you should be especially aware of is the Extensible Authentication Protocol-Transport Level Security (EAP-TLS), which provides certificate-based encrypted authentication. It is the authentication protocol you would need to enable smart card support.

With VPNs, a remote access client connects to a remote private network using either the Point-to-Point Tunneling Protocol (PPTP) or the Layer Two Tunneling Protocol (L2TP) with IP Security (IPSec). A VPN connection allows you to tunnel packets securely using standard networking protocols such as TCP/IP, IPX/SPX, or NetBEUI (if present).

Data encryption is supported between remote access clients and RAS servers using either the Microsoft Point-to-Point Encryption (MPPE) or IPSec. IPSec is

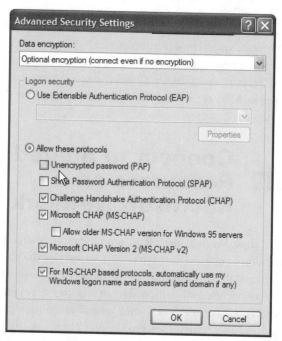

FIGURE 7.18 Additional security configuration

a set of security protocols and cryptographic protection services that ensure private communication over IP networks and can be applied to any TCP/IP connection, including the LAN connection. IPSec provides L2TP with encryption services so that data is transmitted securely from the remote access client to its final destination on the remote network. L2TP is a tunneling protocol; with IPSec, L2TP operates as a VPN. IPSec ensures that data sent through the L2TP connection can be read only by the intended recipient.

Travel Advisory

You must choose an authentication protocol that meets or exceeds your security requirements, and that is supported by the client and the remote access server.

Troubleshooting Dial-Up Networking

Several troubleshooting aids help solve configuration problems with the dial-up facility. One of these is PPP logging, but you must first enable it on a client, as it is not enabled by default. To enable PPP logging on a client, use the Netsh dial-up scripting utility. Type **Netsh /?** at the command line for information on using this utility.

If you are able to establish a connection with the remote network but are unable to communicate with remote resources, run **Netdiag** to review a summary report of network communications. If a dial-up device is unavailable for configuration in the Network and Dial-Up Connections window, check the dial-up hardware in Device Manager and use the Add/Remove Hardware Wizard to install the device.

Objective 7.03

Connect to Shared Resources on a Microsoft Network

In the first two objectives, we looked at the ways and means that computers use to send information to one another. We've been examining the physical connection components and the languages used to send packets of data over these connections. Now we turn our attention to the end result of getting these computers to talk to one another. What is being accessed when we enable communication?

We touched on many of these topics in Chapter 2 as we set up what was being shared and how we could then secure those resources. So just to review (and so you're not flipping back and forth for an earlier reference), the following are several methods for connecting to a shared resource:

- Browsing through My Network Places
- Mapping a network drive through Windows Explorer
- Using the NET USE utility from the command line

These methods require that you understand an important syntax for identifying resources on a network: the universal naming convention (UNC) syntax. The UNC syntax locates the resources in the network and the servers they live on, like this:

```
\\servername\sharename
```

This syntax is used by the NET USE utility and when mapping a drive, and it is also used under My Network Places.

Windows operating systems also include a service, called the Computer Browser, that works in the background to collect and publish information about the servers and the shares available on a network, so that users can obtain a graphical look of what's out there by simply clicking around, rather than using a bunch of UNC pathnames.

Browsing

Now for a quick refresher on regular sharing. As was discussed in Chapter 3, file system resources are made available to network users by creating shares. We do this (unless you're a command-line devotee) by using Windows Explorer. As we do this, there are two services working behind the scenes that are key ingredients in making shares available to network users: the Server service, which we've discussed, and the *Computer Browser* service.

As we've learned, the job of the Server service is to make available a computer's files using the SMB protocol so that clients running the Workstation service can access them. The job of the Computer Browser service, on the other hand, is to make everyone on the network *aware* of all the shares that have been made available and which computers are making them so. In other words, the Computer Browser service exists to manage lists. It all works through a series of browser *roles* that different browser computers play on a network.

Here's how the Browser service works: On every subnet is a Master Browser that keeps the list of all computers running the Server service. Each time a computer boots up on the subnet and is running the Browser service (all NT, 2000, .NET, and XP computers do), it contacts the Master Browser and gives it the updated information. The Master Browser then compiles this and other announcements from the subnet's computers into a Master Browse List and sends copies of the latest edition to backup browsers on the subnet. The backup browsers then do most of the dirty work of browsing the network. Browse clients, when they want to find out what resources are out there, first contact a Master Browser, who sends a list of backup browsers. The client contacts one of the backup browsers and retrieves the browse list, as shown in Figure 7-19. The client then selects one of the computers from the browse list and retrieves directly from that computer the list of resources that are being shared.

I could go on for several pages about the mysteries of the Browser service. For example, it can take up to 30 minutes for a computer that has been turned off to be removed from the browse list. It can also take awhile for your computer to show up on a browse list in the first place, especially if servers in the network are being rebooted. In such cases, the Master Browser role can shift, and it can take awhile for new Master Browsers to update their browse lists, although use of a WINS server can alleviate many of these problems. (But do you *need* WINS in a 2000 network? No.)

Fortunately, this information is not something that you will have to know volumes about for your 70-270 test, or even in a working network for that matter, because the Browser service is self-configuring and self-managing. Just keep this canned answer handy when users ask you about why they don't see certain computers on the network from time to time: "The Browser service is just a little weird sometimes. If it's not there in half an hour, call me back."

Connect to Resources Using Internet Explorer

As has been Microsoft's much-litigated practice with the last several versions of its operating systems, Internet Explorer (IE) is installed automatically when you

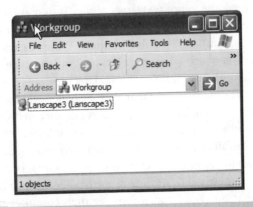

FIGURE 7.19   The browse list for a subnet

install Windows XP. Microsoft isn't shy about its presence, either, and there's almost nowhere you can look and not see the blue Explorer "e" icon. It's there at the top of the Start menu, the All Programs menu, the Quick Launch toolbar, and usually on the desktop (especially if you've upgraded).

The main purpose of IE is to allow you to connect to and retrieve web resources, usually pages that have been saved in the HTML format. Graphic files, such as .jpeg and .gif files, can be displayed from within a browser window, along with a host of other files. Additionally, it can also be used to connect to and download files from File Transfer Protocol (FTP) sites. However, it is not limited to accessing resources on the Internet. IE can also be used just as easily to browse resources that are on the local machine, or on systems within your organization's corporate LAN.

Here are some of the several ways you can connect to resources using Internet Explorer:

- **Enter the Uniform Resource Locator (URL) into the address bar** You can save yourself typing time by cutting and pasting URLs as well. The URL's function is to uniquely identify each and every resource (web page) on the Internet, but the syntax can be used in intranets as well. If you enter just the name of another server on your LAN, for example, IE assumes you are looking for another host in your configured domain and will attempt to connect to that system's web publishing service.

- **Enter a UNC pathname** You can also connect to LAN resources by entering UNC syntax, as described earlier, in the Address bar. This will let you connect to resources made available with the SMB protocol, just as if you had entered this into a Run dialog box or had browsed through My Network Places.

- **Selecting from a drop-down list** The Address box also, by default, remembers the last 25 URLs you've typed into the Address bar.

- **Linking from another web page** The hallmark of web browsing is that you don't have to type to access resources. Through the magic of the Hypertext Markup Language (HTML), you click and the link does the "typing" for you.

- **Selecting from the History or Favorites lists** IE, by default, maintains a record of pages viewed over the past 20 days, which you can access by clicking on the History button in Explorer's toolbar. You can do the same with the Favorites button, accessing a list of links you have told IE to save.

Finally, this test objective requires that you know how shared resources can be protected when network connections are made. If you are reading this book out of sequence, then I refer you back to Chapter 3 for a full discussion of how shared resources are secured. If you are reading in sequence, remember that you can use two separate layers of security: share permissions and NTFS permissions (if the resource lives on an NTFS drive). Know how these two layers of permissions interact for best security implementation and for a maximum chance of test success.

There is another method of making resources available besides via SMB sharing, and we haven't yet talked about it, except for a brief mention in Chapter 3. Fortunately, though, it's one that you already are familiar with on some level, especially given the previous discussion about Internet Explorer: it's Web sharing made possible by Internet Information Services.

Configure, Manage, and Implement Internet Information Services (IIS)

Objective 7.04

W*eb sharing*, put simply, is the sharing of files using the Hypertext Transfer Protocol (HTTP), as distinguished from the Server Message Blocks (SMB) protocol for Server service sharing. Windows XP uses a different software component to accomplish HTTP publication: *Internet Information Services* (IIS). However, the version of IIS installed with XP Professional is a more limited version than the one that will install on 2000 Server or .NET machines. A fully functional IIS installs only on server machines. IIS, as implemented in Windows XP Professional, is designed to act as a small-scale web server for a small intranet or Internet site with limited traffic.

IIS will not be installed by default, unless you have upgraded a machine that was running Personal Web Server. You install IIS by choosing the Add or Remove Programs icon in the Control Panel (Classic view) and then choosing Add/Remove Windows Components. You then check the Internet Information Services (IIS) box, as shown in Figure 7-20.

After IIS is installed, you will see new program items in Administrative Tools called Personal Web Manager and Internet Information Services Manager. You will use these tools to configure and manage your website by right-clicking the node you want to manipulate and choosing Properties. Figure 7-21 shows you how the Internet Information Services Manager will look.

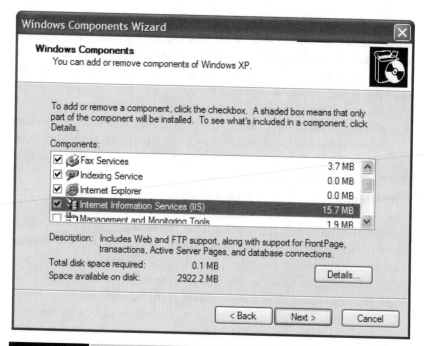

FIGURE 7.20 Installing IIS

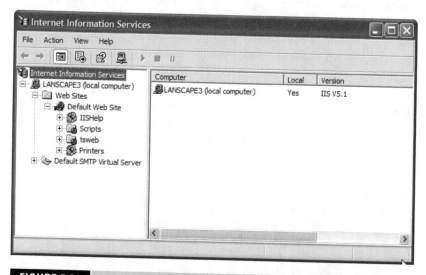

FIGURE 7.21 The Internet Information Services Manager utility

The console tree will represent the logical directory structure of your web and FTP sites, much in the same way that Windows Explorer shows you the directory structure of your regular old folders and files. At the top of this food chain is the computer name whose IIS installation you are administering. You can connect here to other web servers by right-clicking the computer object (you could also select this from the Action menu), and choosing Connect.

Under the computer name entries are the websites, FTP sites, and Default SMTP server objects, although these names are a bit misleading. With Windows XP Professional, you are only allowed to create one site of each type, despite what these parent folder names suggest.

At the next level down are your sites, which are given default names and locations. For example, the default website is called "Default Web Site". What is probably most important at this point about IIS, what you should come away from this discussion with if nothing else, is that these sites are really just pointers to content. In the case of the Default Web Site, the pointer is to this location: C:\Inetpub\wwwroot. (If we assume that XP is installed on the C drive.) Any web pages stored here will be made available by the Default Web Site.

Under the sites, you will see a listing of the folders, or directories, that your site contains. *Ordinary directories* point to corresponding folder locations in the Inetpub\wwwroot directory and are represented with a folder icon. *Virtual directories* are pointers to content that is located elsewhere—either elsewhere on your hard disk or on other computers in the network. The term "virtual" refers to the behavior the user experiences when accessing your website; content looks like it comes from a subfolder of the site, but that content can be physically stored on another computer in a completely different location.

You will configure the parameters of both your sites and directories from each object's Properties dialog box, accessed by right-clicking an object and choosing Properties. With these dialog boxes, you can set the pointer locations, permission and authentication settings, and logging behavior. You are advised to open a dialog box or two to get familiar with what is configurable here.

Travel Assistance

This topic, too, is extensive enough to be the subject of a separate exam. If you want, you could study for the 70-226 Exam, and there are books that are devoted to only developing and designing web solutions using Windows 2000 and IIS. For more information on IIS, I recommend starting with this title: *MCSE Training Kit: Designing Highly Available Web Solutions with Microsoft Windows 2000 Server Technologies,* from Microsoft Press.

There is yet another technology that relies on a working TCP/IP connection, one that allows one user to control another's computer as if it were the user's own. This technology is called Remote Desktop, and is the last 70-270 Exam objective covered in this chapter.

Configure, Manage, and Troubleshoot Remote Desktop and Remote Assistance

As mentioned in the introduction, there have been programs that have been around for several years that allow remote users to connect to your system and take over. They have been popular with computer technicians because the programs allow support staff to fix computer problems without having to make a desk-side visit where the suspect computer resides. The Windows XP version of these programs is called Remote Assistance.

Travel Advisory

These programs are little Terminal Emulation programs, with the *mainframe*, or host, computer being the computer that is being remotely controlled, and the *terminal* computer just sending mouse movements and keystrokes over the network for processing at the host. PC Anywhere, Carbon Copy, and Laplink are popular programs, but you can even perform this operation with free programs like NetMeeting (or even the notorious Back Orifice, but you didn't hear that from me).

Letting a Friend Help Out from a Remote System

With Windows XP's Remote Assistance feature, you get the functionality of a program like PC Anywhere included in the operating system. With this feature, someone sitting at a computer with an Internet connection has the ability to become an extension of the Help and Support Center, allowing you yet another way to get help on the Web.

To use Remote Assistance, both parties must be using Windows XP, both must have an active Internet connection, and neither can be blocked by firewalls. Creating an Assistance session can be summarized in a four-step process:

1. You (the term Microsoft uses for "you" is "the novice"—the one needing the assistance) will enable Remote Access through a check box under the Remote Desktop section on the Remote tab of the System Properties dialog box, as seen in Figure 7-22.

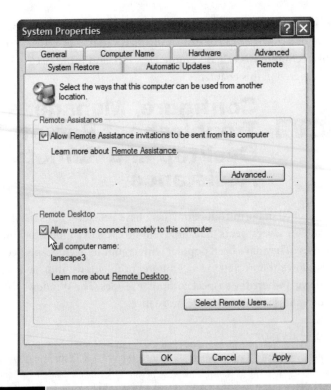

FIGURE 7.22   The Remote tab

The novice will select the option to Allow Users to Connect Remotely to this Computer. By default, the administrator, the account currently logged on, and any members of the Remote Users group can connect remotely. Which users are allowed to connect can be further managed with the Select Remote Users button.

2. The novice must then enable the Allow This Computer to be Controlled Remotely option, which will be set by clicking the Advanced button in the same Remote tab, as seen in Figure 7-23. The expert (see the following) will then have control over the novice's mouse and keyboard as if they were right there at the system. Until the novice enables this option, the terminal window will be a read-only session, allowing viewing and message exchange (including voice) only.

3. The novice then sends out a Remote Assistance Invitation by going through the Help and Support Center. The Invitation is listed as the first task under Ask for Assistance. Click this task, and the next Help and Support Center window, shown in Figure 7-24, lets you send out the request. Alternatively, the novice can use Windows Messenger or e-mail.

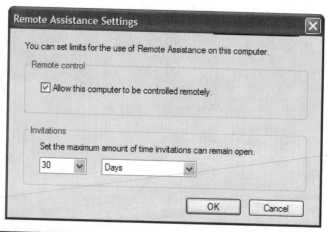

FIGURE 7.23   Allowing remote control

4. If the friend and computer guru agrees to help you (Microsoft refers to this individual as "the expert"—although I'm sure there will be plenty of heated familial debates about who gets to wear which crown), this user will open a terminal window that displays the desktop of the novice's machine. The expert will open the Remote Connection by choosing Start | All Programs | Accessories | Communications | Remote Desktop

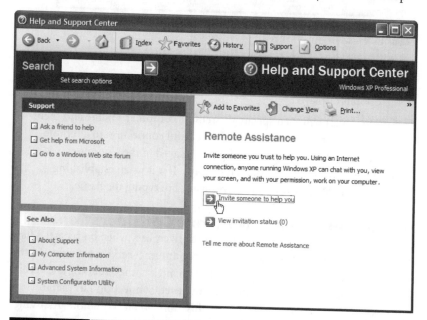

FIGURE 7.24   Sending the invitation

FIGURE 7.25   Establishing the Remote Connection

Connection, opening a dialog box, as shown in Figure 7-25, with all options displayed.

5. The expert will then specify the remote computer's name and then supply user credentials. After a successful connection to a remote desktop, the name of the computer is saved in the Computer drop-down list. You can then simply select it when establishing subsequent remote connections instead of typing the name.

Remote Assistance Network Considerations

Setting up a Remote Assistance session is relatively easy when both parties have a public IP address that has been given by an Internet service provider. In this scenario, the computers connect directly with one another, sending and receiving data on TCP port 3389. Further, the Internet Connection Firewall in Windows XP will automatically open up this port when a Remote Assistance connection is requested. We will discuss the Internet Connection Firewall in more detail in Chapter 8.

However, the aforementioned Internet configuration is not applicable to many home or small office settings, where networked computers are hidden behind Proxy servers or Firewalls. In other words, it's not quite as easy as it sounds for most of these users because of the private IP address settings used in such scenarios.

For instance, many home users, especially those that are sharing their broadband Internet connections using a store-bought router solution, (popular SOHO routers include offerings from Belkin and Linksys) are getting their IP addresses through network address translation (NAT). If you're not sure whether or not you're using NAT, check your IP address (type **ipconfig** at the Command Prompt). If you have an address from the 192.168.*x.y* subnet, something like 192.168.1.100, for example, you are using NAT. NAT is hiding the *real* IP address that is used to connect to other computers on the Internet. With NAT, when you send a request to the www.amazon.com web server to order gift copies of this book for your friends, the amazon.com machine is not sending its packets back to 192.168.1.100. It is sending information back to the public address of your router.

Travel Assistance

For more information on NAT or TCP ports, please see www.webopedia.com, and enter **NAT** or **ports** into the Search dialog box. You can also do a search on NAT from almost any search engine for a wealth of reference information on network address translation.

To use the Remote Assistance feature when NAT is included in the equation, perform the following:

- Get your pal to e-mail you a Remote Assistance invitation and edit the file.
- Under the RCTICKET attribute will be a NAT IP address, one beginning with 192.168 (as mentioned earlier).
- Replace this private address with your chum's real IP address—they can find this out by going to www.whatismyip.com. This is a great little site that will let you know what IP address other computers are using to reach yours—even if it is hiding behind NAT or a proxy. (There are many others that do this, but I'll let you find those on your own.)
- Finally, get them to make sure that they've got port 3389 open on their firewall and forwarded to the errant computer.

Travel Advisory

As a final troubleshooting note, if your network is using a computer as an Internet Connection Sharing server that is running Windows 98 or Windows 2000, Remote Assistance will not work properly.

CHECKPOINT

✔**Objective 7.01: Configure and Troubleshoot the TCP/IP Protocol**   In this objective, we looked at the central components of TCP/IP and the ways that Windows XP Professional clients can be configured to receive an IP address. We examined the significance of the DHCP server and the default gateway in day-to-day network operation. We also examined what utilities can be used to troubleshoot TCP/IP and some common problems that may occur.

✔**Objective 7.02: Connect to Computers Using Dial-Up Networking**   This objective focused on how we could extend the networking functionality of Windows XP Professional computers across different networks, such as the Internet. We looked at dial-up considerations to Remote Access Servers and looked at how to implement virtual private networks. Finally, we looked at some of the security protocols that can be used in conjunction with these dial-up and VPN technologies.

✔**Objective 7.03: Connect to Shared Resources on a Microsoft Network**   This objective is a continuation of the topics first explored in Chapter 2, when we looked at network sharing and ways we could secure shared resources. We also looked at how Windows XP participates in network browsing, which is an easy, point-and-click way to find out about available resources on the network.

✔**Objective 7.04: Configure, Manage, and Implement Internet Information Services (IIS)**   This objective examined how a Windows XP Professional computer could be set up to host a website and the software that makes this possible.

✔**Objective 7.05: Configure, Manage, and Troubleshoot Remote Desktop and Remote Assistance**   Here we explored the way that TCP/IP networks could be leveraged to allow users of one XP system to connect to another system for purposes of troubleshooting and assistance.

REVIEW QUESTIONS

1. Which of the following services must be configured on a Windows XP server for a Windows XP Professional client to obtain IP addressing configuration automatically?

   A. DNS

   B. DHCP

   C. WINS

   D. None of the above

2. You are the administrator of a small network of 20 Windows XP Professional computers, and you have negotiated a deal with an ISP wherein it will lease you 20 IP addresses. You decide that it will be easiest to assign these 20 IP addresses to all of your clients manually. One of the computers on the network is reporting communication problems. You investigate, run the IPCONFIG utility, and this reports back an IP address with a subnet mask of 0.0.0.0. What's wrong?

   A. The NIC has failed.

   B. A duplicate IP exists on the network.

   C. The computer is a DHCP client that has not been able to contact a DHCP server.

   D. Nothing is wrong; you have accidentally configured the subnet mask this way.

3. There are several protocols that are available for Windows XP Professional. To maximize potential to communicate with multiple networks, which of these will be installed by default on a clean installation? (Choose all that apply.)

   A. TCP/IP

   B. NetBIOS

   C. NetBEUI

   D. NWLink

   E. AppleTalk

4. Your company consists of 25 computers running Windows XP Professional, and the company's chosen means of getting Internet access is through a cable modem connection to an ISP. However, every computer on the network must occasionally access the Internet to get e-mail, conduct research, and so on. You attach the cable modem in one of the computers running Windows XP Professional and create a new logical connection object for the cable modem connection in the

Network and Dial-Up Connections window. What do you now need to do to accomplish your objective?

A. Enable ICS on the computer where the modem resides.

B. Enable ICS on all computers running Windows XP Professional.

C. Manually assign IP addresses on all computers.

D. Configure all the computers to obtain an IP address automatically.

5. Jinni is the administrator for a small network, consisting of 50 networked computers all running Windows XP Professional. Users need to connect to a shared folder that lives on a computer called JIN. The path to the shared folder on that computer is this: D:\Public \Data\Region1\Sales\Seltzer Water. The \Tonic folder has been been shared out by Jinni with the share name of Tonic. What do you type in the Run dialog box to connect to the share?

A. net use Tonic

B. \\Jin\Public\Data\Region1\Sales\Monthly

C. \\Jin\Seltzer Water

D. \\Jin\Tonic

6. You have decided to configure your XP Professional machine with a static address and need to do so manually. Which TCP/IP parameters must be configured so that the computer can talk to other computers? (Choose all that apply.)

A. IP address

B. Subnet mask

C. Default gateway

D. DNS address

7. Jill is a pharmaceutical rep out on a sales call, away from the office. She is making a sale and needs to connect to the home office back in Chicago to retrieve some of the company's inventory of the latest drug. Which kind of connection will she not be able to create from the Network Connection Wizard?

A. Dial-up to a private network

B. Dial-up to a VPN server

C. Dial-up to the Internet

D. Connect directly to another computer

E. She can create all of these connections.

8. You are a part of the IT department and have just been involved in a project that moved large groups of computers from one subnet to another. The next day, one of the users calls and reports that she cannot access Internet resources, even though she can PING servers on her own subnet. Beth runs IPCONFIG and gets back the following information:

```
Subnet Mask:    255.255.192.0
Default Gateway:  55.100.210.1
```

What is likely the problem with this user's connectivity?

A. TCP/IP is not bound correctly to the network card.

B. The IP address is incorrect.

C. The subnet mask is invalid.

D. The default gateway is wrong for her subnet.

9. You are hired to study network traffic and recommend improvements. As you examine log files, you discover that 80 percent of all packets transmitted in the network are using the TCP/IP protocol, and the other 20 percent of traffic is split evenly between NWLink IPX/SPX packets and AppleTalk packets. When you investigate the properties of client workstations, you further discover that the binding order of the TCP/IP protocol is at the bottom of the list. How should you modify this situation with the least administrative overhead?

A. Change the protocol binding order on the domain controllers, since they are accessed at startup time.

B. Change the binding order at all of the client workstations.

C. Change the binding order at the domain controllers, member servers, and client workstations.

D. Do nothing; the lowest listing in the binding order is tried first.

10. You are running a company made up of two Windows 2000 servers, 50 Windows XP Professional computers, and 20 Windows 98 computers. You are using the services of one of your local servers for DHCP. Your existing dial-up Internet solution is becoming expensive and slow, and the local cable company suggests that you install a cable modem and use its DHCP server for IP address allocation. However, you have more clients wanting Internet access than the cable company is willing to give you IPs for. You decide, however, to get an additional NIC for one of your Windows XP Professional computers, install the cable modem on that new NIC, share out the connection, and disable your existing DHCP service. What will this change in network configuration provide?

A. The internal workstations will get their IP addresses automatically.

B. The number of IPs needed by your company will not be exceeded.

C. All workstations will have access to the Internet.

D. All workstations will be able to resolve Internet names without further configuration.

E. All of the above.

11. You live in Seattle. Your friend lives in Portland. You are attempting to use Remote Desktop so that you can fix his computer. You both have dial-up connections to the Internet, and you can see your friend's desktop when you connect. However, you cannot take control of the session to show your friend what to do. What is likely the cause of this problem?

A. Your computer is probably behind a firewall that is preventing the session from being anything other than read-only.

B. Your friend must make sure that the Allow This Computer to Be Controlled Remotely option is checked.

C. This is not possible with a dial-up connection. You must have a dedicated Internet connection to use the Remote desktop feature.

D. Your friend has likely supplied you with the wrong IP address.

REVIEW ANSWERS

1. **D** Okay, this is a bit of a trick question. Here's my e-mail address for complaints: brian@youhavetocarefullyreadthequestion.com. You might have been leaning toward answer B, but in reality none of these services are required; Windows XP Professional clients can still obtain automatic IP addresses from APIPA if there is no DHCP server running. A and C are wrong because these are name resolution and registration services and are not used for IP configuration.

2. **B** The Windows XP Professional TCP/IP protocol stack checks the network to see if the IP address it is assigned is already in use on the network. If a duplicate address is detected, the operating system displays a dialog box explaining that an IP address conflict has been detected. If you run IPCONFIG, the subnet mask will be 0.0.0.0. A is incorrect because no information would appear for the failed adapter when running the IPCONFIG utility. C is incorrect because the client

would have an IP address and subnet mask, one from the APIPA subnet of 169.254.*x.y*, with a subnet mask of 255.255.0.0. D is also incorrect because Windows will not let you configure an illegal subnet mask, such as 0.0.0.0. You're welcome to try.

3. **A** Only TCP/IP is installed on a clean installation. If any other protocols are present after installation, Windows XP Professional has been installed as an upgrade. All other protocols are optional, with the exception of AppleTalk, which is available only on a Windows 2000 or .NET Server.

4. **A** **D** After the modem is installed, access the properties of the connection and, from the Sharing tab, select the Enable Internet Connection Sharing For This Connection check box. Then configure all the other computers to obtain an IP address automatically. The DHCP allocator in ICS assigns IP addresses based on the 192.168.0.*x* subnet and assigns a default gateway of 192.168.0.1, which will be the new IP address of the computer running ICS. Additionally, on-demand dialing and the DNS proxy are enabled. B is incorrect because only one computer on the network will be running the ICS service; all others will be pointed to that computer for Internet access. C is incorrect because ICS runs the DHCP allocator service to hand out IP addresses, and manual configuration is not required.

5. **D** This is the correct syntax to connect to a share. A is a no-go because, while the net use command can be used to make connections, this syntax is incorrect. B is incorrect because this looks like the MS-DOS pathname. The Server services just makes shares available, no matter what drive they live on or how deep in the folder hierarchy. C is incorrect because the folder, Seltzer Water, has been given the share name of Tonic, and you want to connect to the share. This question illustrates the difference between accessing something locally and over the network.

6. **A** **B** These two parameters are required for TCP/IP communication. The IP address uniquely identifies a computer on a network, and the subnet mask divides the IP address into a network section and a host section. C and D are wrong because they are not required. They will most likely be configured for any fully functioning network, but they are not necessary to get data from one IP host to another.

7. **E** All of these network connection options are available through the Network Connection Wizard.

8. **D** The default gateway here is an address that is not on the user's subnet. Any default gateway will be just another host (a network card with TCP/IP bound to it) on the same subnet. This host will have the ability to forward packets to other network cards that live on other subnets. A is incorrect because the user can PING successfully on her own subnet, indicating that TCP/IP is installed and working properly. B and C are incorrect because both the IP address and subnet mask are valid addresses. The decimal 192 in binary is 11000000, which adheres to the rule that subnet masks must be a string of contiguous 1's followed by contiguous 0's. This example's subnet mask would look like this in binary: 11111111111111111100000000000000.

9. **B** The binding order at the client workstations is the determining factor in network communication performance, since the clients initiate the conversation and the servers just respond. A is incorrect because the server binding order is irrelevant. C is wrong because you are doing more than required, causing additional administrative overhead. D is incorrect because the top listing is used first—not the lowest; it's used last.

10. **E** This is an ideal situation where ICS can be a solution. Through its implementation, all of the listed changes will occur.

11. **B** To allow Remote Desktop sessions for remote control, the friend, or target computer, must allow for Remote Control by ensuring the Allow This Computer To Be Controlled Remotely option is checked. As a security measure, the default behavior for Remote Desktop is for a read-only session. Because the Remote Desktop session has been successfully established in this scenario, we can safely assume that the correct IP address has been supplied and that there is not a firewall preventing the connection. Also, Remote Control of a session is possible with a dial-up connection; the means to establish the connection is irrelevant.

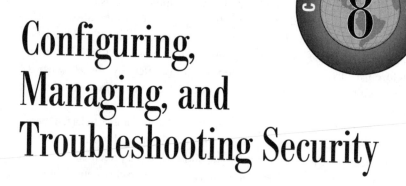

Configuring, Managing, and Troubleshooting Security

	NEWBIE	SOME EXPERIENCE	EXPERT
ETA	6–7 hours	4 hours	3 hours

By the time you've reached this, the last chapter, you might be thinking, "Hey, I've come this far, how important can the last chapter be, anyway? If this really mattered, the author would've put it in the beginning, right? I've already gotten 90 percent of this stuff, and last time I checked 90 percent's an A, and I've heard that I only have to get about a 65 percent or so to pass the 70-270 Exam, and therefore I've already got a pretty good margin of safety by now, so what if I don't carefully study the last part?" That's what all the voices in my head might say, anyway, when I forget my medications.

But a word of advice: Don't skip or skim through this chapter. In fact, if there's one chapter that will require more work on your own time, this is it. Most of the topics related to security are pretty broad, and each topic presented here could very easily merit its own chapter. If you don't believe me, go check out some of the Request For Comment (RFC) white papers posted at www.w3c.org.

Much of this stuff will make a lot more sense if you try it out. So my advice is to take these topics out for a spin, as it were. Configure an IPSec policy for your system and try to PING other computers or browse the Web. Add sites to your restricted sites list. Configure accounts on local machines and, if available, domain controllers and see what success you have. Take away the right to Log on Locally from a user and then try to log on.

The point is, this stuff is important, too. Something has to come last, and in this case, it's last but definitely not least important. (In fairness, many computing books put troubleshooting sections in the last chapter, and you can skim most of those, because there's no way you can recall from a book chapter everything you will need to effectively troubleshoot your particular network anyway.) But as I mentioned in the book's introduction, I've tried to arrange chapters according to how you will actually *use* the operating system, and not by any particular ranking of topic importance. There are no fluff sections here; all material presented maps *directly* to a Microsoft 70-270 Exam objective.

The content in this chapter deals with the security of a computer running Windows XP Professional. The first layer of security applied in an XP Professional environment covers user accounts, because they define who has access to the XP desktop in the first place. If you are a lifelong (in computer terms) Windows 9x user, this is one very noticeable difference between the two environments. In XP Professional, users need to present a valid account to access the system; in Windows 9x, they do not. After discussing accounts, we will explore managing those accounts through the creation of groups and then examine how to configure and manage user rights, which define what a user or group is able to do on an XP system.

We will then move on to a discussion of securing an Internet experience, looking at both Internet Explorer security settings and the configuration of Internet Connection Firewall, which provides a level of protection against hack attacks.

We then move into data encryption, which keeps a user's data private, even when two or more users access the same XP computer—we will learn how Windows XP makes that possible for drives formatted with NTFS (NT file system).

Finally, we will look at many of the security policies available to lock down the XP desktop with the Local Security Policies MMC snap-in. We will examine ways to tighten account and password security, how to configure auditing of system resources, and how to secure network communications through the application of IPSec.

Configure, Manage, and Troubleshoot Local User and Group Accounts

We've spent the greater portion of this book discussing the *what's* and *how's* of the Windows XP Professional environment. Another important consideration, and your first line of defense in protecting access to your data, is *who* gets access to the system in the first place. Setting up your user accounts and then managing them with groups can be one of your simplest yet most effective lines of defense in the effort to secure your computer.

Remember from Chapter 1 that when you install XP, an Administrator account is automatically created. For many XP installations, this is the only account necessary. But, if you want to allow multiple users access to a standalone or workgroup computer, you first need to create user accounts for them. This objective looks at managing who gets to use the Windows XP Professional computer and examines some tasks that can be performed to monitor their activities.

Creating and Managing Local Accounts

You will complete most local user account administration from the Local Users and Groups node, which you access from the Computer Management MMC console, as shown in Figure 8-1. This snap-in contains the Users and Groups subfolders, which are the container objects for your users and groups, respectively.

Alternatively, you can use the User Accounts program in the Control Panel (from the Classic view) to complete user administration tasks. If you use the Control Panel to manage your users, you will see a task-based interface, as seen in Figure 8-2, which will walk you through the process of creating the local accounts. Select the task, and the interface prods you for the rest of the necessary steps.

The User Accounts program is not quite as robust as the Local Users and Groups node in the Computer Management snap-in. For example, from the User

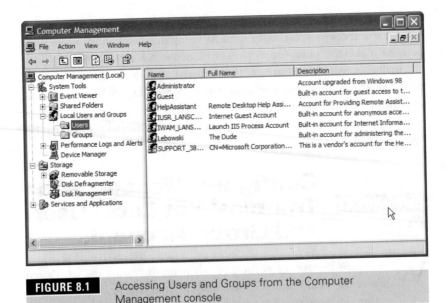

Accessing Users and Groups from the Computer Management console

Accounts interface, you won't be able to set the path to a user's home folder (profiles and home folders is discussed in the section "Creating and Managing Domain

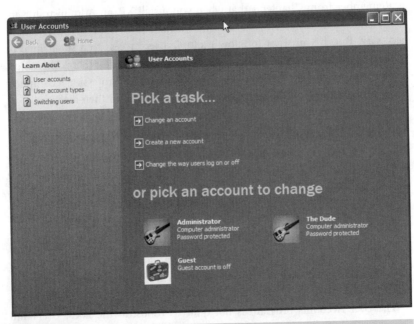

The User Accounts Control Panel interface

Accounts," later in this chapter). When using the User Accounts interface, you can set up new accounts, change passwords, and disable accounts, but that's about it.

The User Accounts program launched from the Control Panel is meant for users with little to no administrative experience or for users just setting up an account or two for standalone use. It takes very little computer skill to manage an account with this interface, which is the whole idea. But, since you will be performing much more complicated account management tasks, and because I have faith in your ability to use task-based, cartoon-like utilities, I won't cover all User Accounts options here. Besides, the Microsoft 70-270 Exam will assume that network administrators will use MMC snap-ins exclusively to manage the Windows XP environment. So, on many levels it pays for you to learn how to use the MMC methods whenever possible.

Managing Built-in Accounts

From the Users folder of the Local Users and Groups node of the Computer Management MMC, you can create, modify, and delete local user accounts, just as in the Control Panel interface. By default, the Users folder contains two built-in accounts that are created at Windows XP Professional installation time:

- **Administrator**   A special account with full control over all resources on the system. This account has the right to perform all system tasks, which include the capability to:
  - Create other user accounts
  - Manage the file system
  - Take ownership of files
  - Install software
  - Install hardware
  - Set up printers
  - Log on in Safe Mode
  - Grant these and other rights to users and groups, including themselves
- **Guest**   Allows a user to access the computer even if the user has no user name and password listed in the computer's Accounts database. This account is disabled by default as a security measure, and even when enabled, the Guest account has few system privileges.
- **Support** *nnnnn* (where *nnnnn* is a random number)   Used for Microsoft Remote Online Assisted Support connections to help resolve issues remotely.

You can rename these accounts (see "Renaming an Account" section later in this chapter), but you cannot delete them.

Travel Advisory

One of those "secrets" that every hacker knows is that the Windows XP
Administrator account is always enabled. For this reason alone, you should
rename the Administrator account as one of your first tasks after installation.
This ensures that hackers won't have one-half of the combination
they need to *completely* wreak havoc on your network. All they
would need for access (the other half) is a good password-
generating program, and eventually they would get in.

And while you can rename the Administrator account, you cannot disable it.
This provides a safeguard against accidentally disabling the only account with
system management privileges. And, in case you're wondering, there really is no
safeguard against forgetting the Administrator password. If forgotten, you
are—well, there's a saying, but I can't quite think of it right now. If memory
serves, it has something to do with a creek and a paddle gone AWOL.

Travel Advisory

...And don't leave the Administrator account blank, or configure it
with a *password* of password—I've seen this in plenty of production
environments. Talk about asking for it.

Creating a New User Account

Because you have limited management capabilities over the built-in accounts,
any additional accounts that the administrator creates mark the starting point
of account management. Creating new user accounts with the Users and
Groups snap-in is pretty straightforward:

1. In the Computer Management Console, right-click the Users folder
   and choose New User. You will then see the New User dialog box, as
   shown in Figure 8-3.

2. Add the User Name. This name must be unique in the Users folder and
   must follow certain naming rules:
   - It must contain between 1 and 20 characters.
   - It cannot match the name of Group accounts in the Groups folder.
   - It cannot include any of the following reserved characters, which
     have special meaning to Windows XP: / \ [ ] ; : | + = , ? < > "
   - It cannot contain all spaces or periods.

3. Add other information in the dialog box as you wish. Table 8-1 helps in
   deciphering the possible options when configuring a new local account.

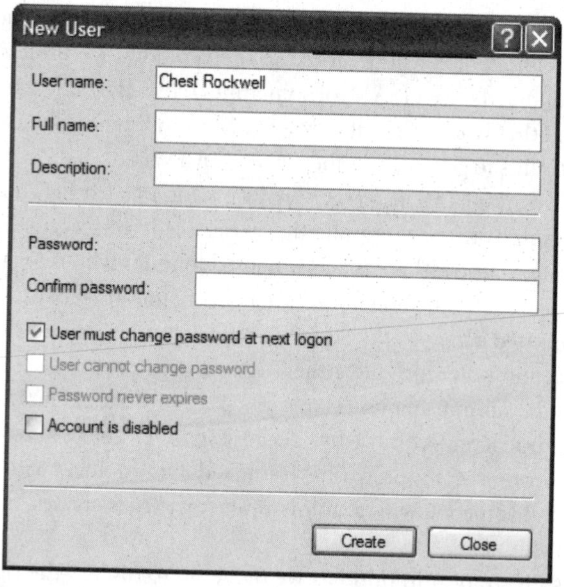

FIGURE 8.3   Creating a new user account

TABLE 8.1   New Account Options

Option	Description
User Name	The only required field; user names are not case sensitive when used to log on.
Full Name	Lets you provide more information about the user; defaults to the User Name if left blank.
Description	Lets you provide more information about the account.
Password	Assigns the initial password for the account; passwords are case sensitive.
Confirm Password	Confirms that you have typed the password correctly.
User Must Change Next Logon	Forces users to change passwords upon first successful Password at logon; selected by default to ensure that password is the individual user's responsibility.
User Cannot Change Password	Prevents a user from changing a password; useful for accounts accessed infrequently by many users, such as the Guest account.
Password Never Expires	Specifies that a user's password never expires; overrides any settings that have been configured with Group Policies.
Account is Disabled	Specifies that account will not be used for logon purposes; helps keep inactive accounts from being used to breach network security.

In this process we have been dealing with the creation and configuration of a *local* user account, which will be stored in the Windows XP Professional's *local* Security Accounts Manager (SAM, or sometimes referred to as just the Accounts) database—in other words, right there on the XP computer's hard disk. If you use local user accounts to get access to the network in a Windows XP setting, you will most likely be working in a *workgroup* environment. In a workgroup, a local user account is required on each computer that a user needs to access in the network.

To illustrate, suppose there is a user named Jennifer who is logging on to an XP system in a workgroup. She submits her user name and password to that system and is granted access to the desktop. But what if Jennifer decides to get up and use the computer on the other side of the room, also in the same workgroup? She submits her user name and password again, but this time is denied access. Poor Jennifer. But why? Because Jennifer does not have a local account at the other computer. She is indeed out of luck with the second computer until someone with administrative privileges creates an account for her at that machine.

Keep this illustration in mind as we move on to discuss the significance of logging into a domain.

You may give accounts names like Jennifer, but as far as the operating system is concerned, when you create a new user account, you create a new *security identifier* (SID), which is a unique number stored in the system's SAM database. This SID has many attributes, including the user name you just specified. In other words, the SID *is* the account as far as the operating system is concerned. Understanding this important aspect of account creation will help you appreciate what's going on under the hood when accounts are renamed, disabled, and deleted.

Creating and Managing Domain Accounts

Now let's contrast the method for the creation of a local account with the creation of a *domain* user account. (Although you don't need to know all the specifics of domain accounts for this exam, you will for other exams, so it helps to get a background now. Plus, if you understand a domain account, it will help you better understand a local account.) You create a Windows XP domain account in the Active Directory database, which is the central repository of account information in a domain environment. Because the account is stored in a central location, the account needs to be created only once, and it allows users to access network resources from any computer in the domain.

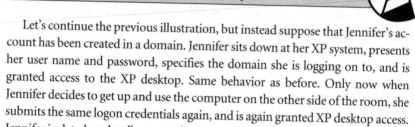

Travel Advisory

Although not a recommended practice, you *can* create a local account on the local machine's SAM database even if a user has a domain account. However, doing so violates many of the tenets of domain creation and can be confusing, because a single user might have many user accounts, each with different sets of permissions assigned.

It is important to keep the two types of accounts straight when working in a Windows XP network. It's especially important to keep them straight when you're troubleshooting.

Let's continue the previous illustration, but instead suppose that Jennifer's account has been created in a domain. Jennifer sits down at her XP system, presents her user name and password, specifies the domain she is logging on to, and is granted access to the XP desktop. Same behavior as before. Only now when Jennifer decides to get up and use the computer on the other side of the room, she submits the same logon credentials again, and is again granted XP desktop access. Jennifer is elated, and walks across the room to thank her domain administrator.

And why is the logon attempt successful this time? Because Jennifer's account has been created (once) on the domain controller (and more specifically in the Active Directory database, housed on all domain controllers, so we could also accurately say that the account was created in the Domain), and not on either of the local machines. Now when she logs on, her credentials are submitted to the domain controller's Active Directory database, where her account lives—not to the local machine's SAM, where it does not.

Other Account Tasks

Now that you've created your user accounts, there are several tasks that fall under the umbrella of account management. You typically won't do these often on a Windows XP local account, but they will be core tasks in the maintenance of domain user accounts.

Renaming an Account   After an account has been set up, you can rename it at any time. When you rename an account, you are simply changing one of the descriptors associated with the SID. The account still retains all its settings and group memberships. This is an ideal administrative step to use, for example, when an employee is leaving a company and is being replaced by another person who will be performing the same job and will need the same security group access.

Renaming a user account is simple:

1. Right-click the account you want to rename and choose Rename from the context menu.

2. Type in the new name for the account and press ENTER.

Deleting an Account   You should delete a user account only if you are sure that it will never be needed again, because when you delete a user account, you are 86-ing the account's SID. If you were to then create a new account with the same name, an entirely new SID would be created, whose properties would need to be completely reconfigured. Because this is such a drastic action, you are warned with the dialog box, shown in Figure 8-4, when trying to delete a user account.

To delete a user account, right-click the account name and choose Delete.

Disabling a User Account   You can disable an account when the account won't be needed for a while—such as when a user is away from the office on a leave of absence. When a disabled account is reenabled, the user resumes normal network activity with minimal administrative overhead.

You might also disable an account for security reasons. Say, for instance, your dot-com is doing another round of layoffs while managers figure out a way to make money on products they don't currently charge for. In such a case, you could disable the soon-to-be ex-employees' accounts before handing out the bad news. That way, disgruntled users could not do any harm to the network on their way out the door.

You disable a user account from the account's Properties page. On the General tab, as shown in Figure 8-5, checking the Account Is Disabled check box will disable the account.

Changing a Password   It may be hard to believe, but it's true: users forget their passwords. When this rarest of circumstances happens, the administrator

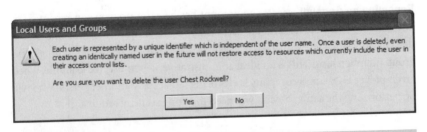

FIGURE 8.4   Deleting a user account

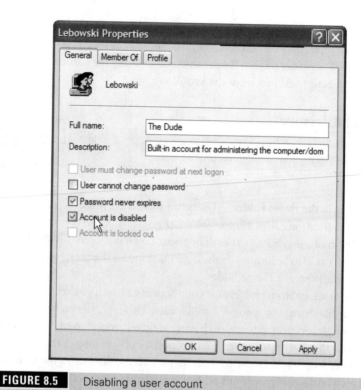

Disabling a user account

cannot simply look at the Properties page to see what the password is. The password must be changed.

1. Right-click the user's account from the Local Users and Groups snap-in.
2. Choose Set Password.
3. Type in the new password and then confirm to reset.

Using Logon Scripts   Logon scripts have done for years what user profiles do in Windows XP Professional. Logon scripts set the user environment, including setting up drive mappings or specifying that certain executables, such as a virus check, run every time a user account logs on to a computer. Logon scripts are also useful in configuring compatibility for clients that do not support Windows XP profiles but still want to maintain consistent environment settings with their native operating systems. Logon scripts aren't heavily emphasized in Windows XP, because their function has been largely replaced by user profiles. In a pure Windows XP environment, logon scripts should not be necessary.

That doesn't mean you don't have to know where and how logon scripts would be configured for an account. Logon scripts can be specified for a user by accessing the Properties page of the account and entering the name of the script in the Logon Script text box from the Profile tab.

Travel Advisory

In a Windows 2000 or .NET Active Directory domain, logon scripts can be more easily administered via Group Policies.

Storing Files in the Home Folder   Users can store their working files in a private network location called a *Home folder*. This setting is also configured from the Profile tab of a user's Properties dialog box. You'll notice in this tab that the Home folder can also be located on the local machine for the user, but this really defeats the purpose of a Home folder.

When you set up Home folders for your network's users, you set up a central location for file storage by using a shared folder. This way, all you have to do is back up a single location, rather than having to travel around to many computers to ensure that backups are being completed for all working data.

To specify a path to a Home folder, enter a UNC pathname in the Connect textbox located on the Profile tab in the user account's Properties dialog box. Make sure that the folder to which you are connecting already exists and has been shared. (If you're wondering about User Profiles, flip back to Chapter 4, where they are covered in painstaking detail.)

Using Groups to Administer Accounts

The purpose of groups is to streamline permission and rights administration. Groups simplify your life as an administrator; it's much more efficient to manage a few groups instead of many individual user accounts. Rather than add individual accounts to an Access Control List (ACL), you can add members to a group and then add the single group to the ACL entries page. Any permissions given to the group affect all members of that group.

Groups are also used to manage what permissions and rights a user has on the system. Although you were exposed to these concepts back in Chapter 3, it might be beneficial to define the terms a little further here:

- **Permissions** define the level of *access* a group (or user) has to a resource. An example of permission would be the Change permission, which allows users to change or delete the data in a file.

- **Rights** provide the user with the ability to *perform some action*, to interact with the operating system. A right might include the power to shut down the system.

It's important to understand the distinction between these two concepts, as groups are instrumental in administering each.

In Local Users and Groups, you use the Groups folder to create, modify, and delete group accounts. Groups are container accounts—a security identifier (SID) to the operating system, just like user accounts—that contain other accounts. To illustrate this point, try creating a group (the steps are outlined later in "Creating a Group") with the same name of an already existing user account. You'll get an error message notifying you that an account already exists with the same name (just a little insight as to what work all those mice are doing in your computer case as we continue).

And just like user accounts, a few Group accounts are created at installation time. At setup, the following Groups are created on a Windows XP Professional machine, visible from the Groups folder in the Computer Management MMC:

- **Administrators**   Have full permissions and rights to the system. Membership in this group is like having an American Express card; it has its privileges. Members of the Administrators group, as we have seen, can take ownership of any object on the computer and then manage that object. They also have all rights granted to the built-in Administrator account, as mentioned earlier. For reasons that (after seven chapters) should be obvious by now, membership in this group should be most carefully guarded. Its default members include the Administrator local account and, in domains, the Domain Admins global group.

- **Backup Operators**   Have the right to back up and restore all files and folders on a system. This right is significant because the Backup Operators also have the right to back up files they would not normally have any access to. However, members of this group can access the system only through the Backup utility. No members are included in the Backup Operators group, by default.

- **Guests**   Have limited access to the computer. This group is built-in, so that its members have occasional access to the computer, even if they are not regular network users. One account is a member by default: the Guest account.

- **Network Configuration Operators**   Can have some administrative privileges that allow them to set up and configure network connections and protocols. There are no default members.

- **Power Users** Have almost every right that Administrators do, but not quite. Members of the Power Users group can create local users and groups, set up local printers, change the system clock, and stop and start services. Unlike the Administrators group members, they do not have the power to take ownership and manage anything they want. Power Users come in handy when distributing administrative work in a workgroup environment.

- **Remote Desktop Users** Are granted the right to log on remotely for purposes of using Remote Desktop Assistance. This group is relevant only if Remote Assistance is enabled.

- **Replicator** Supports directory replication (directory replication is used by domain servers to synchronize directory information). There are no members, by default.

- **Users** Have accounts that are created outside the built-in Guest accounts. The settings of this group generally keep users from harming themselves, as they cannot tamper with the operating system or program files. Any user that is set up automatically becomes a member of this group.

- **HelpServices Group** Used by Microsoft when it establishes a Remote Assistance session to your system.

Special Groups

Membership in special groups is automatic and will be determined by how a user account is interacting with the computer. Accounts become members of these groups based on operating system activity.

Several of these special groups are built into Windows XP, but, as mentioned, administrators cannot manage the membership of each special group. The one special group most administrators need to be cognizant of on a day-to-day basis is the Everyone group (see Chapter 2).

The Everyone special group includes anyone who can possibly access the computer. Compare this with the built-in group Users. What's the difference? The Users are the accounts that you create, while the Everyone group includes all of those plus any accounts that you did not create.

Users become members of special groups through system use, not because they are added to the group by an administrator.

Travel Advisory

Because you cannot influence the membership of the special groups, you will not see them listed in the Local Users and Groups utility. To verify that these groups exist, you must access the ACL for a file folder and then add a group to the list.

Creating a Group

When creating a group, many of the same rules apply as for creating User accounts. To create a group, you must first be logged on as a member of the Administrators or Power Users group.

1. Right-click the Groups folder (found in Local Users and Groups) and choose New Group.

2. In the New Group dialog box, shown in Figure 8-6, specify the name and description of the group.

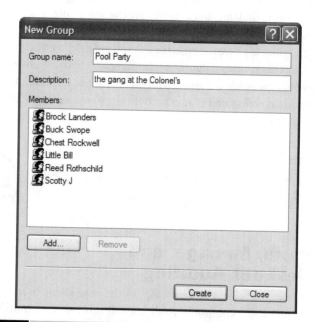

FIGURE 8.6	Creating a new group

3. As with user accounts, the only required part is the Group name, and it must be unique.

4. You can modify the membership of the group you are creating by clicking the Add button and then choosing the accounts you want to make part of the group.

5. When you're happy with the configuration of the group, click Create and you're done.

If you change your mind later, you can always make changes by double-clicking the group in the Groups folder of the Local Users and Groups snap-in and adding user accounts from the General tab. You can also access the Properties of a user account and add the user to a group or two on the Member Of tab.

Deleting and Renaming Groups

Because groups are accounts in the computer's local security database, the renaming and deleting considerations for group accounts are exactly the same as they are for user accounts. You can rename a group by right-clicking the group name and choosing Rename. Because you are changing only an attribute of the SID, renaming a group does not affect the group's membership in any way.

Deleting a group is a permanent action, as you are deleting that all-important SID. If you delete a group and then create another later with the same name, you will still have to repopulate the group with user accounts. However, the deletion of the group has no effect on the user accounts it contains. They will still reside in the SAM database.

Exam Tip

Groups cannot be disabled, as user accounts can. You cannot delete a built-in group account.

Configure, Manage, and Troubleshoot Auditing

By implementing auditing, you gain a Big Brother-like ability to monitor what users are doing on the computer. Auditing will show you what activities are happening on a system, who is doing the activities, and what time they were doing it. You configure audit policy from the Audit Policy folder under the Local Policies node in the Security Settings console, as shown in Figure 8-7.

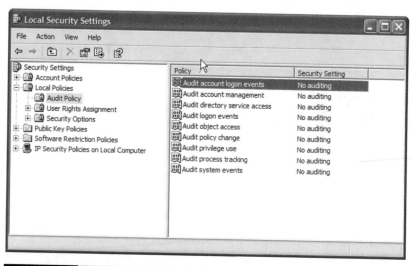

FIGURE 8.7   The audit policies

When you define an audit policy, you get to choose what events to track and whether to track the success or failure of those events. Whether you should track success or failure events depends on the activities you are trying to capture. For example, do you really want to audit each and every successful logon? Probably not. Do you want to audit failed logon attempts? In a secure environment, you probably do. Keep in mind that auditing does generate overhead on the computer, so you want to audit the events that are most likely to indicate a security issue. Unnecessary auditing can be a drag on performance, so you want to focus your audits appropriately.

By default, nothing is audited, so you must configure auditing manually, and it is done on a per-computer basis. It can also be a two-step process, as in the case where you would want to audit who is accessing a confidential file. You would first audit the *success* of object access, and you'd then set the auditing on an individual resource by accessing the Properties dialog box of that resource and configuring auditing on a per-group or per-user basis through the Advanced button, as shown in Figure 8-8.

Travel Advisory

Remember, you need to ensure that Simple File Sharing is turned *off* before you can see the Security tab on an NTFS resource. Verify that SFS is unchecked by looking at the View tab in Folder Options.

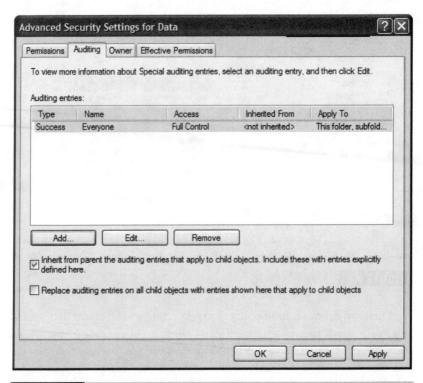

FIGURE 8.8   Auditing a resource

Exam Tip

You can only audit access to resources on *NTFS* partitions.

Finally, the audit policy settings dictate which security settings the Event Log service should log in the Security log. The Security log will identify either the failure or success of audit events. To get detailed information on the events, such as who did what and when, simply double-click the particular event to see the Event Properties window, as shown in Figure 8-9.

I gave this speech in the introduction, and here it is again: it is good practice to use Local Security Policies to get familiar with some of the Group Policy settings. This is a tool that may seem overwhelming at first because of the number of settings that can be configured. Finding exactly what you want to configure will require patience, repeated use, and trial and error. Remember, as the man says, you can't make an omelet...

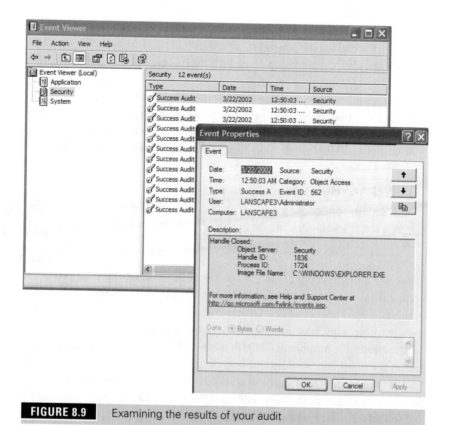

FIGURE 8.9 Examining the results of your audit

That being said, you will hardly ever configure Local Security settings in the real world. That's because most security settings that are important enough to set at the local level should also apply to the network as a whole. So that's what you do: set most, if not all, of your security settings at the domain level in Active Directory rather than at the local computer level. A perfect example of this would be password policies. Does it make sense to require an eight-character password on one computer and not on another? Usually not. So you would set this password policy at the domain level, so that all users of your network would need an eight-character password to log on. Moreover, domain policies will, by default, override local policies, so that even if you set a ten-character password requirement at the local computer using the preceding scenario, the effective setting would still be for an eight-character password.

The most important thing to remember, both in testing and in real life, is that in Windows AD domains, Local Settings are low man on the totem pole—local settings are overridden by site settings, which are both overridden by domain settings, which are all overridden by OU settings. ("LSD is a trip to OU" is what I tell my students, which, granted, is a dumb little mnemonic, but they never forget the order of Group Policy application.)

While all this is not crucial information for the Windows XP Professional exam, it is required understanding as you progress through the MCSE exam series. It can only help if you enter this test with a basic understanding of Group Policies and how they might apply to an Active Directory environment.

Travel Advisory

Local Security settings are the only GPOs that can be applied to a standalone or workgroup Windows XP computer. All other GPOs are domain-based.

So, when might you want to change any of the local Group Policy settings? Well, it is your only Group Policy lever that is available in a workgroup setting. In this configuration, the Local Group Policies can be quite effective on securing a machine, especially one that is shared by many people.

The greater the number of GPOs that are configured for a computer, and the greater the number of settings within each GPO that are configured, the longer it takes for a computer to start and complete the logon process. Therefore, best practice is to minimize the number of GPOs applied to a computer in a domain and to minimize the number of settings applied to a computer in a workgroup or a domain. Configure only what you need.

Configure, Manage, and Troubleshoot Account Settings

It sounds like a line from Mission: Impossible, but it is nonetheless applicable: if you are to access *anything* in a Windows XP environment, you must first obtain the proper credentials and be authenticated. How so? These credentials are obtained through the logon process, and you can do this in a couple of ways. You are probably most familiar with entering a user name and password combination at the Logon dialog box and have done this many times, but you can also insert a smart card and PIN to be authenticated if your computer supports it.

Once you supply the proper logon credentials, an access token is generated by Windows XP and attached to the user account. This access token is really just a list of the user account and all of the groups the account is a part of.

You can think of the access token as being like one of those magnetic-strip keys you get at a hotel. You first present your credentials (credit card and drivers license, let's say) and then a key is generated for you. This key defines which hotel resources you have access to: the room, the laundry facility, pool, workout room, and so on.

When you log on to the computer, the access token generated acts in very much the same way. This token is matched against Access Control Lists (ACLs) set for various system resources, which in turn define those resources you have access to and what level of access you have. This process—generation of an access token—is the same no matter whether you are logging on with a domain account or a local account, although there are some other fundamental differences between the two account types, as we have touched on before and will now discuss in more detail.

Local User Accounts vs. Domain User Accounts

As we discussed earlier, a valid user account can be stored in two locations: in the local security accounts manager database or in a domain security accounts manager database. The local database, as the name implies, is stored on the local machine. Local accounts can access the operating system on the computer. The domain database is stored on a domain controller, in the Active Directory data store. The domain database defines which user accounts have access to the domain, including which of the domain's computers the user may log on to.

> **Travel Advisory**
>
> One of the chief benefits of an Active Directory domain is that you have to create only one account for each user to access the domain. In a workgroup setting, you have to set up multiple accounts for the same user if that user is going to access several machines.

Two separate logon processes are used when accessing resources in a Windows network. You first log on *interactively* to a computer (if you have the proper user rights to do so) to gain initial access to the machine. Logging on interactively means that you are sitting down at the machine and using it, even if your account is being submitted to a domain controller over the network. For instance, as I write this book, I am logged on interactively to the computer in front of me. Logging on interactively can be done by entering a user name and password, and then selecting the domain or the computer name to which you are logging on.

Now that I'm logged on interactively, the chapter file I am working with does not need to live at this computer; it can be accessed on another computer on my network (which is indeed the case, for those curious). So, after the interactive logon process is complete, I access network resources using a *network* authentication method. When I am establishing a connection to the server that the aforementioned chapter files live on, I am actually submitting a user name and password, even if there is no visible way of knowing this.

The account and password used to access the network resource will be the same account used to log on interactively, and these credentials will be checked against the ACL of the resource I am trying to access. In most cases, this will be transparent to the user logged on. Several security measures can be applied to this network logon process. The network authentication method used by default in Windows XP networks is called *Kerberos version 5*.

If you log on locally to the local computer, you must provide separate network authentication credentials to access network resources. When you are logging onto a domain, the interactive logon credentials are used transparently to authenticate you to network resources.

If you intend to log on interactively to a standalone or workgroup computer with a user name/password combination, you will choose the name of the computer in the Log On To text box in the Logon dialog box when the computer starts up. After a computer joins a Windows XP domain, the Log On To textbox is populated with the name of the domain of which the computer is a member, as well as all of the domains that are trusted. On a Windows XP Professional computer, the local computer name will appear there as well.

A convenient logon "tip" keeps a user from having to select the appropriate logon domain from the drop-down list in the Log On To text box. Windows XP domain users can log on using their User Principal Names (UPN), which, just to remind you, is *username@domainname*, where *username* is the account name and *domainname* is the fully qualified domain name defined in the Active Directory store. In other words, domain logons can be sent to domain controllers the same way e-mails are sent. The only difference between an e-mail login and a domain login is which records are searched for in the Domain Name Service (DNS) hierarchy: rather than searching for a Mail Exchange (MX) record to find the address of a mail server, a search is made for a Service (SRV) record that identifies a domain controller in the domain where the logon request is being sent. Sound easy? It will be, if you understand DNS, which you will by the time you pass the Network Infrastructure exam. You won't be able to pass that exam without a thorough understanding of DNS.

> ### Exam Tip
>
> If what I just mentioned sounded a little too much like someone trying to explain the Electoral College, you can be comforted that you really don't *need* to know DNS that extensively for now. Like the Electoral College, sometimes things work best as long as you don't have to think about it too much. As long as you recognize that logging on to a domain is similar to composing an e-mail to yourself, you should be fine.

Secure Authentication Methods

You should know that there are ways to secure log on credentials as they are passed from domain client to domain controller. We'll talk about these secure authentication methods in this section.

To log on to a Windows XP domain using a smart card, you begin the process by inserting the smart card into a smart card reader. This prompts the user for a PIN, which is used to authenticate to the smart card (it is the "combination" to the smart card), not to the domain. A public key certificate is stored on the smart card, and that key is used to authenticate to the domain using the Kerberos version 5 protocol. To use a smart card logon over Point-to-Point Protocol (PPP)—in other words, to log on remotely—Extensible Authentication Protocol-Transport Level Security (EAP-TLS) must be used.

The security protocols available consist of the following. Take special note of which authentication forms use encrypted passwords and which do not:

- **Unencrypted Password Authentication Protocol (PAP)**   Uses a plain-text password and is the least secure authentication type.

- **Shiva Password Authentication Protocol (SPAP)**   Used to dial into and be authenticated by Shiva servers.

- **Challenge Handshake Authentication Protocol (CHAP)**   Negotiates a secure form of encrypted authentication.

- **Microsoft CHAP (MS-CHAP)**   Uses one-way encryption with challenge-response method. This protocol was designed for Windows NT 4 and Windows XP, but it can be used by Windows 9x as well.

- **Microsoft CHAP version 2 (MS-CHAP v2)**   A more secure form of MS-CHAP.

Configure, Manage, and Troubleshoot Account Policy

Account policies are used to indicate the user account properties that are specific to the logon process, such as settings for passwords and account lockout options. To implement account policies, you need to configure the Local Group Policy for a particular machine by adding the Group Policy snap-in to the MMC.

From the MMC, access the Account Policies folders, as shown in Figure 8-10. You can see two subfolders: Password Policy and Account Lockout Policy.

Password policies ensure that security requirements are enforced on the computer, and they apply to all users who access that computer; they are not set on a per-user basis. The policies here are all fairly self-explanatory.

The account lockout policies are used for specifying how many invalid logon attempts should be tolerated before the account is disabled. This is a good way to prevent possible security compromises by a password-guessing user or program. You may also configure how long the account is locked—from several minutes to indefinitely (until the administrator unlocks the account). The account lockout policies are shown in the right pane of Figure 8-11.

As always, it is important to note the defaults. The default Account Lockout Threshold is 0, which means that accounts will not be locked out no matter how many bad logons are attempted. Once you set *any* Account Lockout Threshold, the default time an account will be locked out will be 30 minutes, which means that a user could come back and try again after waiting 30 minutes. If you reset this Account Lockout Duration to 0 (after enabling an Account Lockout Threshold), the account will be locked out indefinitely until an administrator unlocks it.

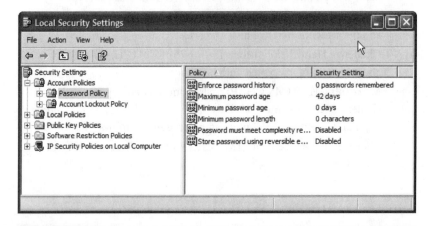

| FIGURE 8.10 | The Account Policies node |

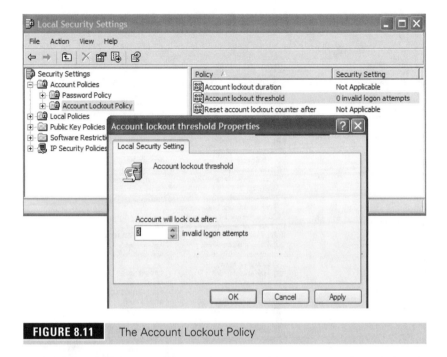

FIGURE 8.11 The Account Lockout Policy

Configure, Manage, and Troubleshoot User and Group Rights

User rights assignments dictate what a user is able to do on a computer. As discussed earlier in this chapter, rights are different from permissions, which define *access* to a resource. A good deal of the function of built-in groups is that members of these groups have predefined rights, which makes rights administration easier. For example, the Backup Operators have the right to back up and restore any file on any file system, regardless of the permissions assigned to the operator. This does not mean, however, that the backup operator has access to open the files he is backing up—just that he has the right to back them up. Administrators can easily delegate the administrative task of regular backups to a user or users without extensive rights assignment.

Travel Advisory

One of the hallmarks of the Administrators group is that its members have virtually every possible right on the computer. This is one reason you must carefully guard the membership of this group.

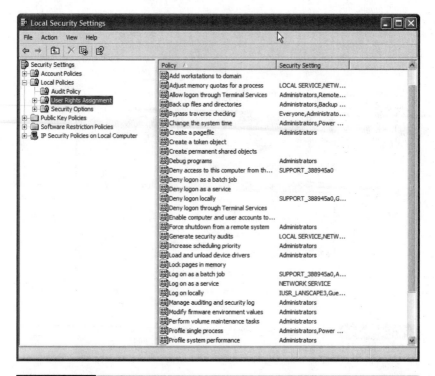

While certain rights are granted to certain groups by default, no rights are explicitly granted to any user accounts. This includes the Administrator account, which is assigned its rights by virtue of its membership in the Administrators local group. You will configure user rights from the User Rights Assignment folder under the Local Policies node, as shown in Figure 8-12.

Objective 8.02

Configure, Manage, and Troubleshoot Internet Explorer Security Settings

By its very nature, browsing the Internet with Internet Explorer poses some inherent dangers. All content is downloaded to your computer before it is displayed by the browser (excuse me, the *operating system*, as Microsoft's legal team would be quick to advise). This content can sometimes contain some fairly chancy stuff, and I'm not talking about pictures of dancing ladies here. Some downloaded content—in the form of ActiveX controls, Java applets, and scripts—is meant to cause tomfoolery on your computer.

Local Lingo

ActiveX, Java Applets, and scripts are all things meant to execute on the client side—your computer—rather than on the server side, as is the case with Active Server pages (.asp pages). Because of where they execute, these three items, while providing great functionality, are considered a potential threat, whereas .asp pages do not pose any security risk.

Because Microsoft realizes that not every piece of Web content was created with the best of intentions, Internet Explorer provides a wide range of features that help you browse the web safely. The purpose of these features is much like that of the Windows Hardware Quality Labs: it tries, where possible, to ensure that only safe content enters your XP system.

Travel Assistance

For full explanations of ActiveX, Java Applets, and scripts, please see www.webopedia.com.

Determining If Content Is Safe

When ActiveX controls are downloaded to your system, IE displays a Security Warning dialog box, asking whether or not you approve of the download. You will have three choices when presented with this screen: Yes, No, or More Info. (The More Info won't be much aid, as it is just a vanilla message about the choices you have.)

Microsoft uses a signing technology called *Authenticode* that works like a driver's license for the control that's being installed. It ensures that the software item comes from the source it says it's from and that it has not been tampered with since leaving the publisher's issuing authority. Now, this signature doesn't necessarily guarantee that the software is safe; just that it has come from the vendor listed in the signature, and that it has not been altered since. It's up to you to decide which software providers to trust.

If you download other content, such as a program from a site such as microsoft.com or download.com, you are presented with a dialog box asking you to either Save or Open the program. Choose Save for the safest computing environment. That way, you can perform a virus scan to the file before deciding to install.

Using Security Zones

If you right-click the IE desktop icon and choose Properties, you will see the Internet Properties dialog box. From this dialog box's security tab, as seen in Figure 8-13, you can partition the Internet into four separate categories, then adjust security settings for these zones according to taste.

For each zone, there is a set of predefined security settings appropriate (in Windows' opinion) for the particular zone. These predefined settings can be easily managed with the slide bar, and a description about how content is handled will be displayed next to the bar.

You can add sites to any of the zones except the Internet zone, which is a grab bag of everything that is not in one of the three other zones. By default, there are no sites defined for these zones, but it is easy to change this. Just click the Sites button to bring up the Sites dialog box—if, for instance, you implicitly trust everything a site has to offer, you can add it to the Trusted Sites list, as seen in Figure 8-14. The default settings for Trusted Sites is Low.

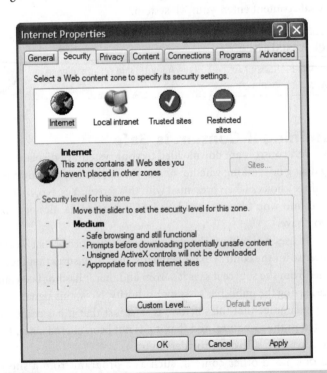

| FIGURE 8.13 | The Internet Properties security zones |

FIGURE 8.14 Adding a site to a zone

Travel Assistance

The refrain here is the same that you heard after the section on IIS in the previous chapter: there is much more that could be said about IE, and it used to be a separate elective test, but you're just not going to be hammered on the minutiae of the IE tabs on the 70-270. For further information, please see the *Internet Explorer Resource Kit* from Microsoft Press.

Configure, Manage, and Troubleshoot an Internet Connection Firewall (ICF)

Objective 8.03

Internet Connection Firewall (ICF) is a software component that prevents unhindered access from other Internet hosts. It accomplishes this by listening to all outbound and inbound traffic, comparing this traffic to a list of filters, and then finally by taking action based on the contents of these filters.

Inbound traffic—any data packet sent to your system—is dropped if ICF does not recognize it as a response to outbound traffic sent from your computer. When a packet is dropped because ICF does not recognize it as being a reply to a request, there is nothing you will notice as an end user. However, you can configure a log file of these events, so that you are able to track down what packets are attempting to hit your system and from whom. (Most will be innocuous.)

Further, you can set up ICF so that certain types of traffic are always allowed or are always blocked. If you were using XP Professional as your web server, you would certainly want to allow unsolicited HTTP traffic to hit your computer.

Setting Up ICF

Microsoft's recommendation is that you use ICF for each direct web connection, that is, a connection where you are using a public IP address. (If you are using a SOHO router or Proxy Server on your home or small office network, you are almost certainly not, and the ICF service is not necessary, as the router is providing that function already.) Remember, you can determine if you are using a public or private IP address by typing **ipconfig** at the Command Prompt.

If you are using Internet Connection Sharing, as discussed in Chapter 7, it is good practice to configure that system to use the Internet Connection Firewall. Systems that are getting their IP addresses from the ICS machine are not considered to be directly connected to the Internet. In fact, enabling ICF on the other systems, which are getting their Internet access from the ICS system, will cause network communications to fail.

Here's how to enable the Internet Connection Firewall to protect a system that is directly connected:

1. From the Network Connections window (one way of accessing is to right-click My Network Places, then Properties), right-click the connection where you will enable the firewall and choose Properties.

2. Click the Advanced tab and then, from the Advanced tab, as shown in Figure 8-15, select the check box labeled Protect My Computer and Network by Limiting or Preventing Access to This Computer from the Internet.

That's really all there is to setting up the firewall. Now, all unsolicited packets are dropped. However, as mentioned, there are instances where you might not want this to be the case. If you are running a website, you certainly are going to fine tune the settings. Here's how:

1. On the Advanced tab of your connection's Properties dialog box (we just saw how to get here, so I won't repeat myself), click the Settings button at the bottom of the screen.

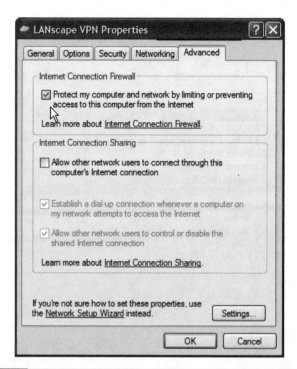

FIGURE 8.15   Enabling Internet Connection Firewall

2. The Advanced Settings dialog box appears, as shown in Figure 8-16. With a check box or two, you will configure the services that the Internet Connection Firewall should allow.

You can even set the ICF to pass certain types of traffic to other computers on the network if the Internet connection is being shared. For example, if there is another machine on the private network that is hosting an FTP site, you can choose the FTP Server service and then choose Edit, which displays the dialog box shown in Figure 8-17. You will then add the IP address of the machine hosting the FTP site.

Configuring Log Activity

As mentioned, the ICF will not generate a log of unsolicited attempts by default. To be able to see what packets are being dropped, you need to enable logging. To do so, perform the following:

1. From the Advanced dialog box of the Network Connection, choose Settings, just as before.

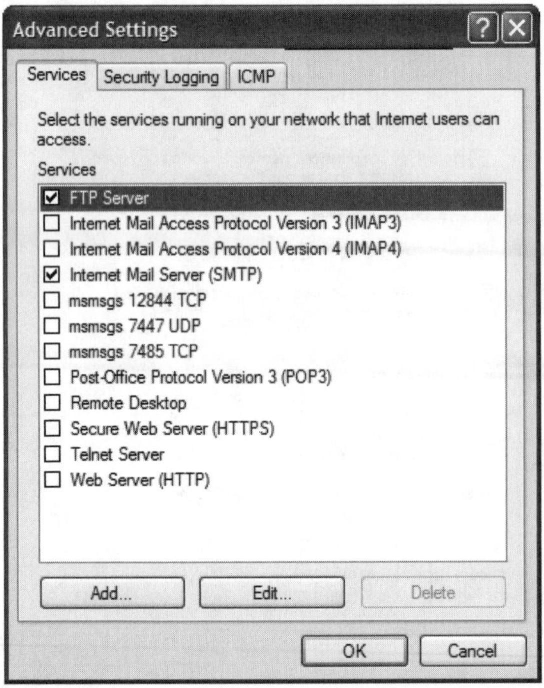

FIGURE 8.16 Enabling services to be found with unsolicited requests

2. Choose the Security Logging tab, as shown in Figure 8-18, and click the check boxes for the events you wish to document.

3. When you have made your selections, choose a file name for the log file (the default is *systemroot*\pfirewall.log), and then a maximum log file size.

4. Click OK to complete the logging set up.

Now with logging enabled, you'll be better able to determine whether someone is trying to scan open ports on the system. To read the contents of the log file, open it in any text editor, like Notepad. Because the log file is in the W3C (WWW Consortium) format, it can also be ported to a number of third-party applications to help cull meaningful information.

FIGURE 8.17   Setting the ICF to pass traffic to another system

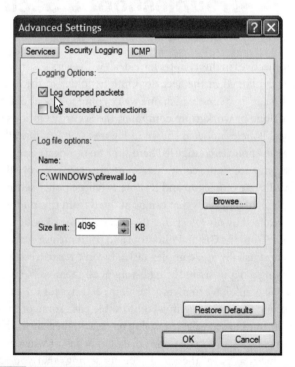

FIGURE 8.18   Configuring ICF logging

ICF's Limitations

As difficult as it is to believe, ICF is not a catch-all security solution for all networks. The firewall provided with XP Professional provides a basic set of protection capabilities against hacking over the Internet. However, it does not monitor outbound communication, which is one of its major drawbacks when compared to most commercial firewall products. And, it should not be thought of as a replacement for a good antivirus program. Many viruses attach themselves to e-mails or to other programs, and you almost always invite those items into your computer, so ICF is of little use against these types of threats.

Speaking of security, there is a powerful set of tools you can leverage to tighten down any XP Pro system, which is the focus of our next objective.

Implement, Configure, Manage, and Troubleshoot a Security Configuration

So far, the objectives in this chapter have dealt with every security policy, save one: those contained in the Security Options folder of the Local Security Policies MMC snap-in. Guess which one we're going to talk about now?

On a standalone or workgroup computer, the Security Options are located under the Local Policies node, as shown in Figure 8-19. Just like all other local group policies, the policies configured here apply to the local computer only but affect all users who access the computer. Some are extensions of other policies, such as the Audit Use of Backup and Restore Privilege policy settings. You can also add supplementary events that can be audited from this node.

As you've realized by now, learning the sheer volume of policy settings that are configurable from the Group Policy tool and configuring security on a computer can be, and usually are, complex tasks. I won't waste trees or risk carpal tunnel generating a hypnosis-inducing listing of all the possible configuration settings, and you won't have to memorize all the settings for the exam. But you will have to spend some time getting comfortable with some of these settings. Start clicking around to see what the dialog boxes say, then apply them to your own system to see what differences they make on behavior when enabled.

Table 8-2 shows a few of the Local Security settings that you are likely to change most often.

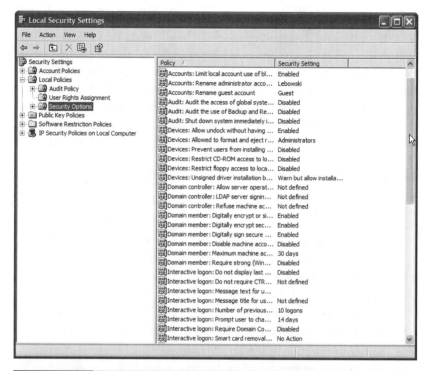

FIGURE 8.19 The Security Options node

TABLE 8.2 A Few of the Local Security Settings You Are Most Likely to Use

Setting	What It Does
Message Text For Users Attempting to Log On	Displays a message, such as a legal notice or welcome message, to users even before they are presented with the Logon dialog box
Restrict CD-ROM Access to Locally Logged-On User Only	Prevents unauthorized software from being installed on the system
Unsigned Driver Installation Behavior	Prevents the installation of unsigned Installation Behavior drivers, even if the user has said it's okay with the driver signing options
Rename Administrator Account	Sets the Administrator account to the name you specify
Allow System to Be Shut Down Without Having to Log On	Can eliminate the requirement that allows a user to first log on with a valid account before shutting down the system

Security Templates

Wouldn't it be great if there were a tool that let you make tons of Security Options changes all at once, rather than have to enable or disable each individual security option you want configured. Wouldn't it be great if there were a template that let you make wholesale security changes quickly? Well guess what?

A neat little MMC snap-in makes the application of multiple security settings much easier. The Security Configuration and Analysis tool allows you to test and apply wholesale changes to the security settings with just a few clicks of your mouse through the use of security templates. The predefined security templates were designed to cover common requirements for security and include four basic security levels: basic, compatible, secure, and high. The predefined security templates are as follows:

- **Basic workstation, server, and domain controller**   Defines the default security level for Windows XP. These templates can be used as a base configuration for security analysis and should be applied to any upgraded computer.

- **Compatible workstation**   Provides a higher level of security but still ensures that all the features of standard business applications will run.

- **Secure workstation or server**   Provides an additional level of security, but does not ensure that all the features of standard business applications will run. Some applications might need a lower level of security to operate properly.

- **Highly secure workstation or server**   Ensures the maximum level of security on a Windows XP machine, without any regard to application functionality.

Travel Advisory

Systems configured with a highly secure template will not be able to communicate with computers running operating systems other than Windows XP, .NET, and 2000.

A security template is an .inf file containing security configuration settings, and Microsoft includes a number of them in the *systemroot*\Security\Templates folder. You can apply a security template directly to a local computer policy when the computer is not part of a domain. You do this to a standalone or workgroup computer by first importing the template into a database of Group

Policy security settings. To apply a security template to a local computer, you need to perform the following tasks:

1. In the Security Configuration and Analysis snap-in, right-click Security Configuration and Analysis and choose Open Database. This will be your working database of settings that will be either analyzed or applied.

2. Name the database and then select the security template you wish to apply to the database. Click Open.

3. Now that the database of settings has been created, you can use this database to either *configure* or just *analyze* your system's security settings, as seen in Figure 8-20. To configure the system with the template's settings, right-click Security Configuration And Analysis and then select Configure System Now.

The first time you use this tool, tips appear in the details pane that will help you apply a security template for analysis. When you use the tool for analysis, Windows XP will compare the database settings against the currently configured settings and then display progress with a series of icons. When the processing is complete, any discrepancies between the local computer settings and the database settings will show up marked with a red flag. Settings that match will show as a green check mark. Settings that do not have either are not configured in the database you have created with the template.

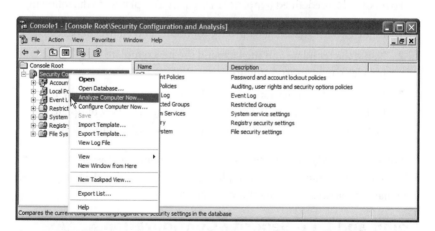

FIGURE 8.20 The Security Configuration and Analysis tool

Exam Tip

You should be aware that the security templates can be applied only to Windows XP computers. What's more, some of the security settings configured involve encryption technologies not available on earlier versions of Windows. As a result, applying secure or highly secure templates should occur only for communication among Windows XP computers.

When you apply the secure or highly secure templates, communication attempts that do not conform to the rules of the template are rejected, and some of these connection and encryption rules are not even available on Windows 9x or NT 4 systems. To ensure compatibility with these operating systems, you should use either the Compatible or the Default security templates.

You can also use the Security Configuration and Analysis snap-in to import more than one security template. This tool allows you to merge multiple security templates to create a composite template and apply configurations for event logs, restricted groups, system services, and file systems. You can also use this snap-in to analyze a computer's security configuration against an existing security template or a composite template.

If you determine that none of the predefined security templates meets your needs, you can create your own templates using the Security Templates MMC snap-in. With this snap-in added, you can start with a new template and modify away, or save a copy of a preexisting template and make changes to the copy.

To modify the predefined templates in Security Templates, do the following:

1. Right-click the template you want to modify and choose Save As.

2. Name the template and then expand the new template to select the policies you want to configure.

3. Double-click a policy name in the details pane to configure the policy, then click OK to save changes to the template. The new template will be immediately available for import into a security configuration.

You can also make changes to existing security templates by selecting an existing policy from the Security Templates snap-in, as outlined in step 3, and then making the desired configuration changes.

Command-Line Security Configuration

In addition to the Security Configuration and Analysis graphical tool, Windows XP Professional includes a few command-line utilities you can use to perform security configuration and analysis using script files as opposed to the MMC interface, as discussed earlier.

SECEDIT   With the SECEDIT utility, you have access to several features that are not available with the graphical tools. Secedit.exe is the command-line equivalent of the graphical tool Security Configuration and Analysis, and is used with the following syntax:

```
secedit /switch /db filename /cfg filename /additional switches
```

where the switch will provide one of the functions mentioned next, the db will specify the path of the configuration database, and cfg will specify the path for the security template to be used. Additional switches will be used to direct behavior.

Four general functions are provided by the secedit.exe utility, with each function performed with different switches used after the secedit syntax. As always, don't forget the /? to reference the full syntax when first getting comfortable with this tool:

- **/analyze**, **/configure**, and **/export** switches correspond to the equivalent tasks that are possible through the Security Configuration and Analysis graphical tool. These switches require that you specify a database to analyze against (by using the /db switch).

- **/validate** verifies the syntax of a template created by using the Security Templates tool.

GPUPDATE   With the GPUPDATE utility, you can refresh both Local and Active Directory-based Group Policy settings, including security settings. This command replaces the SECEDIT /refreshpolicy command option, but accomplishes the same objective. The GPUPDATE is more flexible than the command it superseded and can be used with the following switches:

- **/target:{computer|user}**   Lets you specify that only Computer settings or current User settings get refreshed, depending on the switch used. By default, the GPUPDATE processes both the computer settings and the user settings.

- **/force**   Ignores all processing optimization settings for Group Policy Objects and reapplies all settings.

- **/logoff**   Logs off after the refresh has completed. This is required for those Group Policy settings that do not process on a background refresh cycle but that do process when the user logs on. For instance, when you have configured a new Software Installation and/or Folder Redirection policy, the settings will not take effect until the user logs back on—thus the need for the switch.

- **/boot**   Restarts the computer after the refresh has completed. This is required for Group Policy settings that do not process on a background refresh cycle but that do process when the computer starts up. A perfect use for this is when you have configured a new *computer* Software Installation policy.

Objective 8.05 Configure, Manage, and Troubleshoot Encrypting File System (EFS)

Up till now, it has been drilled into your head that if you want to restrict access to files and folders locally, you should store them on an NTFS partition and protect them with NTFS permissions. Well, I've got good news and bad news. Start with the bad news? Fine. Local NTFS permissions can be compromised when resources are accessed locally by operating systems other than NT or Windows XP. That's right—it is possible for a user booted into an OS other than NT or XP—say, an installation of Windows 98—to bypass NTFS permissions. It takes third-party tools, like NTFSDOS (www.sysinternals.com), to do this, and most users have no idea that this is possible, but such tools are accessible to a determined user. Remember that your first line of defense against a potential NTFS security breach is that, under normal conditions, a Windows 9x user can't even *see* an NTFS partition.

Now the good news: Microsoft includes Encrypting File System (EFS) support with Windows 2000 and XP machines to counter this security vulnerability. EFS provides file encryption services by using a security algorithm and a file encryption key. You must be running NTFS version 5 or later (the version that ships with Windows 2000 and XP—you can't use EFS on an NT 4 machine because its version of NTFS does not support it) to support encryption. Encryption is simply another attribute that is assigned to a resource on an NTFS partition, no different from a compression attribute or the List Folder Contents attribute. Functionally, encryption behaves like the NTFS Deny permission to a file or folder and is totally transparent to the end user. That's not to say that it *is* the NTFS Deny permission, because a user could very well have Full Control permissions to a folder that has been encrypted by another user. But when the user tried to access the encrypted file, he or she would see an Access Denied message, without further explanation.

A user with the proper access key can open and use encrypted files. Any other normal user will get an Access Denied error when trying to access the same file, and Windows XP will not tell the user the reason for the error.

You can set encryption for a file or folder on an NTFS partition in two ways: either from Windows Explorer (as we examined earlier in Chapter 3 when setting the compression attribute), or by using the CIPHER.EXE command-line utility.

To enable encryption from Windows Explorer, open the Properties dialog box of a file or folder and then click the Advanced button from the General tab to open the Advanced Attributes dialog box. As shown in Figure 8-21, you can choose either to encrypt or compress the resource. Remember that these two operations are mutually exclusive—it's either/or.

An installation of Windows XP includes the CIPHER utility, which is more flexible than Windows Explorer. The utility allows you to view the encryption settings on files and folders as well as encrypt and decrypt them. Also, with the CIPHER utility, you can force encryption and create a new encryption key. The syntax of the CIPHER utility is

```
cipher /[command parameter] [filename].
```

FIGURE 8.21   The Advanced Attributes dialog box

Table 8-3 shows some of the command parameters of the CIPHER tool and how each one modifies CIPHER's behavior.

When you set the encryption attribute, you will have the option of encrypting just the folder or all its contents, including subfolders. If you encrypt a folder, any new files created in that parent folder are automatically encrypted.

Moving and Copying

Here's where EFS behaves a little different from other NTFS attributes. The rule of thumb is that encryption is sticky. That is, encrypted files remain encrypted almost everywhere they go, as long as the destination drive is formatted with NTFS. That makes sense, because you wouldn't want a file to be decrypted if it was copied—that would defeat the purpose of encryption. Even if you send an encrypted file to the Recycle Bin, the restorable file will remain encrypted.

Really, the only concern is if the destination folder is on a partition that does not support encryption, such as a FAT32 partition, any partition on an NT 4 machine, or a floppy drive. So, you still have to be very mindful about other aspects of NTFS access.

Recovering Encrypted Files

One of the Policies set for a computer or a domain is the data recovery policy, which covers what will happen if the key used to decrypt the file in the first place is no longer available. This policy identifies one or more users who can access encrypted files no matter who performed the encryption.

If you are part of an Active Directory domain, the default recovery agent will be the Administrator account for the domain. If your computer is not part of a

TABLE 8.3	Command Parameters of the CIPHER Utility

Parameter	Description
/e	Encrypts files and folders
/d	Decrypts files and folders
/s:dir	Specifies that subfolders and files should also be encrypted or decrypted
/I	Causes any errors to be ignored
/q	Quiet mode displays only the most important information

domain, there is no recovery agent created by default, and good administrative practice mandates that you create one.

To create a data recovery agent, you must first generate a data recovery certificate and then designate a user or users to be the recovery agent. Here's how:

1. Log on as the Administrator and then type **cipher /r:filename** at the Command Prompt.

2. You will be prompted for a password to protect the data recovery files you will generate.

3. Two files will be created, a .pfx file and a .cer file, and these files allow anyone to become a recovery agent. You should copy these files to floppy disk and then erase the originals from the hard drive.

Now you are ready to designate a user (or users) as a recovery agent. To do so, compete the following:

1. Log on as the user you want to be the recovery agent and open the Certificates MMC. Navigate to the Current User\Personal node.

2. Right-click this node and choose All Tasks | Import to launch the Certificate Import Wizard. Click Next to begin.

3. The File To Import Page appears where you specify the path to the .pfx file that was just created. Click Next and then you will be prompted for the password.

4. Click Next again and then choose Automatically Select The Certificate Store Based On The Type Of Certificate and then click Finish.

   You're almost done. You haven't forgotten about the .cer file, have you?

5. Now open the Local Security Settings MMC and navigate to Security Settings\Public Key Policies\Encrypting File System. Right-click the node and then choose Add Data Recovery Agent.

6. On the Select Recovery Agents page, find the location of the .cer file you created, then click Open.

7. The Select Recovery Agents page now appears, showing the Agent as USER_UNKNOWN. This is expected behavior—the user name is not stored in the file. Just click Next and then Finish.

Now the currently logged on user is the recovery agent for all encrypted files on the system. You can repeat the procedure if you want additional users to be recovery agents.

Remember, this is a procedure that in real-world situations is applicable more for Workgroup or standalone computers. If a computer is a part of a Windows AD domain, the Domain Administrator account is the default recovery agent, so there is usually little reason to change this behavior. The Domain Administrator account is designated as the data recovery agent in the Default Domain Policy Group Policy Object (GPO). Additional recovery agents are added to any domain-based GPOs, such as an organizational unit (OU) GPO.

If all of this encryption stuff proves too much to manage, you can also disable the use of EFS altogether, although it takes a Registry edit and is beyond the scope of the book and the exam. Just thought you should know.

Travel Advisory

There are several pages of procedure I could have included about the creation and importance of Encryption Certificates for user accounts. Instead, I will point you to Microsoft's white papers on EFS, at www.microsoft.com, for the cookbook instructions. Page count and all.

Objective 8.06

Configure, Manage, and Troubleshoot a Security Configuration and Local Security Policy

As we've touched on already in this chapter, Windows introduced in its 2000 incarnation a new way to manage user environments: Group Policies. Group Policies are a powerful, flexible, granular way to administer your network environment, and they allow you to manage a wide variety of computer and user settings ranging from software distribution and password restrictions to the appearance of the desktop. Group Policies will be the focus of many lessons about Windows 2000 and .NET, especially those concerning Active Directory.

Most of the time, you will be working with Group Policies at the domain level in Active Directory. Policies at the Active Directory level can be applied to sites, domains, and OUs. These objects represent logical and physical structures within an Active Directory enterprise that can be used to break apart an Active Directory installation into separate administrative entities.

However, the focus of Group Policies on the Windows XP Professional exam is mainly on the local level, which means that the policies we will discuss here apply to the local machine alone. You apply local Group Policy to a workgroup or standalone computer that does not use Active Directory to apply security settings.

Exam Tip
This does not give you license to know *nothing* about Active Directory level GPOs, because, after all, these policies are *applied* to computers running Windows 2000 and XP. However, conceptually there is not much difference about *what* can be set in the Group Policy. It's just that for most administrative tasks, it would be pointless to set local policies—you will want policies to apply to more than just one machine or user.

Local Policies

Four categories of local security policies exist: account policies, local security policies, public key policies, and IP Security policies. We looked at one of these policies—public key policy—earlier in the previous section when we examined the EFS recovery policy. By administering the public key policies, for example, we could configure additional recovery agents on a system. This objective covers the other three policy categories:

- Account policies, categorized by password policy and account lockout policy.
- Local security policies, categorized by audit policy, user rights assignment, and security options.
- IP Security (IPSec) policies, categorized by types of IPSec rules.

We have already dealt with the Account policies earlier in the chapter, as well as audit policies, user rights, and security options. Remaining in this discussion is IPSec.

IP Security (IPSec) Policies

The Internet Protocol Security policy settings allow you to configure IPSec. IPSec in Windows XP is designed to protect sensitive data from being intercepted and stolen on a TCP/IP network. It can be most useful when communication between two computers is not secure, such as when data needs to be exchanged using a public network like the Internet. It provides confidentiality, integrity, and authentication of each and every packet of IP traffic crossing the network.

When using IPSec, the two communicating computers first agree on the highest common supported security policy. Each computer then handles the encryption of IP traffic at its own end. In other words, once IPSec communication has been negotiated, each computer's IPSec driver handles the grunt work of securing traffic. Before sending data, the initiating computer transparently encrypts data by using its IPSec policy. The destination computer then transparently decrypts the data before passing it on to the receiving application or process. Because the traffic is encrypted at the IP level, the same security packages can be used for all protocols (think of the application layer protocols such as FTP, SMTP, and HTTP) in the TCP/IP stack.

The IP security policies are implemented from the IP Security Policies on the Local Machine node of the Local Security Settings snap-in. Three policy templates are preconfigured there:

- **Client (Respond Only)** This policy uses the default response rule to negotiate with servers that request security. It will communicate normally (unsecured) with untrusted servers, but will use encryption when requested by a server that requires it. Only the requested protocol and port traffic with that server is secured. This option will give you the most flexibility when negotiating security.

- **Secure Server (Require Security)** For all IP traffic, always require security using Kerberos trust. This policy does not allow unsecured communication with untrusted clients. Most traffic, because it will be unsecured, will be denied, and the number of computers you can communicate with will be limited. However, this is usually exactly the behavior you want when applying this setting.

- **Server (Request Security)** For all IP traffic, always request security using Kerberos trust. Allow unsecured communication with clients that do not respond to a request. This setting will always attempt to negotiate secure communication, but it will not prohibit data exchange with unsecured clients.

Notice that none of these policies is assigned to the computer by default. To assign a policy, right-click the policy name and choose Assign, as shown in Figure 8-22.

You can also adjust the settings of the IPSec policies by accessing the Properties dialog boxes of the given policies. For example, you can change the behavior of the IP filters for a given policy by either choosing to edit an existing IP filter rule or by adding one. An IP filter will direct action on a TCP/IP packet

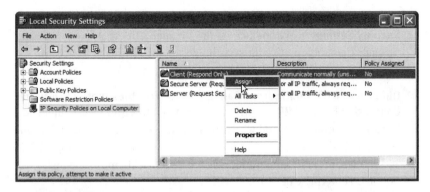

based on the destination of the packet. When enabled, an IP filter checks each incoming packet against the IP filter, and, if a match is found, the properties of the policy are used to send the communication.

Travel Assistance

I told you that you would have to do your homework for a better understanding of this and other security mechanisms beyond the exam. For a more detailed discussion of IPSec, please see *IPSec: Securing VPNs*, by Carlton Davis, (McGraw-Hill Professional Publishing; ISBN 0072127570) or you can search www.microsoft.com for articles on IPSec.

CHECKPOINT

✔**Objective 8.01: Configure, Manage, and Troubleshoot Local User and Group Accounts** Configure, manage, and troubleshoot user and group rights. In this objective we spent time answering the question of *who* is able to access our Windows XP Professional installations. We configured accounts locally, in the local Security Accounts Manager database, and also looked at domain accounts. We used groups to help administer our accounts and then went on to audit user activity. Finally, we configured an account policy, helping define such things as password requirements and lockout settings.

✔**Objective 8.02: Configure, Manage, and Troubleshoot Internet Explorer Security Settings**   We looked at how to make Internet browsing safer through the configuration of security zones and through the settings for downloaded content.

✔**Objective 8.03 Configure, Manage, and Troubleshoot an Internet Connection Firewall (ICF)**   In this objective, the Internet Connection Firewall was examined, and we learned its purpose in helping keep out unauthorized Internet traffic. We learned about where best to configure ICF and about some of its limitations, which keep it from being a thorough solution in an enterprise network.

✔**Objective 8.04: Implement, Configure, Manage, and Troubleshoot a Security Configuration**   In this objective, we learned in greater detail about the security settings that are available from the Local Security Policy MMC snap-in. We also looked at how to customize the templates that can be applied, and looked at the command-line utility for applying security settings and for refreshing security policy changes immediately. Here we also examined how to apply security templates to make many different security settings at once.

✔**Objective 8.05: Configure, Manage, and Troubleshoot Encrypting File System (EFS)**   This objective introduced the topic of encryption, a new feature that is available with Windows XP on a partition that has been formatted with NTFS. We looked at the two ways in which encryption can be set on files and folders and then looked at what role the recovery agent plays in encrypted file recovery.

✔**Objective 8.06: Configure, Manage, and Troubleshoot a Security Configuration and Local Security Policy**   This last objective cleared up a topic not looked at in the previous discussion of Security policies: applying security to IP traffic through IPSec policies. These policies can be used to prevent certain traffic from hitting our computers.

REVIEW QUESTIONS

1. There is a way to encrypt files and folders using a graphical interface, and there is also a command-line utility. What is the command-line tool used to encrypt files on an NTFS partition of a computer running Windows XP Professional?

    A. efs.exe

    B. cipher.exe

C. crypto.exe

D. ntfsadmin.exe

2. You are the domain administrator for a Windows 2000 domain. One of the users, Scott, has set up a home folder location of his files on a Windows 2000 Server. For additional security, Scott encrypts the files stored in this NTFS folder location. Scott is performing confidential research, but he is now taking a three-month sabbatical. Before he leaves, he needs to move his files into his manager's folder so that research can continue. However, the manager gets an "Access Denied" message when she tries to open Scott's files. What can be done to correct this situation?

A. Grant the manager NTFS Full Control permission to the files.

B. Grant the manager NTFS Take Ownership permission; she will then give herself access to the files.

C. Log on as the local Administrator and recover the files.

D. Log on as the Domain Administrator and recover the files.

3. Farah is administering a Windows XP system that many users share. For security purposes, she wants to prevent users from using passwords that are the same as their user account names. Which GPO should she configure to accomplish this task?

A. Enforce Password History

B. Minimum Password Age

C. Minimum Password Length

D. Passwords Must Meet Complexity Requirements

4. Paddy O'Brien is the administrator of a workgroup of Windows XP Professional computers called LUCKYCHARMS. Because he does not want people accessing his LUCKYCHARMS computers, he wants to configure the computers to lock out accounts after four invalid logon attempts. He has configured the Account Lockout Threshold policy setting value to 4. Paddy also wants those accounts locked out indefinitely so that he can investigate the cause of a locked-out account. What should Mr. O'Brien do?

A. Set the Account Lockout Duration to 0.

B. Set the Account Lockout Threshold to 0.

C. Set the Account Lockout Duration to 99,999.

D. Take no action.

5. You are working in a workgroup environment and are in the Administrators group of that machine, but there are others in that group

as well. All systems are running Windows XP Professional. You notice over the course of several weeks that someone keeps changing the system time. You reset the time again, but now want to find out who is doing this if it ever happens again. What do you need to configure?

A. Enable auditing of the Audit Logon Events policy setting.

B. Enable auditing of the Audit Privilege Use policy setting.

C. Enable auditing of the Audit Object Access policy setting.

D. Enable auditing of the Audit System Events policy setting.

6. Allen is concerned that laptop users are logging on to the domain as the Guest account and then introducing viruses on the network. For added security, he wants to implement a smart card logon process in order for laptop users to log into the Windows Active Directory domain. Which protocol should Allen use?

A. PAP

B. Microsoft-CHAP

C. Microsoft-CHAP v2

D. SPAP

E. EAP-TLS

7. You have just installed a new software package on your Windows .NET Server that, for auditing purposes, runs in the context of a user account. Your company presently has a security setting in the Domain Group Policy that requires users to change passwords every 60 days. Not coincidentally, this just happens to be the time that the application fails, until you run over and change the password of the account that the application uses. What's the best way you can avoid this problem?

A. Configure the account so that the password does not expire.

B. Place a user account in the Account Operators built-in group and delegate the task of resetting the application account password to that user.

C. Configure the application so that it uses the Administrator account.

D. Configure a local policy on the computer where the application runs so that account passwords never expire.

8. You are administering a network with a mixture of Windows .NET Servers along with some NT 4 Servers that are running legacy applications. You configure all the Windows .NET Servers to use the Highly Secure template with the Security Configuration and Analysis MMC snap-in. You receive calls almost immediately after you do this,

saying that users of Windows 9x and NT 4 Workstation computers cannot connect to the .NET Servers anymore. They can still connect to the network's NT 4 Servers, however. How could you address the situation? (Choose all that apply.)

A. Add the highly secure template to the Windows 9x and NT 4 workstations.

B. Upgrade the Windows 9x and NT 4 workstations to Windows XP Professional.

C. Give all users Administrator level access to the servers configured with the highly secure template.

D. Remove the highly secure template from the Windows XP Servers by reapplying the basic security template.

9. Navin R. Johnson is the administrator of a network supporting a fast food chain. The Culinary department is concerned that unauthorized users might be able to access and then e-mail confidential recipes, like the one for the company's special sauce, so he is planning to place the Culinary department on its own restricted network segment. The chain's network consists mostly of Windows 98 and NT 4 Workstation computers, but he has recently purchased ten Windows XP Professional computers for the Culinary department. Navin wants members of the Culinary department to communicate with each other, but does not want these computers to be accessible by any non-Culinary computers. What should Navin do to configure this special purpose for the Culinary department users?

A. Use the Security Configuration and Analysis snap-in to apply the Securews.inf security template.

B. Use the Security Configuration and Analysis snap-in to apply the Securedc.inf security template.

C. Use the Security Configuration and Analysis snap-in to apply the Hisecws.inf security template.

D. Use the Security Configuration and Analysis snap-in to apply the Hisecdc.inf security template.

10. You have decided to set up Internet Connection Firewall on a shared Internet connection for your small office network. One of the other computers on the network is set up as an FTP server, and you want outside users to continue to have access to this FTP site. What do you do?

A. Configure the FTP site properties to allow for unencrypted authentication using the Everyone group.

B. Tell your ISP to configure a filter that will allow TCP ports 20 and 21 to hit your shared connection's public IP address. The ICF will then automatically pass through FTP requests.

C. From the Settings page of ICF, you should enable the FTP service on your network, and then add the address of the FTP server to the list of servers running the FTP service.

D. You won't be able to do this without Internet Security and Acceleration (ISA) Server.

11. You have installed ICF for your office XP installation machine, and want to configure it so that objectionable content requests are blocked. How do you configure this behavior?

A. From the Internet Explorer's Security tab, set the Internet Zone's default security setting to High.

B. From the ICF Settings dialog box, configure a filter to block any content that is not rated or that is rated with any objectionable content.

C. From ICF's Logging Options tab, enable a log of successful connections. You can then see what sites have been accessed and configure ICF filters as appropriate.

D. This is impossible without a third-party firewall solution.

REVIEW ANSWERS

1. **B** The CIPHER command-line utility allows you to create file encryption keys and view, encrypt, and decrypt files and folders on an NTFS partition. Several switches will be used to modify this utility's behavior. None of the other command-line utilities exist.

2. **D** Here it is important to note that the computer is a part of a domain, and you should know who the default recovery agent is in a domain. As it stands, only Scott or the Domain Administrator can access Scott's files. When a Windows XP Professional computer becomes part of the domain, the domain Administrator account becomes the recovery agent. This is so because of the Default Domain Policy GPO. A is incorrect because the encryption attribute is separate from NTFS permissions. Changing the ACLs on Scott's files will not change who is the recovery agent. B is incorrect for the same reason. C is incorrect because the local Administrator account is the recovery agent when the computer is either standalone or is part of a workgroup. This changes when the computer becomes part of a domain.

3. **D** The Passwords Must Meet Complexity Requirements policy setting can be set to enforce the contents of a password by verifying that it meets a set of complexity requirements. One of the requirements is that the password cannot contain all or part of the user's account name. This policy is disabled by default in the Default Domain Policy GPO and in the Local Security Policy of a workgroup computer running Windows XP Professional. A and B are incorrect because these settings do not enforce the content of a password. C does enforce the content of a password, but not to the extent that Passwords Must Meet Complexity Requirements does. Minimum Password Length specifies the least number of alphanumeric characters in a password.

4. **A** By setting the Account Lockout Duration setting to 0, the account will be locked out until an administrator unlocks it. This policy setting is not defined by default because account lockouts are not defined either. It has meaning only when an account lockout policy is set. B is incorrect because you want to configure what happens after the account is locked out. This setting defines when and if an account will be locked out in the first place. Setting the Account Lockout Threshold to 0 means that the account will never be locked out. C is incorrect because the Account Lockout Duration of 99,999 sets the duration to about 69 days, which, while a long time, is not indefinite. D is incorrect because a setting of 4 invalid login attempts and an indefinite lockout duration are not defaults, so action is necessary to configure this behavior.

5. **B** A is incorrect because Audit Logon Events allows you to audit each time a user logs on or off a computer where the computer was used to validate the account. C is incorrect because Object Access allows you to enable auditing of objects on an NTFS partition. D is also wrong because System Events allows you to audit when a user shuts down or restarts a computer or when an event has occurred that affects either the system security or the Security Log.

6. **E** EAP-TLS uses transport layer security when a PPP connection is established. Mutual authentication and encryption services are provided between client and server using certificates. All the other protocols are wrong because, while they are all authentication security protocols, they are not used in the smart card logon process.

7. **A** This is the easiest way to reach a solution for this problem. Answer B would work, but it requires much more effort than answer A. C is incorrect because the Administrator account would also need to change its password because of the domain policies in place. D is wrong because the local policy would be overridden by the domain policy.

8. **B** **D** The highly secure template configuration is supported only between Windows XP/2000 machines. B would be a solution, albeit a potentially expensive one. D will also work, but of course you would then lose all the secure configuration options that were applied in the first place. The basic security template does support communication with Windows 9x and NT 4 systems. A is incorrect because these computers do not support security template configurations. Answer C is incorrect because the user logged on does not impact the communication channel required between server and client. It is also never a good idea to give users Administrator privileges indiscriminately.

9. **C** You should use the Highly Secure security template file, hisecws.inf, to ensure that IPSec encrypts any communication over the network. After the template is applied, the Windows XP Professional computers will require IPSec encryption for all communication. And, because only Windows XP supports IPSec, no communication will be possible with pre-Windows XP computers. Answers B and D can be thrown out because they are templates for domain controllers, and the scenario is asking about Windows XP Professional computers. A is incorrect because the Securews.inf template increases Account Policy and Auditing security settings but does not require encrypted communications— you would know that only from spending some time exploring some of the template settings with the Security Configuration and Analysis snap-in.

10. **C** These are the steps you should take for any service running on the private network, not just FTP. A is wrong because this will not cause the ICF to pass through any FTP requests. B is wrong because FTP traffic will hit your public interface, but that traffic will be dropped if you have not taken the steps outlined in answer C. D is wrong because you do not need the full-fledged ISA Server product to enable this feature.

11. **D** Internet Connection Firewall has no capability to filter outbound traffic; it only takes action on incoming Internet traffic, blocking any packets that aren't responses to requests. If someone requests objectionable content, the ICF does nothing to stop the response to the request. A, B, and C are all incorrect for this reason, and are all smokescreen answers—a lot of configuring and button pushing, but none of them effective because of the built-in limitation of ICF.

About the CD-ROM

Mike Meyers' Certification Passport CD-ROM Instructions

To install the *Passport* Practice Exam software, perform these steps:

1. Insert the CD-ROM into your CD-ROM drive. An auto-run program will initiate, and a dialog box will appear indicating that you are installing the Passport setup program. If the auto-run program does not launch on your system, select Run from the Start menu and type *d*:\setup.exe (where *d* is the "name" of your CD-ROM drive).

2. Follow the Installation Wizard's instructions to complete the installation of the software.

You can start the program by going to your desktop and double-clicking the Passport Exam Review icon or by going to Start | Program Files | Passport | MCSE Professional.

System Requirements

- **Operating systems supported** Windows 98, Windows NT 4.0, Windows 2000, and Windows Me
- **CPU** 400MHz or faster recommended
- **Memory** 64MB of RAM
- **CD-ROM** 4X or greater
- **Internet connection** Required for optional exam upgrade

Technical Support

For basic *Passport* CD-ROM technical support, contact

Hudson Technical Support

- Phone: 800-217-0059
- E-mail: mcgraw-hill@hudsonsoft.com

For content/subject matter questions concerning the book or the CD-ROM, contact

MH Customer Service

- Phone: 800-722-4726
- E-mail: customer.service@mcgraw-hill.com

For inquiries about the available upgrade, CD-ROM, or online technology, or for in-depth technical support, contact

ExamWeb Technical Support

- Phone: 949-566-9375
- E-mail: support@examweb.com

Career Flight Path

The Microsoft Windows certification program that you will be joining when you take the 70-270 Exam includes an extensive group of exams and certification levels. Passing the Windows XP Professional exam is all that is required for Microsoft's baseline certification—the Microsoft Certified Professional (MCP).

Microsoft's premier certification is the Microsoft Certified System Engineer (MCSE), and the 70-270 Exam is a great place to start on your path toward gaining this certification. In total, seven exams are required for obtaining the MCSE: four core exams, one core elective exam, and two elective exams.

Additionally, the 70-270 Exam will count toward Microsoft's new Microsoft Certified Systems Administrator (MCSA) certification, which requires three core exams and one elective.

For the latest information on the requirements of the MCSE and MCSA certification, please refer to the Microsoft Training and Certification website at http://www/microsoft.com/traincert.

Core Exams

Every MCSE candidate must pass four core exams. These exams test your knowledge of Windows both as a server and as a client operating system, and they also test your ability to implement a network based on Microsoft technologies. The core exams are

- **70-210** Installing, Configuring, and Administering Microsoft Windows 2000 Professional, or
  70-270 Installing, Configuring, and Administering Microsoft Windows XP Professional
- **70-215** Installing, Configuring, and Administering Microsoft Windows 2000 Server, or
  70-275 Installing, Configuring, and Administering Microsoft .NET Server

- **70-216**   Implementing and Administering a Microsoft Windows 2000 Network Infrastructure, or
  70-276   Implementing and Administering a Microsoft .NET Server Network Infrastructure
- **70-217**   Implementing and Administering a Microsoft Windows 2000 Directory Services Infrastructure, or
  70-277   Implementing and Administering a Microsoft .NET Server Directory Services Infrastructure

The MCSA candidate must pass three core exams. The core tests are

- **70-210**   Installing, Configuring, and Administering Microsoft Windows 2000 Professional, or
  70-270   Installing, Configuring, and Administering Microsoft Windows XP Professional
- **70-215**   Installing, Configuring, and Administering Microsoft Windows 2000 Server, or
  70-275   Installing, Configuring, and Administering Microsoft .NET Server
- **70-218**   Managing a Windows 2000 Network Environment

Core Elective Exam

The four core required exams of the MCSE certification test your ability to *do*, while the core elective exam tests your ability to *plan*. These core elective options are sometimes referred to as the "Designing" exams. Four elective exam options are available for you to choose from, and this is the first point at which you can begin to customize your MCSE certification around the topics that interest you.

- **70-219**   Designing a Microsoft Windows 2000 Directory Services Infrastructure
- **70-220**   Designing Security for a Microsoft Windows 2000 Network
- **70-221**   Designing a Microsoft Windows 2000 Network Infrastructure
- **70-226**   Designing Highly Available Web Solutions with Microsoft Windows 2000 Server Technologies

Those interested in working as an Active Directory specialist, a security specialist, a network designer, or an Internet specialist will know exactly which exam to take. For those of you not so sure, Exam 70-220 may be your best bet, as knowledge of network security is always a valuable commodity.

Elective Exams

With the core elective/design exam, you are given a bit of choice, but with the last two elective exams, you can really customize your certification around your interests and knowledge. Microsoft lists more than 20 exams to choose from, and these can include any of the unused design exams or any of a number of exams on Microsoft server applications.

If you have a particular interest in SNA server (70-085) or SMS server (70-086), for example, then go for those exams. In most cases, though, a certification seeker who is looking to make him or herself marketable to a broad range of employers should concentrate on a core group of elective exams that relate to Microsoft's most common server applications. Probably the two best electives for MCSE candidates who are on a job hunt are these:

- **70-028**   Installing, Configuring, and Administering Microsoft SQL Server 2000 Enterprise Edition
- **70-224**   Installing, Configuring, and Administering Microsoft Exchange 2000 Server

Users with Windows NT 4.0 knowledge can leverage this into their Windows 2000 MCSE by taking exam 70-244, which covers support and integration of Windows NT 4.0 networks.

The MCSA candidate must select one of the following electives:

- **70-028**   Installing, Configuring, and Administering Microsoft SQL Server 2000 Enterprise Edition
- **70-081**   Implementing and Supporting Microsoft Exchange Server 5.5
- **70-088**   Implementing and Supporting Microsoft Proxy Server 2.0
- **70-216**   Implementing and Administering a Microsoft Windows 2000 Network Infrastructure
- **70-224**   Installing, Configuring, and Administering Microsoft Exchange 2000 Server
- **70-227**   Installing, Configuring, and Administering Microsoft Internet Security and Acceleration (ISA) Server
- **70-228**   Installing, Configuring, and Administering Microsoft SQL Server 2000 Enterprise Edition
- **70-244**   Supporting and Maintaining a Microsoft Windows NT Server 4.0 Network

.NET and Beyond

One thing to remember, of course, is that computer technologies change rapidly, and most certifications therefore require you to regularly update your certifications. With the Windows 2000 MCSE, we are actually getting a reprieve, as Microsoft has declared that the .NET and 2000 exams can be used interchangeably, so recertification for XP/.NET won't be necessary. Consult the Microsoft website for more information on which Windows 2000 exams map to which XP/.NET exams.

And, what about all those Windows 2000 exams? Are they still good or do I have to keep testing? There really is no 2000 or XP/.NET distinction when discussing the MCSE certification. You either are or are not an MCSE, and right now both sets of exams will count toward certification. If you have started your journey toward the MCSE by taking the Windows 2000 tests, you have the option to complete your certification with either Windows 2000 or Windows XP Professional/Windows .NET Server exams. In other words, it won't make any difference if you mix and match exams; you will still be an MCSE.

Furthermore, the understanding needed to run either version of Microsoft's operating systems will be highly portable. In fact, Microsoft recommends that test candidates should continue to pursue training and certification in Windows 2000, as skills acquired for Windows 2000 will be highly relevant to Windows XP Professional and .NET Enterprise Servers. In other words, if you know Windows 2000, you are going to have an excellent starting point for Windows XP; and if you know XP, you are going to have a solid grasp of Windows 2000 as well. So again, nothing to worry about.

Index

441

INTERNATIONAL CONTACT INFORMATION

AUSTRALIA
McGraw-Hill Book Company Australia Pty. Ltd.
TEL +61-2-9417-9899
FAX +61-2-9417-5687
http://www.mcgraw-hill.com.au
books-it_sydney@mcgraw-hill.com

CANADA
McGraw-Hill Ryerson Ltd.
TEL +905-430-5000
FAX +905-430-5020
http://www.mcgrawhill.ca

GREECE, MIDDLE EAST,
NORTHERN AFRICA
McGraw-Hill Hellas
TEL +30-1-656-0990-3-4
FAX +30-1-654-5525

MEXICO (Also serving Latin America)
McGraw-Hill Interamericana Editores S.A. de C.V.
TEL +525-117-1583
FAX +525-117-1589
http://www.mcgraw-hill.com.mx
fernando_castellanos@mcgraw-hill.com

SINGAPORE (Serving Asia)
McGraw-Hill Book Company
TEL +65-863-1580
FAX +65-862-3354
http://www.mcgraw-hill.com.sg
mghasia@mcgraw-hill.com

SOUTH AFRICA
McGraw-Hill South Africa
TEL +27-11-622-7512
FAX +27-11-622-9045
robyn_swanepoel@mcgraw-hill.com

UNITED KINGDOM & EUROPE
(Excluding Southern Europe)
McGraw-Hill Education Europe
TEL +44-1-628-502500
FAX +44-1-628-770224
http://www.mcgraw-hill.co.uk
computing_neurope@mcgraw-hill.com

ALL OTHER INQUIRIES Contact:
Osborne/McGraw-Hill
TEL +1-510-549-6600
FAX +1-510-883-7600
http://www.osborne.com
omg_international@mcgraw-hill.com

ExamWeb is a leader in assessment technology. We use this technology to deliver customized online testing programs, corporate training, pre-packaged exam preparation courses, and licensed technology. ExamWeb has partnered with Osborne - McGraw-Hill to develop the CD contained in this book and its corresponding online exam simulators. Please read about our services below and contact us to see how we can help you with your own assessment needs.

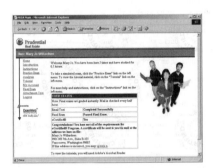